CADOGAN GUIDES

"Cadogan Guides really need no introduction and are mini-encyclopaedic on the countries covered ... they give the explorer, the intellectual or cultural buff—indeed any visitor—all they need to know to get the very best from their visit ... a good read too by the many inveterate armchair travellers."

—The Book Journal

"Standouts these days are the Cadogan Guides ... sophisticated, beautifully written books."

—American Bookseller Magazine

"Entertaining companions, with sharp insights, local gossip and far more of a feeling of a living author ... The series has received plaudits worldwide for intelligence, originality and a slightly irreverent sense of fun."

—Daily Telegraph

"Imaginatively devised and entertainingly written."

—The Independent

Other titles in the Cadogan Guides series:

CADOGAN CITY GUIDES

PRAGUE

SADAKAT KADRI

CADOGAN BOOKS
London

THE GLOBE PEQUOT PRESS
Chester, Connecticut

Cadogan Books Ltd
Mercury House, 195 Knightsbridge, London SW7 1RE

The Globe Pequot Press
138 West Main Street, Chester, Connecticut 06412, USA

Cover design by Ralph King
Cover illustration by Faranak
Maps © Cadogan Books, drawn by Thames Cartographic Services Ltd
Index by Dorothy Frame

Series Editor: Rachel Fielding

First published in 1991

British Library Cataloguing in Publication Data
Kadri, Sadakat
    Prague.—(Cadogan city guides).
    1. Czechoslovakia.
    I. Title
914.37120443
ISBN 0–947754–25–3

Library of Congress Cataloging-in-Publication-Data
Kadri, Sadakat.
    Prague/Sadakat Kadri: illustrations by Oldřich Dufek; Pavel Bezděk (Introduction).
        p.   cm.—(Cadogan guides)
    Includes index.
    ISBN 0–87106–152–X
    1. Prague (Czechoslovakia)—Description—Guide-books.
    I. Title.   II. Series.
    DB2607.K33   1991   91–3732
    914.37'120443–dc20   CIP

Photoset in Ehrhardt on a Linotron 202
Printed on recycled paper and bound in Great Britain by
Redwood Press Ltd, Melksham, Wiltshire

CONTENTS

Food and Drink *Pages 270–86*

Where to Stay *Pages 287–301*

Entertainment and Nightlife *Pages 302–9*

Shopping *Pages 310–14*

Sports and Activities *Pages 315–18*

Children's Prague *Pages 319–20*

Living and Working in Prague *Pages 321–7*

Day Trips from Prague *Pages 328–50*
Karlovy Vary (Carlsbad)—Telč—Terezín and Litoměřice
—Karlštejn and Křivoklát Castles—Kutná Hora

Language *Pages 351–57*

Chronology *Pages 358–60*

Further Reading *Pages 361–2*

Index *Pages 363–70*

LIST OF MAPS

ABOUT THE AUTHOR

Sadakat Kadri was born in Fulham in 1964 of a Pakastani father and a Finnish mother. He studied history and law at Trinity College, Cambridge, and took a Masters degree in law at Harvard University. He is a qualified barrister and New York attorney. He visited central and eastern Europe on many occasions during the 1980s, and lived in Prague for a year while writing this book. His hobbies include cooking chicken.

ACKNOWLEDGEMENTS

My first thanks must go to Hana Syslová, for limitless friendship and help, and also to her husband Vojtěch Sysel. Boundless gratitude to my mother and father, for space, food, coffee and support, and to my sister, Mariya, for unearthing dull facts in my absence. Special thanks also to Jana Bryndová and her mother for giving me a flat; to Mrs Procházková for another; to Jiří Kučera particularly for his help during my frenetic last days; and to David Chirico for constant encouragement, and company on weekend binges in Újezd. Much love to my merry cohort on the Charles Bridge: Little Pavel Bezděk, Big Pavel Bezděk, Dana Peřinová, Pavlina, Renáta, Pavla, Zuzana, Roman, beautiful little Zuzanka, Marta, Ivan, Linda, and Georg Hodek. Similarly, thanks to all those foreigners who sang and danced with me through the magical city, especially Mark Kuzmack, Marianne Decleire, Miranda Rhys-Williams, Sari, Tuuli and Pekka the Finns, Sylvaine Willaume and Cécile Challier, and proto-walkers Rachel Malik and Marion Dewar. On the home front, vast thanks to Rachel Fielding, for editing me with compassion, and hello to Tristram Fielding who pipped this book at the post. Thanks also to Vicki Ingle, for last-minute help; Chris Schüler, for copy-editing the book; Eric Smith for zealous proofreading; Dorothy Frame for indexing it; and Vanessa Letts without whose string-pulling I wouldn't have got this job. I'm also grateful to Mary Harper and Biram Sow for having produced a quasi-god son, Johnny Abdoulaye Sow, during my absence. Thanks to Jan Kolarik at the London branch of Čedok; the Čedok staff at Kutná Hora and Karlovy Vary; the staff at the Clementinum library and the Bibliotecka Pragensia; Dr Frank Kadlec for opening up the secrets of Prague Castle; and all the so-called minor employees who put their bureaucracies to shame by bending and breaking rules on my behalf.

INTRODUCTION

'Prague, wrapped in its legendary magic, is truly one of those cities that has been able to fix and retain the poetic idea that is always more or less drifting aimlessly through space'.
—André Breton to the Prague Surrealist Group 1935

The flim-flam of hundreds of tourist brochures now makes Breton's homage sound almost clichéd, but there is something mighty surreal about Prague. Floating in the architectural flotsam of a thousand years, its domes, dungeons, rickety rooftops and spires are about as close as life gets to fairyland. Its central bridge is bent, one of its clocks turns backwards, an entire 13th-century town is buried three metres under its alleys, and surveying its domain from the hill above the river is a castle in the air. The city lies at the crossroads of Europe, and its spirit has been formed and deformed by the cataclysmic pressures of a millenium of continental madness. Dogs of war have dumped on it from every direction, its streets are filled with the petrified dreams of dissembling monks and cuckoo monarchs, the Communists practised their jiggery-pokery behind an iron curtain for four decades—and yet it survived the hulla-balloo to emerge as one of the most enchanted cities in Europe. The spell that it evokes isn't some two-bit trick with a slipper and a pumpkin, but the almost tangible energy of images, ideologies and myths with which

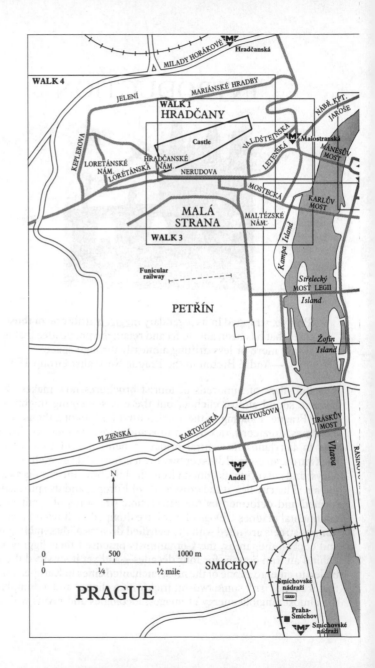

WALK 4

WALK 1
HRADČANY

Castle

MILADY HORÁKOVÉ   Hradčanská

MARIÁNSKÉ HRADBY

JELENÍ

KEPLEROVA

LORETÁNSKÉ
NÁM.

HRADČANSKÉ
NÁM.

LORETÁNSKÁ

NERUDOVA

VALDŠTEJNSKÁ   Malostranská

LETENSKÁ

NABŘ. KPT.
JAROŠE

MÁNESŮV
MOST

MOSTECKÁ

KARLŮV
MOST

MALÁ
STRANA

MALTÉZSKÉ
NÁM.

WALK 3

Kampa Island

Funicular
railway

PETŘÍN

Střelecký
Island

MOST LEGII

Žofín
Island

Vltava

MATOUŠOVA

JIRÁSKŮV
MOST

PLZEŇSKÁ

KARTOUZSKÁ

Anděl

N

0   500   1000 m

0   ¼   ½ mile   SMÍCHOV

PRAGUE

Smíchovské
nádraží

Praha-
Smíchov

Smíchovské
nádraží

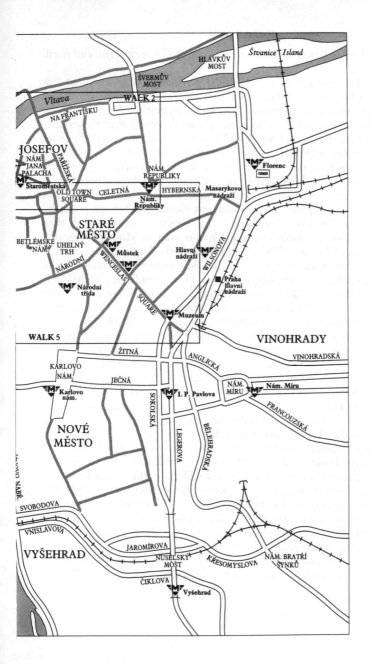

every European has grown up. Give it an inch of imagination, and it will unleash a mile.

Years of smears and smokescreens have added to the mystery that now surrounds Prague. It is the capital of Bohemia, which has been a byeword for outlandishness for centuries. The kingdom began its ascent into the clouds in the mid-1400s: the pope spread the word that Bohemians made love on the streets, while in France, a group of expelled gipsies waved their safe-conducts as they passed through, and the French duly noted that *un bohémien* was a gipsy—as he still is today. By the early 1600s, Shakespeare could get away with describing the landlocked and forested kingdom as 'a desert country near the sea' (*The Winter's Tale*); and in 1938, disingenuous ignorance was elevated to foreign policy by Neville Chamberlain. Ten years later, Prague—further west than Vienna, and considerably closer to Dublin than to Moscow—became lost in 'Eastern Europe'. The city of dreams turned into a forty-one year nightmare, but in the west, Bohemia did little more than to hover across from Bloomsbury to somewhere between Hampstead and Haight-Ashbury. And then in 1989, a few million people pinched themselves, the tin-pot emperors of Communism shivered, and Prague, Bohemia and Czechoslovakia returned to where they belong—the heart of Europe.

The city now has some 1,190,576 inhabitants, with the proportion of men steadily and inexplicably decreasing (48.7 per cent last count); it contains 503 spires, towers and sundry aerial protrusions; and it comprises 495 sq km, ten districts, eight islands, seven hills (like most legendary cities), and an agglomeration of what were historically five separate towns. The city is now the capital of Czechoslovakia (made up of the provinces of Bohemia, Moravia, Slovakia and a slice of Silesia), or the 'Czech and Slovak Federal Republic' as it has been known to officialdom, and virtually no one else, since mid-1990.

The barbed-wire wounds of the cold war still scar Prague, but you couldn't choose a better time to visit. It is still one of the cheapest cities in Europe, and as it busks, dances and kisses its way back into the light, the division of the continent is being repaired on its streets. The magical metropolis doesn't *always* feel so dreamy—particularly as you chew through Prague's accursed dumplings, or cross swords with a charmless hob-goblin of the bureaucracy—but if you pack your senses of humour, adventure and romance, a visit is an unforgettable jaunt into a city where history is in the making, and where a thousand years has already been made.

For Natasha, all the way.

Travel

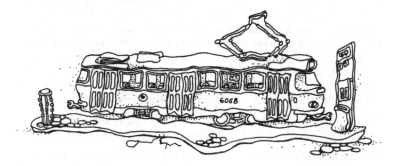

Arriving in Prague

The best source of general information on holidaying in Czechoslovakia is still Čedok, the state-run tourist agency. It's been around for almost as long as the country itself (over 70 years), and although sloth and inefficiency have characterized it for too long, it still organizes by far the largest range of holidays to Prague. They generally cover flights, hotel bookings, and a series of entertainments ranging from nights at the opera to dire evenings of 'traditional' beer and sausages in five-star hostelries. You pay a hefty premium for Čedok's services, but its monopoly, only now beginning to crumble, means that it knows the tangled ropes of Prague's service industry better than anyone. For further information on what it has to offer, contact your local office. In the UK, it's at 17–18 Old Bond St, London W1X 3DA, tel (071) 629 6058, and in the USA at 10 East 40th St, New York NY 10016, tel (212) 689 9720. You could also contact London's **Progressive Tours**, another organization with a long experience of the vagaries of Communist bureaucracy, having had a special relationship with the old regimes for many years. Most of its jaunts are for groups, but it also organizes trips for individuals, progressive or otherwise. It's at 12 Porchester Place, London W2 2BS, tel (071) 262 1676. Cultural tour organizers are listed under Specialist Holidays (see p. 6).

1

By Air: Čedok's tours are often booked solid for months in advance, but finding your own flight to Prague presents few difficulties, although early booking is advisable during holiday periods and throughout high season. British Airways flies daily from London, Manchester, and Edinburgh; and has regular flights from Belfast, Dublin, Glasgow and Newcastle. The airline also has services to many major North American cities. Pan-Am used to fly to the city, but at the time of writing it has sunk to a dangerously low financial altitude; if it recovers, it may resume its Prague route, but otherwise you could contact whichever carrier takes over. Czechoslovak Airlines (ČSA) has a daily service out of London, and twice-weekly flights from New York and Washington DC.

BA: tel (071) 897 4000 (London); tel 800 247 9297 (New York).
ČSA: tel (071) 255 1898 (London); tel (212) 682 5833 (New York).

Both airlines offer roughly equivalent fares, with cheaper deals if you're prepared to accept limitations on your length of stay and book sufficiently far in advance (usually 14 days). Economy return fares range from £210–240 from London, and $750–1100 from New York. BA has special fares for anyone under 26. Bucket-shop bargains and chartered flights to Prague are rare as yet, but it's always worth scanning the Travel section of London's *Time Out* magazine to see what's on offer (try New York's *Village Voice* in the USA). Students and young travellers could also contact **STA Travel** at 86 Old Brompton Rd, London SW1, which offers a range of fairly cheap flights to the city, tel enquiries (071) 937 9921; US residents could go to **Council Travel**, 205 East 42nd St, New York, NY 10001, tel (212) 661 1450.

Prague's small international airport is **Ruzyně**, situated some 20 km to the west of the city centre. The terminal isn't on a metro line, but it's linked to Dejvická station (line A) by buses 119 and 254. Pick up a ticket for a few pennies at the souvenir stand in the airport lobby. You can also catch the shuttle operated by ČSA which runs to and from Hlavní nádraží, via the ČSA offices at Revoluční 25 and Dejvická station. The bus runs at least once every half hour. Plenty of taxi-drivers loiter outside the airport building, and unusually for Prague, will almost certainly use their meter. Expect to pay £3–4 ($5.40–7.20) for the ride into the Old Town.

Airline Offices Telephone numbers in brackets are those of the airline's desk at the airport. Most are open on weekdays only and close by 4 pm.

Aeroflot: Na příkopě 20, tel 26 08 62, 22 46 90 (36 78 15).
Air France: Václavské nám. 10, tel 26 01 55.
Alitalia: Revoluční 5, tel 231 05 35.
Ariana: Ruzyně Airport, tel 334, ext 31 72.
AUA: Pařížská 1, tel 232 27 95, 232 64 69 (36 78 18).
Balkan: Pařížská 3, tel 231 49 96 (36 77 63).
British Airways: Štěpánská 63, tel 236 03 53 (36 77 31).
ČSA: Revoluční 1, tel 231 25 95, 235 27 85.
Finnair: Štěpánská 2, tel 22 64 89, 22 30 12 (32 11 80).
KLM: Václavské nám. 37, tel 26 43 62/9 (36 78 22).
Pan-Am: Pařížská 11, tel 232 47 72.
Sabena: Ruzyně Airport, tel 36 78 13.
SAS: Štěpánská 61, tel 22 81 41 (36 78 17).
Swissair: Pařížská 11, tel 232 47 07 (36 78 09).
Tarom: Pařížská 20, tel 231 07 00 (36 77 65).

By Train: There are three time-honoured routes from England to Prague. The timetable changes little from year to year, but double-checking is advisable. One leaves London Victoria in the morning and early afternoon, crosses to Ostend and after a possible change at Köln, arrives in Prague in the morning or late afternoon of the next day. Another possibility is to travel via Paris, picking up the Paris-Praha night express from the Gare de l'Est. The third capital combination is to stop off in Berlin, and then take one of the many Prague-bound trains from Berlin (Lichtenberg), a journey of about 7 hours. A return journey from London via Paris costs £182 at the time of writing, and you can check that, along with other information on all the routes, at any major British Rail station, or on (071) 834 2345. All international rail tickets are valid for up to two months' worth of stopovers.

Residents of countries outside Europe can also get to Prague on a Eurail Pass, which now covers most of the continent save the country that you buy it in and the Soviet Union. A 15-day pass costs £226 ($390 in the US), a 3-month one £618 ($1042), and there are three compromise lengths and prices in between. All permit unlimited 1st-class travel for the period concerned. 2nd-class passes are only available if you're under 26 (see p. 4). In London, you can buy the passes from **Campus Travel** (Eurotrain) at 52 Grosvenor Gardens, London SW1W 0AG, tel (071) 730 3402; and in New York, you can pick one up from **Council Travel** (see p. 2).

Anyone under the cursed age of 26 is eligible for the set of bargains that transform Europe's trains into mobile youth hostels during the summer. The most comprehensive deals are provided by Campus Travel, which sells direct tickets via Köln for £82 one way, as well as rovers covering a clutch of European capitals including Prague for £182.50. Czechoslovakia is now also part of the Inter-Rail system, which since 1989 has extended to cover virtually the entire continent. The passes cost £175 and are the best way of barnstorming Europe on a budget (although your price calculations should take account of the fact that you only receive a 50 per cent discount out of the country in which you buy the pass). You'll need proof of youthfulness to buy all of the above tickets, but Campus Travel also offers deals to even the most grey-bearded student, and can even book tickets for ageing non-students. Non-European residents can buy the 2nd-class Eurail Youth Pass, which is valid for either one or two months at both Campus and Council Travel. Even more popular are the Eurail Youth Flexipasses, which permit 15 or 30 days' worth of rail travel within a three-month period (not available in the UK). There are no reductions for either the young or the studious within Czechoslovakia—but anyone connected to the British or US educational systems (including over-25s, academics and accompanying spouses and children) can buy a Czech Explorer Pass *before leaving the UK*, which lets you travel the length of the country in a week for £18.50 (2nd class) or £26.50 (1st class). You can buy the pass in many UK travel agencies including Campus Travel. You'd have to spend your entire holiday on a train for it to save you money—but it will avoid plenty of queuing time if you intend to use the rail system a fair amount.

If you're chugging into Prague, you'll arrive either at **Hlavní nádraží** ('Main Station') or **Nádraží Praha-Holešovice**. Both are on line C of the metro network. Hlavní nádraží is the bigger, four floors' worth of station, three of which somehow emerge onto the street. You can change your money and find accommodation at 'AVE', on the second level (May–Sept 6 am–2 am, Oct–April 6 am–10.30 pm). Timetable information is provided in an office near by (6 am–10 pm), but maps and city information are given out in the booth of the Prague Information Service (PIS) in the main hall below (8 am–8 pm). There are two cavernous eating and drinking halls on the top floor (6 am–11 pm). The taxi rank is to your left as you enter the station interior from the platforms. The

4

left-luggage counter is in the basement, and is open 24 hours a day (minus short but potentially disastrous breaks—check the notice board to make sure that you aren't caught short as your train pulls out). The nearby lockers are a cheap way of avoiding having to queue when you reclaim your bags, but they've been known to be rifled. If you use one, fix a combination on the inside of the door before slamming it—and don't forget to note it, along with the locker location. Grimy travellers can clean up in the station showers, in the lonely subterranean corridor under the station's main hall (Mon–Fri 6 am–8 pm, Sat 7 am–7 pm, Sun 8 am–4 pm)—bring your own towel.

Nádraží Praha-Holešovice is less sprawling and has fewer facilities, but it's a short metro ride to the main station. If you arrive at either station after about midnight, you may have a fairly unpleasant first night in Prague unless you have a firm reservation in a hotel. The addresses of accommodation agencies are on pp. 288–9, and Agentura claims to have a 24-hour office at Holešovice station, but experience of darkened doors at 5 am suggests that it can't always be relied upon. If you find yourself up the creek as you stagger off your Berlin milk train, do whichever of the following seems fit.

* Stay put. The police usually leave distressed tourists relatively unmolested, early morning alarm calls notwithstanding. However, the same can't be said of the crazies and psychopaths who flock in as dusk descends, and this is generally a bad option. Hlavní nádraží has got a particularly slimy nightlife.

* Set off for the Jalta Hotel on Wenceslas Square, where you can change money through the night. It's a five-minute walk from the main station, and a 45-minute expedition from Holešovice. Alternatively, gingerly remove the smallest bill from your wad, and ask the most normal-looking freak that you can find if he or she will give you some crowns in exchange.

* Phone every hotel in this book. However, if it's late, the cheaper ones will probably hang up; and if it's summer, all will almost certainly have no beds until at least check-out time the next morning.

* Check your baggage into the left-luggage counter and go for a walk. All that you'll lose will be a few snatched and unpleasant dreams, and Prague will begin to wake up at around 5 am.

Specialist Holidays

Since the 1989 revolution, several small companies have begun to organize trips to Prague for culture buffs. Explorations of the musical traditions of the city are run two or three times a year by **Travel for the Arts** at 117 Regent's Park Rd, London NW1 8UR, tel (071) 483 4466. The trips are a melodious romp from Mozart to Janáček, and for about £750 upwards, you'll get a flight, hotel accommodation and up to a week of operas and like-minded conversation partners. Anyone who's a Friend of Covent Garden is eligible for a discount. Art lovers could also contact **Cadogan Travel**, which has established a Warsaw–Prague itinerary in conjunction with the Victoria and Albert Museum. Unfortunately, Saddam Hussein's attack on the tourist industry threw a spanner in the works, but the trips may be resumed in late 1991 and you can obtain the latest information at 159 Sloane St, London SW1X 9BU, tel (071) 730 0721.

Customs Formalities

A full British passport will get you into Czechoslovakia, although if it's got less than a year to run you could have problems. A Visitor's Card won't be accepted. West Europeans and US citizens no longer need a visa for stays of up to three months. The requirement that tourists register with the police has been abolished. However, if you plan to stay for longer than a month, the bureaucracy still wants to know. You can register at a local police station; or at the foreigners' office at Olšanská 2, just past the unmistakeable television tower on the route of tram 9 (the opening hours are notoriously unreliable—call 24 51 84/7 for the latest details). See Living in Prague for further details on long stays.

Since 1989, Czech customs officers have undergone an almost miraculous transformation. Entry and departure used to involve running a gauntlet of psychological warfare techniques, complete with Mutt-and-Jeff teams, rivet stares, and very sweaty moments while passports were examined and occasionally taken away for questioning. Not all the bad guys have reformed, but you're very unlikely to face more than the most perfunctory examination these days. On arrival, you're allowed to import as many personal effects as you want and up to 250 cigarettes, two litres of wine, a litre of spirits, and half a litre of perfume. Any extra should be declared, and duty paid, although the happy-go-lucky customs information service claims that long-term visitors can bring in any amount that's proportional to their stay—a suggestion that sounds ludicrous, but could possibly be offered in mitigation if you're nabbed. Gifts worth up to 1000kcs can also be imported duty-free. Anything you buy at Tuzex (see p. 327) isn't subject to duty when you leave, although there's a 500-kc limit on other exports from Czechoslovakia. As inflation rots the currency, the limits will either change or become even more meaningless than they already are. The standard prohibitions apply to both arrival and departure—no hard porn, no heroin, no Semtex, etc.—and Czech currency is still not meant to be imported or exported. If you're flying out of Ruzyně Airport, you have to cart your luggage through to customs yourself. X-ray machines can cumulatively damage films, and a single exposure can conceivably wipe out computer data. If you have either, it's a good idea to pack it separately and have it inspected by hand. For more information, contact the laid-back customs bureau at Havlíčkova 11, tel 232 22 70.

Getting Around Prague

The curves and cobbles of central Prague have a mobile life of their own. Most of the streets are no more than the patches of ground that no one has ever wanted to build on, and in their medieval madness, they often lead you on a merry dance and occasionally pull off the startling trick of coaxing you back to your starting-point after a 30-minute meander. Things aren't made easier by the name-change mania that gripped the nation in the months after the 1989 revolution. Countless streets, metro stations, parks and buildings were renamed in the first wave of anti-Communism—and then a fair proportion had their older names restored when it was decided that not all the Communists' friends deserved oblivion. The messy result is that many people in Prague aren't quite sure where they live, while Lenin has apparently retained his interminable airport road for the simple reason that changing all the street signs would cost a small fortune. No one really knows the names of several Prague streets yet, and at the time of writing, you need at least three maps to master the permutations involved. However, the most recent should be adequate for a short visit, and you can pick one up from a PIS office (see p. 34). Check by looking for nábř. Karla Marxe in the index—if you find it, you're holding a dud.

The only specific source of **transport information** is the enquiry centre at 22 92 52, but you'll be very lucky to speak to an Anglophone. Daytime routes of buses and trams are marked on most city maps. There's a standard ticket ('*lístek*') for the buses, trams and metros, costing 4kcs, which you can buy from the yellow machines in metro stations and on street corners (make sure that the green light on the top is on). You can also get them in tobacconists, newsagents and several cafés, but you *can't* buy them on trams or buses, so it's worth getting a bunch at a time. Validate them by punching them in the machines which you'll find on board the tram or bus, and in the vestibule of metro stations. The system relies on your honesty, backed up by occasional inspections by plain-clothed guards and on-the-spot fines of about £2 ($3.60). Each ticket is valid for one journey (although changes are only permitted on the metro), up to 90 minutes long. **Day passes** covering all three services can be bought from the red machines in most stations; and you can get passes up to a week from almost any *tabák*. Don't try to validate them. If you're under 10 or over 70, you have a free ride—and if you're not, you should be particularly careful not to cross one of Prague's most distinctive sub-cultures, female pensioners with time on their hands. Although the *babičky* congregate wherever there's a moral priority to be claimed—in supermarket queues, for example—you're most likely to encounter them joyriding on the transport system. Trams are their favourite. By law they're entitled to your seat, and may raise hell if you don't offer it spontaneously. During rush hours, the best policy is to stand throughout, unless you can somehow trump them. Physical disability obviously works; schizophrenia is another possibility.

Metro: This is the easiest of all ways to get around town. The chrome-plated Soviet-built network still has the legendary efficiency of totalitarianism, and the three lines and three intersections present few difficulties to even the worst sense of direction. Trains run from around 5 am to midnight, every few minutes at peak hours, and stops are scattered all over the centre of town. The junctions are at Muzeum (lines A and C), Můstek (lines A and B) and Florenc (lines B and C). The authorities do their best to make sure that things run smoothly; as on the trams, a recorded message announces the name of each stop (which has led to mass confusion on the rare occasions that it's slipped out of synch), and an unseen eye even watches the platforms to snap at you if you look as though you might leap off.

Trams: These quaint beasts shudder across Prague in droves. They're slower and less comfortable than the metro, but are useful if your destination or departure point isn't on the subway. An added pleasure on winter nights is that most seats are heated. The timetables are so simple that they look incredibly mystifying. Each of the city's hundreds of stops has its own, regularly updated, and the times given apply only to that

PRAGUE METRO

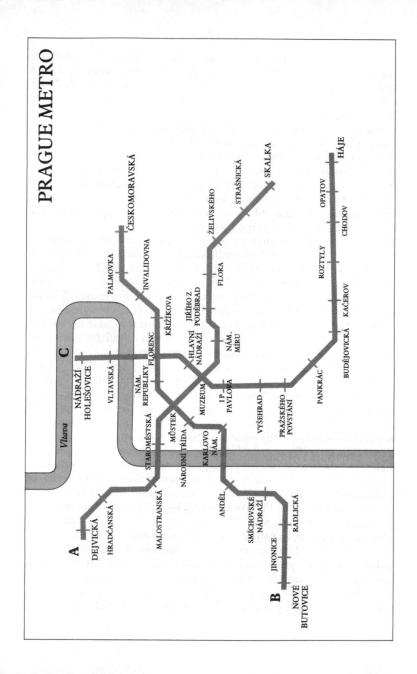

stop. You can usually rely on them almost to the minute. In summer, the regular service runs from 5 am–midnight, in winter until 10 pm. A system of **night trams** then takes over all the major routes; there are nine of them (routes 51–59), and they all pass through Lazarská, in the New Town. Night tram routes aren't marked on street maps, but there's a simple plan on most stops. To find one near you, look out for a white number on a blue background on your local stop.

Buses: These tend not to go through the centre of the city, but otherwise most of the same rules apply as for trams. The timetables are less reliable (tram jams are rarer); and if you're working from a map, take into account that the stops are much further apart. Night buses are marked on the bus-stop plans, but are only really useful if you're living in one of the hellhole housing estates in the suburbs.

Taxis: The main taxi-ranks are in Wenceslas Square; on the corner of Národní and Spálená; in Malostranské nám.; on the Old Town side of the Charles Bridge; at the top of Pařížská, next to the Old Town Square; and next to the Powder Tower. Cab drivers are required by law to use their meters, but during the lucrative tourist season they usually drive off in a huff if you press the point (unless they have recently bought a zapper from Berlin). Most of them, especially those waiting outside the swanky hotels in Wenceslas Square, delight in extracting exorbitant sums from foreigners, and unless you speak some Czech, you shouldn't set off until you've established the cost of your trip. A fair price, allowing for a moderate level of extortion, is about £1 ($1.80) for 3 miles. Humble Škoda cabs are about 10 per cent cheaper than their saloon cousins. Since you're almost certainly going to pay over the odds, tipping is generally neither expected nor justified, but if you meet a driver who's worth it or—exceptionally—one who turns on the meter, the going rate for foreigners is 10 per cent. Haggling and settling is generally a fairly amicable game, but if you have real problems, take the driver's number and let him know that you're doing it. Licences are priceless, and an understanding will be reached if a cabbie thinks that there's even a chance of him losing it. There's a useful **24-hour minicab service** at 20 39 41 and 20 29 51–9, with 500 radio-controlled cars, and controllers who can usually speak enough English to send one in your direction.

A ragged army of buccaneer cabs also cruise the streets at night. They will often reveal themselves if you look homeward bound, but in the small hours it's fine to wave down anything that moves (the police cars won't stop). They're often cheaper than the real thing, but bear in mind that you're not covered by the driver's insurance policy and may well be breaching a term of any holiday insurance cover you may have. Although motorized maniacs are rare in Prague, lone women should be wary of unofficial cabs.

By Car: Cars drive on the right in Czechoslovakia, and automobile anarchy is rarer than in many other European countries. The speed limit in towns is 60 kph (just under 40 mph), but from 11 pm–5 am, that goes up to 90 kph (about 55 mph). On open roads the second limit applies all the time, and on motorways you can travel at up to 110 kph (70 mph). Seatbelts are compulsory outside built-up areas; and driving with *any* alcohol in your bloodstream is strictly illegal. The rest of the road rules are pretty standard, except for those governing relations between cars and trams. The guiding principle is that you don't mess with a tram. It has right of way, even if that involves careering across your lane at full speed; and at stops in the centre of the road, you should never pass on the right while passengers are being disgorged unless a special route for passing traffic has been marked out. Disembarking tram passengers comprise a fair proportion of Prague's dead pedestrians each year.

Until the 1970s, motor traffic trundled uninterrupted through the winding alleys and broad boulevards of Prague. Large tracts of the capital have since been closed to traffic or restricted to those with special permits; and driving in the city centre is now more trouble than it's worth. You can buy a good driving map which shows which roads are navigable (*Praha pro motoristy*, available from all good map shops) but the best rule of thumb is to park on the periphery and continue your journey by public transport. Wenceslas Square and the surrounding streets are closed unless you're staying in one of the major hotels, in which case you should pick up a parking permit when you check in.

The influx of second-hand Mercedes following the collapse of the Berlin wall has helped destroy much of the mystique that once surrounded western motors, but snazzier makes and paintworks still attract discussion groups of auto-enthusiasts, and can be no less interesting to villainous types. If you own an obvious rustbucket, you needn't worry, but otherwise you should at least consider keeping your car in one of Prague's guarded car parks. There are three underground garages which may have space—next to the National Theatre, next to the Smetana Theatre (Smetanovo divadlo), and next to the Kotva store on nám. Republiky. In any case, you should always park in one of the city's car parks, or you run the risk of being towed—in which case, you'll probably find your baby at Černokostolecká street, 15 km outside Prague, although the police will provide more precise information if you call 158.

Petrol pumps are few and far between in Prague. Queues are getting shorter as the Soviets, who used to fuel the Warsaw Pact at knock-down rates, now bill their one-time allies in hard currency. Filling stations are marked on most maps, and the streets on which you'll find 24-hour garages are listed below:

Kališnická—neither super nor diesel.
Olšanská—no diesel.
E14 motorway (in Nusle).
Plzeňská.
Leninova/Dr Benešova.
Argentinská.
Karlínské nam.
Českobrodská—self-service, with vending machine (bring along a pile of 100kc notes).
Poděbradská.

Czechoslovakia's trunk-road surfaces are usually as smooth as any others that you'll find in Europe, but if your engine explodes or you otherwise sputter to a halt, call 154 and a patrol car full of so-called Yellow Angels will charge to the rescue. The Angels arrange for your hulk to be towed to the **24-hour repair service** for tourists and foreign cars at Limuzská 12 (tel 77 34 55); and if you haven't entirely run out of steam, you can drive there directly. After a **road accident**, you should go through the usual formalities of exchanging details, apologies, blows, etc., and you're also expected to report the news to the police on 236 64 64.

Car Hire: The state-owned Pragocar company is based at Opletalova 33, tel 22 23 24, and is open 365 days a year from 7 am–6 pm. Self-drive and chauffeur-driven cars are available (from a Škoda to a Renault), and if you want to drop your car off outside Czechoslovakia, Pragocar also acts as the agent for Avis. Its basic rates run from £19–39 ($33–69). Slightly more expensive is Czech Auto Rent, tel 683 21 65, whose offerings run up to chauffeur-driven Mercedes. Hertz operates out of the Palace Hotel, tel 236 16 37, but you'll also find offices for all the major western companies in most of the larger hotels and at the airport. All take major credit cards.

Motorbikes: The same driving rules apply as for cars, and the maximum speed limit is 60 kph (40 mph) during the day in built-up areas, and 80 kph (50 mph) in other situations. Driver and passenger have to wear helmets; and dipped headlights should be kept on throughout.

Bikewheels and tramlines may find it particularly hard to get on in wet weather—beware. If your dream machine is damaged, basic repairs are carried out at Jeseniova 56, tel 27 90 21.

Inefficient Travel: Messing about on the Vltava is one of the most useless ways of getting from A to B in Prague, since you have to go back to A eventually, but it's fun. See pp. 316–7 for **boating** details. A **horse-and-carriage** is only marginally more functional, and you can mount one at the Old Town Square during the summer. Almost no one rides a **bicycle** in hilly and holey Prague, but if the manager of Tempo-servis at Rybná 3 manages to win over the new private owner of his shop, he'll be opening a bike-hire centre there in the late summer of 1991. Alternatively, you can take a bicycle rickshaw ride courtesy of the entre-preneurial Little and Large Pavel Brothers. You'll find their customized tandem and busy shoe-shine stall at the Malá Strana end of the Charles Bridge.

Long-Distance Travel

Travelling beyond the city limits will involve either choo-choo trains or coaches. Prague's main coach station is at Florenc (on lines B and C of the metro), and there are smaller termini at Želivského (line A—beyond the local bus platforms after you leave the metro station) and Nádraží Holešovice (line C). Tickets sometimes have to be bought in advance, so arrive with time in hand; queues often build up well before the bus leaves, and if you find yourself at the back of one you might spend most of the journey on your feet.

Trains going vaguely northwards usually leave Hlavní nádraží or Nádraží Holešovice (see above); and those to the south run from Smí-chovské nádraží on line B of the metro. Trains also shoot off in all directions from Masarykovo nádraží. The entrance is on Havlíčkova, in the New Town. Tickets should be bought in advance, but if you're in a hurry, just jump on board and pay the small supplement to the conduc-tor. There are timetables on rollers in all the stations; look up your route on the map, and then refer to the corresponding table. The word for 'arrival' is *příjezd*; 'departure' is *odjezd*.

Fares within Czechoslovakia are still among the cheapest in Europe at the time of writing. Sample 2nd-class fares are £1 ($1.80) for 50 km, £1.50 ($2.70) for 100 km and £2 ($3.60) for a 200-km journey. There's a standard supplement of about 60p ($1) on fast trains, which you can identify on timetables by the abbreviated number of stops. The difference between 1st- and 2nd-class carriages is negligible on short journeys, but on longer trips the extra legroom is sometimes worth the 50 per cent premium. Couchettes and sleepers are a bargain—even a night of 1st-class comfort will only set you back an extra £2.50 ($4.50). There are no student or youth fares for travel within Czechoslovakia, but see page 4 for details of the Explorer Pass.

Prague may be only one stop on your grand tour—in which case, there are several worthwhile travel options available in the country. As links with the ex-Warsaw Pact decline, Czechoslovakia's once legendary travel bargains (Moscow for £2/$3.60, for example) are following it into the dustbin of history, but travelling east remains cheap. The journey to Warsaw costs about £25 ($45) and to Budapest, under £10 ($18). There are also 25 per cent reductions to ISIC-card holders travelling to Poland and the Soviet Union (and if you didn't get a visa in advance, you can get one for at least the former country at the embassy in Prague—see p. 25). You can book onward international rail tickets at the ČSD agency, near the taxi-rank at Hlavní nádraží (Mon–Fri 7.30 am–6 pm, Sat 7.30 am–1 pm). The friendly (unless beleaguered) staff can also get you back to London, and even organize a trip to Beijing on the Trans-Siberian express, subject to the average waiting-list of five weeks. The best coach bargains in Prague can be picked up at Bohemiatour on Zlatnická 7 (Mon–Fri 8 am–3.30 pm). It offers a rock-bottom service to London (£55/$99); as well as the chance to join a mob of Czechs on the often surreal day- and weekend-trips that have become popular since the 1989 revolution. They're usually dirt-cheap returns, with rough accommodation provided, and allow once travel-starved Praguers to go shopping and sightseeing for a few hours in a range of cities which include Venice and Paris.

Travellers with Disabilities

Even the most powerful electric wheelchair is likely to whine to a halt when confronted with some of Prague's hills, and over the last 40 years, very little has been done to make travelling across the city easier for people with limited mobility. There are no lifts in any of the metro stations, and it's sometimes difficult for even the most able-bodied to push into the crush of a tram before the doors close. Prague's new mayor has begun a long-needed review of disabled facilities, but a sign of how much needs to be done is the fact that only now are the first public toilets for non-walkers being installed in the capital. Kerbs are being smoothed in the Old Town, and more ramps are being constructed, but for the foreseeable future you can't expect an easy ride in any sense.

The best source of general information about travel across Europe in the UK is RADAR at 25 Mortimer St, London W1N 8AB, tel (071) 637 5400, which publishes *Holidays and Travel Abroad—A Guide for Disabled People* (£3). In the US, get hold of *Access to the World—A Travel Guide for the Handicapped* by Louise Weiss ($16.95 from Facts on File, 460 Park Avenue South, New York NY 10016). While planning your holiday, you should get in touch with **Metatur**, at Štefánikova 48, tel 55 10 64 (fax 55 10 49), run by the English-speaking Petr Marek. The agency organizes tours within Czechoslovakia, and is more than happy to cater for anyone with a physical disability. At the moment, its primary concern is to earn the hard currency to help home-grown disabled people, and its tours are also open to the able-bodied. It's just finished remodelling its own boarding house, a Renaissance palace with space and facilities for 100 people—but at the time of writing, the former owner (dispossessed by the Communists) is making threatening noises about wanting his lucrative and much-improved property returned. He may not succeed, and even if he does, Metatur is still the best (albeit only) source of information for anyone with visual, audial and dietary difficulties as well as the wheelchair-bound. The organization unfortunately has no priority on the few hotels in Prague with wheelchair access, which are the following (see Where To Stay for addresses):

Atlantic—four rooms, with adapted baths/WCs on each floor.
Atrium (under construction)—will have five rooms.
Belvedere—four rooms, and steps peppered around the building.
Diplomat—five rooms, and one non-smoking floor.
Forum—a single bathroom on the fifth floor.
Olympik—two rooms.
Palace—two rooms.

Czechoslovakia's spas are also said to help scores of medical conditions, from cerebral palsy to psoriasis. Each watering hole has its particular specialities, and most have therapy centres. For further information, contact Čedok before leaving home, or **Balnea** in Prague at Pařížská 11, tel 232 37 67 (fax 232 19 38).

Practical A–Z

Calendar of Events

Like street names, the significance of many dates in Prague has become very unclear since the 1989 revolution. Most Communist commemorations are very definitely *passé*, but they've been branded into so many heads that it's almost certain that pastiche celebrations will continue to occur. Four new memorial days have been added to the calendar as of 1991. Judging from those that have already passed at the time of writing, no one yet knows what you're meant to do on them, so if you pull into Prague on one of the days marked with a star, expect the unexpected. If you arrive on one of the days in bold on the other hand, you can at least be sure that every shop in the capital will be closed.

January
1—**New Year's Day**.
19—Anniversary of Jan Palach's Death*.

February
28—Victorious February. Anniversary of Communist takeover in 1948. Used to involve 'vast popular manifestations' in the Old Town Square.

March
7—Tomáš Masaryk's Birthday*. The first president of the Czechoslovakian republic, stooped, bearded, intellectual and much loved. This

damp squib is about as likely to be publicly celebrated as Victorious February.

April
Easter Monday. The year's excitement begins. In the fortnight before Easter, street vendors sell willow switches (*pomlázky*) bedecked with ribbons, and grandmothers to granddaughters across the country suck eggs. The preparations reach fruition on Easter Monday (Pondělí velikonoční) when, until midday, Prague's men thrash their women with the sticks to keep them fresh for the coming year. The newly-fertilized women then give their menfolk the hand-painted eggs, and are also allowed to pour buckets of water over them. The bizarre ritual takes place behind locked doors—but according to most reports, it's almost universal.

May
1—**Labour Day**. Likely to revert to another day of feasting and fecundity. This was one of the most enjoyable holidays of 1990, with a dawn-to-dusk dancing party held in the Old Town Square. However, mass unemployment may spoil the fun.

5—**Anniversary of Prague Uprising** (see page 47).

9—**Liberation Day**. Many thousands of Soviet soldiers died liberating Prague, and thankfully no one has dared cancel this holiday. However, the contribution of the US Army under Patton, ordered to stop short of Prague by General Eisenhower pursuant to the Yalta Agreement, was celebrated in Plzeň for the first time in 1990.

12—Anniversary of Smetana's Death. Musicians walk from his grave in Vyšehrad to Obecní dům and play his masterpiece, *Má Vlast*. Prague Spring music festival begins.

June
Very few scheduled entertainments, and most are of the most stupefying kind. However, the city's streets turn into a summer theatre of mime, puppets and guitars, and you could while away the entire month amidst the peaceful anarchy of the Charles Bridge.

July
Karlovy Vary International Film Festival (every even year).

5—SS Cyril & Methodius Day*.

6—Anniversary of Jan Hus's death (and birth)*.

August
Another month-long party of mime, music and theatre is usually held on

Prague's Střelecký ostrov (Marksman's Island). There were a few hiccups in the organization of the event in 1990, but it's long been an annual event.
21—Anniversary of 1968 invasion. An unknown quantity. In 1990 Prague went wild—a Soviet tank was upturned in Wenceslas Square, a yellow submarine was sighted in several spots, while a platoon of Praguers dressed up as military machines and attacked the Charles Bridge.

September
Proposed date of an annual Mozart festival, beginning in 1991. It's the brainchild of Italians, and promises to be a lavish city-wide extravaganza. You'll have to book for most concerts, but the Wolfgang-fest will either begin or end with a multimedia party on the Charles Bridge, with far-out patterns beamed onto the swirling Vltava below.

October
28—**Independence Day**. The only new workless day, replacing Victorious February and commemorating the foundation of the first republic in 1918.

November
17—Anniversary of the first demonstration of 1989 revolution. Very tepid ceremonies, followed by general retreat to cafés to discuss what went wrong.

December
Throughout the month, baths containing carp appear on Prague street corners, and the roads foam with rivulets of blood and water. The creatures are the Czech equivalent of the British turkey, and normally placid Praguers spend several minutes each day watching gizzards being removed. Don't stand too close—the *coup de grâce* generally sprays fishy brains across a wide radius.
6—St Nicholas's day. Troops of children dress up as St Nick or Old Nick (with attendant angels) and, led by their parents, stalk the streets of Prague handing out coal to evildoing tots, and sweets to the good ones.
8—Anarchists and youth protest John Lennon's death. The march should culminate at the John Lennon Wall (see p. 190), although in 1990 it set off from there to a particularly good nightclub.
24—Christmas Eve. Children apparently spend most of the day trying to fast, in the hope of seeing golden pigs. Carp is fried in batter and eaten. Baby Jesus brings the presents. St Nicholas makes the occasional surprise appearance.

25—**Christmas Day**. Nothing happens. More carp is eaten.
26—**St Stephen's Day**. More carp is eaten.
31—New Year's Eve, a.k.a. St Sylvester's Day. Half of Europe comes to Prague; the other half is in Berlin.

Climate and Best Time to Go

There's nothing too extraordinary about Prague's climate. The average temperature hovers around freezing point between December and February (and is often considerably below), climbing into T-shirt weather from May. July and August are the hottest months, reaching the high 20s fairly regularly; and the chill of autumn usually sets in towards the end of September. Rain isn't much of a problem, as Prague is surrounded by usefully absorbent mountains. The driest month is February, and the wettest July, when summer showers have a habit of dropping lazily in the late evening.

Average Temperatures in °C (°F)

January	*February*	*March*	*April*
−4/1 (25/34)	−2/3 (28/38)	1/7 (33/45)	9/13 (48/56)
May	*June*	*July*	*August*
9/18 (48/64)	13/22 (56/72)	14/25 (58/78)	14/25 (58/78)
September	*October*	*November*	*December*
11/20 (52/68)	6/12 (43/54)	2/5 (34/40)	−1/1 (30/34)

Baking afternoons and lingering twilight make the summer the most popular time to visit Prague, but if you have any control over your annual holiday, avoid the city in August. A fair proportion of Europe descends on the capital, along with globe-trotting Antipodeans and transatlantic Eurailers. Praguers take fright and leave for their country retreats every weekend; but you'll be left at the mercy of a snarled-up service industry that's inefficient at the best of times. Heat-seeking visitors should aim to arrive in late June or early July; or best of all, early September, when the almost-statutory holiday periods of much of Europe are over but the cobbles remain warm. Prague's buskers are still out in force on the streets, its gardens and islands are in late bloom, and the city heaves a sigh of relief at having survived the deluge. As autumn turns to winter, pensive types can watch leaves yellow and die, or head for the city's cafés and restaurants, which develop a jolly intimacy that lasts throughout the big chill. The capital closes down almost completely between Christmas Eve and Boxing Day (St Stephen's Day); but since 1989, New Year's Eve has been transformed into one of Europe's happiest fiestas. February is the cruellest month, but also the time that you're most likely to see Prague swathed in snow, not the mushy rubbish of the west, but the creaking stuff of Good King Wenceslas. Buds pop, sap rises, and public displays of affection reach new heights at the beginning of April (it's generally limited to kisses on the Charles Bridge, but many still remember a legendary performance under the St Wenceslas memorial in the spring of 1990). The end of the month is another of the optimum times to come to the city. When the Prague Spring music festival begins in early May, the tourist season has turned full circle.

Communications

Prague's **Main Post Office** is in the New Town at Jindřišská 14, tel 26 41 93, and is open 24 hours daily. Postal services are provided in the main hall; and when that's closed, in the small room on the left of the vestibule. Fax and telegram counters are in the room to the right. During the night, the public telephones are also there, but otherwise they're in the bigger room on the left. Counter 17 of the cavernous main hall will keep correspondence for you if you don't know where you'll be staying—letters should be addressed to you at 'Poste Restante/Jindřišská 14/110 000 Praha 1'. Have your passport when you collect your mail (Mon–Fri 6.30–11, Sat 7.30–1).

There are several other post offices in the city centre, including one in the Old Town at Kaprova 12 (Sat 8–1; Sun–Fri 8–6, and 8–8 for telegrams and telephoning); another in Malá Strana at Josefská 4; and one opposite St Vitus's Cathedral in the Third Courtyard of the castle (8–7).

Post: The lingering effect of pre-1989 friendships mean that it's still cheaper to send a letter to Beijing than to Bonn, and the Czechoslovakian postal service divides the non-Communist world into three zones: eastern Europe, western Europe and the rest. At the time of writing, sending a postcard costs, respectively, 0.50kc, 3kcs and 5kcs; a letter costs 1kc, 4kcs and (up to 10g) 6kcs. Expect prices to increase. Stamps can be bought from tobacconists, souvenir shops and the like, as well as from post office counters. Correspondence can still take anything from five days to two weeks to reach the west; there's an express service which doesn't cost much and can halve that time.

Sending a parcel can be an interminable chore. You're expected to take any packages destined for abroad to the post office at Plzeňská 139, tel 53 29 50, for inspection. Few post offices will let a parcel through otherwise—but you can sometimes avoid the red tape if you're only sending printed matter (in which case the local postmen and women will still want to have a peek). As a general rule, you should never expect post offices to sell anything as obvious as envelopes or wrapping paper, for which you should look for a shop marked *papír* or *papírnictví*.

Telephones: About half of Prague's public call boxes were disembowelled during a thieving frenzy that followed the 1989 revolution, and trying to find one that works can be frustrating in the extreme. With the orange phones (a disappearing breed, having proved structurally weaker than the others), place a 1kc coin in the groove, and it will drop automatically when the phone is picked up at the other end. The same applies to the small black phones. The grey phones also take larger value coins—flick the coin in immediately *after* you're connected. A high-tech phone with digital display is slowly being introduced—it takes your money in advance, and should regurgitate unused coins. Public telephones generally gurgle for a while before connecting you, so don't assume that the first noise you hear is an engaged tone. **Local calls** cost 1kc for an unlimited time, and you can make them from any of the three types of callbox. Prague telephone numbers can be from four to eight digits long; and the word for extension is *linka*. **Long-distance and international calls** can be made from all but the 1-kc phone boxes. The modern phones are the best for calling home (you can find a couple along Wenceslas Square), but you can also use the grey boxes if you're deft with a pile of 5kc coins. You can chat to an international operator by dialling 0135—and to reverse the charges, call 0132 and say 'na účet voleného (London/New York etc.)'. If you find that impossible, the operators all speak English, although 'collect call' is more widely understood than 'reverse charge call'. The dialling code to the UK is 0044, and to the USA it's 001; the code *for* Prague is 01042(2) from the UK and 01142(2) from the USA. You can also make international calls from a post office; the procedure varies, but generally you leave a deposit and dial the number yourself from a booth. There are more useful phone numbers on p. 000.

Faxes: Slimy sheets of paper can be sent from the Main Post Office and the one in the castle (non-stop and 8–7, respectively). The central office also acts as a reception service at 232 08 78, 232 09 78, 26 04 46 and 26 04 60 (all prefixed by the relevant code).

21

Telegrams: These can be sent from all the post offices listed above.
International Courier Service: DHL Couriers can be booked at the Forum Hotel (see p. 297).

Crime

As in the rest of one-time Communist Europe, an increase in (usually) petty crime has been an unwelcome side-effect of Czechoslovakia's Velvet Revolution. There's a basket of sociological explanations for the phenomenon; and one of the more concrete reasons is the fresh start that Václav Havel (an ex-con himself) magnanimously offered the hoodlum community in the heady first days of his presidency, when he signed an amnesty releasing some 200,000 villains. They've made the most of it, helped along by the fact that a demoralized police force (VB) virtually went into hiding for several months after the 1989 revolution. It was held in almost universal contempt for its zealous support of the old regime, obsessive enforcement of jay-walking legislation, and legendary depths of stupidity. They patrol in threes, and Praguers used to claim that one was there to write the arrest warrant, another to read it, and the last to keep an eye on the two intellectuals. Most people still harbour a healthy suspicion of the boys in green, which erupts into anger with regular revelations that many former secret police (STB) officers remain on the payroll; but as crime rises, Praguers are slowly having come to terms with the time-honoured quandary of who else to call when the flat gets burgled. Although the police have given up most of their thuggish ways, they can still be remarkably unhelpful. If you really need help, however, look for a patrol car with the sign 'VB' or 'Policie'. You can distinguish the law's long arm from army conscripts by the guns and truncheons that it carries. Prague's central police station is at Konviktská 14 in the Old Town; and the **emergency telephone number** is 158.

Praguers aren't used to the idea of anti-social types, and many are convinced that their city has become the New York of central Europe. In fact, it's still one of the safest capitals in the world, and elementary precautions should keep your property and person intact. The most common form of thievery is the gentle art of pick-pocketing. Crooks usually operate in pairs, and are particularly active wherever tourists gather—be especially careful on the Charles Bridge in the summer. Distraction and commotion are the nastiest weapons that you're likely to face. Before leaving home, make a separate note or a photocopy of your passport details (number, date, place of issue); and keep travellers' cheque receipts well away from the cheques themselves. It's also a good idea to jot down the numbers of your credit cards, and the emergency telephone numbers for reporting losses, failing which you have to brave the chaos of the Čedok office at Na příkopě 18—although it will probably take the thief as long to find somewhere to use a card in Prague as it will take you to plough through Čedok's bureaucracy. Most holiday insurance policies require you to file a report within 24 hours of a theft; go to the main police station at Konviktská 14. Optimists could also try the lost property office at Bolzanova 5 (Mon and Wed 7.30 am–12 noon, 12.30–6 pm; Tues, Thurs and Fri 7.30 am –12 noon and 12.30–4 pm, tel 236 88 87). If you're waylaid—or forgetful—on a train, each station also has its own lost-property office.

Physical violence is rare in most parts of the city. However, ugly situations may occur during the early hours in Wenceslas Square and the main station, the green in front of which has become known as Sherwood Forest (although the men who fill it are merry only in the worst sense). If you're a lone woman, you'll probably find Wenceslas Square doubly uncomfortable at night, since it's a well-known promenade for prostitutes, pimps and sad men (the same applies to Perlova Street), but otherwise don't worry too much about wandering around the rest of the city. Keys, knees and umbrellas are useful weapons to keep in reserve, and Czech hairspray is apparently a particularly effective blinding agent.

Finally, anyone black or even marginally off-white should expect to come across a certain degree of racism. It's often of a fairly innocent kind (much of the former Warsaw Pact seems unaware that the word 'nigger' is impolite), but it can create the occasional uncomfortable situation. The concept of a black American is widely understood (although it's best if he or she knows a lot about rapping), but anyone who's British but not white is still something of a riddle to many in Prague. However, it's the native non-whites who bear the brunt. One of the most unpleasant of the genies to slip out of the velvet bottle in 1989 is an open dislike of the 30,000-strong Vietnamese population, and most notably of all, the racism shown towards the country's several hundred thousand gipsies (*cikány*). The latter can be raucous and probably commit more than their fair share of the country's crime, but it's very difficult to find a Praguer who could even preface his stereotypes with the assertion that one of his best friends is a gipsy.

Customs and Traditions

Praguers tend to be polite and shake hands a lot, but there are only a few peculiar habits which you really need to know. They can be mastered in a day, and often ease social intercourse considerably.

* If you are staying in a private flat and find yourself receiving strange looks as you walk around your tenement, say *dobrý den* (good day) and smile. The greeting is ubiquitous even among perfect strangers, and elderly folk can get particularly cross if they're ignored.

* As you leave a café table which you have been sharing with Czechs, say *na shledanou* (au revoir).

* When entering a Czech house, make as if to remove your shoes. Your host may well waive the requirement, but the reflex will be seen as a sign of good breeding.

* When in a pub, *never* pour beer from one glass into another. If you do, an awestruck hush is almost certain to descend over the table, and in extreme cases, you may be asked to leave.

* Women can expect to be treated as sex objects and/or helpless creatures by almost all male Praguers. Feminism hasn't taken off yet, and you'll come across a huge amount of soft-porn and vile-looking tissue paper magazines during your stay.

Electricity

Prague's voltage is usually 220 AC, but you'll need a plug with two round prongs before anything will fire up. Buy adaptors before you leave, as they're next to impossible to buy in the city. The best is the universal kind, because it can deal with the earthing prong that sticks out of some sockets. If you're staying in private accommodation in an older part of town, the voltage may be 110 AC. That's fine for US equipment, but UK hairdryers will work at half-speed, while high-voltage equipment won't work at all. Pack a transformer, if in doubt.

Embassies

Austria: Viktora Huga 10, tel 54 65 57.
Belgium: Valdštejnská 6, tel 53 40 51.

Bulgaria: Krakovská 6, tel 26 43 10.
Canada: Mickiewiczova 6, tel 32 69 41.
Denmark: U Havlíčkových sadů 1, tel 25 47 15.
Federal Republic of Germany: Vlašská 19, tel 53 23 51–6.
France: Velkopřevorské nám. 2, tel 53 30 42.
Hungary: Karoliny Světlé 5–7, tel 22 73 32.
India: Valdštejnská 6, tel 53 26 42.
Israel: Milady Horákové 84, tel 37 39 60.
Italy: Nerudova 20, tel 53 14 43.
Netherlands: Maltézské nám. 1, tel 53 13 78.
Poland: Valdštejnská 8, tel 53 69 51.
Romania: Nerudova 5, tel 53 30 59.
Spain: Pevnostní 7, tel 32 71 24.
Sweden: Úvoz 13, tel 53 33 44, 53 38 65.
Switzerland: Pevnostní 7, tel 32 83 19, 32 04 06.
USSR: Pod kaštany 1, tel 38 19 40.
United Kingdom: Thunovská 14, tel 53 33 47/70.
USA: Tržiště 15, tel 53 66 41.
Yugoslavia: Mostecká 15, tel 53 14 43, 53 30 97.

The British Embassy acts on behalf of citizens from Australia, Ireland and New Zealand.

Insurance

Travel insurance policies rarely come in useful, but when they do, you're very glad you took them out. Almost every travel agency has forms lying around, and your cover can begin from the moment you sign the dotted line and hand over your premium. The extent of coverage varies, and it's generally worth while to compare at least a couple of policies. The ceiling of medical coverage is less important for holidays in Prague than in some other cities, since British citizens receive free treatment, and prices for everyone else are more than reasonable. More important are the theft and loss provisions. Check whether stolen cash is reimbursed, and go through the even smaller print detailing exclusions and the minimum and maximum losses covered. The latter is often the sneakiest clause of all, and may result in your recovering only half a camera, and an even more tiny fraction of a lost suitcase. US students with an ISIC card have free and automatic (albeit limited) coverage from the moment they venture out of the home of the brave.

Medical Emergencies

Ambulance—tel 333
Doctor—tel 155
Fire—tel 158

As stated above, British citizens can have most minor ailments treated free of charge in Czechoslovakia, thanks to a long-standing reciprocal arrangement between the two countries, which covers almost any treatment short of liposuction and plastic surgery. The USA hasn't yet offered Czechs the dubious benefits of Medicare, and US passport-holders will be billed in full for any treatment that they receive, with a 50 per cent deposit payable prior to treatment. All poorly foreigners should head for the Fakultní Poliklinika, on the second floor at Karlovo nám. 28 (Mon 7.15 am–5 pm, Tues–Thurs 7.15 am–3.45 pm, Fri 7.15 am–2.30 pm). If you need emergency treatment after hours, the best policy is to call the doctor or ambulance at the above numbers, but you could also go straight to the Nemocnice Na Homolce on Roentgenova, off V úvalu, tel 52 92 1111—ask for the foreigners' department. There's a dental service for tourists at the Poliklinika. If your agony doesn't coincide with its opening hours, Prague's **emergency dentist** at Vladislavova 22 will temporarily cap or permanently extract the offending tooth, from Mon–Fri 7 pm–7 am and all through the weekend, tel 26 13 74. The waiting room alone can be a harrowing vision of purgatory, and the services provided are surrounded by so many Prague folk legends that you should probably grin and bear it until the Poliklinika reopens. There are plenty of **opticians** around; look for a sign saying *oční optika*, or feel your way to Mostecká 3, tel 53 11 18, or Národní 37, tel 22 10 71. There are scores of pharmacies (*lékárna*) where you can redeem your prescriptions. Several are open for business 24 hours a day, but the dozy apothecaries almost invariably have to be banged awake during the wee hours. The most central is the non-stop shop at Na příkopě 7, tel 22 00 81/2, and the others are listed below.

Ječná 1, tel 26 71 81
Koněvova 150, tel 89 42 03
Nám. bratří Synků 6, tel 43 33 10
Štefánikova 6, tel 53 70 39
Pod Marjánkou 12, tel 35 09 67
Milady Horákové 48, tel 37 54 9
Nám. dr Holého 15, tel 82 44 86

Sokolovská 304, tel 83 01 02
Moskevská, tel 72 44 76

One particularly pressing type of emergency can be dealt with by the
condom machines in the vestibules of most metro stations, all open 24
hours. Look for the boxes with the sign 'Men's Shop'. On a similar
theme, women spending some time in Czechoslovakia might note that
while the Czechoslovakian contraceptive pill is less fearsome than it once
was, it's still more hormone-unfriendly than western varieties.

Money

The Czech currency is the crown (*koruna*), mystifyingly abbreviated to
kc, which is made up of 100 heller (*halér*). At the time of writing, the
country's banks offer about 55kcs to the UK£ and 30 to the US$, but as
economic reforms push the currency towards full convertibility and
prices inflate, those figures will become laughable. To a large extent, the
exchange rate is likely to adapt itself to price increases, and **almost all of
the current prices in this book are given in western currency**.
However, goods which were heavily subsidized for social reasons by the
Communists, such as food, drink and transport, will probably increase at
a higher rate than inflation. All this means that it's only possible to give
very rough estimates of how much your stay in Prague will cost. The
following prices should give you some idea. They all assume 20 per cent
inflation and an exchange rate of £1 = $1.80. In the case of food,
anticipate planned across-the-board rises in mid-1991.

Private flat, per person per night—£10–£30 ($18–54).
Double room in hotel (cheap)—£16 ($29).
Double room in hotel (expensive)—£130 ($234).
Full dinner for two—£8–30 ($15–54).
Loaf of bread—20p (36¢).
Bottle of beer—25p (45¢).
Bottle of wine—£1 ($1.80).
Kiwi fruit (ubiquitous)—15p (27¢).
Packet of Czech cigarettes—15–50p (27–90¢).
Taxi-ride for three miles—£1.20 ($2.16).
Ticket for major opera or play—£1.00+ ($1.80+).
Weekly travel pass for bus, tram and metro—£1.50 ($2.70).

Although it's still impossible to buy Czech currency before leaving
home, the once-legendary maze of compulsory exchanges and triple-

tiered rates has been abolished, and the only paper-work you still face is folding up the bills concerned. Don't even bother with the black market any more. The rate on the street used to be twice that on offer in official banks, but since currency reforms, the difference is only a few crowns. Moneychangers often try to make up for declining profits by handing over inflation-infected or otherwise useless currencies—the Polish *zloty* is a particular favourite. If you insist on dodgy dealing, don't accept anything that doesn't have the word *Československých* on it; and if your partner isn't prepared to hand you his money first, something is rotten in the state of the deal. Also beware of being handed small 100kc notes marked with the ugly mug of ex-Communist president Klement Gottwald—they were withdrawn from circulation for ideological reasons in early 1991. If you're of a charitable bent, you could also bear in mind that although foreigners no longer face jail for dealing on the black market, your spiv business partner may go down for months or years if caught.

Exchange offices now exist all over Prague, and almost every hotel and accommodation agency will be happy to relieve you of your hard currency. Fast, convenient and horribly incongruous Chequepoint branches also gleam out of the medieval centre of the town at Staroměstské nám. 27, Celetná 18 (8 am–8.30 pm) and the Third Courtyard of Hradčany Castle (Mon–Sun 9 am–6 pm). There's also one at Václavské nám. 1. You can change money (at a lower rate of commission) at almost any of the many banks in the centre, such as the Komerční banka at Václavské nám. 42 or the Živnostenská banka at Na příkopě 20. The second is open until 12 noon Sat, but bank opening hours tend to be Mon–Fri 8 am–6 pm. There are 24-hour exchange facilities at the larger hotels, the most central being at the Jalta on Václavské nám. 45. Before deciding how much to change, check that you'll be able to reconvert any excess back into western currency (at the time of writing, the procedure is still expensive and time-consuming, but that's likely to change).

Cash: The plastic revolution has yet to reach Prague, and cash is still required almost everywhere. A small wad of western currency is useful for emergency situations, since it's usually easy (if illegal) to spend it directly. There's no longer the mystical premium attached to the US dollar that there was before 1989, and £ sterling and Deutschmarks are just as well understood by most people now. Despite a long-standing fascination with *valuta* (hard currency), Czechs can become very annoyed if tourists treat the crown as a joke, and although young Germans seem rarely to change their D-Marks at all, it's always best to pay in Czech money unless absolutely desperate. (On a similar theme, avoid

loud comments on how cheap everything is—penny-pinching Praguers often understand enough English to get hot under the collar.) Western cash can also be useful for bribery—but although the practice, along with tit-for-tat backscratching, is still ubiquitous in Prague, it's not something that you should try while in the city unless you're with a Czech friend who suggests it. The etiquette and unspoken language of corruption means that foreigners almost invariably get the wrong end of the stick.
Credit cards: Major cards can still only be used in the swankiest restaurants, shops and hotels. (See Food and Drink, and Where to Stay.) However that's changing as privatization proceeds, and it's also now possible to get cash advances on certain cards. Go to Čedok at Na příkopě 18 if you have an Access/Mastercard; and to the Komerční banka (see above) if it's a Visa. Diners' Club and American Express are also handled by Čedok; call 231 04 06 for the latest details.
Travellers' cheques: Few if any shops are yet prepared to accept these in payment, but cheques are the only safe way to carry around small fortunes in Czechoslovakia. American Express, Visa and Eurocheques are the only ones that you can be sure will be easily recognized by Prague's suspicious bank staff (although they will eventually cash any major cheque). At the time of writing, it's only possible to get hard currency for a cheque in some banks, such as the Komerční banka at Václavské nám. 42. If your cheques are pilfered, the following addresses provide what passes for an instant refund in Czechoslovakia.

American Express—Čedok, Na příkopě 18, tel 22 42 51.
Visa, Eurocheque—Živnostenská banka, Na příkopě 20, tel 22 35 51 (Mon–Fri 8 am–6 pm).

Telegraphic transfers: Most major western banks have hitched up with at least one of their Czech cousins, and having money wired over is no problem. The best policy in an emergency is to call your western benefactor (reversing the charges) and have him or her find out when and where you can lay your hands on the loot. Barclays Bank sounds the most efficient over the phone. It's soon to open up a branch in Prague, and until it arrives you can have money sent from any of its offices abroad to either the Komerční banka or the Živnostenská banka. Make sure to find out which branch.

Packing

Prague makes few sartorial demands on tourists. Blue jeans have been the acme of popular fashion for two decades, and until 1989 a pinstripe either signified a trader from the west, a member of the secret police or a Party official. Václav Havel's heroic struggle with his suit is a sign that the times are a-changing, but the city remains far less formal than most other European capitals. Smartness is expected in the more expensive restaurants, and if you're planning a night at the opera, something elegant might be appropriate; otherwise, wear just what you want. Bring walking shoes to tackle the city's cobbles and hills; an umbrella is usually enough for what the heavens might throw at you.

Other objects worth tossing into your suitcase are a knife (for picnics), an alarm clock, and basic medicines for emergencies. Travel light—you can still pick up most day-to-day items in the shops for less than they would cost at home. A set of passport photographs is useful for student cards and onward visas. If you've got Czech friends, it's a nice idea to phone them before you leave and ask if they'd like a present. Most people will have peculiar desires for obscure objects that haven't yet reached Prague: Monty Python videos, bottles of Guinness, etc.

Religious Affairs

Religion has been through strange times in Czechoslovakia. A population that was 90 per cent Protestant by the early 1600s reverted to Catholicism *en masse* over the next century, faced with a daunting combination of late Baroque churches and cruel and unusual punishments. More recently, an anathema was pronounced on religion by the Communists during the 1950s: churches were looted and closed, anti-Zionism was often used as a cloak for anti-Semitism, and a subject called Scientific Atheism became a compulsory part of the national curriculum. Even though religious policies were less repressive from the early 1960s, few would publicly admit their faith to the government, which was even less likely to admit the admissions; but the most recent survey (by the Catholic church) suggests that 65% of the population are Catholic, and about 5% Protestant.

Czech Catholics have always had to face the uncomfortable fact that the national hero, Jan Hus, was burned with the connivance of a pope. As a result, the religion has never had the stridency or nationalistic leanings that it acquired, for example, in Poland, although Prague's Cardinal Tomášek became a much-admired figure of the opposition to Communism. For corresponding reasons, nonconformism has recovered considerable ground since the dark days of the Counter-Reformation. The Czech national church is the Unity of Czech Brethren, established in

1918 as a gentler version of the almost-Calvinist Unity of Bohemian Brethren (the successors of the Hussites—see p. 36). Prague's Jews have dwindled to a minority of less than a thousand; in 1700, they formed 25% of the city's population, and before the war one in twenty Praguers still described themselves as Jewish.

After years during which proselytizing was heavily discouraged or banned, there's also been an upsurge of interest in sects and cults since 1989—sometimes charming, sometimes alarming. Václav Havel spent a day meditating for peace when the Dalai Lama visited Prague in mid-1990; and Prague's Hare Krishnas now sing *mantras* to polite applause in Wenceslas Square on summer weekends. Bands of pearly-teethed American evangelists are often to be found on the Charles Bridge, interspersing their ditties with political lectures and good news, usually with the help of sign language or a brainwashed Czech. Jehovah's Witnesses have also arrived—hundreds of happy families (all sporting identification badges) came to a convention in the city in 1990. It's going to be an annual event, but despite initial sympathy for the lucky elect, their foot-in-the-door techniques seem so far to have caused more bafflement than enlightenment.

Church services were only banned for a short while in the 1950s, but immediately after the revolution there was an upsurge in churchgoing among all ages and sections of the population. For a while, crucifixes became a popular fashion accessory among Prague's youth, but now that religion has lost its image as a symbol of anti-Communism, the wave of interest is dying down again. The times of services are listed below. Sunday Mass is held in English at St Joseph's Church, and you can confess your holiday sins to a Czech priest who'll more or less understand at 10 am, 30 minutes before the service begins.

Roman Catholic
Our Lady Before Týn, Staroměstské nám. Mon–Fri 5.30 pm, Sat 9 pm, Sun 11.30 am and 9 pm.
Our Lady of the Snows, Jungmannovo nám. 18. Mon–Sat 8 am and 6 pm; Sun 9 am, 11 am and 6 pm.
Our Lady of Victory, Karmelitská 9. Mon, Tues, Thurs, Fri 9 am; Sun 9 am, 10.30 am and 7 pm.
St Francis's, Křížovnické nám. 2, Sun 9 am.
St Giles's, Husova 8. Mon–Sat 6.30 pm; Sun 8.30 am, 10.30 am and 6.30 pm.

St James's, Malá Štupartská 6. Mon–Fri 6.45 am; Sat 8 am; Sun 8 am and 11 am.
St Joseph's, Josefská Sun 10.30 am.
St Nicholas's, Malostranské nám. Mon–Sat 7.30 am; Sun 8 am and 11 am.
St Vitus's Cathedral, Prague Castle. Mon–Fri 5.45 pm; Sat 7 am; Sun 7 am, 9.15 am, 11 am and 3 pm.

Greek Orthodox
SS Cyril & Methodius, Resslova 9. Tues and Thurs 8 am; Sat 8 am and 5 pm.

Czech Hussite Church
St Nicholas's, Staroměstské nám. Sun 10.30 am; Wed 5 pm.

Methodist
Ječná 19. Sun 9 am; Tues 7 pm; Wed 7 pm.

Baptist
Vinohradská 68. Thurs 6.30 pm; Sun 9 am and 6 pm.

Seventh-Day Adventist
Korunní 60. Sat 9 am and 2 pm.

Jewish
Orthodox: Staronová Synagoga, Červená ul.
Conservative: Jubilejní Synagoga, Jeruzalémská 5.
Services are held on Friday and Saturday evenings at the beginning and end of the sabbath. The precise times are pinned up in the vestibule of the Staronová Synagoga (Old-New Synagogue).

Muslim
Neither the Iranian, Iraqi nor Kuwaiti embassies knew of a mosque in Prague.

Services

Laundries and Dry Cleaners: There are no laundrettes, but laundries are common. Look out for the sign *prádelna* or *prádlo*. Two useful ones in the centre are at Václavské nám. 17 (Mon–Fri 6 am–8 pm), and Mostecká 2 (Mon–Fri 7 am–7 pm).
Photographic Services: You can buy most standard brands of film in all major hotels, and plenty of smaller shops. If you need something more complicated, try Foto-Kino-Optika-Video at Lazarská 6 (Mon–Fri 8 am–12.30 pm and 2–6 pm), the first and still the largest private camera

shop in the capital. Express film labs, of varying quality, are springing up to meet the demands of snapshooters; the Fotoexpress Minilab, on Lázeňská 15 offers a 1-hour service (Mon–Wed 9–7, Thurs 9–8, Fri 9–6, Sat–Sun 10 am–6 pm). You can get passport photographs in the 'Polaroid Studio Express' shops. There's one in the subway half-way down Wenceslas Square (Mon–Fri 8 am–7 pm); but traditionalists might prefer the black-and-white studio at Bartolomějská 1 (Mon–Fri 8 am–6 pm). There's a photocopying shack at the back of the Máj department store on Národní.

Express Shoe Repairs: There are several while-you-wait cobblers in the centre of town. You could hobble to either the shop inside the arcade at Panská 4, or that at Václavské nám. 62, tel 235 19 93 (Mon–Fri 9 am–7 pm, Sat 9 am–1 pm).

Smoking

Prague lives under a sooty coat; its pollution is said to be about as bad as that of central London, which is no mean feat in a city where a traffic jam has been known to make the news. Deep breathing will provide plenty of carbon monoxide, but if you need nicotine as well, you'll find Prague a highly congenial retreat from the passive smoking lobby of the UK and US. The first thing to do is to divest yourself of your duty-frees, which are still a sure sign that you've just stepped off the plane. Czech cigarettes are far cheaper than those of the west, and often only slightly more destructive to your health. The mildest are probably the Bulgarian *Select*, but *Femina* also provides a smooth drag (blue packs; the reds are slightly stronger, and green are menthol). *Milde Sorte* are Austrian, and have a certain cachet among the upwardly-mobile; but Prague's favourite has to be *Petra*, as endorsed by 40-a-day President Havel. *Sparta* are the Marlboros or Camels of the country, rugged, manly and frightfully strong. The Constructivist lettering of *M20* make them useful as souvenirs; but the closest thing to genuine Soviet cardboard has to be the filterless *Start*, the humble favourite of penniless conscripts and addicts past the point of no return.

There are only a few other things that smokers need to know. You should be very careful about asking a Czech for a light ('mate oheň?'). If you're proferred a lit cigarette, never remove it from the other person's hand unless you're sure about what you're doing. To take it is usually regarded as very bad manners, but can also be construed as an erotic suggestion. Similarly, never scrounge someone's last cigarette, and don't press yours onto someone else, as Czechs have a colourful phrase for such situations. Finally, almost all Czech beer joints ban the weed in their dining rooms for a couple of hours at lunchtime. Waiters hurl ashtrays onto the table the minute that it's over, and almost enough nicotine emanates from the furnishings to keep addicts going throughout, but it's the closest thing to a smoke-free zone that you're likely to find in Prague.

Students

Despite the insistent claims of many UK youth-orientated travel agencies, there are no travelling discounts to students already within Czechoslovakia, unless you're travelling on to Poland or the Soviet Union (25 per cent reduction). However, there are several deals available before you leave (see p. 4), and holders of an ISIC card are also eligible for reductions on almost all Prague's museums and galleries. You can buy the card at most student union offices, as well as a number of travel agents, including London's STA Travel and Campus Travel, and New York's Council Travel (see page 2). In Prague, a scrap of paper that vaguely suggests that you're enrolled somewhere should persuade the staff of the International Students' Union to issue you with the card. See p. 326.

Toilets

You'll find toilets in every subway station; and if you're desperate, it's acceptable to rush into a café or wine bar and ask for the *záchod*, a.k.a. WC (*ve tse*). 'Men' is *muži*; 'women' is *ženy*. Paper is rarely provided—if you're a woman, you'll usually receive one scrap from an attendant in exchange for a compulsory payment of one or two crowns, but it's generally advisable to carry spare supplies. Apart from that, there's very little difference between Prague's loos and those of NATO countries.

Tourist Information

The official **Prague Information Service** (PIS) has offices all over Prague, for example on Na příkopě 20, and Staroměstské nám. 22: open Mon–Fri 8 am–8 pm, Sat–Sun 9 am–6 pm (April–Oct); Mon–Fri 8 am–6 pm, Sat–Sun 9 am–5 pm (Nov–Mar). Someone can usually be found who speaks English, and although it can be strangely dificult to persuade them to divulge much information during the frenzy of high season, you can pick up some idea of what's going on in Prague and fill in the gaps with the sources listed below. PIS also runs sightseeing tours (by coach in summer), as does Bohemiatour on Zlatnická 7, and IfB next to the Hotel Evropa at Václavské nám. 25.

The best cultural overview is *Přehled kulturních pořadů v Praze* ('Summary of the Cultural Programme in Prague'), which you can buy in most newsagents. It's published at the beginning of each month, but it usually sells out within days. The listings are largely self-explanatory; but if you find its detail and lack of English translations intimidating (or if you can't get hold of it), pick up a 'Cultural Events' booklet from a PIS office. Several new listings magazines in English have appeared since the revolution, which you can buy in most hotels, and at Chequepoint exchange offices (see page 28).

No single booking agency covers all of Prague's venues, but they're often useful sources of information and can save you time and effort—if an English-speaker is behind the desk. IfB (see above) is one of the only agencies to sell advance tickets for all the grand venues, including the Národní divadlo, Nova Scena, Smetanovo divadlo and Laterna Magika, but you have to pay in hard currency. Service is efficient and friendly, but the surcharge that's added (£10/$18) is about ten times the box-office price of most tickets at the time of writing. You can buy your own tickets directly from the four theatres listed above. All the smaller theatres, and most concerts, including pop music and the cheap and cheerful balls that are often held in the city, are dealt with by two agencies hidden in shopping arcades: SLUNA on Václavské nám. 28 (Mon–Fri 10 am–12.30 pm and 1.30–6 pm) and Melantrich at Václavské nám. 38 (Mon–Fri 9 am–7 pm). Cinema tickets can be bought at the SLUNA office in Panská 4. The last three bureaux all charge a 10 per cent commission. The only place in Czechoslovakia to buy tickets for the Prague Spring music festival is at Hellichova 18. It's only open for a month from mid-April onwards, but advance information and tickets can be ordered by post from Bohemia Tickets International/ P.O.B. 534/ Praha 1—111 21.

History

> Those who lie on the rails of history must expect to have their
> legs chopped off.
>
> Rudé Právo (Communist Party newspaper) 1979

The thousand-year history of Prague is one of the most inspiring and
tragic of any European city. Glory, betrayal and martyrdom litter its
pages, while its magnificent skyline has grown to maturity, bloodied but
unbowed, through centuries of invasion and war. Prague's citizens—
who conceived nationalism before it even twinkled in the eyes of the rest
of Europe—now stand on the threshold of freedom once again. What
they'll do with it is anyone's guess—but if history is any guide, it's not
going to be dull.

The First Přemysl is Found

The story begins with the establishment of Bohemia's first ruling dynasty, the Přemysls, at some time around the end of the 8th century. Myth
and history are intertwined, but according to the former, the Čech tribe
had established itself at Vyšehrad ('higher castle'), a rocky outcrop on the
Vltava river that still bears the same name. Čech himself was a mass-
murderer on the run; but it was his son, Krok or Crocus, who went down
in legend as the putative founding father. However, he had one funda-
mental weakness—try as he might (and he tried at least three times) he

times) he was unable to produce a male heir. Of his three daughters, Libuše, Kázi and Teta, Libuše was the most impressive and the one who succeeded him. According to Bohemia's venerable chronicler, Cosmas of Prague (c. 1045–1125), she was:

> ... a wonderful woman among women, chaste in body, righteous in her morals, second to none as judge over the people, affable to all and even amiable, the pride and glory of the female sex, doing wise and manly deeds; but, as nobody is perfect, this so praiseworthy woman was, alas, a soothsayer.

Cosmas tells a good story, even if chastity and morality don't seem to have been Libuše's strong points—it's said that when she tired of her lovers, she destroyed the evidence by having them hurled off the Vyše-hrad into the Vltava. As for the soundness of her judgments, even Cosmas admits that the unpopularity of one of her decisions (over a boundary dispute) caused something of a crisis. The losing party complained that only a husband could knock some sense into hysterical Libuše, and the cry was taken up by the men of the tribe. Libuše's response was to go into a trance. Pointing towards the distant hills, she told them to follow her horse, which would take them to a ploughman whose descendants would rule over them for ever. The horse trotted off, the people dutifully followed and a sturdy farmer named Přemysl was brought back to wed Libuše. A dynasty had begun.

The city of Prague (as distinct from the settlement at Vyšehrad) also owes its legendary origins to one of Libuše's prophecies. According to Cosmas, she was overcome by a vision involving two golden olive trees and 'a town, the glory of which will reach the stars'. Again the loyal subjects trooped off to a spot described by Libuše, where they found a man building a door-sill (in Czech, *práh*—hence the name Praha or Prague) for his cottage. Legend has it that this spot was on what is now Hradčany, or the Castle District. Building started in earnest and the rest, as they say, is history.

Archaeological finds and other scanty evidence suggest that the first people in the area were a Celtic tribe known as the Boii, who lived here at the turn of the Christian era and stayed long enough to leave behind the name 'Bohemia'. In the 2nd century AD, Marcus Aurelius briefly considered incorporating the region into the Roman empire but thought better of the idea—the place was just too wild. In about the 5th century, the Čechs, a Slavonic tribe from Croatia, are thought to have established a powerful presence in the area, but there's no record of Crocus, and it's only in the later 9th century that the first historically-attested Přemysl, **Bořivoj**, appears on the scene as ruler of Bohemia. The little princedom was still an insignificant cog in the Greater Moravian empire, which included most of the Slavs of central Europe, and which was engaged in endless bloody tussles with the German Frankish state—known as the Holy Roman Empire—to the west.

The Great Schism between the Roman and Byzantine Churches had already begun to open up, and German monks were scurrying across the Moravian empire with their version of the Good Book. As far as the Slavonic kings were concerned, that represented enemy propaganda—but Christianity was clearly the coming thing, and in about 863, the empire's ruler, Rostislav, turned to the eastern Church for help. Emperor Michael sent along **Brothers Methodius and Cyril**, two Greek Holy Rollers who arrived with a Bible and a liturgy written in a new Greek-based alphabet (Glagolitic, or Cyrillic script) that could deal with the grunts peculiar to the Slavs. Jealous Germans levelled the usual charges of heresy, but the two men remained on fairly good terms with Rome until their death. In Bohemia, Bořivoj was dunked into the new religion by Methodius in about 874. Mass abandonment of storm and fertility gods followed.

Bohemia Takes Off

Although the Slavs had little sympathy for the Holy Roman Empire, its power couldn't be ignored. As the Přemysls struggled to control Bohemia, they began to turn away from the east—and the influence of Germans in Bohemian affairs, which was to become a tragic motif over the next millennium, began to grow. In 885, Pope Stephen V declared the Slavonic liturgy to be heretical. The Přemysls took his word for it and began the switch away from Cyrillic, for which western tourists can be eternally grateful. Bohemia remained subservient to the Moravian empire until the beginning of the 10th century, when that empire suddenly disappeared from the map, seized by rampant Magyars who had recently marauded across from central Asia. The invaders' conquests included Slovakia, the province to the east of modern Czechoslovakia; it was to stay under Hungarian control for almost all of the next thousand years, but little Bohemia was left untouched. No one knows why it was spared, but it's from this point that its history hots up.

In about 921, **Prince Wenceslas** (Václav) became Bohemia's sovereign. A gentle Christian who seems to have spent his life attending church foundation ceremonies, he may have been a suitable subject for imaginative 19th-century carols but he just wasn't up to the rough-and-tumble of Dark Age intrigue. In 935, he was murdered on the way to mass by his brother, **Boleslav the Cruel**. What Boleslav lacked in kindness, he made up for with political skill: by selective extermination, he removed the remaining rivals to the Přemysls in Bohemia; he extended his dominions massively, punching a large hole into Magyar territory and marrying his daughter into the Polish ruling family; and he successfully resisted political pressures from Rome. In 973, under the rule of his less cruel son, Boleslav the Pious, Bohemia's strength was acknowledged by the pope, who finally consented to the founding of a bishopric in Prague. Two more Boleslavs followed—Boleslav the Third, who reverted to type and murdered several unruly nobles at a banquet, and his brother, Boleslav the Brave. The last was called in from Poland by the Bohemian nobility to sort out his sibling, which he did by blinding him.

Over the next two centuries, Bohemia was pulled ever deeper into the tangled web of the Holy Roman Empire, and its interminable struggles between power-hungry popes, German princes and whoever had mustered the support to be elected emperor. In the early 13th century, both pope and emperor allowed Bohemia's princes to call themselves kings and wear a crown—which was as unimpressive as it sounds, and laid the ground for future emperors to claim the right to appoint Bohemia's king. An explosive brew was also building up at lower levels of society. Under the reign of King Wenceslas I (1230–53) German merchants were invited to Prague and other parts of Bohemia, where they were allowed to govern themselves according to their own laws. Native nobles eyed the influx with growing suspicion. They had accumulated a great deal of power thanks to the murderous tiffs of the Přemysls, and had no intention of letting it pass by default to the Germans.

Wenceslas' successor, **Přemysl Otakar II**, gave further ground to the colonists, quite literally, by founding Malá Strana on the left bank of the Vltava for their benefit in 1257. During his reign (1253–78), the city developed into three autonomous units—the Old Town, the Castle District itself on Hradčany, and Malá Strana. A Jewish community in the area around Malá Strana was expelled to make way for the Germans—if Jews wanted to stay in town, they joined another Jewish community in the north of the Old Town which had been walled into a ghetto some years before. Gipsies are thought to have first come to Bohemia at about this time in the wake of the short but savage incursions of the Tartars in 1241–42—although, somewhat inexplicably, Romany lore claims that they arrived from Egypt, far from the Tartars' route of conquest across Russia. Trade and finds of silver deposits around nearby Kutná Hora helped to fund Prague's first building boom, and its Romanesque basilicas and houses gave way to Gothic grandeur.

However, the city's expansion was soon stopped in its tracks—a victim of Přemysl Otakar's own success. By the early 1270s, his skills at marriage, politicking and war had created a Bohemian kingdom that stretched from the Baltic to the Adriatic; which did nothing to satisfy the country's nobles that they could control their all-devouring king, but was more than enough to shake Germany's princes out of their internecine struggles. Otakar made a last-minute lunge for the emperor's throne in 1273. He missed—and Rudolf, count of Habsburg, stepped into the imperial driving seat. Three centuries later, Rudolf's descendants would burn their name into Bohemian history—and he made a memorable initial impact in 1276, when he led 100,000 soldiers into Bohemia. He was greeted by an emissary offering Přemysl Otakar's unconditional surrender. According to Thomas Carlyle, the Bohemian king tried to retain a shred of dignity by begging to be allowed to genuflect in the privacy of a tent. Rudolf agreed, only to have its walls whisked away at the crucial moment. Otakar was allowed to stay on his throne, but the powerful empire that he had built lay in ruins.

Anarchy and Chivalry

In 1306, the Přemysl dynasty sputtered to a halt with the murder by persons unknown of the 17-year old Wenceslas III. Libuše's foresight had turned out to be finite, and finding a successor was no easy matter—the German townspeople had their own axes to grind, and the nobility was split in several directions. The issue was temporarily solved when the Emperor Albert stepped in and suggested that his son, another Rudolf of Habsburg, would found a new hereditary dynasty for Bohemia. It was an offer that, in the light of recent events, was hard to refuse; but young Rudolf failed to live up to his father's expectations and died a year later. By now, tensions were high. Albert invaded to protect the good name of the Habsburgs, and was promptly assassinated; while one stormy Diet in Prague ended in mass murder after an Austrian suggested that if the Bohemians wanted a native king, they should get on their horses and find a peasant relative of Přemysl the Ploughman.

Anarchic Bohemia badly needed a monarch, and by 1310, everyone was longing for a strong hand. Their favour settled on 14-year old **John of Luxemburg**, the son of the new German emperor, Henry VII, who seemed well suited to provide the stability required.

The young king confounded everyone's expectations. Henry died on his way home from the coronation, and some blame John's oddball character on lack of parental control during his formative years. He spent most of his reign on a warring spree across Europe: for a time, he conquered northern Italy; he occasionally helped out with the pope's crusades against the tenaciously pagan Lithuanians; and he skilfully bagged Silesia a few days after it had foolishly thought his absence in the Baltic made it safe to declare war. He cared little what Prague got up to so long as it kept the royal coffers full, and burghers and nobles all made the most of the new opportunities: during John's reign, the Old Town got a town hall, a legal code and formal supremacy over every other town in the kingdom. John's interest in Bohemia waxed briefly around 1319: he invited Europe's most celebrated knights to Prague in order to re-establish Arthur's Round Table (no one turned up); and he had his baby son imprisoned, because a friend suggested that his wife would put the child on the throne while he was away making war. Although John's errantry took him far across Europe, he was an obsessive Francophile, and any gains that Bohemia made were a by-product of his desire to serve French interests. He happily paid the price in the end, dying a surreal death in 1346 at the Battle of Crécy, fighting for the French against the Black Prince's English army. Old and blind, John tied himself to two Czech noblemen and charged into the heart of the enemy ranks, leading 500 horsemen to annihilation under the arrows of Welsh archers. A Bohemian historian reports the highly dubious news that on hearing of his death King Edward III burst into tears and cried: 'The crown of chivalry has fallen today; never was anyone equal to this King of Bohemia'.

The Golden Age

John's son also fought at Crécy and narrowly escaped with his life. He could hardly have been less like his father. The German princes certainly agreed: scatter-brained John had been repeatedly blackballed for the imperial throne, but they had just elected his son **Emperor Charles IV**. On his return from Crécy, he was also offered the Bohemian crown. He doesn't seem to have borne his father a grudge for having imprisoned him, and loyally joined most of his mad dad's crusade. But Charles's reign was to be the mirror-image of that of his father.

John had been sure to give his son a good French education, but Charles systematically used the skills that he picked up at the Parisian court in a way which would have been entirely alien to the bluff Francophile. In 1356, he finally regularized the imperial electoral system, putting power squarely in the hands of the princes, thereby undercutting those who had voted against him, and dealing a body-blow to the temporal ambitions of the papacy, which had had an effective veto for centuries. (Future popes would find plenty of other ways to stick their oars into the empire's affairs.) He repaid the French debt by taking advantage of the battering that the country was receiving at the hands of the English (the Hundred Years War had only just begun) to reduce it almost to vassal status. The decline of both France and the papacy was symbolized by Charles's ability to persuade Pope Urban V to return to Rome from his Avignon 'prison' in 1367. The French looked on aghast as their man left; Charles met Urban's boat, and accompanied him to Rome where the pope crowned the emperor's fourth wife Elizabeth of Pomerania.

For Prague, having a calculating and ambitious monarch on the throne after a series of gamblers and crazies was a godsend. Charles may or may not have been a good patriot—but like any king with a family to consider, he acted like one. Charles hoped that by making a power base out of Bohemia he would enable his successors to continue his good work. He spoke fluent Czech (along with several other languages); he encouraged the development of the country's language and traditions; and he wrapped his reign in a series of legends, going back to Libuše and St Wenceslas (his mother was the daughter of King Wenceslas II, and he milked the Přemysl connection for all it was worth). Charles's dreams for Prague were spectacular. He had adopted his name at the age of 30 in honour of Charlemagne, the first Holy Roman Emperor and the last to rule over an undivided empire, and he had hopes of recovering all the ground that had been lost over the years. With the help of his friend and former tutor, Pope Clement VI, Prague had already been elevated to an archbishopric in 1344, and Charles got permission to invite monastic orders from the furthest-flung reaches of the eastern Church. Prague wasn't the capital of Europe for long—but under his reign it enjoyed a brief heyday as one of the most vital centres of Gothic art and architecture; and as befitted a medieval town with pretensions of grandeur, it got a new bridge, cathedral and the first university in Central Europe. For decades this was an academic vortex, sucking in scholars from as far away as Oxford. In the same year (1348) Charles founded the New Town, incorporating the straggling settlements outside the city walls into a system of broad streets and marketplaces that must count as the most successful and lasting piece of urban planning since the efforts of the Romans.

Nationalism and Hussitism

The peace and prosperity enjoyed by Bohemia during Charles's reign weren't to last. For two centuries tensions had been building between the country's German and Czech populations. The native nobility, although far from homogenous, resented the political influence wielded by the Germans; traders and workers were jealous of their economic influence in Prague and other cities. Popular anger soon found potent expression in a movement for religious reform—one which began a century before the birth of Martin Luther, and which was one of the first signs of the conflict that was to tear Europe apart.

Charles probably could have done little to prevent the forthcoming explosion—unfortunately, he actually did his bit to shorten the fuse. While distancing himself from the political influence of the Papacy, he relied heavily on the support of Bohemia's clergy, which grew particularly fat under his reign. His policy of inviting scores of religious orders to Prague also aroused hostility. Monasteries and convents were set up across the city, and Praguers realized with angry fascination not only that medieval monks and nuns were as prone to screw around as anyone else, but that here they were being subsidized to do it. The Church was brought further into disrepute by one of Charles's personal obsessions, a mania for collecting religious relics. He spent a small fortune on saintly organs, pieces of the True Cross and the like, and even persuaded the pope to create a Day of Relics, on which his collections would be exhibited to huge crowds in Prague's main squares. The fetishistic fairs were extremely popular. Apart from the fact that indulgences were sold at knock-down prices by special agreement with the pope, hundreds of miracles were regularly recorded—but the gatherings usually degenerated into drunken orgies, and in the cool light of day, many began to wonder if the Church's time hadn't come.

In reaction to its excesses, reformist clerics began to flood into Prague during the 1350s and 1360s. One of the most influential, and symptomatic of the times, was **Jan Milíč of Kroměříž**. As the Black Death marched across Europe, and ill omens piled up in Prague, he became convinced that Apocalypse was imminent (a standard view among the reformers), and even more ominously, that Charles IV was the Antichrist. He announced his conclusion to a startled imperial court in 1366, and spent the next eight years in and out of jail. He was wrong—Charles died peacefully in 1378—but although the seven seals stayed closed, the next decades saw the struggle for reform reach new heights.

Charles IV's eldest son, **Wenceslas IV**, took over as both emperor and king of Bohemia. The new ruler wasn't the man demanded by the difficult times. He was liked by the hoi polloi (he went on regular pub-crawls through the Old Town, and had a flair for populist gestures, including the old favourite of dressing up in paupers' clothes and then executing anyone who sold him short measures), but his relations with the high and mighty were fraught with difficulties. He tended to give jobs to his lowly chums, so the Old Town nobles imprisoned him in 1394; he got out eventually, but watched haplessly as he was stripped of his imperial title by the German electors in 1400 and constantly outsmarted by his replacement as emperor, wily half-brother **Sigismund**.

In 1402 a young priest, **Jan Hus** (John Huss), much influenced by the teachings of the Oxfordshire parish priest, John Wycliffe, was appointed rector of the Charles University. Although Hus would never have regarded himself as anything but a Catholic, his fiery sermons moved further and further from the party line. His assertion that clerical and even papal decrees had to be tested against scripture amounted to a direct political attack on the power of the church—there were hundreds in Prague alone who lived off the notion that contact with the Almighty was cheapened if it wasn't made through duly-appointed intermediaries. Like the Protestants who were to follow, the Hussites preached in the vernacular, and in about 1414 began the practice that was to characterize the movement, allowing the congregation not only the bread, but also the wine of the Eucharist. They became known as the Utraquists (from the Latin for 'in both kinds'), and adopted the chalice as their emblem. The Church was not pleased. A sentence of excommunication against Hus was published in 1411, and in 1414 he agreed to appear before a General Council of the Church at Constance to defend his views. He should have set them out in a letter. A safe conduct provided by the fiercely orthodox Emperor Sigismund proved to be worth considerably less than the paper it was printed on. Hus was locked up on arrival. The emperor issued a mild public protest, while urgently warning the assembled bishops to barbecue Hus without delay. The inquisitors actually gave Hus several chances to recant everything that he'd ever said, but he refused—and on 6 July 1415, he was burned at the stake. His ashes were scattered into the Rhine to discourage souvenir hunters.

News of his death enraged his supporters back home. Wenceslas and his wife made clear their sympathies for the nationalists, but many pro-Roman officials remained, and Wenceslas was under constant pressure from his brother to keep the heretics under control. In 1419 things went from bad to worse when councillors at the New Town Hall were **defenestrated** and killed by a Hussite mob—a novel form of political violence that was to become a regular feature in Bohemia's history. The pressure finally became too much for Wenceslas; later that year he bowed out of history by succumbing to repeated apoplectic fits.

In 1420, sneaky Sigismund tried to succeed his brother as king of Bohemia. No one quite knew what had happened at Constance, and the delegation of Prague citizens and noblemen who received him weren't initially averse to his claim. It became clear, however, that he intended to restore Church privileges and suppress the Utraquists, and the last straw came in 1420 when Pope Martin V declared a crusade against Bohemia. During the next decade he would anounce four more, while the Turks merrily hammered into Christendom. Bohemia found itself at war with most of Europe; even Joan of Arc took an interest in 1429, warning the Hussites in doggerel Latin that once she'd finished with the English, she'd come to sort them out. However, she herself was sizzled two years later by ungrateful Catholics; and the brilliant one-eyed general, **Jan Žižka** (c. 1360–1424) developed an almost invincible army that successfully repulsed each crusade, and made 'Hussite' a word that Catholic mothers across Europe would frighten the kids with. At the same time, Catholic propaganda successfully tarred the Hussite movement with the brush of the Adamites, a breakaway movement (brutally suppressed by the Hussites themselves) who practised a medieval form of free love involving arcane nudist rituals, and the word 'Bohemian' entered the vocabulary of several European languages as a synonym for weirdo. As early as 1421 a more important division developed among the Utraquists, between moderates who sought a compromise with Rome and a more radical group who were beginning to think in terms of a total break with the Church. Many Bohemian nobles, and a large part of the Old Town, allied themselves to the more moderate cause; while the others were based in the poorer New Town and outside Prague at a camp and commune known as Tábor, giving rise to their nickname, the Táborites.

The conflict between the two groups came to a head in 1434. The new pope, Eugenius IV, reluctantly granted the right to administer and receive communion in both kinds (an agreement known as the Compacts of Basle). The extremist Táborites rejected the proposals as insufficient, so the moderate aristocrats wiped them out at the Battle of Lipany in 1434.

Sigismund, finally recognized as sovereign of Bohemia, died a few months later. His successor, Albert of Habsburg, followed suit in 1439, time enough for him to impregnate his wife, Elisabeth, who produced Ladislav the Posthumous in 1440. Ladislav reigned briefly from 1453–1457 when he died of the flu; but the real ruler of Bohemia from 1440–1471 was an Utraquist nobleman, **George of Poděbrady** (Jiří z Poděbrad), who ruled as king from 1458. George staunchly defended the new religion against a backsliding Holy See, which tried to steal the Compacts of Basle at one point (1448) and excommunicated George at another (1466). Although he had high hopes of establishing a native dynasty and expanding an independent Bohemian empire, he was living in messy times and found himself concluding a treaty with the pro-Catholic **Vladislav II of Jagellon** of Poland, in order to fight off the equally pro-Catholic Matthias Corvinus of Hungary.

Vladislav was elected king in 1471, and it was under his reign that the last flickers of popular Hussitism went out. Anti-Catholic feelings still ran high among the population—a riot against Vladislav's officials in 1483 produced Prague's second defenestration (along with the lynching of several Germans and Jews for good measure)—but the nobility began increasingly to look after their own interests. Taking advantage of the king's long absences (he preferred Hungary's Buda castle), nobles introduced serfdom in 1487, and began to brew beer (a long-standing privilege of the towns) on their feudal estates. Many nobles kept to the Utraquist faith, but in their hands it came to signify little more than a tipple at communion. The Hussite mantle was largely taken over by the Union of Bohemian Brethren, an ascetic bunch who subscribed to a mixture of predestinarianism and resistance to the Antichrist (i.e. Catholic kings). The movement grew in strength among ordinary Czechs, but it was rarely in favour with authority, and Protestant nobles tended to sniff at it with suspicion. But even if the first flowering of Czech nationalism was over, Prague and Bohemia had nevertheless established themselves as a centre of anti-Catholicism—and were to pay heavily over the next centuries.

The Habsburgs Arrive

Although vacillating Vladislav managed to produce an heir, Ludvik, the latter managed to drown in a marsh while running away from the Turks at the Battle of Mohács in 1526. Another would-be dynasty had bitten the dust, and princelings and archdukes from across Europe headed for Prague to vie for the vacant throne. The fateful choice of the divided electors was **Ferdinand I of Habsburg**. He seemed tolerant enough for a Catholic—he had been educated by liberal Erasmus—and after years of fratricide, some had the forlorn hope that a strong monarch might turn his attentions to the Turks, who had strolled ever deeper into eastern Europe during the Hussite wars. The nobles made it clear that he was being *elected* to the throne, and didn't take very seriously his occasional mutterings that the Habsburgs had had the right to rule Bohemia for over 300 years. They had forgotten their predecessors' promises to Albert—and the Habsburg chicken was coming home to roost.

In the 1520s, many of Bohemia's Germans fell under the Lutheran spell, while the Bohemian Brethren found affinities with Calvinism—and although estimates vary, the population was probably 90 per cent Protestant by the middle of the century. The religious issue came to the fore gradually. Ferdinand began his reign tolerantly enough, while he battled away with the Turks, and his first concern was to consolidate Habsburg rule. He had a minor triumph in 1541, when a fire raged through Prague and destroyed all the state documents. In the absence of the papers which would have proved otherwise, he somehow persuaded the Estates that whatever they'd said 15 years earlier, he had ascended the throne by hereditary right. Peace with the Turks in 1545 allowed him to turn his mind to matters spiritual. Ferdinand was religious and Catholic, but his opposition to Protestantism was strengthened by more mundane concerns: in the empire as a whole, Catholicism was a usefully universal ideology under which to establish centralized rule; and in Bohemia, Protestantism still had a dangerously nationalistic tinge, even though many of the country's Germans now shared the religion of the Czechs. He had long been trying to forge an alliance between Catholicism and old-style Utraquism—but although Prague's Protestants had been suspicious since his trick with the documents in 1541, it was only in 1547 that he laid his cards on the table.

In that year he sweet-talked them into financing an anti-Turkish army, which then marched westward to attack Protestants in Saxony. Representatives from across the country met in Prague and decided that enough was enough—the king would respect the Estates' privileges and their right to elect the monarch, or else. They could have chosen a better time to make a stand. Ferdinand's troops massacred the Saxons in weeks, and were back in Prague before the Estates had got their own army off the drawing board. They made the best of a very, very bad job, and surrendered unconditionally. Ferdinand held a meeting with them at Prague Castle, and after chopping off the heads of three of the most troublesome leaders, convinced them of what he'd long believed—that his family was to rule Bohemia for ever, and that the powers and privileges of Prague and other Bohemian towns were to be cut down drastically.

It was dramatic stuff, but in 16th-century Bohemia, agreements were made to be broken, and Ferdinand made sure to have his eldest son **Maximilian** crowned king while he was still alive. The Habsburg family had recently had a squabble, and its Spanish section had hived off, so Ferdinand was particularly anxious to consolidate his western empire. That meant coming to terms with Germany's Lutheran princes, and at the Peace of Augsburg (1555), it was established that a territory's religion would depend on the preferences of its ruler. The unsteady compromise did little to help Bohemia, ruled by the Habsburgs themselves. Ferdinand introduced the fiercely proselytizing Jesuit order into Prague in 1556 to counteract the spread of Lutheranism, and in 1563 Pope Pius IV launched the militant programme of the Counter-Reformation at the Council of Trent. It was to be another half century, however, before the interests of the Habsburgs and those of the Papacy were fully to coincide, in an explosive fashion.

Ferdinand died in 1564, to be succeeded as emperor by Maximilian (who was already king of Bohemia). In return for continued funding for his anti-Turkish forays, Maximilian granted Bohemia's Lutherans the right to organize independently of the old Utraquist church. The concessions enabled him to have his son elected king of Bohemia with little difficulty in 1576, and when Maximilian died later that year, the same son succeeded him as **Emperor Rudolf II**.

Rudolfine Prague

The Turks were now within 100 miles of Vienna, the traditional seat of the Habsburgs. The Czech Estates offered to pay off a fair chunk of the empire's debts, and rebuild the castle, if Rudolf moved to Prague. By 1583—despite frantic lobbying by Viennese nobles—the emperor had decamped to his new capital. Prague became the centre of an empire for the first time in two centuries.

Rudolf was the most singular monarch that Prague had seen since Charles IV. In a very different way from his predecessor, he too presided over a cultural rebirth in the city (see pp. 66–8). The Papacy had high hopes for the young emperor—educated in the powerfully anti-Protestant atmosphere of the Spanish Habsburg court, he seemed just the man to give Bohemia its comeuppance. Unfortunately for the Catholic Church, Rudolf turned out to be a very strange fish indeed, imbued with an almost mystical spirituality that was far from the new orthodoxy the Church was trying to promote. Fanaticism was almost entirely alien to him—the Lutheran astronomer Johannes Kepler was just one of those who found a haven at his court—but his education left him torn between the ideal of a universal truth and the reality of a Christianity that was being reduced into two armed camps. High in the castle, his artists and scientists tried to transcend a world that was falling apart, but the deeper his court delved into the esoteric mysteries of the symbolic and the occult, the heavier grew the burden of the religion into which Rudolf had been born. The sensitive emperor was never able to resolve the dilemma, and teetered between profound pessimism and mild insanity for most of his reign. He sought absolution regularly, but his public pronouncements were rarely confessions of faith—in 1605, an increasingly perplexed papal nuncio reported back to his boss that Rudolf had just declared, 'I know that I am dead and damned; I am a man possessed by the devil'.

Legend and history came to remember Rudolfine Prague as a fantastic city of alchemy and astrology, suspended in time, but its surreal atmosphere was very much the product of the moment. The Counter-Reformation was gathering force in neighbouring Austria and Styria; a part-time lunatic and full-time melancholic was on the throne; and mystics and zealots of every hue were massing in the city. Prague had become the nerve-centre of Europe's schizophrenia. Although Rudolf's reign was remarkably peaceful for two decades, waves of panic regularly spread across the capital. As the silver-tongued Jesuits made slow but steady advances in the capital, rumours grew that they were planning an armed insurrection; alarmed fury greeted the pope's theft of 11 days in 1583, when the Gregorian calendar was introduced into Bohemia; and in 1588, the sun entered the fiery trigon for only the second time since the birth of Christ. As the century drew to a close, Prague's seers shivered like animals before a storm, and issued the time-honoured announcement that the world was coming to an end.

It would have taken a genius to steer the empire peacefully through its crisis, and Rudolf's temperament, though unique, was ill suited to the job. His Spanish education had given him a powerful belief in the Habsburg mission, but his interest in politics was combined with an utterly irrational set of policies. He was terrified of popes and monks, and although he passed several anti-Protestant laws in the later years of his reign, he rarely enforced them—a combination which made few friends and plenty of enemies. Another problem was the succession issue. While in Spain, Rudolf had spawned a brood of bastards (including Don Giulio, a clockwork-obsessed sexual deviant and psychopath), but in Prague he tenaciously refused to marry, and withdrew at the last minute from unions with two hopeful princesses. As the years passed and his nobles clucked nervously, he would fly into a rage if the subject was publicly mentioned—although as late as 1608, he had his henchmen go on a furtive trawl through Europe's marriage market to see 'what sort of nubile princesses or even high-ranking countesses are available'.

But by then, the game was almost up. His younger brother **Matthias** had been intriguing against him since his first major bout of insanity in 1600. Matthias steadily picked up support from other princes, whose patience with madcap Rudolf had reached an end. By 1606, Matthias had launched an open mutiny, and two years later he forced his brother to hand over all his realms save Bohemia, which was to be Rudolf's posthumous gift. Prague's nobles were happy with the compromise, having stayed loyal to Rudolf with the aim of extracting concessions in his moment of weakness. They were disappointed. The would-be autocrat had become a failed has-been, and in the last years of his reign, Rudolf swung wildly from promises to threats against his Prague nobles while making frenzied plans for revenge. It all ended when he offered his cousin, Leopold, the empire, just to deny it to Matthias. Leopold mysteriously acted as though Rudolf still had something to give, and his armies marched into Prague in 1611. Matthias did the same, Leopold left as swiftly as he had come, and an exhausted Bohemian nobility recognized Matthias as king. Rudolf was forced to abdicate and died alone in his castle a year later, and his brother was elected to the imperial throne.

From Defenestration to Massacre

In 1617, Emperor Matthias, as heirless as his brother had been, proposed his cousin **Ferdinand** as his successor to the crown of Bohemia. Ferdinand had made a name for himself as a rabid anti-Protestant while archduke of Styria, and it's hard to understand why the electors agreed to recognize him as king. As the policies of both Matthias and their new monarch turned more militant, the Bohemians began to ask themselves the same question—and on 23 May 1618, they finally took their stand against Catholic rule. The two most hated of Ferdinand's councillors were William of Slavata and Jaroslav of Martinic (the latter was known to chase his serfs into Mass with dogs, and to have wafers stuffed down the throat of anyone who insisted on a spot of wine at communion), and it was decided to give them a traditional Bohemian lesson. In full armour, the Protestant Estates entered the Court Chancellery in Prague castle and, egged on by a crowd, hurled the two royal councillors and a secretary through the window. All three survived the 50-foot drop—the Catholic Church attributed it to a miracle, others claimed that their fall had been broken by a dungheap. Prague's third defenestration threw Europe into the religious fratricide of the Thirty Years War. By its end in 1648, the continent was in ruins.

Bohemia didn't have to wait that long. Prague's nobles swiftly set about looking for a royal champion. Europe's Protestant princes had long expected the lid to blow on the Peace of Augsburg, but although Ferdinand and allies were massing their forces against Prague, no one was yet sure if this was the Big One. Only one was eager to take up the gauntlet—**Frederick of the Palatinate**, who had had his eye on the Bohemian crown for some time. He arrived in 1619, accompanied by his English wife, Elizabeth—who was, incidentally, pregnant with Prince Rupert, later to be an impetuous if unsuccessful scourge of the Roundheads. Everyone agreed that Frederick had excellent manners (although the low dresses of Elizabeth's English maids set tongues a-wagging for several years) but it's hard to see how the Bohemians could have made a worse choice. The allies he was expected to carry with him, including Elizabeth's father, King James I, flaked away as he spent the winter in Prague. By the following November (1620), Ferdinand's Bavarian allies were within reach of the city, and Bohemia's nobles had resorted to frantic negotiations with the Turks. It soon became apparent that the 'Winter King' had never fought before in his life—and the morale of his Bohemian army gently collapsed as he nervously shuttled from battlefield to castle and made repeated attempts to persuade his wife to leave town (she was made of sterner stuff, and refused). The two armies finally met at the **White Mountain** (*bílá hora*) just outside Prague, on 8 November. It was the mother of all Bohemian battles, and a sorry end to over two centuries of anti-Catholicism in the country. The Czech and Hungarian allied armies scattered into headlong retreat. They can't altogether be blamed—their enemies included Polish Cossacks, who charged into Protestant ranks with a sabre in each hand as they held their reins between their teeth; and the Virgin Mary apparently made an appearance—but Frederick emerges with no credit whatsoever, unless love of life counts for something. He had already virtually deserted his troops; and when news of the rout reached the banquet he was holding in the castle, he decided to scarper. His wife persuaded him to stay firm, and he uncertainly agreed to rally his forces for an orderly withdrawal— but as he watched her and little Rupert ride off in a carriage, he cracked and gave the signal for mass flight.

There's one strange postscript to the battle. Among those who fought with the Catholics was **René Descartes**, who was sowing his wild oats as a mercenary before settling down to his epistemological enquiries. His presence at the battle has given rise to Prague's most absurd legend. He's said to have been wounded, and on recovering from unconsciousness, to have declared with relief, 'I think—therefore I am'—a reflection which, when honed, would transform the course of European thought.

The Bohemian Counter-Reformation

Ferdinand, who had become emperor after Matthias's death in 1619, proceeded to exact a terrible revenge from the upstart Bohemians. A few days after the battle, he was given some advice by one of his court favourites, a Capuchin friar called Brother Sabinus. Quoting Psalm 2:9, the holy man ventured to suggest that, 'Thou shalt break them with a rod of iron; thou shalt dash them in pieces like a potter's vessel.' In March 1621, judges were sent to Hradčany Castle from Vienna to consider cases against 27 Protestant leaders. Two months later, on the anniversary of the defenestration, all were sentenced to death. 24 were beheaded, the longstanding privilege of the nobility (although two suffered the discomfort of having a tongue and a hand chopped off before getting it in the neck), while three commoners went to the gallows, all in Prague's Old Town Square.

The Thirty Years War ravaged Europe until 1648. It began as a struggle to assert Habsburg power, but by the 1630s almost the entire continent was sorting out its political differences by fire and sword. Germany's princely armies made mincemeat of each other; Sweden's Gustavus Adolfus made a spectacular entry on the Protestant side in 1630; and pragmatic Cardinal Richelieu of France busily encouraged the anti-Habsburg cause and threw his country into a pussy-footing war with Spain in 1635. As Richelieu's policies testify, the battle-lines were far from cleanly religious—but in Prague that made little difference. Bohemian Protestantism and nationalism were inseparable; while Ferdinand soon hitched the imperial cause firmly to that of the Church. Even before the war's end, he and his monkish allies extinguished the city's ancient powers. In 1624, he removed the court to Vienna and sent in German-speaking bureaucrats to carry out the metropolis' edicts; while in 1627, a new constitutional settlement finally established hereditary Habsburg rule over Bohemia. Protestantism was made a capital offence, and the independence of the Czech Estates was destroyed. Thousands of families emigrated for ever, while turncoats and parvenus decended like locusts on vast tracts of confiscated land. The **Peace of Westphalia** (1648) was a compromise not far removed from the Peace of Augsburg a century before—but no one disputed Habsburg control over Bohemia any more, and its Protestants were denied even the very limited religious freedoms guaranteed elsewhere. The last battle of the war was fought on Prague's bridge, between the Swedes and a motley crew of soldiers, newly-Catholicized students and Prague Jews. When the dust settled, Bohemia was left with its population reduced by over a third, and the country plunged into a decline that lasted two centuries.

Nothing Happens

Frederick the Great invaded Prague twice in the mid-18th century; but otherwise the city became a backwater where you went when the bright lights of Vienna became too much. The spiritual shock troops of the Counter-Reformation, the Jesuits, led the consolidation of the new faith with a Baroque building programme that transformed the face of the city, but even the monks had to leave town when the work was done. The Jesuits were placed under a worldwide ban by a jealous pope in 1773; and in 1781, the despotically enlightened **Emperor Joseph II** abolished most of the empire's other monasteries and convents. The corollary was the restoration of individual religious freedom for all save the weirdest sects. Prague's Jewish population was finally allowed out of its ghetto, but just in case they got any uppity ideas, an imperial decree of 1789 prohibited all males save the eldest son from receiving a marriage licence.

The Nationalist Revival

During the early 19th century, Bohemia began to breathe again. Europe's tide of nationalisms swept across the country; and after centuries of German meddling and oppression, Czechs began to hanker for a purely Slavic alternative. The Czech language, which had all but died out since the Battle of the White Mountain, was resuscitated by a handful of writers and researchers—František Palacký and Josef Jungmann being among the most notable—whose painstaking efforts can almost be compared to those of Eliezer Ben-Yehudah in creating modern Hebrew. In 1848 the citizens of Prague were up in arms again, this time joined by the rest of the empire in a revolt against Metternich's iron rule from Vienna. Prague's Czechs split with the German revolutionaries by refusing to take part in the German National Assembly at Frankfurt, and a Slavic conference was held in the city in June. Imperial forces soon shot their way through the barricades, but although it was not apparent at the time, the Habsburg empire was slowly dying. Composed of a score of different peoples, it was to prove incapable of adapting itself to growing nationalist sentiment. But as it sickened, Czechoslovakia quickened. On the cultural front, composers such as Smetana and Dvořák dug deep into the national consciousness to emerge with a music fit for a new country. On the political front, nationalists wrested a series of concessions from Vienna towards the end of the 19th century, including language ordinances and the creation of an autonomous Czech division of the Charles University. Within Slovakia, nationalism also emerged in reaction to Hungarian rule; but despite common pan-Slavist sympathies, few in either state had yet developed a clear programme of autonomy, let alone joint independence.

From Independence to Dependency

As the pattern of European alliances emerged in the years before 1914, many Czechs and Slovaks felt with apprehension that in any future war, their interests lay firmly in the enemy camp. Lingering pan-Slavism encouraged sympathy even for the corrupt Russia of Nicholas II, while democratic ideals and anti-German sentiment made others look towards

France and Britain. When war broke out, two men—**Tomáš Garrigue Masaryk** and **Edvard Beneš**—set out on a four-year tour to persuade the world that Czechoslovakia was an idea whose time had come. In 1918, Masaryk was in the United States. President Woodrow Wilson had made clear his support for the principle of self-determination, but neither he nor anyone in the White House was quite certain which European tribes existed, let alone which should get independence. Masaryk signed a deal with Slovak emigrés in Pittsburgh, and although he very quickly reneged on his promises, that was enough to persuade Wilson to give 'Czecho-Slovakia' the green light.

Masaryk and Beneš wasted no time. On 28 October 1918—while artillery fire still thundered in the west of the continent—independence was declared. Within two weeks, Masaryk had been elected president of the new Czechoslovakian Republic. As the western allies pondered how to neutralize the losing powers and contain the Bolshevik incubus, Masaryk and Beneš, now Foreign Minister, unilaterally staked out the borders of the new state. These encompassed the largely German-populated Sudetenland to the west, as well as areas claimed by the Hungarians and the Poles, but at the peace conferences the victors ratified the *fait accompli* with little discussion and no plebiscite.

The youthful democracy flourished economically and culturally, and its capital embraced the new age with vigour; but the 1920s weren't the best of times to consolidate democracy. Although the country's political structures rode the Depression with a stability astonishing in a country so young, the latent and ancient problem of the German minority was soon to explode with unparalleled ferocity. An ongoing separatist movement in the Sudetenland found a champion in Hitler, and Czechoslovakia became the eye of the building European storm. Under the notorious 1938 **Munich Agreement** Britain, France and Italy gave Hitler *carte blanche* to seize the Sudetenland. The disingenuousness of the British Prime Minister, Neville Chamberlain, has made a contemptuous reference to appeasement obligatory for visiting western politicians ever since—although Hitler was sweet about him, saying that, 'He seemed such a nice old gentleman that I thought I would give him my autograph as a souvenir'. In Czechoslovakia, many gave up hope on the west and in a strange echo of pan-Slavism came to regard the Soviet Union as Czechoslovakia's last best hope—an attitude which was fatefully to influence Beneš's policy during and immediately after the war. Within six months, the 'quarrel in a faraway place of which we know nothing' (as Chamberlain described it in a BBC radio broadcast) had led to the invasion of Czechoslovakia by the German army. Britain and France remained silent as the **Reich Protectorate of Bohemia and Moravia** was declared in March 1939 (Slovakia was made a puppet republic), and only after the invasion of Poland six months later did they declare war on Germany.

The war left Prague's buildings almost unscathed. Its population was less fortunate. Tens of thousands of intellectuals, politicians and gipsies were imprisoned or killed, while of the 90,000 Jews who remained in the Protectorate in late 1939 (about 26,000 had emigrated in the six months after March), only some 10,000 survived the war. The town of Terezín (Theresienstadt) in northern Bohemia was turned into a 'model' ghetto to show the Red Cross—while 140,000 other visitors passed through on the way to Auschwitz, Ravensbrück and Treblinka. Hitler chose Prague's old Jewish Quarter to be the site of an 'exotic museum of an extinct race', to which artefacts from exterminated Jewish populations throughout Europe were sent. The macabre decision has meant that, thanks to the Nazis, Prague now has the saddest and finest memorial to pre-war European Jewry on the continent.

Beneš had taken over as President in 1935, and fled three years later, having received indications that Hitler personally wanted his head. He was making the twilight rounds of the North American lecture circuit when war broke out, and swiftly crossed back to London to establish a government-in-exile. Czech units, evacuated at Dunkirk after the fall of France, were integrated into the British army, and many Czech pilots fought and died in the Battle of Britain. Within the Protectorate, somewhat to the surprise of the Nazis, whose armies had invaded without even token resistance, armed underground movements began to operate, directed largely by the London government. Some Czech Communists were also active, but had to play a doubly surreptitious role, as the Party was stymied by the tortuous logic of the Nazi-Soviet pact. The resistance annoyed Hitler sufficiently for him to appoint **Reinhard Heydrich** as *Protektor* in place of the namby-pamby Von Neurath in late September 1941. Heydrich proceeded to liquidate the resistance by wholesale public executions and the banning of all public gatherings on pain of death. He lived for nine more months, time enough for him to chair the Wannsee Conference in Berlin in January, at which he ironed out the administrative aspects of what he called 'the coming Final Solution of the Jewish problem'. In June 1942 he died from infected wounds after an assassination attempt by London-based Czech parachutists. Hitler ordered savage reprisals. 1331 Czechs were summarily executed; while the parachute squad, along with 120 members of the Czech resistance, were holed up in a Prague church where they died to a man. **Lidice**, just outside the capital, was the scene of one of the first well-publicized massacres of the war. It was chosen at random to be wiped off the map. After burning down the houses, Gestapo and SS troops shot dead its 172 male inhabitants. The 195 women were sent to Ravensbrück; seven babies out of 90 children were judged sufficiently Aryan to be sent to German adoption homes. None was ever found. Not only did the Nazis kill the village's current inhabitants, they also traced all those who had been born there in order to execute them. A story told by the Czech writer, Josef Škvorecký (and fictionalized by another, Bohumil Hrabal) is that they missed one man, who was serving a jail sentence at the time. On his release, he returned to his village only to find it a desert of asphalt, and went insane. The local Gestapo refused to shoot him as he demanded, and he died of drink a few years after the war.

On 5 May 1945, the capital's resistance groups broadcast a call to arms and thousands rose up against the remnants of the occupying Nazi forces in the city. The **Prague Uprising** lasted only four days, but street fighting and last-minute executions left up to 5000 Czechs dead—plaques and graves throughout the city mark where they fell. On 9 May 1945 the Soviet Red Army entered Prague to a rapturous reception. A provisional national assembly, under Beneš as president, was set up in October, and set about solving the problem of the German minority for one last time. While mobs lynched collaborators, the country's three million Sudeten Germans were expelled, resulting in the deaths of thousands. The policy was official, indiscriminate (Jews were included), and approved by the Allies at the Potsdam Conference.

Communist Consolidation

The Czechoslovakian Communist Party led by **Klement Gottwald** swept the board in the 1946 elections, with 38 per cent of the votes. (Even before the war, it had been one of the strongest in Europe, winning 10 per cent of the votes in 1935.) Beneš appointed Gottwald prime minister of a coalition government, but Uncle Joe Stalin had no intention of letting his protégé go to bed with a bourgeois. Gottwald's rabble-rousing skills and Beneš's weakness led to the former's assumption of the presidency in February 1948. Within a month the popular foreign minister, **Jan Masaryk**—son of Tomáš—who was less accommodating to the Communists, had died in a mysterious fall from his office window late one night. A fourth defenestration began 40 years of Communist rule, and the Party was pleased to report 89 per cent support in new elections in May.

Within a year the Terror had begun. Gottwald, prodded on by Stalin, imprisoned thousands of political opponents, and executed over 200 after show trials which were as fraudulent as the best of Moscow's in the 1930s. The most notorious was the **'Slánský Trial'** of 1952, in which 11 high-ranking Party members (almost all of whom were Jewish) were condemned as 'Trotskyite Titoists, bourgeois nationalist traitors and enemies of the Czechoslovak Republic and of socialism', and sent to the gallows. (The trial has been dramatized in a moving French film, *L'Aveu*.) Slánský (who was actually guilty of far worse than the ludicrous charges on which he was tried), wasn't rehabilitated until 1990. Rudolf Slánský Jnr. became a respected figure of the opposition to Communism, and is now Czechoslovakia's ambassador to the Soviet Union.

From Socialism with A Human Face to Normalization

Gottwald caught pneumonia at Stalin's funeral, and followed his mentor into oblivion nine days later. His death of 'Moscow flu' still brings a smile to the face of many Czechs when they talk of their 'first working-class president', as he was invariably referred to in official publications until 1989. During the mid-1960s reformers at the lower levels of the Party began to work on revitalizing its links with the rest of society. In 1963, the Kolder Commission published a terrifying report on the 'violations of socialist justice' of the 1950s. Large numbers of victims were rehabilitated, posthumously in all too many cases. In January 1968, **Alexander Dubček** was elected to the post of First Secretary. During the so-called **Prague Spring** of 1968, Dubček proposed ever-more radical reform of the country's political and economic institutions, partly out of personal conviction but largely at the urging of more powerful forces and individuals both within and outside the Party. At this point the Soviet Union, in the form of General-Secretary Brezhnev, decided that the Czechoslovak proletariat needed help to stave off 'a return to the bourgeois-capitalist system'. He took soundings of all the other leaders of the Warsaw Pact, and on 21 August, Czechoslovakia was invaded by five armies. Maverick Nicolae Ceausescu was the only Communist leader to stick to the principle of non-interference. Molotov cocktails greeted the tanks, while road signs were reversed and street names removed in a quixotic attempt to disorientate the invaders, who killed scores of civilians on Prague's streets. On the day of the invasion, the reformers were bundled onto an Aeroflot jet and taken to Moscow for urgent discussions, and the Prague Spring suddenly turned very cold.

The cultural and political renaissance of the mid-1960s had been strangled in its cradle. The times were desperate. Fourteen philosophy students at the Charles University drew lots, and agreed to burn themselves alive one by one until press freedom was restored. 'Torch No. 1' was **Jan Palach**. On 16 January 1969, the 20-year old emptied a can of petrol over himself in Wenceslas Square, and set light to himself. Before he died, three days later, Palach begged his doctors for news of the reaction to his act. They told him that flowers and phone calls ran into the thousands—and that the government had said nothing. Palach died asking that none of his friends follow him. Two weeks later, Jan Zacíc, not connected to the group, immolated himself in northern Bohemia. Over the next month, so too did many others. Their names, reasons and number are still unknown.

Dubček had lingered on, racked by a sense of responsibility for the invasion and half-heartedly dismantling his reforms, but he had become yesterday's man. The Soviets began looking for a stooge. Several Central Committee members applied fairly directly for the job, but even Brezhnev could see that they were too widely loathed. In April 1969, Dubček was replaced by **Gustáv Husák**—resistance hero, victim of the Terror and supporter of the Prague Spring. Few understood how he got the job. Brezhnev was among them. He's said to have murmured, 'If we can't use the puppets, we'll tie the strings to the leaders'; and within a year, Husák began to dance. Some 500,000 people were deprived of their Communist Party membership, either for what they had done pre-1968 or, in the case of those who wouldn't publicly support the invasion, for what they now refused to do. The process was called 'normalization' (*normalisace*); and when it was finished, the government declared that Czechoslovakia had achieved a state of *realní socialismus*, an eerie phrase that's usually translated as 'real existing socialism'.

A new generation grew up without even the memory of hope. The signatories of the 1977 human rights manifesto, **Charter 77**, were ruthlessly persecuted, and apathy led tens of thousands of non-Party members to sign a government-backed petition condemning the organization. The possibilities for change seemed less than zero.

The Velvet Revolution

Even as late as mid-1989—with Hungary and Poland well on the path to reform—few observers saw Czechoslovakia as likely to follow in the near future. But as the East German regime tottered, refugees from the country began to flood into the West German embassy in Prague. The revolutions of 1989 had begun. On 9 November the world woke up to the news that bulldozers were demolishing the Berlin Wall, and on 17 November Prague's students confronted a baton-wielding police force on the streets of the New Town. The filmed scenes of police brutality, against students armed with candles and flowers, aroused the population from two decades of torpor. Within a week a million people had taken to the streets of the capital to demand that the government resign. For the next six weeks, Prague was enfolded by a 'Velvet Revolution', an anarchic hubbub of strikes, pickets and celebrations which culminated in the election of playwright and recently-released political prisoner, Václav Havel, to the presidency on 29 December 1989.

The Rebirth of History

Free elections to the Federal Assembly were held in June 1990. The turnout was 96 per cent—a figure that would have done the old regime proud—but although the Communists clung onto about 13 per cent of the vote, over half the seats went to **Civic Forum** (*Občanské fórum*), and its Slovakian counterpart, Public Against Violence. The movement, created within days of the first demonstrations of November 1989, offered a far-from clear manifesto—the result not of duplicity, but of utter confusion. Its candidates included pop stars, penitent ex-Communists and monetarists with steel-rimmed glasses, and to no one's surprise the rainbow coalition has been fading to grey ever since. In early 1991, it split into left- and right-wings, and **Václav Klaus**, the Finance Minister, has emerged as the party strongman. Klaus has confessed to boundless respect for Margaret Thatcher's impact on the British economy. Many Czechs still idolize the ex-Leaderene, but they may soon think twice; spines are beginning to shiver as economic reforms bite. It's currently estimated that by 1992, dole queues will be 300,000-long and stretching.

Waking up from half a century of night and fog has also revealed a Pandora's box of social problems. Between them, the Habsburgs and the Communists helped to destroy class divisions among Czechs, but in Prague you're sure to come across the widespread and sometimes violent contempt for the gipsy minority and the handful of Vietnamese immigrants. In the east, Slovakian nationalism has become a powerful political force—and it harks back to the only political precedent that it has, the Nazi-sponsored puppet government of 1938–45. Even the spirit of Communism is far from dead: although some 600–800,000 had already left the Party by February 1990 (about 40 per cent of its total membership), ex-Communists still dominate managerial and teaching positions throughout Czechoslovakia. Root and branch dismissals would bring society and the economy to a shuddering halt, and would have rather unfortunate resonances in a country that has seen rather too many purges for its own good; but popular resentment is widespread and likely to grow as Communist opportunists become capitalist entrepreneurs. Cruellest of all the historical twists since 1989 is the fate of the November revolution. In early 1990, it emerged that the 'dead' student was alive and well, and had been living on the payroll of the secret police (STB). The clash of 17 November was organized by the KGB and STB, with the intention of replacing the Husák regime with one more in tune with Gorbachev's Soviet Union. Fortunately for Czechoslovakia, matters soon slipped out of the conspirators' hands, and Communist rule died. The bloody fate of the Romanian revolution a month later, also thought to have been hatched in the Kremlin, shows the forces that could have been unleashed had the Czech government fought back.

If you say 'Velvet Revolution' in Prague today, you're likely to get a very wounded look—but hope survives. The Warsaw Pact has been wound up, Soviet troops have been withdrawn, and although there's apprehension at the thought of millions of refugees flooding westwards from a crumbling Soviet Union, few expect that 'fraternal assistance' will come their way again. With the thoughtful, if sometimes morose, help of President Havel, Prague, Bohemia and Czechoslovakia are piecing their history together once again, and feeling their way into an uncertain future. The penultimate word belongs to Havel, pronounced in December 1990. 'The happiness is gone. The second act is called crisis. The crisis will be chronic and then the catastrophe will happen. Finally the catharsis will come, and after that everything will start to go well.' Prague has been through it all before.

Czech Culture

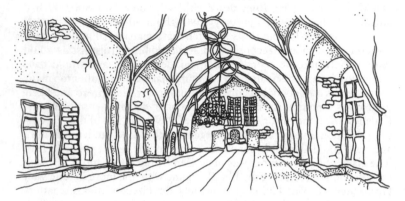

Art and Architecture

The Golden Ages of Prague have been short and few, and yet the city has emerged with one of the richest architectural legacies in Europe. Purists may object that it's a visual cacophony; anyone with an ounce of romance will be dumbstruck. Czech painters have perpetrated some atrocities over the years, but Bohemia's Gothic art and the riot of modernism of the first half of this century were superb. Catholic oppression helped, by providing the city with an unforgettable Baroque skyline; the Nazis spared it their artistic efforts, but did their little bit by holding off the tanks until the last week of the war; and the city is now one of Europe's most complete if haphazard selections of a millennium of cultural endeavour.

Romanesque

A century was a tender age for a town in 10th-century Europe—but in 965, at a time when most urban centres in the north of the continent comprised a few wooden hovels, Prague was already a thriving town of stone and mortar. The Jewish merchant Ibrahim Ibn-Jacob said as much in his travelogue, noting also that it was very rich and that man and beast would easily find enough to live on. The earliest architecture was Romanesque, deriving from what Europe could remember of the old

62

empire's building skills, and the first churches follow a standard basilican ground plan, with nave and aisles separated by a colonnade. Stone was heavy, but no one yet understood how the clever Romans had supported the weight of their roofs. As a result, Romanesque buildings were either covered with wood or supported with massive pillars; narrow church naves might be given simple tunnel vaults; tiny rotundas, whose tops were supported by a circular wall, were built. Prague's best surviving example of a Romanesque church is St George's Basilica; and three of the mushrooms survive, one of them on Konviktská. The structural deficiencies of these building methods were slowly solved across Europe after about 1100, but Prague stuck with crude Romanesque architecture for two centuries after that.

Gothic

The style of architecture that spread from French cathedral design of the later 12th century was named 'Gothic' centuries later by Renaissance-minded Italians who felt that it could only have been produced by vandals. Weight problems were solved by the realization that pointed arches could redistribute stresses throughout a building; that ribs could be used to hold up a vault and then filled in with light material; and that external walls could be bolstered with exposed flying buttresses. These engineering feats were only the means by which a new spirit was brought into architecture: pointed arches and tremendous steeples drove heavenwards; walls, which no longer had to support the weight of the building, became a field for rich sculptural decoration; and sheets of glass, framed only by decorative tracery, flooded the interiors with light.

The first glimmers of the new architecture arrived in the mid-13th century with the building of St Agnes's Convent, and Gothic features also crept into Prague's Old-New Synagogue. Its effect on the city had been delayed, but it was to be complete. Prague owed its existence to its river, but this had its disadavantages. In the late 1200s, the Vltava submerged the town once too often, and the burghers retaliated with the drastic step of burying their town under three metres of earth. Romanesque Prague became subterranean Prague (much of it still in existence under the Old Town), and a new one was built in Gothic style, using decoration and glass to a greater extent than ever before.

It was under the reign of Emperor Charles IV (1346–78), that Prague entered the European stage. Charles was well-travelled (he studied at the French court and invaded northern Italy while a youth); had a deep reverence for relics, gemstones and painting; and was driven by a proud determination that before he was through, his capital would outshine Paris. Under the influence of his hare-brained Francophile father, he imported a French architect, **Matthew of Arras** to begin his new cathedral; but by the mid-14th century, it was Germany that was leading the continental field in church design, and in 1353 Matthew's timely death brought 23-year-old **Peter Parler** to Prague. The Swabian's father, Heinrich, had just completed the first of Germany's great hall churches at Schwäbisch Gmünd; but Peter outdid him with St Vitus's Cathedral, one of the grandest late Gothic churches of continental Europe. It would take five centuries before the finishing touches were put to the work; but Parler, who was also an accomplished sculptor, assembled a team that left an indelible imprint on the capital.

Bohemian artists also began to produce the first work that was recognizably unique to the country. Its earliest art had come from Constantinople, along with Christianity, and Byzantine art continued to be the model even after Bohemia threw in its lot with the Pope (see p. 38). The oldest paintings to survive, however, date from the first half of the 13th century, and show how artists were beginning to break free of the rigid rules of Byzantium. The lead followed was that of Siena, where the grace of the older tradition was maintained but its strict iconography gave way to personal interpretations of the tales and characters concerned. The individualist trend in Bohemia manifested itself in ever-heavier modelling, which reached a peak in the work of Charles's court artist, **Master Theodoric**—whose outstanding portraits of saints in Karlštejn Castle (see p. 345) ranks as some of the most distinctive work of any royal artist in 14th-century Europe. The emperor's mystical taste for glass and precious stones spills out of Theodoric's work; and the expensive fashions set by Charles were reflected in the creation of Prague's first artistic guild in 1348, which united painters with goldsmiths and glass-blowers.

Charles died in 1378, and although Peter Parler and sons continued to hammer Gothic Prague into existence for another two decades, the assertive spirituality of Charles's art was replaced by a mood of self-indulgence among the court and clergy of his son, Wenceslas IV. Painting and sculpture moved towards a sophisticated and idealized style; while sculptural decoration grew ever-more personalized, erupting occasionally into fantastic beasts or obscene tableaux. They added richness and colour to the city, but were out of tune with the popular mood. In 1420, the outbreak of the Hussite Wars called an abrupt halt to cultural development. Although the Hussite movement called for spiritual regeneration, art and architecture weren't high on its agenda—paintings represented idolatry, Church property was theft, and the clergy was the enemy. St Vitus's Cathedral, which had got as far as its central tower, was ransacked; most of the city's other churches were looted or burnt; and only two of its religious orders were left *in situ* after they took the revolutionary and cowardly decision to side with the masses.

When the dust settled in the 1470s, under the reign of Vladislav II, Prague's Gothic architecture ended in a series of splendid explosions. The king gave his name to the last phase of late Gothic architecture in Bohemia—and the magnificence of the structure that best exemplifies it, the Vladislav Hall, shows that by the end of the 15th century Prague Gothic had gone just about as far as it was possible to go. The ribs of the vault, flowing with gay abandon, have less in common with the structural supports of early Gothic architecture than with the spatial invention of Prague's late Baroque (see below); and the hall is filled with features from the Italian Renaissance, working their way up from Italy via the court of Matthias Corvinus in Hungary, decades before its influence was to be felt in western Europe.

The Renaissance

The Italian Renaissance had a haphazard effect on Prague's architecture. The coronation of Bohemia's first Habsburg monarch Ferdinand I in 1526 encouraged the flow of Italian ideas to Prague, but they made limited headway through the narrow lanes of Gothic Prague. Ferdinand built his sublime Royal Summer Palace (1538–63), and when land prices on the left bank plummeted after a huge fire in 1541, a series of imposing Renaissance palaces were built by nobles anxious not to appear unfashionable; but the town's burghers were a more conservative bunch. Windows might be enlarged and straightened, *sgraffito* was often plastered over façades, the more adventurous might even build a miniature courtyard at the back; but the sturdy Gothic structures themselves stayed firm until the tidal wave of the Baroque. North Italian craftsmen poured into Prague towards the end of the 16th century, but they were second-rate peddlers of an architectural style that was already old hat at home.

Mannerism

During the reign of **Emperor Rudolf II** (1576–1611), Prague became one of the leading centres of Mannerist culture in Europe. The term, like so many others in the vicious world of art appreciation, was originally one of abuse; when the new style emerged in northern Italy at the beginning of the century, its apparently distorted and unnatural proportions were often seen as no more than an affected (or untalented) departure from the classical beauty of the High Renaissance. Mannerism was a clear retreat from the notion that art could best capture the essence of the world by trying to reproduce it in its most noble form. In a troubled century of religious uncertainty, the attempt to penetrate beyond the appearance of things was part of a widespread and urgent search to find a more solid basis for a universal truth. Rudolf's court crossed national boundaries and modern-day disciplines. The old order was collapsing, and no one really knew what its replacement might look like. Alchemists and astrologers were just as likely to have useful ideas as painters and sculptors, and the fine arts of Rudolfine Prague are packed with the symbolism of the esoteric and the occult.

Rudolf's art collection was one of the largest of its time, and as well as buying works, he summoned artists to Prague from across Europe. The Milanese painter, **Giuseppe Arcimboldo** (1527–93) followed the emperor to Prague, having loyally served the Habsburg court since the days of Ferdinand I. He is best known for his allegorical portraits, surreal compositions which drew on an arcane system of correspondences between man and nature. They began when Ferdinand, with Habsburg humour, had asked him to draw the syphilis-ravaged face of the court doctor. Arcimboldo produced a likeness made up of animals and cooked fish, which impressed everyone, not least the Surrealists, who rediscovered the artist some four centuries later. He created many more of the heads while in Prague, and organized Rudolf's pageants in the castle. Many of the emperor's other favoured painters came from the Low Countries. Among them was **Bartholomeus Spranger** (1546–1611), who proved central to the development of the court's art. He settled in Prague in 1581 after travelling across France and Italy. Spranger's style—shimmering with colour and movement, and highly sophisticated in form and composition—expressed itself not just in classical and religious themes but also in a series of allegorical paintings which pulled together motifs from alchemy and astrology to glorify the emperor and the imperial mission. The apotheosis of Rudolf—Christian hero against the Turks and patron of the arts against dark ignorance—was a theme to which most of his artists turned their hand at some point. **Hans von Aachen** (from Köln—1552–1615) was appointed to the imperial service in 1597. Aachen had spent a decade in northern Italy, during which he had kept Rudolf up to date with developments in the art market (the emperor sent him across Europe to snap up Dürers and the collections of the recently deceased); and one of his occasional jobs was to travel to foreign courts to paint pubescent princesses during Rudolf's doomed search for a suitable match. His work comprised elegant portraits and religious scenes; but like Spranger, he also painted nudes, tinged with an eroticism which sometimes went beyond a respectable Renaissance fascination with the human form. The trend permeated the art of the court—largely due to sad Rudolf himself, who often stipulated his preferred views. An almost morbid voyeuristic spirit lurks behind many of the classical love scenes which he commissioned, usually drawn from myths telling of deception and weakness, and generally capturing highly advanced stages of courtship. The emperor's sculptors came from Italy on the recommendation of Giovanni Bologna, who stuck with the Medicis despite repeated Habsburg attempts to buy him out. **Hans Mont** gave up the art after being blinded while watching a game in Rudolf's tennis court; but **Adriaen de Vries** (1545–1626), a talented student of Bologna, stayed in Prague until his death.

Rudolf's curiosity stretched to the natural world, and among his still-life artists were the Flemish **Roelandt Savery**, who arrived in 1604 and developed his skills in portraying plants and beasts in the emperor's fabled menagerie and gardens (he's thought to have been the first European to paint a dodo). The emperor's court was also the centre of one of the grandest collections ever assembled, rivalled only by that of Uncle Ferdinand in Ambras Castle. As well as a panoply of 15th- and 16th-century art, Rudolf's thirst for knowledge led him to amass clocks, perpetual motion machines, gemstones and endless lists of curiosities—including a homunculus pickled in alcohol, remnants of the clay used by God to create Adam, Brutus' dagger, and four stones which fell from a clear sky onto a Hungarian battlefield.

Rudolf's court was an ephemeral Camelot which began to evaporate from the moment of the emperor's sorry downfall in 1611. His successor, Matthias (with whom Rudolf had fought a long battle over a unicorn horn), spirited parts of the collection over to Vienna a year later; and almost all the rest was systematically removed in 1648, when Swedish troops invaded Prague specifically to steal the collection for their own

unbalanced Queen Christina. Although engravings of Spranger's paintings were an important influence on the earliest work of the Haarlem
Academy, Rudolfine Mannerism was a vortex of talent, rather than an
explosion; and its mood was far removed from that of the city below.
Prague's visual arts were going through another crisis in an atmosphere
of quasi-Calvinism, and the Estates sold off an unknown amount of
Rudolf's collection in 1619. Local engravers gave some of the emperor's
art a wider audience, but the reasons for their popularity were sometimes
dubious—as was widely noted after 1612, when a local artist died and
was found to have painted a varied collection of pornographic works for
unidentified patrons. The court's introverted intellectualism led it to an
interest in the Jewish cabala, and its contacts with ghetto scholars
reinforced the otherworldly image of Rudolfine Prague that has been
fixed in the city's popular imagination. It began with *Satyricon*, a trashy
but influential 17th-century satire, which reached its high point when
the narrator was led to a thinly-veiled Rudolf, engrossed in conversation
with a sinister type clutching formulae and retort—and was told by a
courtier, 'That, my lord, is the most favoured person in the whole
palace—a Jew'.

Rudolf's architecture has also been lost. Much of what was built still
clung on to Gothic motifs (the church of St Roch is a good example that's
still around); and the few grand schemes of the emperor, such as his
rebuilt castle, have been all but destroyed by later remodelling. There
are remnants of his summer palace at Stromovka (see p. 268), and its
artificial pond is fed by a mile-long tunnel, one of Rudolf's pet projects.

The Baroque

Mannerism asked imponderable questions; the style that followed declared violently that it had the answer. The Baroque emerged in Rome in
the late 16th century, at almost exactly the same time as the Council of
Trent laid down its demand that art was to glorify the Church. It took
some time to get to Prague and by the time it did so, its Counter-
Reformatory zeal had been all but spent in its home town. But here it was
part and parcel of the Catholic reconquest of Bohemia, and within a
century it had utterly transformed the face of the city.

There was no return to the balanced harmony of the Renaissance, but
the Baroque used ideas such as movement, disproportion and unnatural
light with a consistency that overwhelmed rather than intrigued. The
new architecture elbowed its way into the vast **Waldstein Palace**, which

represents a transition between the two styles; but while the Thirty Years War progressed, most Catholic orders and newly-rich nobles bided their time. When it ended in 1648, building began in earnest, helped along by another burst of land-clearance in 1689 when a fire destroyed most of what remained of the Gothic Old Town.

The first Baroque architects in Prague were imports, usually shadowy figures about whom little is known. **Carlo Lurago** (1615/18–84) was born in Tessin, but seems to have worked only in Prague; some trained in Rome itself, such as the classicizing Frenchman **Jean-Baptiste Mathey** (*c.* 1630–95); but the majority came through Vienna, which had become a centre of the new architecture since Ferdinand II had stormed back to his ancestral home in a post-White Mountain huff (see p. 53). Of the latter group, the most prolific were **Francesco Caratti** (?–1677/9) and **Giovanni Alliprandi** (1665–1720). All brought some of the most distinctive features of Roman Baroque to Prague. Ovoid halls and domes stretched through their palaces and churches, replacing the serene circles of yesteryear; and the huge dramas of their palatial façades loudly announced that Prague had lost the war, and the victors had come to stay.

By the beginning of the 18th century, northern Europe had firmly snatched the baton of the Baroque from its homeland; and Prague and Vienna were setting a scorching pace, each encouraged by the inventiveness of the other. Two of the city's greatest architects were **Kristof Dienzenhofer** (1655–1722), born in Cuckoo Hill, Bavaria, who settled in Prague around 1685; and his native-born son **Kilian Ignaz Dienzenhofer** (1689–1751). Kristof's contemporary, the Viennese court architect **Johann Fischer von Erlach**, also designed several works in Prague. All three men were heavily influenced by the undulating rhythms of Borromini's work in Rome and the quivering geometry of Guarino Guarini, who had visited Prague and drawn up unrealized plans for a church in Malá Strana in 1679. The influence of the two Italians appears most strikingly in the Dienzenhofers' joint masterpiece, the Jesuit Church of St Nicholas in Malá Strana, one of 18th-century Europe's finest.

Prague Baroque has been called 'the fruit of oppression' and 'the flowers of evil' by the modern Czech author Milan Kundera, and it has an ideological element that took it to a realm of deception and power that it rarely reached elsewhere in Europe. It's apparent in the vast palaces built on confiscated lands, but most especially in the city's churches. A population which was 90 per cent Protestant and had started the Thirty Years War had to be taught a lesson—and the city's religious orders knew that if you yanked the heartstrings violently enough, the mind would follow. The Jesuits were the most notorious masters of the Baroque propaganda exercise, and produced St Nicholas's Church as the evidence, but all the religious architecture of the period is permeated with missionary zeal. The mysterious abstraction of Gothic vaults was replaced by vast illusionistic paintings and frescoes; the Marian cult and miracle-working icons found their way into almost every church; and splendid but fake marble, gold and silver appeared throughout. The trick worked; Praguers headed like moths towards the Catholic flames, and by the 18th century, a majority of the city had reverted. It's sometimes difficult now to appreciate the hypnotic power of the churches—to the modern mind they often appear little more than tacky works of triumphalist propaganda—but the greatest can still reduce you to a moment of stunned silence.

The architecture wasn't entirely alien to the city's traditions. Even in St Nicholas's, the flowing vault harks back to the Gothic style; and the work of the third great architect of Bohemian late Baroque, the Prague-born **Giovanni Santini** (1667–1723), is even more explicitly Gothicizing. His churches—especially outside Prague (see Day Trips—Kutná Hora, pp. 346–50)—are replete with tall towers and pointed arches, and the ribbed vaults of many look like nothing so much as the floral extravagance of the Vladislav style.

Throughout Europe, the Baroque saw a reintegration of architecture and sculpture, after the Renaissance insistence that both were independent elements of a building. Baroque statuary became one of the most distinctive features of Prague's architecture. Coming so soon after the tail-end of a long late Gothic phase, the Baroque established a tradition that influenced design into the 20th century, and has given Prague's streets one of the highest concentrations of sculptured façades in Europe. Baroque sculpture began with the relative restraint of **Jan Bendl** (1620–80) and **Matthias Jäckel** (1655–1738), but at the end of the 17th century, a combination of lessons learnt from Rome and the accelerating pace of the Counter-Reformation gave rise to the epic works of **Matthias Braun** (1684–1738), born in the Tyrol, and **Ferdinand Maximilian Brokof** (1688–1731), born in Prague of Slovakian origin. Neither ever attained the virtuosity of Rome's Bernini, but their work—Madonnas brimming with sexuality and atlantes straining with their spheres—shows the superhuman sensuality with which the Catholic conquerors titillated and ultimately subdued the natives.

Baroque painting in Bohemia isn't up to the sculpture. **Karel Škréta**

(1610–74) was the first of its early Baroque artists. Škréta studied in Rome—and developed a style which made use of most Italian art of the previous century, rounded off with the classicist restraint of Nicolas Poussin, whom he's thought to have bumped into briefly. He had left Prague a Protestant exile, and returned a fervent Catholic; and apart from portraits, he produced vast amounts of work for the busy monks of the day. **Michael Willmann** (1630–1706) was another convert, who produced messy (albeit deeply-felt) moments of religious anguish and passion, which were sorry homages to the exuberance of Rubens. The most accomplished works of Prague Baroque were the experiments with light and colour of **Petr Brandl** (1668–1735); but even in the 18th century, the most important development in the painting of Germanic countries, their ever-more-glorious frescoes, found few worthy practitioners in Prague. The only notable exception is the work of **Franz Anton Maulpertsch** at the Strahov Monastery (see p. 198).

In the second half of the 18th century, the enervating force of the Baroque had almost eaten itself up. Prague's architecture was briefly affected by the **Rococo**, which transformed the mobility and dramatic light-effects of the earlier style into playful elegance. Its most characteristic features were the use of pale colours and asymmetrical motifs, most notably in the dangling stucco decoration of the Goltz-Kinsky Palace (see p. 146) and the Sylva-Taroucca Palace on Na příkopě. The fey creature only lasted a few decades in Prague, before both it and the Baroque were finally extinguished in the late 18th century.

From Neo-Classicism to Neo-Gothic

Under the reign of Emperor Joseph II, the city's culture suffered a series of rapid blows. Fripperies had no place in the monarch's coolly rational world. What remained of Rudolf's collection was auctioned at giveaway prices in 1782; while most men of the cloth were turfed out of their monasteries, which were then turned into barracks (see p. 53). The Jesuits had already been disestablished in 1773, and the disappearance of religious orders from Prague had particularly serious consequences. As the wealth of the aristocracy had flowed towards Vienna, the Church had emerged as the most important patron of art and architecture in the capital. Although the monks had arrived as conquerors they had made a huge contribution to its cultural life. In the last years of the century, this all but ended.

There was little originality in the few buildings that appeared in

Prague in the years between 1780 and the middle of the next century. Architecture was typified by a dry classicism inspired by France. Buildings continued to use many of the motifs rediscovered during the Renaissance: triangular pediments and Grecian pillars or, more often, pilasters. But they were no longer piled together with the bombast of the Baroque and sculptural decoration was no longer used on façades. The change was particularly noticeable in Prague, which had taken to the earlier style so completely, but neither classicism nor the Empire style which followed had much impact on the centre of the city. The cool façade of the Philosophical Hall of the Strahov Monastery, housing the last flourish of the Baroque in the form of Maulpertsch's ceiling fresco, represents the transition; the genteel Tyl Theatre shows the new style at its best. The late 1700s also saw the greening of Prague. The palaces of Malá Strana were given the gentle lawns and terraced slopes that characterize the area today; avenues were planted; and the city's first parks were tamed for the great Prague public over the next decades.

Nation-Building

In the middle of the 19th century, Prague's architecture became engulfed in the national revival movement (see p. 54), which demanded monuments to reflect Bohemia's glorious past. Like the rest of Europe, the city was swept by a vogue for rehashing older architectural styles; and the favoured choice for buildings of national significance was the Renaissance. It didn't matter that Prague had been little touched by the real thing and non-existent in the age of antiquity, nor that what little had appeared was imported by the Habsburgs. Huge pediments were triumphant, and stacks of disordered columns were thought to be noble. The result appears most clearly in Prague's National Museum. The later 19th century also saw a wave of restoration of Bohemia's Gothic architecture, which (with more reason) was also seen as an expression of the national spirit. However, the zealous bunch concerned, led by **Josef Mocker**, often destroyed more than they created, since they frowned on anything that had appeared in the intervening centuries—which, given Prague's messy architectural history, was often most of the building concerned. One exception was St Vitus's Cathedral, to which the same architects began to add a western half some 550 years after construction had commenced. Artists also played a heroic role in the national revival, adorning the new buildings with mythological and allegorical works to express the aspirations of the patriotic movement. The work was a useful

72

visual aid for a public whose literacy in the recently-revived Czech language was often shaky, and you can see it in the National Theatre, Municipal House (pp. 139–40) and the museum at St Agnes's Convent (p. 165).

Opening the Doors to Europe

By the turn of the century, Habsburg rule had begun to crumble, and directly political concerns gave way to introspection over what the future held in store for little Bohemia/Czechoslovakia. As interest in Vienna declined, many self-consciously turned for inspiration to the rest of Europe. Artists and architects went shopping for ideas across the continent, and France in particular was to be a decisive influence on the country's cultural development until the Nazi invasion in 1938.

Art Nouveau and Symbolism

Prague's architecture at the turn of the century was dominated by Art Nouveau—or rather, the Europe-wide search for a new decorative style that came to be known by a bewildering variety of names (the sartorially-minded Italians named it after Regent Street's Liberty store). This book uses the term 'Art Nouveau' throughout, but the Bohemian *secese* was actually a mixture of two fairly distinct trends. One came from France and Germany, and used foliage-inspired motifs, with a particular fondness for whiplash curves; while the second attempted to escape the slavish historicism of the dying century's architecture, and looked instead to far more abstract angular structures, self-contained and stripped of ornamentation. The latter came to Prague from Vienna, and had a powerful influence that ran through the next four decades. Even before the First World War, **Jan Kotěra** designed a series of severe buildings that have more in common with post-war Constructivism (see below) than the popular idea of Art Nouveau, notably his own house on Hradešínská. The two varieties of Art Nouveau jostle one another in the bourgeois mansions of the northern Old Town, which saw a high tide of slum clearance around 1900. There are plenty of the houses in suburbs such as Vinohrady and Vršovice, although some succumbed to a burst of bourgeois mansion-clearance during Allied bombing raids at the end of the Second World War.

Art Nouveau found decorative expression in the work of **Alfons Mucha** (1860–1939), who began as an innovative poster designer for (and apparently, lover of) Sarah Bernhardt in Paris, but spent the rest of his life producing hackneyed tributes to the Slavic race; and in the sculptures of **Ladislav Šaloun** (1870–1946) and **Stanislav Sucharda** (1866–1916). Two of the most original artists to emerge during the 1890s, however, were mystical types less concerned with the new forms that had been developed by Art Nouveau than with the spiritual values that could be expressed with the greater level of abstraction. The first was the sculptor **František Bílek** (1872–1941), who studied in Paris in the early 1890s. Using a huge variety of techniques and materials, Bílek linked ideas spanning music, literature and religion to produce a complex and fascinating body of work. His house has now been turned into a museum (see p. 251). **František Kupka** (1871–1957) settled in Paris after 1896, but much of his most important work has found its way back to Prague. Kupka's earliest paintings concentrated on ideas of rebirth and renewal; but after several years as a medium, he moved on to produce some of Europe's first intentional abstract art, such as his *Amorpha, Fugue in Two Colours* (1912). His better-known contemporary, Vassily Kandinsky, shared similar beliefs in visual music, but is thought to have painted his first non-figurative composition one year after Kupka.

Cubism

In 1902, a belated exhibition of the French Impressionists and a Rodin retrospective caused a storm among the city's artistic community. Three years later, however, all eyes were on an exhibition of the anguished work of the Norwegian Edvard Munch. As a result, Prague took a crash course in the clash of philosophies that had been building in Europe over the last decade, between the view that art could and still should show what the world *looked* like, and the idea that it should express the emotions of the artist and the subject. Drawing inspiration from the two very different starting points, the capital's painters, sculptors and even architects were soon immersed in the artistic ferment of pre-war Europe.

Prague's first modernist painting came out of *Osma* ('The Eight'), a group of artists founded in 1907. Its initial inspiration was the raw force of Munch, but as early as 1910, Czech artists such as **Emil Filla** (1882–1953), **Bohumil Kubišta** (1884–1918) and **Antonín Procházka** (1882–1945) had picked up on Parisian Cubism. For the next decade, Prague was to be perhaps the most important centre of the new art outside its birthplace. For a time, Czech artists developed a form of Cubo-Expressionism, using Cubist methods but packing their work with a powerful psychological punch. The most interesting paintings of Czech Cubism were produced in these first years, but Filla and Procházka left to set up the more formally Cubist *Skupina* ('Group') in 1911, and began to move away from capturing moments of existential crisis, to more orthodox examinations of structure (and later, movement). Kubišta wouldn't join the Skupina, and his fascinating work, riddled by dark questioning, was cut short only by his death in the 1918 flu epidemic. Two other artists to emerge during this period—**Josef Čapek** (1897–1945) and **Jan Zrzavý** (1890–1977)—also dabbled with Cubism, but were more concerned with the primitivism that had inspired it. Each produced a set of simple and beautiful paintings, with a lyricism that in the case of Zrzavý in particular, signposted the way to developments in the 1920s.

Kubišta notwithstanding, Prague's painters largely followed the lead set by Picasso and Braque, but the sculptors and architects in the Skupina produced maverick works that are unparalleled in the world. The leading sculptor was **Otto Gutfreund** (1889–1927), who studied under Bourdelle in Paris, but returned in 1911 to create a series of works that are uncatagorizable. Most of his early work exemplifies the ideas of Cubo-Expressionism. The disciplined coherence of Cubist planes and angles was used to explore emotional states (*Angst* and *Hamlet* were two of his earliest efforts); but he also explored Czech Baroque's use of imbalance to express energy, and the Futurist fascination with movement, to develop ways of capturing tension in sculpture. The most extraordinary three-dimensional experiments of Czech Cubism were made in architecture. Three members of the Skupina—**Pavel Janák** (1882–1956), **Joseph Gočár** (1880–1945) and **Josef Chochol** (1880–1956)—openly rejected the harshness of their teacher Kotěra's work, and tried to restore depth and human proportions to their buildings by using three-dimensional geometrical forms on the façades. The idea was to translate one of Prague's oldest architectural traditions into the idiom of Cubism; how far they succeeded is open to question, but in Prague you can see examples of the only systematically theorized and practised Cubist architecture in the world. (You'll find examples of the strange results at Celetná 34 and Neklanova 2 and 34.)

Devĕtsil and Surrealism

The inter-war years were among the most exciting in the history of Prague's cultural life, spiced with a political content with which the post-war Communist government had serious problems. Some of the best work of the period has been under wraps for decades and is only now emerging.

Clean breaks are rare creatures in history, but in 1918 much of Prague's artistic community thought that it had just lived through one. The old world didn't look too good after the carnage of war; Czechoslovakian independence had finally been won; and over in the east, a rosy Bolshevik dawn was rising. In 1920, a group of young artists, led by the breathtakingly energetic **Karel Teige** (1900–51) founded *Devĕtsil* ('Nine Forces'), which was to throw itself into the van of the European avant garde during the next decade.

There was probably never a time when the old cliché of Prague laying at the heart of Europe was as directly relevant to developments in the city. With a population that was almost 10 per cent German-speaking, influences from the north and the south were unavoidable (though Germany became more important than Vienna); French contacts continued unabated; and the spectacular explosion of creativity in the east was to have cultural effects in Prague long after it had been snuffed out at home. One of the most significant arrivals was **Roman Jakobson** (1896–1982), who came as Soviet press attaché in 1923; the ideas he developed in the Prague Linguistic Circle were seminal to Structuralism, and he was an active member of Devĕtsil during the inter-war years.

The firmly-stated political philosophy of the group was Soviet-style Marxism, but after a very brief tinker with the idea of 'proletarian art', Devĕtsil spent the rest of the 1920s bobbing and weaving through a maze of artistic experimentation that led one exasperated Party critic to describe the group as 'the fruit of late capitalism'. The roller-coaster began in 1924. Teige hurled the group into the mêlée of European -isms with his First Manifesto of Poetism. In it he embraced the abstract beauty of the machine age—transatlantic liners, lightbulbs—an idea at the heart of Soviet Constructivism; but also began to lay down his own theory of 'Poetism', 'the art of pleasure', which was to condition the art produced. The balancing act was precarious—technology had just happily slaughtered millions—and Devĕtsil never consistently united the two elements of its philosophy. The general feeling was that art should be accessible to everyone, and not just an élite. Machine-made goods were favoured because 'their midwife is not art', and there were plenty of them, to boot. But, on the other hand, Devětsil came up with some work that would have been incomprehensible to anyone who hadn't read every manifesto published.

Despite the fact that Teige spent most of the early 1920s calling for 'the liquidation of art' (and the Artist), Poetism was characterized in its first years by a joyful celebration of creative imagination. A strong influence was the French theorist and writer Guillaume Apollinaire, who had visited Prague in 1902. To the dismay of many Poetists, he had passed through unrecognized, although he apparently met Ahasuerus, the Wandering Jew, when asking for directions. There were few constraints more rigid than free association, and the ideal was to cross sensory boundaries. The lyrical poets **Jaroslav Seifert** (1901–86) and **Vítězslav Nezval** (1900–58) worked on 'film poems' (i.e. scripts); the sculptor **Zdeněk Pešánek** (1896–1965) created visual pianos and perhaps the world's first neon fountain; and Teige turned his hand to almost every field save painting. One of the most common forms of art in the group was the collage, or 'pictorial poem' in Teige-talk. It was a democratic game that anyone with scissors could play, and appealed to the Poetists' fascination with modern images and the feelings that could be inspired by combining pictures on a certain theme. Holiday pictorial poems were a favourite—apart from allowing plenty of opportunities to use pictures of transatlantic liners, they also stressed the new international mood of the country. Not surprisingly, photography was favoured by the movement, which took the view in the early 1920s that it should and would replace the dying bourgeois art of painting. Most of the group walked around with cameras for a while, although its photography section contained only one full-timer, **Jaroslav Rössler** (b. 1902). Two other photographers emerged during the 1920s—**Jaromír Funke** (1896–1945) and **Josef Sudek** (1896–1976), and although they were never confined by the ideological posturings of the group, their pre-war interests included beautiful machines and suggestive patterns of objects. One-armed Sudek also began a life-long expedition through the light and shadow of Prague, with a beautiful series of shots of dusty St Vitus's Cathedral, taken in 1924, as the builders were putting the finishing touches on Peter Parler's masterpiece.

Devětsil's love of cameras meant that its early attitude to movies was equally celebratory. Cinema's popular appeal almost gave it the edge as a non-élitist medium (Charlie Chaplin and Douglas Fairbanks Jnr were both drafted into Devĕtsil, although neither found out); and the big screen seemed an excellent way of linking images and ideas and communicating them to the masses. The group's members turned out endless film poems, and the first Structuralist film analysis took place in Prague, but it came to virtually nothing. The conservative studios would have nothing to do with avant-garde urchins and Teige sadly had to warn that the industry would 'probably perish on its unforgivable sins' if it didn't start producing some of the works 'alas, only on paper, in the desks of modern authors'. Although it didn't perish, it certainly wasn't very vital until after the war (see pp. 82–5), but it enjoyed one international success with Gustav Machatý's *Extase* ('Ecstasy'—1933), one of the world's first erotic films that was also artistic (honest, guv). Devĕtsil had more success with the stage, and in 1926 it set up the Liberated Theatre, which was taken over three years later by the comedy and cabaret duo of Jiří Voskovec and Jan Werich (V and W), whose work remains popular today.

Outwardly Devĕtsil had many interests in common with French Surrealism, but the two groups kept at arm's length during the 1920s. Teige had issued his manifesto a month before André Breton, and he was probably jealous of the wider attention the French movement was getting, but towards the end of the decade, the darker questions raised by Surrealism began to make heavy inroads into the happy-go-lucky early Poetism of Devĕtsil. This was exemplified in the work of two of the group's painters, **Toyen** (1902–80) and **Jindřich Štyrský** (1899–1942). During the 1920s, both moved from painting geometrical abstractions to a far more personal and introspective style that relied on half-remembered images and semi-conscious associations. In 1926, during a three-year stay in Paris, they tiresomely christened their new work 'Artificialism', but their increasing concern with buried levels of consciousness was only a short step to Surrealism. Another Devĕtsil member, **Josef Šíma** (1891–1971), settled in Paris in 1921 and hovered on the fringes of the movement for a decade. He was regarded as heretical by the French group for his concern with the collective rather than individual unconsciousness (the result of an epiphany after a close encounter with a bolt of lightning); but although he painted too many cosmic eggs and crystals for the Surrealists' liking at first, he became an important contact between the two movements.

The supposed obstacle between the groups was political, and after the French made a doubtful pledge of allegiance to the Communist International in 1930, the way was free for increased contacts. In 1932, one of the first international exhibitions of Surrealist art was held in Prague, and in 1934 the Prague Surrealist Group was established. Teige hopped on board and took over in the same year; and giving free rein to his unconsciousness, he produced some of his most amazing and alarming collages, a series of women's bodies penetrated by machinery or otherwise dismembered. Breton and Paul Eluard boosted the troops by visiting in 1935; and Poetism had established an imaginativeness and co-operation between the branches of the arts that made Prague's Surrealist movement the second most active in Europe outside Paris through the 1930s.

Surrealist architecture would have been a fine thing. There was none of that, but Prague (and to an even greater extent the town of Brno) saw huge activity in the field of design. In the immediate post-war years, the pre-war Cubist architects developed a short-lived 'Rondocubism' which it was hoped could become a distinctively national style for the new republic. The theory was impressively realized in the bizarre Banka Legii on Na poříčí, designed by Josef Gočár. It was still the façade that was emphasized but, in a manner harking back to the Baroque, its elements were amassed and pushed outwards in repetitive curves. Another distinctive use of a Prague traditional feature was the integration of figurative sculpture on the building. The friezes, by **Jan Stursa** and Otto Gutfreund, are far removed in their simplicity from Gutfreund's earlier Cubist-inspired work. Although he died in 1927—the Vltava got him as he took a dip on a hot day in June—the friezes were an important move towards a form of social realism that influenced many other sculptors in the later 1920s.

Rondocubism was the last effort to create a Czech national architecture for the 20th century. Between the wars, internationalism and ideology led most of Prague's architects (again, often involved in Devětsil) towards Constructivism and Functionalism. The basic difference between the two was that the first claimed that mass production and modern materials were beautiful; the second theoretically didn't give a hoot, so long as a building served its purpose. Both theories found willing adherents in Prague, and by the 1930s, the aesthetic differences, although still loudly argued over, were little more than nuances. Prague hurled itself into the brave new world of glass and concrete. In 1924, Teige organized Czech participation in the first international Bauhaus exhibition; Le Corbusier came to Bohemia three times, skirting around Prague after Teige attacked him for betraying Functionalism by worrying too much about the looks of his buildings; and the Brno-born Adolf

Loos built his Müller Villa on the outskirts of the capital, on Nad hradním vodojemem in Střešovice. The ideal of many of the city's architects was to use the new ideas to house the poor. Teige went the whole hog and suggested abolishing the family and socializing education in collective blocks. The most significant modernist housing built in Prague, though, was the Baba Housing Estate, a private project for well-heeled professional types. In the jaded light of the 1990s, it's less exciting than it must have appeared at the time, but if you want to see how transatlantic liners influenced the city's designers, the houses are around Na Babě in Prague 6.

From Nazism to Normalization

The Nazis rolled into town in March 1939, and Prague's cultural life was crushed. Functionalist architecture wasn't glorious enough; most contemporary Czech art fell squarely within the category of degenerate art. Exile and extermination decimated the city's intelligentsia, and three years after liberation another tyranny moved in.

With the accession of a Communist-led government in 1948, creativity in painting and the plastic arts was sacrificed on the altar of Socialist Realism. The doctrine, invented by Moscow in the 1930s, was a monolithic officially-controlled programme of extolling the class-struggle and the onward march to socialism. Sometimes defined by Czechs as 'art so simple even the Central Committee can understand it', it produced monumental buildings and Stakhanovite murals and sculptures that still disfigure parts of the capital. The best architectural example is the formidable Hotel International, Prague's homage to the even more mammoth University of Moscow (which Muscovites used to claim wasn't all bad, since it was the only place in the city from which you couldn't see the University of Moscow). The hotel now has a perverse splendour, and if you're in the area, pop in for a vodka. The pre-war avant-garde was an abomination in Communist eyes; not only was its work too unReal, but the Surrealists had spent the later 1930s flirting with Leon Trotsky. Turncoats were granted dishonourable rehabilitation; those who resisted were tempted back into the fold by a variety of means, notably spells of hard labour in Czechoslovakia's uranium mines. Karel Teige lived long enough to see his dreams turn to dust. He's said to have committed suicide in 1951, with a warrant out for his arrest.

In the late 1950s, after the death of Stalin, a slow thaw set in. One of the most impressive of the artists to emerge was **Mikuláš Medek** (1926–74), banned during the 1950s for his association with Teige's post-war Surrealist group; and the activities of a new generation of writers and filmmakers pulled the city into the Swinging Sixties after two decades of austerity.

On the night of 21 August 1968, 200,000 Warsaw Pact troops turned the Prague Spring into winter. Within two months, Louis Aragon (who had been one of the first French Surrealists to make the leap to Stalinism) had coined a phrase that was to haunt the next two decades, when he warned that Czechoslovakia was on the path to becoming a 'Biafra of the spirit'. Within two years, the government had launched a programme of 'normalization', that was more of a threat to independent thought than anything since the Counter-Reformation. Potential centres of ideological resistance—theatre companies, the Writers' Union—were dissolved and reconstituted; individual artists who had supported the Prague Spring were anathematized; and most importantly, the government all but gave up the idea of promoting the Party line through art. The form of cultural control was far more insidious than Socialist Realism, or even Baroque churches. So long as artists were prepared publicly to recant earlier errors, they were often grimly snatched back into the bosom of the Establishment; and what they said subsequently in their art was often less significant to the government than the persona that they presented to the public. In the case of those artists whose work was only tangentially political, official acceptance (and a livelihood) might depend only on being prepared to utter a few words; and the characteristic feature of the country's officially-sanctioned art over the next two decades, most especially the 1980s, isn't a slavish portrayal of the Party line, but a coy evasion of thorny issues. The government had learnt to smile at gentle experimentation; and those who kept quiet could now even include the occasional in-joke at the regime's expense.

Those who wouldn't play the game weren't sent to uranium mines—just prevented from ever using their skills again. Ph.Ds and artists found work as stokers and taxi-drivers, and were harassed for 'parasitism' if they couldn't find anyone brave enough to employ them. The most courageous signed the **Charter 77** manifesto (see p. 59).

Resurrection

Since 1989, the whole of Czechoslovakia has been piecing together its cultural history. Two generations have grown up with a mangled view of their past, broken only by some years of truth in the 1960s, and few are yet able to assess it. The work of Devětsil is a particular puzzle to many, since it doesn't fit neatly into either the Communist or anti-Communist camp—which may not be the best way of judging a work of art, but it's one that's as popular in contemporary Prague as it's been in many other places and times. Many of the city's most talented young sculptors and artists have spent much of their time since the revolution exhibiting their work abroad, but the city's galleries are nevertheless filled with new work, as well as newish work which has been languishing in drawers for decades. The Bell House in the Old Town Square (see pp. 146–7) has some of the best exhibitions. The glorious architecture is there for all to see. Even the Communists didn't dare tamper with that.

Film

Early Czech cinema produced *Extase* (1933), a classic of cinematic erotica starring Hedy Lamarr; but it was only after 1945 that the medium took off in Czechoslovakia. It's had a chequered history, but its high points have given Czech film and animation an international reputation for excellence.

Prague's Barrandov studios emerged from the war as Europe's largest functioning film complex outside Italy and France—all thanks to the Nazis, who had confiscated it and expanded the facilities considerably, with an eye on what was expected to be a post-war audience in serious need of relentless propaganda. Their cinematic dreams fell through, but it soon became clear that others had similar ideas. In 1945, Barrandov was nationalized. The decision was taken for honourable reasons, and supported by many film-makers, but it meant that when the Communists took over in 1948 they could, and did, swallow it whole. The studios began to churn out classics of Socialist Realism, a gooey mess of sanitized folk traditions and heroic furtherance of Five Year Plans, often with a romance thrown in (e.g. handsome Party official meets naïve but zealous peasant-ess, CIA plot to destroy tractor factory, sabotage thwarted, hands held at sunset). The films were never popular, and haven't seen a screen since the 1989 revolution—but there may be a kitsch revival, in which case you could keep your eyes open for *Tomorrow There Will be Dancing Everywhere*.

The 1950s were lean years, but even then talented film-makers began to break free of the censors' stifling attentions. Czechoslovakia's huge international reputation in the field of animation began to develop with the work of three directors, **Hermína Týrlová**, **Jiří Trnka** and **Karel Zeman**, which combined animation, live-action and puppetry to an extent that was then all but unique. The films won kudos at a time when little else in Czechoslovakia's cultural life was celebrated abroad, and were sometimes even lauded by the government. The jittery camera and savage cuts of **Jan Švankmajer** added a new punch to the genre when he produced his first short feature in 1964. By then, the liberalization that was to culminate in the Prague Spring was in full swing, and for some five years an extraordinary generation of Prague film-makers created and rode the crest of what became known as the **Czech New Wave**.

Most of the new directors emerged from Prague Film School (FAMU), where, in the words of one of the best known, **Miloš Forman**, the students 'first learnt to read between the lines, and then to write between the lines'. Working in close collaboration with talented new authors such as Bohumil Hrabal (see p. 90), they produced work which broke entirely from the conventions of the recent past. The casting of amateurs presented a world that remains spontaneous even today; while a playful eroticism replaced the heroic and chaste embraces of the previous decade.

Simply by representing a real world, the new directors found themselves making political statements from the outset. Forman's first two films, *Lásky jedné plavovlásky* ('Loves of a Blonde'—1965) and *Hoří, má panenko* ('Firemen's Ball'—1967), were both examinations of society in microcosm, where entire villages were drafted in, and bumbling officialdom presented in all its gentle mediocrity. **Věra Chytilová** had her film, *Kopretiny* ('Daisies'—1966) banned for misrepresenting Czech youth, whom the authorities seemed to believe, were immune to the summer of love. It was in 1967 that the outside world first realized that something special was happening in Prague, when another FAMU graduate, **Jiří Menzel**, won an Oscar for Best Foreign Film with his *Ostře sledované vlaky* ('Closely Observed Trains'—1966), the celluloid version of a novel by Bohumil Hrabal. This superb film is a surreal variation on the favourite Communist theme of anti-Nazi struggle, centred around issues of premature ejaculation. In one celebrated scene, a station-master advances up the thigh of pretty Jitka Zelenohorská with a selection of official rubber stamps. Menzel was strongly advised to remove the shot, but arranged for a private screening at the village where the film had been made. The inhabitants insisted that it should stay, and the Bottom Stamping Scene is now a legend. It's also one of the most touching scenes of Czech cinema.

In the years leading up to the Prague Spring, several films stepped beyond gentle mockery into powerful allegory. **Jan Němec**'s *O slavnosti a hostech* ('The Party and the Guests'—1966) was set at a grim outdoor feast, where straying guests are brought back by worried diners; eventually, dogs are used to make sure that no one misses out on the fun. Few Czechs were in much doubt as to whose Party it was, least of all beleaguered President Novotný, who considered a libel suit. **Jaromír Jireš**'s adaptation of Milan Kundera's ascerbic novel, *Žert* ('The Joke') was filmed while tanks rumbled through the streets in August 1968. One of the last, and most daring, films was *Nezvaný host* ('The Uninvited Guest'). This 1969 graduation film by FAMU student **Vlastimil Ventzlik** revolved around two sets of neighbours, each of which finds that a lumbering and unknown visitor has decided to stay indefinitely. Each is uncouth—but one eventually wins over his hosts by buying them a better present than the next. It was an accurate assessment of the social divisions that were to arise over the next 20 years, and Prague's real guests took offence. The film was seized, much of the rest of the work of the previous five years was banned, and FAMU's teachers were dismissed.

The New Wave sank into the quagmire of the 1970s. Many directors took their chances and fled to the west. Among them was Miloš Forman, whose 1975 *One Flew Over the Cuckoo's Nest* gave him the security of an international reputation. That reputation, and perhaps more importantly the US passport that he acquired, enabled him to return to Prague in the early 1980s to film *Amadeus*. Menzel decided to stay, and after signing a statement in support of the 1968 invasion, was permitted to make anodyne films during the 1970s. In the 1980s, Chytilová and Menzel both produced work which had a better popular reception, but although Czech cinema of the last decade had a wryly critical humour which could easily be understood by the Czech audience, it was far from the exuberant spontaneity of the New Wave.

After the 1989 revolution, several films which had been locked away since 1969 were shown for the first time. Apart from most of the works listed above, they include **Karel Kachyňa**'s *Ucho* ('The Ear'); Menzel's adaptation of another Hrabal novel, *Skřivánci na niti* ('Larks on a

String'—1969); and Evald Schorm's *Konec faráře* ('The End of the Priest'), based on a story by Josef Škvorecký. But the future of Czech cinema remains very unclear. The whims of the censor have been replaced by those of the investor. A penny-pinching government has cut back on public funding, while Barrandov itself has been put out to rent. Menzel and others are working on new films, but there's little sign of a renaissance at FAMU, most of whose students you'll find lounging around at the Café Slavia (see p. 307).

One of the most intriguing survivors of the 1960s is the animator Jan Švankmajer. He still claims allegiance to Surrealism, as well as to the Mannerist Prague of Rudolf II and Arcimboldo, and his eerie use of puppets shows the influence of both. Since 1989, he has begun to do some long-overdue cinematic violence to Czechoslovakia's recent history, and along with the classics of the Sixties, his is among the best work now showing in the city.

Literature

A common complaint of modern Czech writers is that their country's literature has never been given the international audience that it deserves. It's a fair comment—albeit one that applies to most other small nations—but modern Czech writing has actually done remarkably well on the crowded world stage, particularly when you consider its late start.

Until 150 years ago Czech literature was all but non-existent. After the suppression of Cyrillic script in the late 11th century (see p. 48), Latin remained the usual written language until the mid-1300s. There are very few earlier examples of Czech literature, and one of them consists of obscene doodles on a prayer book scrawled by a bored nun at St Agnes's Convent. Charles IV (1346–78) encouraged the use of the language; and the Hussites produced a series of Bibles in the vernacular, later given definitive form in the Kralice Bible (1579–94). In 1623, the exiled Protestant and pedagogue **Jan Ámos Komenský** (Comenius) published his *Labyrinth of the World and the Paradise of the Heart*, a questing allegory which plodded through most of the mortal coil—and then what little there was of a Czech literary tradition fizzled out. The cause was the Thirty Years War, which left Bohemia devastated and saw German replace Czech as the language of the educated classes. It was only with the linguistic revival of the early 1800s that modern Czech literature began.

85

Romanticism and Nationalism

The founding father, acknowledged as such by almost every writer who followed, was the dashing **Karel Hynek Mácha** (1810–36). He cut a Byronic figure even unto death: the Englishman had been cut down by a malarial mosquito in the fight for Greek freedom; Mácha lay lingering with pneumonia after hurling himself at a blazing building. In true Romantic style, he left a fiancée, pregnant with his illegitimate son, and an epic poem, *Máj*. Although it was prefaced with a message to the Czech nation, Mácha's passions lay far from the progressive-minded nationalism of his day. The lyrical poem is a macabre examination of a doomed love; and the May of the title isn't so much springtime as one of the months which comes before winter. That didn't stop patriots seizing on it as an expression of the national genius—but Prague's Surrealists of a century later were almost closer to the mark when they declared him a kindred spirit.

In fact, although the nationalist current of the 19th century flowed through every other area of the arts, it inspired very little literature of note. **František Palacký** (1798–1876) published a seminal Czech history, but the only major novel to draw on the rural themes so dear to the hearts of the patriots was *Babička* (Grandmother—1855) by **Božena Němcová** (1820–62). The journalist and writer **Jan Neruda** (1834–91) snatched realistic vignettes from Prague life, particularly Malá Strana—which aimed to be accessible to the new reading public, but were closer in spirit to Charles Dickens than to the blood and soil of Czech nationalism.

Back to Civilization

Armed with the neologisms and background reading that had been provided by 19th-century linguists and translators, Czech literature was finally ready to tackle the world. French Symbolism was the first modern movement to affect Prague. The poets concerned centred around the journal *Moderní Revue*. This morbid crowd was typified by **Karel Hlaváček** (1874–98), whose last years were spent dying of tuberculosis and capturing the experience in verse. Over the next 40 years, Prague's avant-garde went on an exhausting trek from Cubism to Surrealism, and had little time for the outworn conception of the novel; but the work of Guillaume Apollinaire remained a powerful influence on the Devětsil group (see pp. 76–80), which produced the poets **Jaroslav Seifert** (1901–86) and **Vítěslav Nezval** (1900–58). Nezval, whose career ended rather ignobly after the war, turned the language into liquid with lyrical poetry which—along with the work of Vladimír Holan—is still often regarded as the best Czech poetry after Mácha. Seifert's work tends to attract loyal affection rather than acclaim nowadays, despite the fact that he picked up a Nobel Prize in 1984.

The first major Czech writer of the 20th century was **Karel Čapek** (1890–1938), whose work was infused with the democratic spirit of the inter-war republic that died in the same year as he did. A recurrent theme was a suspicion of technology, and the angry young men and women busy celebrating the machine ethic despised his vocal anti-revolutionary attitude. Another preoccupation of his was a fascination with presenting all sides of a story—a technique which he developed with a triple-faceted set of novels—*Hordubal, Meteor* and *An Ordinary Life* (1933–34)—each independent but each contributing to a whole truth. Čapek attributed the typically liberal idea to the Cubist paintings of his almost-as-famous brother, Josef Čapek (see p. 75). The writer's best-known work is his 1920 science-fiction play, *R.U.R*, standing for the English phrase 'Rossum's Universal Robots'. A smash on Broadway and in most of Europe's capitals, it gave the world the word 'robot', from the Czech *robota*, meaning 'hard labour'.

A very different character was **Jaroslav Hašek** (1883–1923). A fair portion of his classic *The Good Soldier Švejk*, chronicling the archetypal anti-hero's perceptive bumblings through Europe's 1914–18 war, is assumed to have been written while drunk. The novel broke new ground in Czech, simply by ignoring most of the established differences between the spoken and written language. Hašek was no cerebral moderate like Čapek, but he was an even more isolated figure, uninterested in the pretensions of the avant-garde and unable to focus his radical temperament on anything for long. He lasted 30 months as a Commissar in the Red Army—but far more typical was his swift dismissal from his editorship of *Animal World*. It came after he wrote an article on a recently discovered fossil of an antediluvian flea, and offered to sell readers two thoroughbred werewolves. (See also Visionary Prague, pp. 100–101).

Čapek and Hašek notwithstanding, it was Prague's Germans who made the literary running in the first decades of the century. So many of this 35,000-strong, 8 per cent minority were authors that, according to the popular journalist **Egon Erwin Kisch** (1885–1948), 'If people hear you're from Prague, it's simply taken for granted'. An even more distinct subset existed: 85 per cent of the city's Germans were Jews and Prague, along with Vienna, was a centre of the last flowering of Jewish culture in Europe. (Among the many who passed through was Albert Einstein, Professor of Theoretical Physics at the Charles University from 1911–1912.) Only one non-Jewish German writer is much remembered today—**Gustav Meyrinck**—and even his one-hit wonder was a best-selling retelling of the story of the golem, the Prague ghetto legend *par excellence*. In German countries, **Franz Werfel** (1890–1945) is still read; **Max Brod** (1884–1968) was a highly successful novelist in his day; and one of Kisch's schoolmates, less well known than any of his contemporaries while alive, was **Franz Kafka** (1883–1924), who has probably done as much to influence modern thought as any other author this century.

Kafka's universe—so distinctive that it gave birth to an adjective—was created in Prague, where he lived for all but a few months of his life. The effect of the city on his work is often overstated, most audaciously by the foreign tour guides who tell visitors that museum-like Hradčany inspired the mental labyrinth of his novel *The Castle*—but it had a powerful psychological impact. Prague was known familiarly to Czechs as *matička* ('mama'), and in 1907 Kafka wrote to a friend, 'This mama has claws. We ought to set fire to it at both ends ... and maybe then it would be possible to escape.' Like the hapless insects and litigants of his fiction, he spent a lifetime trying to make sense of the background into which he had been born. In his brutal *Letter to His Father* he analyzed his childhood with a detail that matched his novels' most nightmarish logic. He handed it to mother; she never passed it on.

Towards the end of his life, he finally began to tackle one of the biggest riddles, his Jewish background. He bolted to Berlin in 1923, and having begun lessons in Hebrew, began to make plans to emigrate to Palestine. Six months later he was dying, and back in Prague, he wrote his last story, an allegory of the Diaspora told by one of the mice of the threatened tribe. Mama reclaimed him, and he now lies buried in the New Jewish Cemetery.

Max Brod, Kafka's closest friend, was an extraordinarily appealing character, selfless in his support of the city's artists, some now world-famous, some forgotten. He had Hašek's *Švejk* translated into German, and it found its way to Bertolt Brecht in Berlin; he personally translated the libretto of Janáček's *Jenůfa* (see p. 93) and gave the composer an international audience; and the supreme irony for a man who was a literary star while Kafka was an insurance official is that he lived to see his independent claim to fame evaporate. Kafka's last will asked his friend to burn most of his unpublished manuscripts. As Brod remarked, the author knew that he was perhaps the least likely person in the world to follow the instruction, and as a result he has gone down in history as the man who saved Kafka's work from the incinerator.

The only wartime literature worth mentioning was *Reportage from the Gallows* (1943), which was allegedly smuggled from the condemned cell of the Communist journalist **Julius Fučík**. It was translated into 70 languages after the war, and Fučík became one of the post-war regime's favourite heroes—and as a result, one of the more unfortunate victims of the 1989 revolution. The manuscript may have been forged by the resistance, but it's now quite common to hear Praguers claim (with no evidence whatsoever) that he was a counter-agent who died recently and peacefully, among his ageing Nazi chums somewhere in South America.

Living in Truth

'When an ordinary person stays silent, it may be a tactical manoeuvre. When a writer stays silent, he is lying.'

Jaroslav Seifert

The Communist takeover of 1948 had a more threatening effect on literature than perhaps any other area of Czechoslovakia's cultural life. The doctrine of Socialist Realism (see p. 80) regarded writers as the 'engineers of souls', a phrase usually attributed to Uncle Joe himself. There was no shortage of time-servers prepared to take on the task. The poet Nezval hurriedly excised God and death (favoured themes) from his collected work, and until one or both caught up with him in 1951, he was an eager mechanic for the regime. Few honest authors could accept the job with integrity, however, and after the first revelations of Stalinist misdemeanours in 1956, it became all but impossible. According to the novelist **Josef Škvorecký**, whose first work appeared during the late 1950s, frowned-on writers began to devise ever more ingenious ways of slipping past the censors, such as placing fiction into obscure scientific journals, or handing their work to sympathetic but tolerated fellow-writers who would print it under their own name.

During the liberalization of the early 1960s, the literary thaw was symptomized by an absurd but important conference in May 1963, where literary critics successfully argued that Franz Kafka's work was relevant to the socialist aspirations of modern-day Czechoslovakia. Kafka—a socialist sympathizer himself, in the days when it meant something rather different in Czechoslovakia—would probably have appreciated the irony. It was rather too subtle for the post-1968 government, which denounced the conference as one of the first assaults of the Czech counter-revolution.

Václav Havel's first play (*Zahradní slavnost* or 'The Garden Party') was published in 1963. Many of the country's best new authors, such as Škvorecký, **Bohumil Hrabal**, and **Milan Kundera**, worked in close conjunction with the Czech New Wave film-makers (see pp. 83–5), and Kundera taught at the film school. Much of the new writing was tinged with an eroticism that had been long suppressed in official literature, and which has become one of the more distinctive features of modern Czech novels. Hrabal's fascination with sex is tender, if sometimes bizarre; while in the case of **Ivan Klíma**, the popular Beatle-fringed president of the Writers' Union during 1968, a sadder and less exuberant view of human relationships has tended to come to the fore. Kundera's approach is the best known in the west, as a result of his filmed novel *The Unbearable Lightness of Being*, and is most remarkable for the cerebral world of betrayal and often cruelty in which his lovers are steeped. Kundera has been accused of being a misogynist and an out-of-touch exile; but like the work of Klíma, his novels can be seen as portrayals of an atomized society in microcosm, and are branded with the searing history of the Prague Spring.

Through the 1960s, the influence and confidence of the writers grew. They were among those leading the external pressure on the Communist Party to introduce structural reforms, which reached a head in July 1968 with the publication of the polemical '2000 Words Manifesto', written by the journalist **Ludvík Vaculík**. Leonid Brezhnev got on the phone to ask Alexander Dubček how on earth it could have found its way into the newspapers. Dubček's response was too vague, and within a month, the Prague Spring had been crushed by the fraternal tanks of the Warsaw Pact.

The illusion of reform was over, and the next 20 years saw it replaced by the bread and circuses of 'real existing socialism'. The lies of the post-1968 government were clearer than those of any of its predecessors, but a dispirited population all but gave up caring; and Czech literature now fought the most crucial battle of its short history. Authors engaged the government in a struggle for the country's language, unparalleled in its scale outside post-war Communist Europe. Havel's plays parodied the obscurity and lies of bureacratic speech, while his articles developed one simple theme—that the regime would win if it could change the meaning of words, and would be subverted if people refused to play its semantic game. The idea that truth alone would threaten the government might seem idealistic, but the only common feature of the hundreds of works suppressed was that they made no allowances for the censors' tastes. From the early 1970s, individually typed 'Padlock Publications' (*Edice Petlice*) of banned literature began to circulate. Some, such as Vaculík's *feuilletons* (translated into English as *A Cup of Coffee with My Interrogator*), were direct attacks on the day-to-day injustices of the regime. Others, such as the works of Ivan Klíma were no more than honest stories set in an unadorned Prague. Some writers, such as Kundera and **Pavel Kohout**, left the country. Among them was Škvorecký, who with his wife set up Sixty-Eight Publishers in Toronto. The company published and smuggled hundreds of works back into Czechoslovakia, a contribution to Czech culture which has won him an honoured place in the country since 1989.

Literature Unlocked

At the time of writing, Czechoslovakia is the only country in the world to have as its figurehead a man who has been both a brewery worker and a published playwright. President Havel is potent evidence of the political importance of post-1968 literature—but as he's said in a different context, that's always been a shaky way of judging the work of the time, and it remains to be seen how the country's writers will adapt to a post-Communist world. Havel has announced that he can't write anything other than his (studiously crafted) speeches while he's president. Given the potential subject-matter, many hope that he'll soon conquer this creative impasse. The only writers who will sink are those who found themselves so locked into the anti-Communist struggle that they were defined by it—a catagory which some think includes Havel himself. Bohumil Hrabal, on the other hand, compromised enough to sign a government-organized petition attacking Havel and others; but his lyrical works, loaded with a humanism and sense of the absurd that makes politics almost irrelevant, are widely regarded as the pinnacle of contemporary Czech writing.

Music

Prague music rode the storms that regularly shattered every other area of the capital's cultural life. While the Hussites were stringing up choir masters, they composed some of the first recorded martial hymns; and as the Counter-Reformation burned Bohemia's language and literature out of existence, Prague Jesuits performed mysteries which gave birth to Czech opera. Although many leading Baroque musicians found fame elsewhere—notably the Benda family at Frederick the Great's court—many stayed on, including the organist **František Brixi** (1732–71).

Prague's status as a glorified suburb of Vienna had certain musical advantages. In January 1787, **Mozart** (1756–91) made the first of four visits, and swiftly wrote his *Symphony in D. K504 ('Prague')*. While Vienna never quite understood Wolfgang, Prague fell in love with him: *Figaro* was a roaring success; he conducted the premiere of *Don Giovanni* in the city; and he composed *La Clemenza di Tito* for the Bohemian coronation of Leopold II in 1791. 3000 Praguers attended a requiem (by a Czech) nine days after his death, as he lay little-mourned in a third-class section of Vienna's St Mark's cemetery. The city has revelled in its recognition of Wolfgang's genius, helped by Miloš Forman's cinematic tribute to his home town, *Amadeus*.

However, it was another half a century before Bohemia found a musical language appropriate to Romanticism—in the **polka**. Peasants had been raucously skipping to a 2/4 rhythm for centuries, but in the mid-1800s patriotic composers decided that the dances expressed everything most noble about the country. Simultaneously, the rein-vention of Czech now made home-grown librettos possible. In 1866, rustic traditions brought to life the first great national opera, *The Bartered Bride* by **Bedřich Smetana** (1824–84) in which the composer showed a deftness for comedy and characterization that was compared to Mozart at his best. Two years later, his operatic fusion of rural Bohemia and its legendary landscape reached almost Wagnerian heights in *Dalibor* (1868). His symphonic masterpiece, the six-poem cycle of *My Country* (Má Vlast; 1874–9), transformed national myth into a sweeping and universal lyricism. The composer went deaf in 1874 and never heard it performed. He incorporated the last screeching E note that he ever heard into his autobiographical *String Quartet in E-Minor* (1876). Even in his lifetime, Smetana was regarded as the father of Czech music (though he never quite learnt Czech) and in 1881, he conducted his opera *Libuše* at the opening of Prague's National Theatre. It burned down two weeks later (the firemen were at a funeral), and Smetana died insane and syphilitic in 1884, but his reputation endures.

The second great figure of 19th-century Czech music was pigeon fancier, model-railway enthusiast, and protegé of Brahms, **Antonín Dvořák** (1841–1904). Dvořák spent 1891–1895 in the United States (to which the optimism of his *9th Symphony (From the New World)* was a homage), but he too was strongly influenced by folk music (*Slavonic Dances*). It also permeates his symphonic works, which have the rich melodiousness of Smetana but a more disciplined feel. His chamber music is highly regarded, and his *Cello Concerto* represents the composer at his best.

Prague's critics fiercely debated the merits of Smetana and Dvořák, but showed almost unmixed hostility to Moravian-born **Leoš Janáček** (1858–1928)—in part because he had reviewed a work by the influential National Theatre director as 'so-called music, filled with menacing obscurity, desperate screams and dagger stabs'. Janáček was a close friend of Dvořák, and shared his interests in folk music (*Lachian Dances*). He became convinced that it was born from the cadences of speech, and from the late 1880s he scribbled down sounds in a notebook wherever he went—from the monkey shrieks at London Zoo to the death rattle of his daughter. He never used the notes directly, but his concern for authenticity gave birth to work which, combining spare but extraordinarily powerful melodies with a deeply humane philosophy, is some of the most inspiring classical music of the 20th century. Look out in particular for his operas *Jenůfa* and *House of the Dead*; his orchestral works, *Taras Bulbas* and *Sinfonietta*; and his two rarely-performed but excellent string quartets. His *Glagolithic Mass* is also exceptional.

Even more prolific was **Bohuslav Martinů** (1890–1959), who produced over 400 uncategorizable works, with names like *Thunderbolt P.47*. Czechs admire him; foreigners are often at a loss.

The most notable post-war music in Prague has been that suppressed by the government. To two generations, **Marta Kubišová** is the personification of the 1968 Prague Spring: an outlawed Sandie Shaw whose *Modlitba pro Martu* reduced thousands to tears when she sang it for the first time in 21 years during the demonstrations of 1989. The **Plastic People of the Universe** became the Sex Pistols of Prague—*very* roughly speaking—when in 1976 they were put on trial for singing 'shit' once too often. As a direct result, the capital's intelligentsia founded Charter 77; and as an indirect result of that, Václav Havel became president. He's still friendly with the reconstituted version of the group, **Půlnoc**, who along with **Garáž** are thrashing out the sounds now most in demand among Prague's headbangers, trendies, and loon-pant wearers. If that's not your bag, pick up a recording of Beethoven's 9th Symphony with its concluding *Ode to Joy*, played at the first classical concert of post-Communist Czechoslovakia, and still hopefully called the anthem of the United States of Europe.

Visionary Prague

A cockeyed outlook on the world permeates the history of Prague. For centuries, the capital has stalked wild geese and built monuments to chimeras. What follows is a ramble through a jungle of delusions, from alchemy to Communism, in which only glimmers of sanity have ever appeared.

Seers and Stargazers

The ear of Rudolfine Prague was attuned to speculations on all the highest planes, and soothsayers, croakers, necromancers and prophets of every description found the emperor's court a congenial staging-post. In Rome, the shadow of the stake was a powerful disincentive to weirdness; in Prague, the character of an emperor whose horoscope had been cast by Nostradamus demanded it. His vast curiosity cabinet included mandrake root fetishes (thought to scream when pricked); he apparently carried moss from the bones of a hanged man in his back pocket; and his courtiers were at the sharp end of contemporary scientific thought. Wherever there was a mystery to be pondered, Prague thinkers could be guaranteed to deepen it. The emperor's private secretary published an acclaimed thesis on squaring the circle; others wrote influential works on a Silesian boy reported to have been born with a gold tooth in 1593; and when a bone was unearthed in the capital, the city was consumed by a debate on whether it was an elephant's tusk or the shin of an antediluvian giant.

Two of the earliest visitors to the capital were the extraordinary Jekyll and Hyde duo of John Dee (1527–1608) and Edward Kelley (1555–95?), who pulled into the capital on a coach from Cracow in 1584. Dee, a Fellow of Trinity College, Cambridge, and astrologer to Queen Elizabeth I, was a scholar in search of a question; but quite what drove Kelley, whose experiments in England had included the disinterment and quizzing of a corpse, has never been satisfactorily established. It does a disservice to his warped genius to call him a mere fraud, but Rudolf would still have done well to ask him why he had no ears (they had been shorn for counterfeiting). Instead, the emperor put both men on the imperial payroll.

The partnership revolved around crystal balls. With Kelley gazing, and the doctor asking the questions, they had already clocked up hundreds of hours of crystalline conversations with maverick quasi-Christian angels, all conducted and recorded in Enochian, an entirely new 117,649-character language. Rudolf seems, remarkably enough, to have been uninterested in Dee's outline of the hallucinations, but the duo were to spend five eventful years in and around Prague.

Their unholy alliance came to an end before they left the city, however. In April 1587, while peering into the crystal, an astounded Kelley (32) informed Dee (60) that Madimi, one of the regular cast of angels, was taking off all her clothes. Under protest, Kelley also revealed that she was also ordering the two men to 'share all things in common, including our wives'. Kelley assured Jane Dee (also 32) that 'my heart pales at the arrangement'. Jane was considerably more upset than the earless grave-robber; the thoughts of frumpy Mrs Kelley are nowhere recorded; but a pained John Dee decided that, imponderably mysterious though they were, the angels' commands had to be obeyed. A covenant of sex and silence was signed between the group in May 1587. Kelley then seems to have had problems getting his act together, and tetchily locked himself into his laboratory for several days, but it's interesting to note that Theodore (Gift of God) Dee was born 9 months and 2 weeks later. The angels never spoke again, and Kelley soon fled the lugubrious love-nest. In 1589, the Dees were on their way back to England; at which point Kelley reappeared in Prague and entered another department of Rudolfine science—alchemy.

Rudolf's court was the Los Alamos of the alchemical age. Europe's wild golden-goose chase peaked in the late 1500s, and to questing types

everywhere the emperor was the latest incarnation of Hermes Trisme-
gistus, the mysterious quasi-divinity who had been the first to crack the
transmutation secret. Unfortunately, Hermes' gnomic utterances—notably, 'that which is above is like to that which is below; but that which is
below is like to that which is above'—kept a tight lid on the Hermetic
wisdom. The concept of the philosopher's stone ('the stone which is not
a stone, a precious thing which has no value, a thing of many shapes, this
unknown which is most known of all') did little to advance matters, but its
discovery was one of Rudolf's obsessions. Anyone who could show
proven alchemical ability was given board and lodging, and all the
technology that money could buy. As they slaved over their stills, alem-
bics, crucibles and hot-ash baths, Rudolf's alchemists produced
interesting results—hair-restoring potions, hair-removing potions, laxa-
tives, philtres and new recipes for mulling wine—but the nature of the
experiments (among other factors) ensured that the stone remained
elusive. Congelation, calcination, cibation and mortification were among
the standard processes; when those failed, they could be combined with
ceration, the addition of wax, or inhumation, which generally involved
burying the substance concerned in dung.

The stakes were high in the alchemical quest: possibly eternal life,
certainly ultimate wisdom, and depending on the Hermetic tract that you
read, anything from a million-fold increase in gold to a thousand billion.
The scope for quackery was immense. On one celebrated occasion, a
mysterious Arab drew into the capital and invited hundreds to a banquet
at which he swore to multiply contributions by a thousand; to general
consternation, he and the money exploded into a puff of smoke instead.
The dangers were no less dramatic. Dungeons and mercury inhalation
were occupational hazards, and in Prague unmasked charlatans faced
the added possibility of being paraded in tinsel and hanged from a yellow
rope on a gilded scaffold. Alchemical theory had accommodated the
risks, by suggesting that the philosopher's stone could take up to 12 years
to ripen. By that time a nimble failure could be long gone, leaving behind
only a cooling heap of wax and dung; but for those who talked big and
failed to deliver, time could run out far sooner.

Kelley was one of those who learnt the hard way. The Englishman had
stumbled upon the stone while pottering around the ley lines of Glaston-
bury during happier times with John Dee. Although his claims were
relatively modest (an increase in gold by a factor of 72,330), he was taken
on by Rudolf in 1589. He began impressively, transmuting a pound of
lead into gold with a drop of blood-red oil, leaving a ruby at the bottom of

the pot) and was promptly knighted by the emperor. By 1591, however, he was under pressure. England's Lord Treasurer had written to ask for 'a token, say enough to defray the expenses of the Navy for the summer', and Rudolf was finding that the gold he was receiving was significantly less than the amount he was paying his knight. Kelley was incarcerated on suspicion of heresy and sorcery. He enjoyed an Indian summer in 1593, when he was reported to be at liberty and making gold 'as fast as a hen will cracke nuttes', but his incredible career was drawing to a close. Suitably enough, no one knows where or when (or, say some, if) he died. Legend claims that he lost a leg or two jumping from a tower, and then poisoned himself; a neat variation on the tale is that the fatal draught was an elixir of life that he had prepared for the emperor.

Kelley notwithstanding, alchemists would soon become chemists, and the stargazers of Rudolfine Prague also stood at a turning point in the history of science. In the space of a few decades, the universe had been shaken to its core. For some 1500 years, the moon, planets, sun and stars had orbited the earth attached to Ptolemy's harmonious crystal spheres, but in 1543 the Pole Nicolaus Copernicus had revived the ancient heresy of heliocentricity. No one knew how to look at the universe any more. When a Paduan arrived with a set of concave mirrors, they were snapped up by the thinkers of the court; Giordano Bruno stopped by in 1588 with his theories of infinite worlds; and as comets, a supernova and fateful conjunctions hurtled through the firmament during the last decades of the century, the capital battened down the hatches and prepared for darkness at noon and the end of empires.

Successive imperial mathematicians at Rudolf's court personified the critical juncture to which the heavens had come. The work of the first, the little-remembered Nicholas Ursus, was inextricably linked to that of the second, the Danish Tycho Brahe, who served between 1599 and 1601. While still in Denmark, Brahe accused Ursus of plagiarism, setting off an arcane intra-continental row that became vitriolic even for an age when scientists didn't mince their words. Ursus published a defence from Prague in 1597. It interspersed an erudite survey of astronomy's history with constant references to one of Brahe's supporters as 'Snotface', taunts about Brahe's own disfigured nose, and the observation that the Dane's daughter was 'not yet nubile and so not of much use to me for the usual purpose'. Brahe never quite matched his opponent's invective, but he was no more stable. Some said that his departure from Denmark had been inspired by another dispute over the ownership of a dog; and although his stellar observations did their bit for rationalism by putting the boot into Ptolemy's crystal spheres, in Prague he subjected poor Rudolf to endless astrological prophecies of doom. The emperor was told variously that he would die before 50, that he would be killed by a monk, and that he would follow his pet raven to Hell.

Brahe's successor as imperial mathematician (1601–12), Johannes Kepler, went further than any of his contemporaries in developing a rational philosophy of science, but the wisdom of the ancients continued to permeate his work. His laid down the laws of planetary motion, but linked them to the idea that each of the five planets corresponded to one of the musical ranges from bass to treble. His suspicion of superstition (reinforced when his mother was tried for witchcraft) meant that when it came to astrology, he was cautious. He suggested that the aspects affected the world only in the limited sense that a peasant could affect the shape of a pumpkin, and he sensibly warned that 'one must keep astrology entirely from the emperor's mind' (although he actually cast several horoscopes for Rudolf). His contributions to scientific debate were incomparably more elegant than those of his predecessors, often written in Latin verse or Ciceronian orations. However, neither the mode of expression nor the caution demanded by the dangerous times fully account for their elliptical sound to the modern ear. His comments on those who now questioned Copernicus' views are a suitably oblique memorial to an absurd Prague that has never quite disappeared.

'They castrated the poet
Lest he copulate;
He lived without testicles'.

Rabbi Loew

Every community mythologizes its history, but with the legendary Rabbi Loew, Prague's Jews personified it. Loew (as in 'I just *lurve* sushi') was a celebrated scholar in the relatively tolerant Prague of the late 1500s, but the stories that came to envelop his life encapsulated the centuries-old experience of the ghetto—where pogroms and the evil eye were omni-present dangers, and only the rabbi could really explain why life was so abysmal.

The legends begin on a touching note. When young Loew arrived in the capital, he was smitten by Pearl, daughter of one Reb Schmelke. Schmelke then went bankrupt, but Loew was so in love that he agreed to wait until the dowry could be raised. Impetuous it may have been, but it was only ten years before Reb Schmelke was back on his feet, thanks to a bag of gold which a contemptuous cavalier tossed at Pearl as he stole a loaf of bread. Loew, by now steeped in the Talmud, declared that that had been no ordinary horseman, but Elijah. The stage was set for an extraordinary life.

Certain themes run through all the tales. The ghetto is under constant threat from Christians, the wickedest of whom is Brother Thaddeus, whose very mention brings a hiss to the throat. There is also the occasional good *goy*, most notably the weak but fundamentally sympathetic Emperor Rudolf. Pulling the strings together is mild-mannered Rabbi Loew, who checks Brother Thaddeus at every turn, dares to reveal to the emperor that his real mother was Jewish, and exchanges tips with other super-rabbis across Europe in his dreams. After 300 clerics ask Loew to answer questions like 'Are the Jews guilty of killing Christ?', his eloquence wins them over to a man. On the innumerable occasions that Rudolf begs him for help, he rescues him from jail, dethrones an impostor and overturns expulsion edicts. When a jealous flunky persuades the vacillating emperor to order Loew to hold a banquet, the rabbi transports a shimmering palace from a distant land into his humble ghetto abode; and to the now-jovial Rudolf's uproarious laughter, the luckless lackey pockets a goblet and is rooted to his seat. The picture of Rudolf that emerges is about as far from reality as it's possible to get. The emperor summoned the rabbi to his castle once, to discuss a matter that was never revealed, which was clearly more than enough material for generations of Jewish myth-makers.

The legend now inextricably linked to Loew is that of the golem, or artificial man. The word, meaning 'unformed substance' (or 'unmarried woman') in Hebrew, is first found in Psalms 139:16; and the idea that humanity could create life comes from the mystical cabalistic tradition that it contains a spark of the divine. Jewish history is littered with pre-Loewian golems, and they have stalked Europe's ghettos for centuries. Jakob Grimm found one in Poland in 1808, but Rabbi Loew's has become the most famous, turned into a German silent film (1920), a French talkie (1937) and a tale to alarm good Jewish boys and girls everywhere. It all began while Loew was communing with the cosmos one night. He was warned that a great danger loomed, and told to make a golem, pronto. With his two youthful rabbi sidekicks, he hurried to the banks of the Vltava. Chanting melancholy psalms and working by torchlight, the trio built a man out of mud, walked around it several times, and Loew then placed the unknown name of God (the *shem*) in its mouth. 'Joseph Golem' was born. His adventures are laced with slapstick ghetto humour—such as the moment that he follows orders too literally and floods long-suffering Pearl's kitchen—but most are of a grimly heroic nature. Joseph once rescues a girl from being forcibly baptized; and when the community is on trial for ritual murder, he arrives with the exonerating evidence as the verdict is to be announced. The allegation that Jews kneaded Christian blood for their Passover *matzoth* (unleavened bread) echoes throughout, and as well as thwarting the remorseless Brother Thaddeus, Joseph constantly intercepts shadowy Christians wheeling dead babies into the ghetto in order to lay the ground for a pogrom.

Joseph was eventually laid to rest in the roof of Prague's Old-New Synagogue (see pp. 160–162). The annihilation of the capital's Jews gave rise to the last golem legend. It had been said that he would return when needed, but as the Nazi cattle trains filled and emptied, those Jews who remained declared that he had died forever. It sounds likely, but Praguers still claim that on stormy nights, Joseph's footsteps can be heard on those streets of the ancient ghetto that survive.

Švejkism

20th-century literature in Prague has produced two -isms that go far to illuminate the absurdity of Czechoslovakia's modern political experience. The first was Kafkaism, which a literary lackey of the Communist Party dismissed in 1963 as 'a knife severing the veins of progressive traditions'. The comment contained its own unintended admission of moral harakiri; but it's with Švejkism that authority generally, and the Communists in particular, faced irony in its purest form.

The Good Soldier Švejk, written by the Czech Jaroslav Hašek in the years around the First World War, became the first great anti-hero of the modern age; and via the theatres of Berlin took the continent by storm (Bertolt Brecht died with the book by his bed, admittedly along with 60 others). Švejk was Sancho Panza and Don Quixote rolled into one and set loose on the battlefields of Europe. Armed with an eagerness to ape formalities and observe rules to the letter, and the ability to shine the occasional shaft of common sense on the hecatomb around him, Švejk survived—which is what the doctrine is all about.

Hašek himself was the first Švejkist. The alcoholic anarchist began with fairly minor journalistic hoaxes: he conducted pseudonymous polemics against himself in the two major party newspapers of the day; and during his time at *Animal World*, Prague's animal-lovers were buffeted with reports of a musk-rat invasion of the capital and rampaging packs of collies in distant Patagonia. The -ism really began to emerge in 1911, when he wrote the earliest Šwejk stories. Hašek announced that his newly-formed Party of Moderate Progress Within the Bounds of the Law would contest the Imperial elections in June. It lost, despite a rousing song (chorus: 'To arms, to arms, to arms!/ Moderate progress is our aim!') and the offer of a pocket aquarium to anyone who voted for the party. Hašek then wrote the party's social and political history. In 1915, he checked into a hotel in feverishly anti-Russian Prague as 'Ivan Fyodorovich Kuznetsov, born in Kiev and coming from Moscow', giving as his reason for visiting 'to check up on the General Staff'. Habsburg secret police cordoned off the block; a relieved Hašek told them that he had been worried about the lax security in the capital, and got away with five days in jail.

Most Czechs now claim that there's a heavy dose of Šwejkism in the national character, but as usual with stereotypes, that's only half the story. The characteristic emerged with full force during the 1968 invasion. The commander of the Warsaw Pact forces, Marshal Grechko (nicknamed El Grechko after his armies strafed a particularly interesting design onto the National Museum) warned Czechoslovakia's president that 'We have all read Šwejk and that's all that's happening here'. Alexander Dubček remained in power, promising everything and doing nothing; Praguers would politely translate road signs for tank crews, not mentioning that they had just reversed them; and according to Milan Kundera, an address to a students' meeting by the new First Secretary, Gustáv Husák, had to be cancelled when the audience wouldn't stop shouting 'Long live the Party! Long live Husák!'.

However, demoralization is the kiss of death to Šwejkism, and it was often a far darker, Kafkaesque, streak that came to the fore under Communism, particularly after 1968. Too many came to believe in the powers-that-were. Although mockery continued behind closed doors, Praguers absorbed the lies and methods of the government rather than hurl them back. It was the Poles who were the true heirs of Šwejk during the 1970s and '80s, and as even many Praguers admit, it's no coincidence that Czechs were so late joining the 1989 revolutions. The symbol of Kafkaism—the man who destroys himself in the search to make sense of another's world—is also the symbol of Prague and Czechoslovakia's modern history. For all his incredible bravery, Jan Palach was Josef K., not Josef Šwejk, when he burned himself to death in 1969.

Communist Kitsch

When the Czechoslovak Communist Party moved into the driving seat in 1948, official culture embarked on a headlong descent that was to last four decades. The fetish of the Five Year Plan, gigantomania, and the celebration of vulcanization processes were to leave no one entirely untouched.

The Party's first plunge into truly execrable taste was the transformation of President Klement Gottwald into a pickled icon when he died in 1953. The procedure was in its infancy in the Communist world, and Gottwald proved too rotten for formaldehyde. An alarmed government replaced the would-be mummy with a dummy. That was soon removed, but the lecherous drunkard then became 'Czechoslovakia's First Working Class President', immortalized until 1989 in a metro station, a bridge, countless roads, museums, banknotes and a town.

Stalin himself was the subject of Prague's most mind-boggling piece of cultural junk, when in 1953 the government constructed a 30-m-high statue in his honour, glowering from a hillside over Prague's Old Town. 600 workers spent 500 days building the colossus, which showed Stalin leading a Soviet worker, woman heroine, soldier and botanist into the future. The designer, Otakar Švec, did the decent thing and shot himself before its completion, but the Czechoslovak Communist Party apparently had every reason to be satisfied with its magnificent display of unctuousness. Triumphant speeches were held as it was unveiled in 1955, and workers from across the country danced polkas at the base. But within a year, things had gone badly wrong. Stalin's successor, Nikita Krushchev, let slip that Uncle Joe had, objectively speaking, deformed socialism—and even worse, that a personality cult had apparently grown up around him. The Party took a quick look at its 14,000-ton masterpiece, and shrouded it in scaffolding. In January 1962, a commission was set up. A panicky Mr Štursa, who had seen the project through, wrote to suggest that Stalin could be sliced off the botanist *et al*, and replaced by 'an allegory—perhaps a woman holding a bouquet?'. The commission never replied, and in October 1962 the dynamite boys went in. The heroes were destroyed by a series of night-time detonations; a single explosion would have ripped away most of the hillside and the bridge below.

Mass activism was essential to many of the bizarre rituals of Communism. Most Praguers now draw a discreet veil over their participation, but as the Party would have said, the statistics speak for themselves (although it confused matters by also saying things like, 'We do not bow to facts'). The Spartakiáda, a quinquennial gymnastic exhibition inaugurated in 1950, continued until 1985, but the 1960 week was typical. 800,000 athletic types filled Prague's Strahov stadium, and displayed synchronized contortions on themes such as 'Towards New Tomorrows' and 'Life Wins Over Death'.

Vast crowds waved red flags at Prague's May Day rallies, where Party luminaries saluted missiles and spoke on peace; work teams would compete, albeit very half-heartedly indeed, for the 'Brigade of Socialist Labour' award, a piece of cardboard which could still be found in Prague factories in early 1990; and the shibboleths of a hollow regime emerged from the mouths of thousands of otherwise-honest folk.

It's hard to tell whether long-term damage has been done to the Prague psyche by the cultural atrocities perpetrated by their side of the Cold War. During the 1950s, many actually believed in the slush and the cant, but it was in the 1970s and 1980s that kitsch very nearly triumphed, by implicating hundreds of thousands in a world of schmaltz. The aspirations were noble, but they were enshrined in hyperbole which threatened to destroy critical functions entirely. The dangers have become clear since 1989: one example is that years of seeing banners attacking racial discrimination have led many to conclude that anti-racism is somehow equatable with Communism.

Visible vestiges of Prague's post-war era have become hard to find. The crimson placards that lined Wenceslas Square (saying things like 'We shall overfulfill the Plan by 143%!') were removed almost immediately, statues have been toppled, and history is being re-rewritten. Ghosts survive in the hundreds of silent megaphones which once blared martial tunes and speeches on festival days, and in the Hotel International, where the standard of service still pays homage to its Socialist Realist inspiration. You could also investigate the latest humiliation inflicted on the Soviet tank that still stands on nám. Sovětských tankistů (see p. 266), last seen painted pink and surmounted with a papier-mâché object that was either a large finger or a penis. A gallery of Communist culture may eventually be opened, and if so, it could incorporate several exhibits from the now defunct Museum of the National Security Corps and the Army of the Interior Ministry. Many commemorated the valour of the border patrol, and the threats faced daily by the Czechoslovakian state. They included packs of strange cigarettes (accompanied by photographs of their bewildered hippy owners), and a home-made helicopter and pretend tank of very hopeful would-be escapees. Most stirring of all was 'Brek', an almost legendary guard dog who pounced on 60 fleeing miscreants, sustained two shot-gun wounds, and was eventually stuffed for his pains.

Prague Walks

The view into Malá Strana from Charles Bridge

A walk through old Prague is a stroll through a labyrinth of the senses. Wherever you turn, you're confronted by come-hither tunnels, lanes disappearing into mysterious curls, or the distant sound of music. Crawling through its hidden staircases and cloisters will take you through a treasure chest of ages, and—on occasion—a *déjà vu* of a childhood dream.

The walks are structured around the ancient divisions of the capital. Prague castle—in fact an entire city of regal follies—is covered in Walk I; and Walk IV is a stroll through the hush of the surrounding district. The higgledy-piggledy Old Town is divided between Walks II (northern half and Jewish Quarter) and V (southern half); and Walk III criss-crosses Malá Strana, the cream of Prague Baroque. Apart from Wenceslas Square (Walk V), the dusty chaos of the New Town isn't covered in the walks. However, despite its name it is 600 years old, and if you're in town for more than a week you could explore its hidden surprises (see p. 257). On the other hand, if you only have a couple of days, the order of the walks corresponds very roughly to their level of interest—although Walk III heads the list for smoochability, Walk IV wins for its becalmed quirkiness (and it contains Prague's best art gallery), and the Astronomical Clock and Charles Bridge in Walk V are the quintessence of the magical city.

Each walk is headed with a list of the main sights on the route, followed closely by possible lunch stops, and details of where it starts and ends. The best time for the walk is also mentioned: in a nutshell, *avoid Walks I and IV on a Monday, Walk II on a Saturday, and Walks III and V if it's raining*. All the walks should be begun by midday if you want to see everything, but Walk III is a good choice for an evening meander. How long each will take is suggested: a fairly brisk approach is assumed, and if you're a dawdler at heart, you can easily add 50 per cent.

There are two minor considerations to bear in mind before setting off. One of the most absurd juxtapositions of past and present in Prague is that two systems of house numbering, on red and blue signs, exist. Only the modern blue numbers are used in this book. Also, you may notice that pedestrians at traffic lights are reluctant to move until they see a little green man. The obsession isn't as developed as in the anally-retentive nations of the north; but even if you dare face the basilisk glares of the grimacing, growling *babičky*, and cross against the lights, you may be summarily fined by a traffic cop.

Pick of Prague

Baroque churches: St Nicholas's Church; St James's Church.
Cemeteries: Malá Strana Cemetery; Old Jewish Cemetery.
Evening drinking: Evropa café in winter; the length of Michalská street in summer; cup of *burčák* on the Charles Bridge in August.
Galleries: Šternberk Palace (European Art); St George's Convent (Czech Gothic and Baroque art).
Gothic architecture: Cathedral of St Vitus; Vladislav Hall; Old-New Synagogue; St Agnes's Convent; Bell House.
Islands: Kampa; Žofín (Slovanský ostrov) and Střelecký ostrov.
Preposterous Baroque shrines: Loretto; *Bambino di Praga*; St John Nepomuk's tomb.
Rides: Funicular up Petřín Hill; tram 22; rowing on Vltava.
Romantic strolls: Winding path down Petřín into Malá Strana; Kampa Island; Nový svět; streets around St Agnes's Convent.
Subterranean spots: House of the Lords of Kunštát and Poděbrady; U bílého koníčka (disco); U zlaté konvice (wine bar).
Views: From a table at Nebozízek restaurant; the orange tiles of Malá Strana from the top of Nerudova street; from a room in the Hotel Praha.
Walled gardens: Waldstein Gardens; courtyard in Clementinum; cloister of St Giles's monastery.

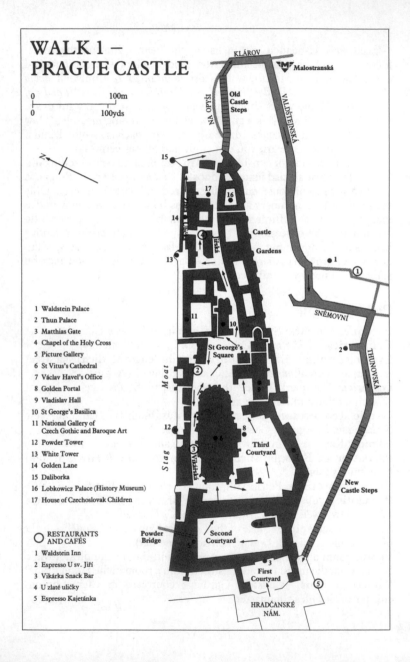

WALK 1 –
PRAGUE CASTLE

0   100m
0   100yds

KLÁROV

◤M Malostranská

Old
Castle
Steps

NA OPYŠI

VALDŠTEJNSKÁ

Castle
Gardens

15

17

16

14

4

Jiřská

13

● 1

① 1

SNĚMOVNÍ

1 Waldstein Palace
2 Thun Palace
3 Matthias Gate
4 Chapel of the Holy Cross
5 Picture Gallery
6 St Vitus's Cathedral
7 Václav Havel's Office
8 Golden Portal
9 Vladislav Hall
10 St George's Basilica
11 National Gallery of
    Czech Gothic and Baroque Art
12 Powder Tower
13 White Tower
14 Golden Lane
15 Daliborka
16 Lobkowicz Palace (History Museum)
17 House of Czechoslovak Children

11

10

St George's
Square

②

2

Moat

12

● 2

THUNOVSKÁ

8

③ Vikárka

6

Third
Courtyard

Stag

New
Castle Steps

○ RESTAURANTS
   AND CAFÉS

1 Waldstein Inn
2 Espresso U sv. Jiří
3 Vikárka Snack Bar
4 U zlaté uličky
5 Espresso Kajetánka

Powder
Bridge

Second
Courtyard

5

3

First
Courtyard

⑤ 5

HRADČANSKÉ
NÁM.

Walk I

Prague Castle

The tomb of St John Nepomuk

New Castle Steps—St Vitus's Cathedral—Vladislav Hall—St George's Basilica—National Gallery of Czech Gothic and Baroque Art—Powder Tower—Golden Lane—Daliborka—Old Castle Steps

From its beginnings as a pagan mound to the day that Václav Havel was sworn in as president, Prague's history has unrolled in Hradčany Castle. Its neo-classical veneer now stretches half a lazy mile over the capital, but it's the onion domes and demented prongs of the cathedral, rising from its core, that hint at what really lies within. This walk uncovers the city's medieval heart and arcane mind. It explores St Vitus's Cathedral, the monument to a monomaniacal emperor and one of the grandest churches of the 14th century; and it takes you through the Vladislav Hall, a late Gothic masterpiece with early Renaissance windows through which three men and the Thirty Years War were launched. By the end, you'll have begun to sense the forces, large and small, that have made Prague tick so strangely for so many centuries. Every building has its secrets, from the laboratory of Emperor Rudolf II's alchemists, to the minuscule pastel cottages of the 400-year-old Golden Lane.

This walk is one of the best for a rainy day—unless that day is Monday, in which case everything is closed. Get moving in the morning—the doors start to shut as early as 3.30 pm. If you have the energy at the end of the walk, you can happily start Walk III through Malá Strana, which is at

its best in the evening. Another possibility is to take tram 22 four stops up the hill, which deposits you neatly at the beginning of Walk IV.
Start the walk at Malostranská metro station. Line A gets you there, as do trams 12, 18 and 22. The walk **ends** about 20 metres from where it begins.
Walking time: 3 hours, longer for gallery addicts.

LUNCH/CAFÉS
Eating opportunities are limited within the castle walls, and in the packed tourist season you're courting starvation if you don't have a healthy breakfast. Some of the spots listed in Walk IV are not far if you're desperate, although they are just as likely to be full.
Valdštejnská hospoda (Waldstein Inn), in Valdštejnské nám., just before you begin the climb up to the castle. Mon–Sat 11 am–3 pm (lunch). Fairly formal; a more varied menu than usual stretching from trout to game. If you're organized, you could make a lunchtime reservation here in advance; if not, expect an hour-long wait at the door in summer.
Espreso Kajetánka, at the top of the New Castle Steps, Tues–Sat 11 am–10 pm, Sun 11 am–8 pm. A pleasant little café-bar perched over the pantiled roofs of Malá Strana. Space is at a premium in the summer, but there's a terrace where you'll get a table eventually. Warm sandwiches, cakes and coffee.
Vikárka Snack Bar, in the lane next to the cathedral. May–Sept 8 am–8 pm, Oct–April 9 am–8 pm, Sun 9 am–3 pm. Not to be confused with the adjoining restaurant, which is bound to be full. Dull surroundings, standard food and service.
Espreso u sv. Jiří, in the square in front of the Church of St George. Tues–Sun 10 am–5 pm. Ersatz pizzas, hamburgers, steaks, all topped with some of the most consistently good service in Prague. The flipside is that it's tiny, although there's an outdoor terrace in the summer.
U zlaté uličky, just before its namesake, the Golden Lane. Tues–Sun 10 am–6 pm. Useful for thirst-quenching, but no food as yet.

☆   ☆   ☆   ☆   ☆

Hills were much in demand in the dangerous Dark Ages. Prague's venerable chronicler, Cosmas, was particularly complimentary about the Hradčany hill, comparing its shape to 'the back of a dolphin or a sea-pig'; and he was writing in the 12th century, when the topography would have been clearer than today. Despite the legend that Prague's history began with the soothsaying of Libuše at Vyšehrad (see p. 37), the castle is almost certainly the oldest continually-settled part of the city. The Přemysls, Bohemia's first dynasty, fortified the area towards the end of the 9th century. They coexisted happily with neighbouring cockerel-worshipping pagans until Prince Bořivoj got Christianity and founded a church. Relations became strained, the infidels revolted, and Bořivoj left town for a while. By the beginning of the 10th century, however, the family was firmly in control. Until the end of Bohemian independence in the 17th century, the castle was home to most of the oddballs to rule the country—and behind the monotonous palatial grandeur of its façade, it's a vast monument to centuries of regal madness.

*To get up to the castle from Malá Strana station, walk along Valdštejnská. To your right are the glorious gardens of the Polish Embassy (Fürstenberg Palace). They are meant to be closed to the public, but you could always lose your way looking for a visa. Gloomy palaces hem you in for the rest of the street, but a drive halfway along on the right leads to the entrance of the **castle gardens**. The terraced greenery was assembled from grounds once owned by the noble Ledebours, Černíns and Pálffys. Welded together by stone staircases and dotted with Baroque follies, it clambers all the way up to the castle and looks down across a magnificent panorama of Malá Strana. The gardens have been closed for longer than anyone can remember; climbing over the entrance gate, to your right past the steps at the end of the drive, is prohibited.*

*At the end of the street you'll come to Valdštejnské nám. The palace of General Waldstein, whose epic gardens and life story you'll find in Walk III, runs along one side. Walk up the cobbled street opposite. Turn left at the quiet leafy triangle, and then right up Thunovská. You'll pass the Baroque façade of the British Embassy (Thun Palace) on your right, lurking at the end of a cul-de-sac. Its deviousness is somehow appropriate—it expands into an unseen Renaissance palace that was the eventual bounty of Major Walter Leslie, one of the assassins of the no-less-treacherous General Waldstein. At the end of the narrow lane in front of you, its buttresses straining to keep the sides apart, you begin the climb up the **New Castle Steps** (Nové zámecké schody). Never trust the word 'new' in Prague—there have been steps here since early 15th century, and the climb follows a 13th-century route from the castle to Malá*

*Strana. At the top of the steps, you'll find the castle gates to your
right. Recover your breath and take in the view of the city.*

The pomp of the castle's façade dates from 1753–1775, when, after
centuries of sieges, fires and royal building projects, it had become a
crazed accretion that sorely displeased pernickety Queen Maria
Theresa. Although the Habsburgs had moved to Vienna over a century
before, she still regarded the palace (and Bohemia) as a pleasant little
possession, and hired her Viennese court architect, Nicolo Pacassi, to
clean it up. He filled in moats and added neo-classical façades with dull
abandon although, behind it all, huge chunks of the medieval castle
survive. At least Maria Theresa tried in her tasteless way to make the
castle pretty; her son, Joseph II, attempted to turn it into a barracks, and
succeeded in part. In the century before Czechoslovakia achieved its
independence in 1918, the castle was all but deserted by the distant
Habsburgs. The last emperor to spend any time here was Ferdinand the
Gracious after his forced abdication in 1848. A. J. P. Taylor claimed that
Ferdinand's most significant statement was 'I am the Emperor and I
want dumplings'. He brought little glory to the castle as he ended his
days here. In 1918 it became the seat of the president—a tradition
maintained by the Communists, and one which continues today with
Václav Havel's occupation of the office.

> *Enter the castle through the main gateway under the Art Nouveau
> Battling Giants, and take a look at the **castle guards**, resplendent
> in their bright blue uniforms.*

Until 1989, they wore dull khaki, but when Havel moved in, he got a
friend, Theodor Pištěk, to design something more jolly. Pištěk's last
major job was as costume designer for *Amadeus*, and the gulping guards
look dimly aware that they are the victims of a presidential prank.
They've even been known to join in the laughter at the hourly changing
of the guard ceremony. Another of Havel's wheezes was to dress the
brass band in red and have them play a tune every Sunday morning. If
you're here at midday, keep your eyes left, and on the first floor you'll see
them emerge onto the window ledges to blast out a lilting classical piece
composed specially for the ceremony by Michal Kocáb, rock musician
and MP for central Prague.

> *Walk through the first courtyard. Between the pine flagpoles is the
> **Matthias Gate** (1614), thought to have been designed by Vincenzo*

*Scamozzi. The Vicenza-born architect worked in the service of
Emperor Matthias and visited Prague in 1599–1600. He was a
close follower of Andrea Palladio, but the elegant serenity of the
master's influence gave way in Scamozzi's later work to some of the
earliest hints of the Baroque—and this grand gateway is one of
the first signs of the new architecture to have appeared in the capital.
The Roman triumphal arch is now unhappily immured in a building dividing the first two courtyards (the public rooms of the president), but it originally stood proud and alone between two bridges
crossing the outer moats of the castle. Directly in front of you is the*
Chapel of the Holy Cross, *designed by Nicolò Pacassi and
subsequently remodelled both internally and externally.*

Since 1961 the chapel has contained the public part of the **St Vitus's
Treasury**, a collection of odds and ends accumulated since the 11th
century. It really took off in the 14th century, during the reign of
Emperor Charles IV; cultured and cosmopolitan he may have been, but
he was truly medieval when it came to saintly relics. He was a man
obsessed—on his jaunts abroad, he begged, borrowed and according to
legend stole (once, from the pope) about 200 sacred objects. When his
nephew, Charles V of France, asked the emperor in 1356 to help him
recover his father (John the Bountiful, who had been confiscated by the
Black Prince at the Battle of Poitiers), Charles agreed to mediate with the
victorious English only after being given two thorns from Christ's crown
and splinters of the True Cross. As well as countless monstrances and
jewelled crucifixes, this chapel contains the choicest fruits from his
collection. Since the war, the po-faced authorities have been steadily
whittling away at the more unusual exhibits, and at the time of writing
full-scale reorganization is under way. However, you may still find
Moses' staff, the Virgin Mary's robe and veil, several shirts worn by Jesus
on the cross, and a crystal pitcher containing the tablecloth from the Last
Supper. Read between the lines.

*From the chapel, walk across to the northern end of the courtyard,
past the Baroque fountain (1686) and the disused well. Through the
gateway in front of you is the* **Powder Bridge** *over what was the
northern moat of the castle (see Walk IV). Turn left at the beginning
of the arch into the* **Picture Gallery of Prague Castle** *(Obrazárna Pražského hradu), containing works of art kept in the castle
since the reign of Emperor Rudolf II (1576–1611).*

111

Rudolf summoned artists from across the continent, and assembled a court that became one of the centres of European Mannerism. Like Charles, he had a mania for collecting that became legendary, even in an age when curiosity cabinets cum art galleries were a dime a dozen among Europe's nobles. No detailed inventory survives, but as well as rhinoceros horns, nails from the Ark and the like, Rudolf is thought to have installed some 3000 pictures and 2500 sculptures. This is a sad tribute. The gallery was pillaged by occupying Protestant forces during the Thirty Years War: a moderate pruning by the Saxons in 1631–32 was followed by a systematic ransack by Swedes in 1648. (Their naughty Queen Christina later sold most of the loot, reverted to Catholicism and lived off the proceeds in Rome.) Lots of what remained was sold off by Joseph II in 1782. However, the gallery is worth a brief visit to get a feel of the eclectic taste of Rudolf—more of whose collection pops up later on this walk—and the decline of his Habsburg successors.

Open Tues–Sun, April–Sept 9 am–5 pm, Oct–Mar 9 am–4 pm, adm. At the time of writing, the collection is temporarily closed, pending a full-scale security review. Two visitors walked off with a Cranach during opening hours and replaced it with a cheap Rembrandt reproduction. The normally hyper-sensitive babičky who guard each room didn't notice that anything was amiss for several hours. However, it should have reopened by the time you're reading this.

The small first room contains the art most closely related to the emperor himself. The portrait skills of one of his court artists, Hans von Aachen, are displayed in two rather atypical works, showing none of the stylized proportions or mild eroticism for which he's best known. It probably had something to do with the subject-matter: his *Head of a Girl* is touched with the affection that a father might be expected to show his daughter, while his full-length *Portrait of Emperor Matthias* flatters the peacock-grandeur of the hated brother who usurped Rudolf's throne. (Aachen waited for Rudolf to die, and then jumped onto Matthias's payroll.) There's a bust of Rudolf himself by his sculptor, Adriaen de Vries; and the strange work of Joris Hoefnagel, who painted innumerable studies of creatures of the deep and crawlers of the earth, showing a fascination with the order (and decay) of things that was typical of Rudolfine Mannerism (see pp. 66–8).

Unfortunately, the audacious sneak-thieves removed the most exceptional work in the room: an *Unequal Couple* by Lucas Cranach the Elder. Cranach was one of the artists whose work Rudolf collected obsessively.

The artist's harsh realism probably appealed to a masochistic streak in the emperor, and this painting of a lecherous man and pickpocketing girl, locked into an eminently equal embrace, offered a glimpse into the mind of a man who never married and sank into melancholy or insanity when the subject was raised. The work may just return, and if not, Cranach's *Mocking of Christ* remains as a hint of the cruelty of which the artist was capable.

The Swedes and Saxons were discerning hordes, judging from what they left behind. The rest of the gallery contains works that lay around in the castle for three centuries and were identified only by scientists with X-ray machines in the late 1960s. Even now the attributions change with disconcerting regularity. However, the next room contains an intriguing *Amnon and Tamar* by Lucio Massari. The saga of incest and rape is mysteriously treated as a story of unrequited love: topless Tamar gazes wistfully at her hunk of a half-brother, while the men at the door look as though they're about to break up a tryst rather than leave the scene of the imminent crime. An Oedipal sphinx sitting cryptic under the bed is about the clearest reminder of the incestuous theme.

The next rooms contain a motley collection of 16th- and 17th-century Italian works, but highlights include Guido Reni's *Centaur Nessus abducting Deianeira*, Gentileschi's *Triumphant Amor*, and a *Flagellation of Christ* by Tintoretto (who is also credited with two mediocrities). There's a pretty work by Titian (*Toilet of a Young Lady*) and four paintings by Veronese; the *Portrait of a Jeweller, Jacob König*, shows his shrewd friend who landed the job of Venetian buyer for Rudolf II. The end of the largest room is dominated by the vast *Gathering on Mount Olympus* by Rubens—an exuberant feast of divine nudity where the gaze of ashen-faced Cassandra, peeking out from the wall of flesh, seems to have been the only concession to a moral message that fun-loving Rubens was able to make.

The stone portal at the other end of the room is a remnant from the days when the gallery used to be Rudolf's stables (housing 300 thoroughbred horses), and leads to some dignified portraits by Jan Kupecký, and an excellent *Still Life with Cards and Letter* by Samuel van Hoogstraten (1627–78). Hoogstraten spent his life exploring the effects of perspective, and this work, an almost abstract composition, is imbued with a sense of experimentation that's immediately apparent to the 20th-century mind.

The last room contains some astonishingly bad portraits of assorted

Austrians and Spaniards. Rudolf II may have not been the healthiest of Habsburgs, but if you take the portraits of Marie Eleonoro and Marie Leopoldina at face value, it was with these two that the inbreeding finally took hold. The museum has taken the unusual step of advertising the paucity of its own collection by showing photographs of paintings that are now elsewhere in Europe. Take a look at the surreal composite heads by the Milanese Mannerist Giuseppe Arcimboldo, court painter for three generations of Habsburgs between 1562–1587. His portrait of Rudolf as a bunch of fruit (*Vertumnus*, Roman god of the garden) was eagerly awaited in Prague, and the emperor loved it. Ageing Arcimboldo, who had served the Habsburgs for decades, was allowed to return home in 1587, but he continued to receive a salary until his death, and he was awarded the highest imperial title, that of Count Palatine.

> *From the gallery, retrace your steps and turn left through the arch into the Third Courtyard—and stop dead before* **St Vitus's Cathedral** *(Katedrála svatého Víta), looming up before you as you emerge from the tunnel.*

Prince Wenceslas (a.k.a. Good King) founded the first church, a rotunda, on the site in 929 after receiving St Vitus's arm as a token of friendship from the Saxon King Henry I. He dedicated it to the saint in honour of the limb, but also because he hoped to convert the local pagans, who worshipped a four-headed war and fertility god called Svantovít (St Vitus in Czech is *svatý Vít*). The trick was made even easier by the fact that Svantovít liked cocks, a symbol shared by Vitus. Between 1060 and 1096 the church was enlarged into a basilica, but it was under Charles IV that the present construction, one of the finest 14th-century churches in Europe, began to take shape. Building commenced in 1344, months after the future emperor had persuaded his ex-tutor, Pope Clement VI, to promote Bohemia to an archbishopric. Charles hoped to make Prague into a great imperial metropolis, and the cathedral was to be its centrepiece. Having been brought up in Paris, he turned first to a French architect, summoning Matthew of Arras from the papal court at Avignon. Matthew built the east end of the chancel on standard French lines, but luckily for Prague's Gothic architecture, he died in 1352. His replacement, called to the court from Swabia, was **Peter Parler**, the scion of a distinguished family of German masons. His new plan for the nave inaugurated a half-century during which Prague became the most significant centre of Gothic architecture in Europe. Although the church was unfinished at his death in 1399, most of its most notable features are his work. The Hussite wars brought construction to a halt, and the building was closed with a temporary wall which stayed for centuries.

The entire western part of the church, including the grand façade you're looking at, was only completed between 1871 and 1929. Prague's neo-Gothic mania at the end of the last century did its fair share of damage to the town, but the architects' efforts here can hardly be faulted. Their work completed a symbol of Bohemian history, and gave Prague's skyline a focus it had lacked for 500 years. Although there's an almost too perfect industrial precision to some of the pinnacles and sculptures on the façade, you'd be hard-pressed to find the joins in most of the building.

As you launch your gaze through the mammoth pillars lining the noble arch of the nave, you're in the monument to the greatest king ever to rule Bohemia. Charles, on his way to becoming one of the most powerful men in Europe, almost certainly hoped to be canonized after his death à la Louis IX and Charlemagne. But he was taking no chances. The Black Death was marching across Europe, and Prague's clerics were warning that the Apocalypse would take place sometime between 1365 and 1375. To add insult to prospective injury, one of the city's leading preachers had recently accused him of being the Antichrist. As well as putting his capital firmly on the medieval map, Charles's magnificent offering to God was private insurance that, when weighed in the balance, he would not be found wanting.

The first three chapels on each side date from the early 20th century. Although topped up with older decoration, they are filled with neo-Gothic sculpture that's as lifeless as St Ludmilla, throttled and serene in the first chapel to your right. The stained glass is another modern addition dating from the 1930s. The original Gothic church is thought to have had only one coloured window, and its bold use of clear light was one way in which architect Parler broke from the church's French origins. The windows have a certain garish splendour, but here at least it's hard not to wonder how different a completed 14th-century church might have been. The window in the third chapel was paid for by an insurance company, and celebrates prudent risk-assessment with the psalm 'Those who Sow in Tears Shall Reap in Joy'.

Walk past the Renaissance tombstones, and the tower of the old cathedral. You're now in the original part of the building. To your left is the **choir** *(1557–61), designed by Ferdinand I's court architect, Bonifaz Wohlmut, and surmounted by a tremendous organ* *dating from the later 18th century. Originally, it closed the western end of the church, but the whole shebang was moved in the 1920s. Just to your right is the shining goldmine of the* **Chapel of St Wenceslas**, *built between 1362 and 1367 by Peter Parler.*

Gentle Wenceslas died at the hands of his brother Boleslav in 935, and has wielded more influence from his grave than he ever did during his life. After killing him, Boleslav cheekily decided that to be the brother of a martyr was no bad thing, and he had the remains transferred to the original rotunda in 939. Charles exploited his ancestor in a far more systematic fashion. From the example of St Louis, he had learnt how useful national cults were in cementing together a kingdom, and even before his arrival in Prague, he began to turn his ancestor's grave into a shrine. He had the old tomb decorated with silver statues of the Apostles (which his father, John of Luxemburg, immediately pawned to finance his latest foreign adventure); and when the cathedral was begun, he had Parler change his plans for the nave to build this chapel on the site of the original grave.

There are two doorways. The northern portal in the nave contains the ring to which the saint allegedly clung as he was hacked to death, although the church where the deed occurred, outside Prague, has always indignantly claimed to have the knocker concerned. The arch is flanked by sculptural warnings—on the left, a crumbling figure of Peter denying Christ, and on the right a vicious devil yanking Judas' tongue from his mouth—but the interior is an inviting mosaic of gilt plaster and semi-precious stones, unevenly framing and crowding over the painted Passion scenes below. The chapel is a Gothic painting in three glittering dimensions, suffused with the shot of mysticism that ran through the otherwise eminent worldliness of Charles. The number of stones (about 1370) corresponds to the date of its construction (and, if Prague's clerics were to be believed, the rough date of the Second Coming); and if you can lay your hands on a Bible, take a look at ch. 21 of the Book of Revelations. The chapel is a literally-conceived model of the Heavenly Jerusalem, whose arrival would herald the end of history.

The full ramifications of the original decoration, which Charles illuminated with 144 perpetually-burning candles, would have been hard for the modern mind to appreciate; but impressive as the chapel is, there have been some changes over the years. The emperor and his wife are still kneeling near the crucified Christ over the chapel altar, but the (heavily restored) paintings on the upper part of the wall date from 1509.

They show scenes from the *Legend of St Wenceslas*, as well as portraits of Vladislav II of Jagellon and his rather unappealing wife Anne, who flank the arched window. The **tomb** in the centre was once as gold-plated and jewel-encrusted as the rest of the chapel (and contained small reliquaries for 18 more saintly scraps) but Charles's sons proved as impious as their grandfather, John of Luxemburg, had been. Wenceslas IV melted down bits and pieces to make gold coins, while Sigismund turfed the saint out and carted away the whole coffin during his occupation of the castle in 1420. Wenceslas' semi-precious home dates from the early 20th-century, and represents one of the rare occasions when Prague's pedantic neo-Gothic restorers didn't even try to match the original work.

The chapel also contains a Gothic statue of the saint by Peter Parler's nephew, Henry; some more odd stained glass (a translucent vision from the late 1960s); and in the south-east corner is a **sanctuarium**, built here by Charles so that Wenceslas could guard the cathedral's wine and wafers. The emperor also gave the chapel tremendous secular significance by establishing a new coronation ceremony linked closely to the cult of the saint. Much of it took place here, and the forged door in the south-west corner leads to a small room containing the old **crown jewels** of Bohemia. You'll have a job getting to see them, though; the door is closed with seven different locks and to track down the scattered keys, you'd have to sweet-talk some fairly imposing figures, ranging from President Havel (No.1) to Cardinal Tomášek (No.7). In any case, any pleb who puts them on signs his own death warrant. The legend was last fulfilled (or just possibly created) in 1942, when *Reichsprotektor* Reinhard Heydrich is said to have sneered with Teutonic arrogance when the grizzled guardian of the jewels warned him of the curse; shortly after trying on the crown, he was cut down by assassins. An extension of the story, which begins to damage its own case, is that Heydrich's two sons also had a go. One died a fairly predictable death on the eastern front, and Nemesis apparently caught up with the other at the end of a mad stallion's hoof.

> *Good King Wenceslas was one of the first buried here, but like any cathedral worth its salt, St Vitus's in its heyday served as a necropolis for the corpses of the high and mighty. In the central aisle is the white marble **Habsburg mausoleum** (1566–89), containing the remains of the first two generations to rule Bohemia.*

Ferdinand I died in Vienna, but the family decided to honour St Vitus's with his posthumous presence to shore up their shaky claim to be the hereditary rulers of Bohemia. His wife joined him, and in 1577 Maximilian II arrived here at the head of a funeral procession that chroniclers noted was the grandest that Prague had ever seen. All three characters were sculpted sleeping on top of the tomb, next to each other and in full regalia. Maximilian's peculiar son, Rudolf II, made his own arrangements (as you'll soon see), as well as those of his mother when she died in 1603. The funeral procession that he organized for her was a suitably lavish affair, marred only by the fact that Rudolf himself failed to turn up, despite plans to attend in disguise.

The Habsburg contingent only topped up a church which was already brimming with human tissue, thanks to relic-mad Charles IV. In 1354 he proudly wrote to Bohemia's first archbishop, 'I do not think that you will find another place in the whole of Europe, except Rome, where pilgrims can seek out so many holy relics as in the cathedral of St Vitus'. Apparently, Prague did not yield second place to Rome for want of trying. The **St Andrew's Chapel**, *next to that of Wenceslas, contains a picture known as the* **vera icon** *(true image). The Vatican also has one—a messy state of affairs, given that the* vera icon *is the miraculously-imprinted hanky used by the (strangely anagrammatical) St Veronica to wipe the sweat off the crucified Jesus. The story goes that Charles set his heart on the thing and asked the pope if he could have it; the pope said no way, so the cunning emperor asked if he could copy it instead. The weak point of the story is that the pope trusted Charles enough to agree—otherwise, it's not hard to believe the punch line, that the emperor handed the copy back to the pope and you're looking at the original. The castle catalogue casts some doubt on the matter by listing the work as a 'Gothic panel painting from about the year 1400'.*

In the next chapel is the entrance to the **crypt of the cathedral** *(open 9 am–4.45 pm, adm). The tour is a confusing journey through the convoluted architectural history of the cathedral. Columns and tombstones unearthed over the years litter your path as you wend through the 11th-century crypt of the basilica, the cathedral's foundations and those of its original choir, 20th-century masonry, and the northern apse of Wenceslas' rotunda. A plan of the two older churches in the penultimate room may help you piece together the puzzle, although it's hardly any less complicated.*

The wooden steps take you back out into the nave, but first take a look at the **royal crypt** *in the room to the right, next to more of the basilica's foundations.*

The spotlit sepulchre is the bizarre resting place of some of Bohemia's greatest kings, silently awaiting Gabriel's trumpet in an avant-garde collection of stainless steel and granite sarcophagi—all were given a postmortem and reinterred here during the final stages of the church's completion in 1928–1935. You'll find Charles IV here, in front of his four wives who've all been tossed into the same stone box. Rudolf is in his original pewter coffin, but he's a lost and lonely character even in death. He's separated from his forebears (in the mausoleum upstairs), his internal organs (in the Saxon chapel), and his successors (who deserted Prague altogether after the Battle of the White Mountain (see pp. 52–3) and now lie in the Capuchines in Vienna).

From the crypt, you emerge back into the centre of the nave, a good point from which to compare the medieval part of the cathedral with its 20th-century extension.

From here you can see one of Parler's most significant contributions to the design of the church, the net-vault of the choir, which breaks free of the purely practical concern of cross-ribbed vaulting, the need to stop the roof from falling down, and shows the move towards abstraction that came to characterize late Gothic architecture across Europe. Parler is thought to have borrowed his ideas from England, possibly after Charles IV's daughter married King Richard II. The work is actually a model of restraint compared to the exuberance of English vault design over the previous century; nevertheless, it was the first time that the ideas had been used in a major continental church. Up in the triforium are a series of busts by Parler and his workshop. They're among the earliest portraits in Gothic art, but you'll need binoculars to see them properly. As well as Charles and family, Parler and Matthew of Arras are represented—an unusual honour for the time which shows the respect that Charles had for his architects.

The line of chapels on the right continues with the **Royal Oratory**, designed for Vladislav II by his court architect, Benedict Ried, and built in 1493. The vault and the entrance are decorated with fantastic branch-like ribs, gnarled stone bows bent across the vault. Ried, like Parler, had radical ideas when it came to vaulting, as he showed to magnificent effect in his design for the Vladislav Hall, which you'll see soon.

Walk past the Waldstein Chapel, containing the Gothic tombstones of the cathedral's two architects. Opposite the chapel is a relief

119

showing what looks to be a very orderly iconoclastic rampage through the cathedral that occurred in 1619. You're now entering the oldest part of the church, but to go any further you have to get round the incandescent Baroque **tomb of St John Nepomuk**, *fashioned from 3700 pounds of solid silver after a design by Fischer von Erlach the Younger.*

What John would have made of it all can only be guessed. Larger-than-life angels support the coffin; the swooning saint clutches a crucifix above the lid; and four heavenly bodies float over it all, dangling from wall-brackets. The cleric had been venerated in an unassuming way from the moment he was lobbed off the Charles Bridge in 1383 (see pp. 245–6), but three centuries later he suddenly found himself at the heart of the Jesuit drive to re-catholicize Bohemia. The monks needed a native saint, and John fitted the bill—he was untainted (to both sides) by any involvement in Europe's religious schism, he was Czech, and he was dead. In 1715, a canonization committee gathered in Prague to investigate the old legend that John had been martyred for refusing to tell King Wenceslas IV what the queen had said in the confession box. When his rotting coffin was exhumed from his chapel (opposite the tomb), the confessor's skull was found to contain a lump of organic matter. The committee's three doctors examined it, solemnly swore that it was John's incorrupt tongue—a useful organ, given the basis of his proposed canonization—and the 100 or so commissioners hurried to Rome with the news. The pope proved uncharacteristically sceptical, and the Jesuits pulled out all the stops. Six years later their doctors declared that not only was his tongue still throbbing with life, but growing steadily. That clinched it, and in 1729 John was canonized. To make his cult even more palatable to Praguers, the Jesuits filled the castle fountains with beer and wine on his annual feast day. They couldn't quite get the cathedral renamed, but after John was reburied in this awe-inspiring piece of kitsch in 1736, it effectively became the high altar. Curious scientists examined the tongue in the early 1980s and declared that it was actually a desiccated brain. Sadly, it's no longer available for public worship, having been removed to an inaccessible part of St Vitus's treasury. It apparently resembled the condom-like object pointed out by the priggish cherub on top of the coffin.

The next chapel along contains yet more bodily remains—the two Přemysl Otakars in tombs sculpted by Parler, and under the slab marked with the Habsburg double-headed eagle, a vault containing Rudolf II's exiled viscera. There are also fragments of a mural painting (The Adoration of the Magi) *which may have been painted by Master Theodoric, court artist to Charles IV—you'll see some of his most exceptional work later on this walk (see p. 128). As you pass the centre of the cathedral, pay your respects to the **altar to St Vitus** on your left, especially if you're afflicted with an annoying twitch or you've been bitten by a mad dog. Vitus hasn't done well over the years, outshone first by Wenceslas and then by John Nepomuk, and his tomb is an insignificant 19th-century affair. At least Charles IV did him the courtesy of cobbling together a full body.*

On the left as you pass the next two chapels are two more **oak reliefs**, dating from 1631, which show the flight from Prague of Frederick of the Palatinate (motto: I Know Not How to Turn) after the defeat of his Protestant armies at the Battle of the White Mountain. Malicious they may be—they were commissioned by the victorious Ferdinand II—but the second is a lovely snapshot of 17th-century Prague, all the king's horses and men galloping in hasty retreat from the medieval castle across the bridge and through the Old Town Square.

On the right just past the choir is an amazing wooden altar (1896–99) by the Czech sculptor František Bílek. Its simplicity, and the pain that it exudes, owes much to the humanistic traditions of late Gothic art in Bohemia, but Bílek's Symbolism developed a spiritual language independent of any single religion or country. His **Crucifixion** is a masterpiece: Christ rising slowly from the ropes and nails of his cross, locked into meditation while a heedless humanity despairs at his feet; and on the altar, the return of hope, portrayed by a single arm stretching up with its offering.

Bílek's sculpture is a modern addition that works; the Art Nouveau stained glass by Alfons Mucha (a 1931 comic-strip celebrating SS Cyril and Methodius) is one that doesn't. You're back in the modern chapels. From the cathedral, turn left into the expanse of the Third Courtyard, where you'll find a large granite obelisk (a memorial to the dead of the 1914–18 war), and at the far southern end, the offices of the president. Once the isolated enclave of Communist greymen, they're now occupied by the livelier (albeit increasingly besuited) entourage of Václav Havel. Every now and then, the corridors of power are opened to the public, and if you get to see the endless Rococo interiors, you'll understand one of the reasons why Havel refuses to live in the castle and still sleeps in his rundown fourth-floor apartment near Jiráskův Bridge (Jiráskův most). On

*the southern façade of the church is the central **tower**, which
marked the front of the cathedral until its modern completion.*

It's almost 100 m high, although a fair chunk of that (38 m) is made up of
the multi-storey Baroque dome added by Pacassi in 1770. Four bells
hang in the tower, of which the largest is **Sigismund**, an 18-ton monster
on the first floor. Bells caused no end of trouble in the 16th century.
They couldn't be touched by anyone impure (a category which included
all women), and pubescent boys dressed in white had to be engaged to
transport them from foundry to belfry. Sigismund, dating from 1549,
was the successor to two earlier bells. The first was dragged on sledges
from the Old Town by hundreds of pretty urchins in 1534; after several
days, they got it to the gate of the castle, only for it to roll out of control
and break into pieces. No chances were taken with the next one, which
was cast in the castle grounds and hung in 1538—three years before
smashing to the ground during the great fire of 1541. Sigismund finally
made it in 1549. Like the carillon of Loretto, it survived the great
Austro-Hungarian bell massacre of 1918 (see p. 203) and can be heard
booming across Hradčany on Sunday mornings. The ornate golden
grille in the arched window dates from Rudolf II's reign (hence the 'R'
just above)—so too do the two clocks, the higher of which shows the
hour, the lower the minute.

*To the right of the tower is the **Golden Portal**, once the main
entrance to the cathedral.*

The emphasis on the southern façade is unusual in church design—
Charles effectively turned the cathedral around, so that Wenceslas could
have the prominence that he deserved (his chapel is just to the right of
the doorway). Another of Peter Parler's notable touches appears under
the bullet-shaped arches, where ribs spray into the air from the door,
again inspired by England and again unique for its time on the continent.
Above the gate is a **mosaic of the Last Judgment** dating from 1370–
1371, pieced together by Italians following a cartoon drawn up by artists
in Charles's court. Kneeling below Christ the Judge are patron saints; to
the left, on Christ's right hand, the luckier resurrected corpses emerge
from their coffins; while to the right, wretched sinners wail and gnash
their teeth as they're herded into Hell. The not-so-humble suppliants on
either side of the central arch, crowned and ermined, are Charles and his
fourth wife, Elizabeth of Pomerania. The 30 colours in the thousands of
glass cubes are covered by a protective film which fades to grey every six

years; at the time of writing, the mosaic is lustreless, but if promises are kept it will be shining in full technicolour by the end of 1991.

Head towards the **Royal Palace** *(Královský palác), connected to the royal oratory of the cathedral by a covered passage, to your right as you face the mosaic. Since the castle was first fortified, this has been the site of the royal residence, and inside are three layers of palace, spanning the Romanesque and the Renaissance. Until it was paved during Rudolf II's reign, the Third Courtyard sloped steeply downwards towards the east, and the older halls are below ground level—a feature you come to expect in Prague. Two storeys down is the huge Romanesque gloom of Soběslav's 12th-century palace. Charles used it to store the wine he brought back from his travels, and built a new palace on top. In keeping with his peaceful megalomania, it was designed to outshine the Paris Louvre. Huge halls and chambers from both buildings survive, but are closed to the public for no good reason.*

Charles's rollicking son Wenceslas IV deserted the palace in 1383 for the high jinks to be found in the Old Town, where he built a new Royal Court. Over the next century the castle was deserted, save for the occasional Hussite mob or invasion by Wenceslas's brother, Sigismund. In 1483, life returned suddenly under Vladislav II of Jagellon. City pressures had become too much for the Catholic monarch—his officials had just been defenestrated by Hussites from the Old Town Hall, and the final straw came when he opened the windows of the Royal Court one morning to be greeted by an arrow carrying the scrawled message, 'Get out of town, Polack'. He left in a hurry, crossing the Vltava by boat at night, and wasted no time in fortifying and expanding the desolate castle.

His northern walls and towers (which you'll see later on this walk) survived Maria Theresa's redecorations, as did his grandest building venture, the **Vladislav Hall** (Vladislavský sál), built between 1486 and 1502 by his court architect, Benedict Ried, over the two earlier palaces. (Open Tues–Sun April–Sept 9 am–4.15 pm, Oct–Mar 9 am–3.45 pm). Vladislav built his new hall above Charles's palace partly because of his belief—all too often disproved in the castle's history—that 'high' meant 'safe'; but it was also the expression of the worldly grandeur that now permeated the court. The palace is the culmination of the Bohemian late Gothic style named after the Polish king (see p. 65). In its magnificent vault, ribs shoot up like monstrous tendrils from its wall shafts, intertwining across five gently articulated bays and somehow meandering into star-like flower petals in the centre. Ried used anything that seemed to fit the opulence required: the broad rectangular windows are pure Renaissance, sneaking into Bohemia years before the Italian influence began to be felt in western Europe; spiralling pillars and classical entablatures frame the doors of the hall.

Surrounded by the almost tangible space of the hall ($62 \times 16 \times 13$ m) you understand the awe of the chronicler who breathlessly recorded, 'There was no other building like it in all of Europe, none that was longer, broader and higher and yet had no pillars'. Horses fitted in here comfortably; mounted stewards and cupbearers lined the sides during banquets, and tournaments were a regular feature. Under the reign of Rudolf II, it became a bazaar; a contemporary engraving shows it full of high-hatted and haggling merchants, and even a small scrum of bargain-hunting Persians. Since 1918, the president of the Republic has been sworn in here, and this was where Václav Havel took the oath of office that ended 40 years of Communist rule in December 1989.

To the right of the entrance is a door leading to the **Ludvik Wing**, *built in similar style by Ried between 1502 and 1509, and named after Vladislav's successor, Ludvik of Jagellon (who ruled from 1516–26). Inside, on the same floor as the hall, are the two rooms of the* **Czech Chancellery**.

Walk through the portal of the first room (marked with Ludvik's initials) into the next chamber, in which the chancellor and the governors used to deliberate under the Habsburgs. It was here that Prague's most significant **defenestration** took place on 23 May 1618. Count Thurn and other Bohemian protestant noblemen confronted the two hated catholic governors appointed by Ferdinand I, and after explaining their grievances, tossed both out of the window to your left (see p. 51). According to a contemporary account of events, 'They loudly screamed "Ach, ach oweh!" and attempted to hold on to the narrow window ledge, but Thurn beat their knuckles until they were both obliged to let go.' Their secretary, Fabricius, protested and followed them down. All three plunged some 50 feet, but landed more or less comfortably in a dungheap. After interviewing a number of witnesses, most of whom swore that they had seen the Virgin Mary parachute the men to safety, the Church declared it a miracle; and following the defeat of Bohemian Protestantism at the Battle of the White Mountain, two obelisks were set up below to com-

memorate the glorious event. They mark where the governors came to
rest. No similar honour was accorded the humble Fabricius.

*From here walk back into the hall, and go through the first door on
the opposite side of the hall.*

The staircase spirals up to the offices of the **New Land Rolls**, a land
registry institution similar to the Norman Domesday Book. The walls
and ceilings are decorated with scores of colourful crests, the emblems of
the clerks between 1561 and 1774. If you walk through to the next room,
you'll see a mid-16th-century cabinet containing the rolls themselves,
highly unofficial-looking hand-painted tomes decorated with rainbows,
planets and various flora and fauna.

*Back in the hall, turn left and take the second door to the left into the
Diet.*

Originally part of Charles IV's palace, it was rebuilt by Ried in about
1500 only to be completely destroyed by the fire of 1541. Ferdinand I's
architect, Bonifaz Wohlmut, designed the present room between 1559
and 1563, copying Ried's vaulting and making his own contribution to
the hall's Renaissance motifs with two mutant Doric pilasters, twisted
like liquorice sticks into three dimensions around the door. The Diet
was the supreme court in medieval times, and the place where the
Estates met until 1848; if the emperor wanted to meet his Czech subjects
(which was not often after the Battle of the White Mountain), they all
assembled here. Nobles and clergy sat on either side of the central
throne. In case the town representatives were in any doubt about their
insignificance in Habsburg Bohemia, they were given one collective vote
and left to stand in the gallery perched high up on the wall to your right.

*As you leave the Diet, to your right is the entrance to the **All Saints'
Chapel**. It was built by Peter Parler as part of Charles IV's palace,
but after the 1541 fire, its vault was rebuilt, and Baroque additions
have left it an unimpressive appendage to the rest of the hall.
Opposite you is an **observation terrace**, where you can try to find
the remains of the defenestratees' dungheap (unfortunately its rough
location is hidden by a covered passage). Leave the hall through the
Riders' Staircase on your left, built by Ried in around 1500.
Knights summoned to amuse the diners with a spot of horseplay
would storm up these shallow steps on their steeds. The pointed*

cutaway section on the portal was to make sure that nothing embar-
rassing happened to their plumes. You'll emerge in St George's
Square (nám. u sv. Jiří), originally much larger and the heart of the
medieval castle (the buildings to the north are neo-Gothic 19th-
century creations). On your right is the charming early Baroque
façade of the **Basilica of St George** *(Bazilika sv. Jiří) and*
neighbouring **Chapel of St John Nepomuk**, *with perky orange-*
on-brown pilasters and dunce's cap of a dome facing the majestic
chancel of St Vitus's opposite.

Open April–Sept 9 am–5 pm, Oct–Mar 9 am–4 pm, and alone among
Prague's churches, this one charges an admission fee (2kcs at the time of
writing). After seeing the Baroque façade, the Romanesque interior
comes as something of a surprise. The church was the second to be
founded in the castle (921), predating the Cathedral of St Vitus. Its
interior was rebuilt after a fire in 1142, but zealous restoration at the end
of the last century has robbed it of gloom and turned it into a spanking-
clean model of neatly hewn pillars and masonry. To your right as you
enter is the Chapel of St John Nepomuk. He and his tongue are in the
cathedral (see p. 120), and the bones and skull grinning below the altar
belong to one of the early abbesses. The church was an even more
crowded cemetery than St Vitus's. Most bones were removed, but at the
end of the nave are the tombs of three early Přemysl rulers. The wooden
tent on the right houses Vratislav II, next to Boleslav II and then
Oldřich.

In front of them, between the Baroque steps winding up to the
chancel, is the 12th-century crypt. It contains the Romanesque tympanum that used to crown the southern portal of the church, with minuscule abbesses and kings attending the coronation of the Virgin. At the
top of the steps is the chancel, decorated with fading Romanesque
frescoes of the Heavenly Jerusalem, and to the right is the **Chapel of St
Ludmilla**. The saint was Prince Wenceslas' grandmother and spiritual
adviser, strangled at prayer with her veil by his pagan mother Drahomirá,
who hoped thereby to coax her son back into the cock-worshipping fold.
It was an optimistic scheme, and it soon collapsed: Wenceslas took
Ludmilla's side, and had her remains transferred here in 925; Drahomirá died, apparently swallowed up into Hell on what is now Loretánská
street. Sadly, the chapel is inaccessible, having been firmly closed off
since a 17th-century German workman temporarily absconded with
some of the saint's bones.

Turn right as you leave the church, and then right again into the neighbouring **St George's Convent** *The Benedictine convent was the first in Bohemia, founded by Mlada, the sister of Boleslav II, in 973. She went to Rome to ask the pope to make Bohemia a bishopric, and he not only agreed but also gave her an abbess's staff to take home. The nuns are long gone though, having thrown off their habits when the fanatically enlightened despot, Joseph II, abolished all the empire's religious institutions in 1782. He turned the convent into a penitentiary for bewildered priests to consider the error of their ways. Despite its venerable age, successive reconstructions have left it a dull building, except that it contains the* **National Gallery of Czech Gothic and Baroque Art.**

Open Tues–Sun, 10 am–6 pm, adm. The collection is divided into two sections, Gothic art in the basement and on the ground floor, and Mannerism and Baroque on the first floor.

The earliest Gothic art in Bohemia dates from the beginning of the 14th century. The slender and elegant Madonnas in the first room of the basement, their faces half turned away, show how Bohemian art was beginning to escape the rigid formality of its Byzantine progenitors. Figures became more robust, with even heavier features, typified by the *Strahov Madonna* (*c.* 1350), almost struggling with her overgrown brat. The break with Orthodox art had begun to occur across western Europe; but the second feature marked the birth of Bohemia's independent artistic traditions, and during the few decades of Charles IV's rule, made its painting unique in Europe.

To your left as you leave the room is the gallant *St George*, plunging a lost standard into the mouth of a downed dragon (the flag's gone missing, but you can see it in the copy of the work that now stands in the Third Courtyard). The bronze statue, which dates from 1373, was designed as a free-standing work, one of the first in Europe to break out of the Gothic inability to conceive of sculpture (any more than painting or architecture) as an independent art form. That said, it's not easy to see what Europe's proto-sculptor had in mind; puny George is dwarfed by a remarkably life-like horse, recast with the rather different techniques and mentality of two centuries later.

In the room to your right is the *Vyšši Brod (Hohenfurth) Altarpiece*. The most notable feature of the nine paintings is their use of contrasting colours to create the illusion of depth, a century before the laws of perspective twinkled in the eyes of the clever Florentines. It's most remarkable in *The Descent of the Holy Ghost*: huddled Apostles swirl in a sea of reds and greens and indigoes,yet the space around them appears almost three-dimensional.

The loudmouthed creature at the bottom of the set of steps with the droopy ears is a gargoyle. It's mysteriously called Capricorn, *though less goat-like a beast you never did see. Walk past its howling canine companion into the room containing the work of* **Master Theodoric**.

Theodoric is the first of Bohemia's painters to emerge from misty anonymity—and as you gaze at the six paintings on display here, you'll understand why. Bohemia's experiments with colour values and facial modelling reach their culmination in these panels, which have a vitality that survives six centuries. Huge saints spread onto the edges of their medallion-studded frames; their powerful human ugliness crowds forward into the small room; and with just the crow's feet of an eye or the downturn of a lip, Theodoric gives them an expressiveness deeper than anything that had come before. The panels are from the Chapel of the Holy Cross at Charles IV's castle at Karlštejn, where there are over 100 more (it's closed until about the year 2000—see p. 345). Theodoric was the emperor's court painter—a radical choice for a man brought up amidst the delicacy of French art, and one which almost makes his other quirks seem unimportant.

Up the stairs there's a café, but hold your horses—a golden age draws to a close in the next room.

With Charles's death and the coronation of his wastrel son Wenceslas IV in 1378, Bohemian art became increasingly refined. Sophistication replaced spiritual mystery, and the paintings of women take on a doll-like charm. Look, for example, at *SS Catherine, Mary Magdalene and Margaret*, languid rosy-cheeked triplets. As you walk along the next corridor, the line of Madonnas become mothers, while motherhood is heavily romanticized in the process. The *St Vitus's Madonna* shows the process in all its treacle, and it's especially apparent in the sculptures. The trend towards humanization takes a different form in most of the men of late Gothic art; the corridor is filled with hirsute and/or bald saints, while Christ suffers and is tortured with a greater intensity than ever before.

Up the steps and to your left is a small room containing the very big Tympanum of the Northern Portal of the Týn Church, *dating from around 1380–90. The central scene is the work of either Peter Parler or one of his team then working on St Vitus's Cathedral.*

Compare its sense of balance and perspective with the clumping neanderthals on either side, flagellating and crowning Christ, which were the work of lesser artists. The tympanum was originally gilded and painted, but the colour has disappeared, along with much of the top scene, where diabolical amphibians struggle with a rather unconcerned angel, ripping a poor soul apart in the process.

The work in the next corridor represents the final period of Gothic art in Bohemia.

By the time you get to the *Žebrák Lamentation*, the regular cast of characters mourning the dead Christ have a restraint that's still utterly Gothic, but they have begun to sprout the extra inches and shrunken pinheads that are characteristic of Mannerist art; and a strange sense of movement pervades the sculpture, from the rolling curtain of drapery to the Medusa-like locks of Christ. The floor ends with the carvings of Master I. P., a shadowy character who lived in Prague between 1520 and 1525, and who left behind a series of masterful woodcuts, showing all the devotion to north European foliage characteristic of the Danube School.

On the second floor, the pace heats up. Despite the Žebrák Lamentation, the gallery's shift from Gothic to the Mannerism of Rudolf II's court painters is abrupt.

As you walk up the stairs, you're ambushed by the rather incredible eroticism of the *Epitaph of the Goldsmith Müller*, by Bartholomeus Spranger. Sex permeated the art of the emperor's court—generally in its kinkier forms—and here Spranger has turned Christ into a coquettish pin-up, sly, pouting and wrapped in the strangest loincloth that you'll have ever seen. It was Spranger's memorial to his father-in-law, and bereaving relatives (rare portraits by the artist) line the bottom of the scene. Spranger himself thought it one of his greatest successes, and its almost reflective iridescence is one of the best examples of the feature that typified his work—but quite what the stern mourners thought about being extras in a Mannerist skin-flick can only be suspected.

The collection also contains a rippling *Hercules with the Apples of the Hesperides* by Rudolf's sculptor, Adriaen de Vries, the only full-length work by the artist to have escaped the attentions of the Swedish art collectors of 1648 (see pp. 67–8). The *Allegory of the Reign of Rudolf II* (1603) by Dirck de Quade van Ravesteyn is typical of the many apotheoses that were produced to celebrate a pipe-dream vision of Rudolf's crisis-ridden reign. Peace, Justice and Plenty fondle each other's breasts, while an iron-clad imperial bouncer keeps a curious Turk at the door. The last paintings of Rudolfine Prague, landscapes by the Flemish Roelandt Savery, show the skills of a man whom the emperor sent to the Alps when he wanted to know what they looked like. The fawns and stags can only hint at Savery's real place in art history, as the first European painter of exotic animals and also, in the case of the dodo that he found in Rudolf's zoo, the last.

Baroque painting begins with the restrained touch of Karel Škréta, but its dubious culmination is heralded by the Last Judgment trumpet in the ear of *St Jerome* by Michael Willmann. Removed from the sensory wonderland of Prague's Baroque churches, Willman's work, and much of that which follows, has all the unpleasant drama of a fish twitching out of water. The heroic proportions and animation of the country's Baroque sculpture make it no less peculiar under the harsh light of the gallery—but it's far more fun. The quiver that begins with Jäckel's *Mary, Mother of Sorrows* becomes an earthshaking crescendo among the statues of Matthias Braun and Maximilian Brokof, the two greatest sculptors of Baroque Prague. Braun's *St Jude* is the most spectacular example. The sculptor studied in Venice and probably Rome, and with this statue, he seems to have made an attempt to trap the ecstasy of Bernini's *St Theresa* in the frame of an octogenarian. It didn't work, and the sculpture is heartstopping in every sense, a whirlwind of frenzied rags and varicose veins. Brokof's armed and arrogant Moors are models of restraint by comparison.

Past the paintings by the Czech Petr Brandl, you'll find the remarkable work of Jan Kupecký (1667–1740), a melancholy Czech exile who spent most of his life shuttling between Vienna and Nuremberg. Kupecký lived off commissions from rich buyers and trod a thin line between flattery and honesty. With his superb *Portrait of the Miniaturist, Karl Brun*, he just about lets the diabolically charming subject, swathed in silk dressing-gown and furry shadow, get away with the concealment of a faraway stare, but he's less sparing of himself. He looks downright shocked by what he found when painting his *Self Portrait with the Artist's Wife*. It might just be what he met in the mirror, but it's worth bearing in mind that his wife was busily being unfaithful at the time. That's her again, clutching a Bible in the next painting, *Penitent Spouse*, and only you can judge what her husband thought of her oath.

From the gallery, walk into the narrow lane ahead of you (Vikář-ská). The present buildings date from the early 18th century, but Rudolf's **alchemists** *used to live in earlier houses here. Sunk in the shadows of the cathedral's flying buttresses and vomiting gargoyles, their main laboratory was in the* **Powder Tower** *(Prašná brána), also known as* Mihulka, *on your right.*

Open Tues–Sun, April–Sept 9 am–5 pm, Oct–Mar 9 am–4 pm, adm. The tower was built as an armoury in the 15th century; a foundry had been set up by the 16th century; and under the reign of Rudolf II, scientists and quacks from across Europe hopefully distilled their aqua vitae and toiled with base metals here. Despite rigid admission tests administered by Rudolf's quality controller Tadeáš Hájek of Hájek, during which applicants had to transmute a pound of lead into gold, a motley crew of adventurers and charlatans were taken on as imperial alchemists. Among them were the incredible English duo of **Edward Kelley and John Dee.** Kelley, who lost his ears in England and his legs in Prague, seems to have been a rather magnificent fraud; but Dee was a true Renaissance scholar. He has gone down in Prague legend as the trickster who wormed his way into Rudolf's confidence by translating bird-warbles; in fact, by the time he arrived in Prague with Kelley in 1584, his Europe-wide reputation was established, thanks in no small part to a giant mechanical dung beetle with which he had amazed the Fellows of Trinity College, Cambridge, some 40 years before. While in the capital, he had his son baptized in the nearby cathedral, but that wasn't enough to placate an alarmed papal nuncio who eventually per-suaded the emperor to expel the English sorcerers from the capital. Kelley was to return, and give birth to another string of Prague legends (see pp. 95–7).

Any alchemy that survived Rudolf's abdication in 1611 ended with the outbreak of the Thirty Years War. The tower was used as an ammunition dump by occupying Swedish forces in 1648, until it blew up. It has since been rebuilt, and now houses a museum devoted to its strange history. The basement (through the gate and down a curving set of stone steps to your left) sinks to sub-zero temperatures for much of the year, and is only open during the summer. It contains a selection of objects from the foundry of Tomáš Jaroš, bell-maker *extraordinaire*. Sigismund the Bell was one of his babies, and there are two of his more minor creations here (you're still not supposed to touch). Another object that you can examine at close quarters is the copy of Rudolf II's pewter coffin, lined with a set of repellent cherubs.

The next floor contains a paltry selection of weapons—two six-foot muskets and a cannon—and no mention of the far more interesting lamprey (*mihule*), who gave the tower its nickname. The creatures were supposedly bred here for the castle kitchens, but apparently the lamprey tank was actually in another tower, which disappeared in the late 1500s. The second level contains retorts, crucibles and stoves used by the alchemists. This was once their laboratory (and the top floor of the tower), as proved by the sooty roof and chimney, which survived the centuries thanks to an unthorough replastering.

The last floor contains an elegant collection of late 16th-century furniture and art, including a typically icy work by Agnolo Bronzino: *Nobleman in Red Coat*. There's also a portrait of the young Rudolf—a rare chance to see his magnificent Habsburg chin before he was able to muster the hairs for a beard.

From the tower, retrace your steps and cross St George's Square. Walk along the road next to the church (Jiřská) and take the first left—follow the path round to the right and then left, and you'll emerge into the **Golden Lane** *(Zlátá ulička), one of the most popular attractions in the castle.*

The huddled cottages date from the later 16th century, and look like a Matisse painting come alive—tiny blocks of colour stretching higgledy-piggledy down the street. There's barely enough room inside to fit a cat, let alone swing one. The cottages are built into the castle fortifications, and originally housed 24 of Rudolf II's marksmen. The minuscule passage used to be even tinier; houses lined the other side until the 18th century, by which time the street had been filled by scores of craftworkers who were fleeing the restrictive practices of the town guilds. The noise from their pub disturbed the abbess of St George's convent, so she destroyed half the street. The last inhabitants were evicted in 1951, and the houses were turned into the souvenir shops you see today, each selling virtually the same rubbish as the next.

The origins of the street's name have long caused controversy. 19th-century mythmakers transmuted the soldiers into alchemists, falsely robbing Vikářská of its claim to fame, and creating one of the most pernicious of Prague legends. In fact the lane seems to have been named after goldsmiths who lived here in the later 17th century, but a Czech

historian recently hurled a thought-provok-
ing cat among the etymological pigeons. It's
well known that the 24 sharpshooters had
been provided with only one toilet between
them. Backed up by lateral thinking (over 100
people lived here before the nuns' demolition
job), he suggested that the 'gold' referred to
was urine, dribbling down the passageway for
generations.

> *Unless it's unbearably full, you may*
> *want to potter around the street for a*
> *while. There's a café in a courtyard to*
> *your left (with Renaissance painted*
> *flowers hiding on the joists), and on the*
> *right as you enter the court is the sheer*
> *wall of the* **White Tower** *(Bílá věž),*
> *built as part of Vladislav II's forti-*
> *fications of the castle.*

For about 200 years after 1584, it was
Prague's central prison. Among those held
here were the 27 Protestant leaders executed
after the Battle of the White Mountain.
During the reign of Rudolf II, the few villains
in his court unlucky enough to be rumbled
were also kept here. Among them was the
already-mentioned Edward Kelley, who
eventually fell foul of the emperor, and was
imprisoned in towers across Bohemia. The
nature of the dispute is unclear, but legend
has it that Rudolf became convinced that Kelley was withholding the philosopher's stone
from him. If he had it, it didn't do him much
good—he's said to have been crippled leaping
from the windows above you in an escape
attempt, and then to have poisoned himself
here.

Back in Golden Lane proper, take a look at
the charcoal-coloured hovel (No. 22) on the
left, a tourist-trap Tardis swallowing up a

coach-load of Germans at a time. Between December 1916 and March 1917, Franz Kafka lived here and wrote most of the short stories published during his lifetime. His sister Ottla, who actually rented the house, deserves to be remembered in her own right. Married to a German 'Aryan', she was exempted from the first anti-Jewish measures passed by the Nazis, but after seeing her two sisters and their husbands taken away to the Lodz ghetto, she divorced him. In August 1942, she was sent to Terezín (Theresienstadt), and died in Auschwitz after volunteering to escort a children's transport there the following year.

*Walk to the end of the street—if the green door is open, at the bottom of the steps you'll find the **Daliborka** tower to your left, built in 1496 as another part of Vladislav's fortifications.*

Open April–Sept 9 am–5 pm. The tower was the work of Benedict Ried, but he has kept his flamboyant tendencies firmly under control here. As you walk down into the main body of the tower, bricks jut out from the crumbling masonry, and the heavy arches and immense walls fiercely announce their function. Between fending off onslaughts, the tower served as a prison for the nobility. It's named after its first inmate, a knight named Dalibor of Kozojed, who landed up here in 1498. The events leading to his incarceration are unclear. They involved a revolt of serfs on a neighbouring estate and dispossession of the landowner concerned. Dalibor may have been no more than a thieving vulture; but over the centuries he's been turned into a Robin Hood figure who returned from distant climes to find that serfdom had been introduced (1487) into once-free Bohemia, and incited a rebellion. While awaiting the chop, he's said to have taught himself to play the violin, attracting huge crowds to the tower—that's the mournful sound you hear if you're around at midnight. The story has minor flaws—the violin was only introduced to Bohemia in the late 16th century—but it was good enough for Smetana to use the motif in his epic opera named after the knight.

Most noble criminals had the privilege of having their heads chopped off when their hour was up, but those who had been especially troublesome were dealt with in less summary fashion. Through the door to the left of the main entrance is a cramped stone staircase, whose worn steps lead down into a dingy cell above the tower's oubliette. Prisoners would be bound and lowered through the narrow hole, and left to starve to death. If they got bored, they could always watch their predecessors putrefy.

If the doorway to Daliborka is closed, retrace your steps to Jiřská and turn left—otherwise, walk straight ahead past the white bricks of

*the **Black Tower** (Černá věž—another debtors' prison) and turn
right as you enter the street. The final stop of this walk is the
Lobkowicz Palace, on the southern side of the street just before
the castle gates.*

The Lobkowiczes were among the staunchest servants of the Counter-
Reformation during the religious cold war of Rudolfine Prague. Zdeněk
Lobkowicz was appointed chancellor by the emperor during one of his
pro-Catholic moods—and his wife, Polyxena, made innumerable contributions to the cause. She gave the capital the incredible Bambino di
Praga (see pp. 187–8), and it was thanks to her fortitude that the 1618
defenestratees survived their plunge from the Vladislav Hall. Fabricius *et
al* were far from home and dry as they emerged from their dungheap—
pistol shots followed, and Count Thurn assembled a posse to complete
the botched job. They fled to the garden door of this palace, and
Polyxena nobly let the stinking trio take shelter. What's more, when
Thurn popped round to ask if he could kill them, she gave him such an
earful that he apparently apologized and left.

*The palace now contains Prague's **Historical Museum**, a small
collection containing one or two exhibits which neatly wrap up the
loose ends of this walk.*

Open Tues–Sun 9 am–5 pm, adm. The museum runs backwards, and
you should start on the second floor. In the second room are copies of the
cursed **coronation jewels**. The crown was designed on the instructions
of Charles IV for his new coronation ceremony. The original contains
the largest sapphires then known to Europe, and a hole to accommodate
the Crucifixion thorns that Charles had just acquired. The emperor also
established a tradition that it was to be stored on St Wenceslas's skull
between ceremonies. There's also the Wenceslas Sword, one of the links
to the older and more bizarre Přemysl coronation rite, in which the
prospective king would be presented to a peasant on a stone throne, who
would slap him about the face and then give him this sword to wave. The
busts of Charles and John of Luxemburg and spouses are visible copies
of those hidden in the triforium of St Vitus's Cathedral. The next room
contains various oddments from the period of the Hussite Wars, including a relief from the Bethlehem Chapel (see pp. 233–4) of an
inelegant bunch of Disciples, sprawled around a table and a very strange
main course. They're all about to polish off the *Last Supper*, which was an
artistic theme especially popular in the Hussite struggle to drink communion wine. The floor ends with exhibits related to the Battle of the

White Mountain, including a portrait of hapless Frederick of the Palatinate, painted during his doomed sojourn in Prague; as well as the engraving of the Vladislav Hall (by Aegidius Sadeler) mentioned on p. 124.

Opposite the museum is the palace that used to be occupied by the burgrave (castellan) of the castle. It's now the **House of Czechoslovak Children***, a useful public babysitting service (see p. 320). The building in which kids now romp used to house one of the castle's execution chambers. At the foot of the lane is the eastern gate of the castle, guarded by two more fidgeting boys in blue—in front of which are the* **Old Castle Steps** *(Staré zámecké schody). As you might expect, they're newer than the New Castle Steps which began the walk, although Na Opyši, curling away on the left is one of the original paths to the castle. Both routes take you down to Malá Strana, and you'll find the metro station some 20 m to the right. Each has its pros and cons: the road is quieter, but it's haunted by a headless driver with a flaming carriage; on the steps, you just might find a worthwhile souvenir among the junk.*

Walk II

Old Town Square and Jewish Quarter

Týn Church

Powder Tower—Church of St James—Old Town Square—Old Jewish Cemetery—Old-New Synagogue—St Agnes's Convent

Founded and fortified in the 13th century, the Old Town is the central European fantasy in microcosm, a topsy-turvy world of Baroque colour and Gothic gloom, public executions, legends and wonder-working rabbis. As you follow the centuries-old route to the market square, you'll shadow the life of the last Jewish storyteller of Prague, Franz Kafka, and then wander among the synagogues and ancient cemetery of the former ghetto itself. Its houses and lanes were demolished to make way for Art Nouveau mansions and avenues; elsewhere in the Old Town, history reeks from every stone, but in the Jewish Quarter, it's the transformation that speaks.

Start this walk by the early afternoon. The museums of the old Jewish ghetto close at 5 pm, and the latest that you can buy a ticket is 4.30; in winter the times are 4.30 and 4 respectively. The convent and gallery at the end of the walk are closed on Monday; on Saturday, the Jewish Quarter takes a rest. Fair weather is a bonus, although there are plenty of stops where you can take shelter from a storm. The southern Old Town is covered in Walk V, and one variation on the present walk is to continue to the Charles Bridge from the Old Town Square.

To **start**, take the metro (line B) or trams 5, 24 or 26 to Nám. Republiky

137

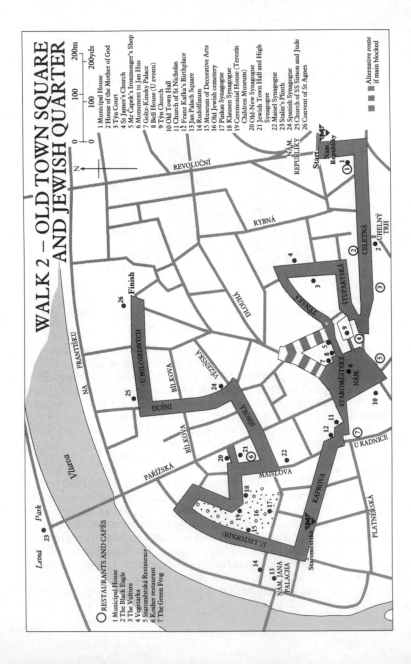

WALK 2 – OLD TOWN SQUARE AND JEWISH QUARTER

1 Municipal House
2 House of the Mother of God
3 Tyn Court
4 St James's Church
5 Mr Čapek's Ironmonger's Shop
6 Monument to Jan Hus
7 Goltz-Kinsky Palace
8 Bell House (U zvonu)
9 Tyn Church
10 Old Town Hall
11 Church of St Nicholas
12 Franz Kafka's Birthplace
13 Jan Palach Square
14 Rudolfinum
15 Museum of Decorative Arts
16 Old Jewish cemetery
17 Pinkas Synagogue
18 Klausen Synagogue
19 Ceremonial House (Terezín Children Museum)
20 Old-New Synagogue
21 Jewish Town Hall and High Synagogue
22 Maisel Synagogue
23 Stalin's Plinth
24 Spanish Synagogue
25 Church of SS Simon and Jude
26 Convent of St Agnes

○ RESTAURANTS AND CAFÉS

1 Municipal House
2 The Black Eagle
3 The Vulture
4 Vegetarka
5 Staroměstská Restaurace
6 Kosher restaurant
7 The Green Frog

Alternative route
if main blocked

(leave the station by the exit marked nám. Republiky rather than Masarykovo). At the **end** of the walk, you can get the same trams from Revoluční, or it's a short walk back to where you began.
Walking time: 3–4 hours.

LUNCH/CAFÉS

Eat and drink during the first part of this walk. There are refreshment stops beyond the Old Town Square, but they're fewer, further between, and more likely to disappoint. You could head back to the square at the end of the walk.

Obecní dům (Municipal House), next to the Powder Tower. Art Nouveau café (7 am–11 pm) and restaurant (11 am–11 pm); the latter serves meals all day.

U červeného orla (The Black Eagle), Celetná. A café popular among Czechs in tourist-free winter. Only serves cold food, but it's cosy.

U Supa (The Vulture), Celetná 22. 11 am–10 pm. This airy arched hall with its palm-tree fronds is a relaxing spot to stop for a beer; if there's no space, try the restaurant to the left of the main entrance. Sausages to go.

Vegetarka, Celetná 3. Mon–Fri 11 am–2.30 pm. Counter service, but the queue can be long. Vegetarian food, of the more uninspired variety, and it's been known for liver sausage and bratwurst to be the only dishes on the day's menu.

U Týna, Staroměstské nám. next to the entrance to the Týn Church. Prague's best coffee-shop, with 18 (largely alcoholic) varieties and a selection of cakes. Small, dark and smoky.

Staroměstská restaurace, Staroměstské nám. (south side). Summer 9 am–11 pm; winter 9 am–9 pm. Grab a seat in the bar, where you can get quick and juicy chicken pieces; or sit outside, where you can watch the square with a beer.

Kosher Restaurant, Maislova 18. (11.30 am–2 pm—see Food and Drink for evening opening times). Nothing to write to mother about, but it can be more interesting than average Czech fare.

☆   ☆   ☆   ☆   ☆

From nám. Republiky look for the ornate Art Nouveau façade of the **Municipal House** *(Obecní dům), built between 1906 and 1911 as an unusually successful contribution to the Czech national revival movement.*

The building stands on the site of the Gothic Royal Court, occupied by

139

Bohemia's monarchs for an unhappy century, deserted for several more, and finally destroyed in the early 1900s. Its replacement, with exhibition halls and auditorium, had the standard patriots' aims of edifying the masses; but unlike all the other dire architectural monuments of the revival movement, it came late enough to express itself in the language of Art Nouveau. As a result, exploring the building is a treat if you enjoy whiplash curves and organic excrescences; and the various sculptural and artistic homages to Czechdom and civic virtues hardly impinge on your enjoyment at all.

Between the wars, the building was the rendezvous for the nabobs of Czech-speaking society in Prague, and at the time of writing there's grim talk that at least part of the voluptuous interior will be transformed into a D-Mark- and dollar-consuming casino. It has never really been clear how much the unwashed public is allowed to see in the so-called Municipal House, but moderate self-assertion should leave you unmolested. Stride purposefully up the stairs and peek into as many rooms as possible. The entire building is a maze of cut glass and mirrors, around a lift shaft wrapped in gilt foliage, and each hall has its surprises.

Highlights include the Turkish delights of the absurd **Oriental Hall** (Orientalní sál); and the **Němcová Hall** (Němcová sál), which contains an Art Nouveau aquarium encrusted with brass snails. Next door is the glittering and inexplicable **Sweetshop**. In the circular **Mayorial Hall** (Sál Primátorský) are violet windows, and paintings by Alfons Mucha: examples of the sombre late work of the man who designed posters for Sarah Bernhardt and produced some of the most distinctive work of Parisian Art Nouveau during the 1890s. Rising through two floors at the core of the building is the **Smetana Hall**. Every year on 12 May, the Czech Symphony Orchestra arrives here hotfoot from a pilgrimage to the composer's grave in Vyšehrad (see p. 265); and the Prague Spring music festival bursts into life with a performance of his symphonic poem cycle *Má Vlast* ('My Country').

*Turn right from the main doors, towards the looming **Powder Tower** (Prašná brána), a Gothic hulk marooned in a 20th-century sea. Joined to the neighbouring Municipal House and confronted by the monumental 1930s façades of the State Bank and the Transport Ministry, it's a stately but forlorn witness to a glory that never was.*

Open April and Oct 10 am–5 pm, May–Sept 10 am–6 pm, adm. As long ago as the 11th century, traders with turbans, pelts, spices and slaves would roll into Prague from the east through a gateway here; and in the later 1200s, they were joined by *nouveaux riches* from the silvery boom town of Kutná Hora (see pp. 346–50), all on the way to Prague market. In 1475, King Vladislav II of Jagellon laid the foundation stone of this tower amid general festivities and merriment. He had just moved into the Royal Court next door, and the elated burghers of the Old Town had stumped up the money for the new tower as a coronation present. However, the Hussites were a mercurial crowd, and eight years later they hurled his mayor out of one window, and shot a death threat through his own. Vladislav beat a hasty retreat to the safety of Hradčany hill. The burghers stopped building. A century later, it was given a temporary roof, a use (gunpowder storage) and an unimaginative name; and in 1757, it was bombarded by Frederick the Great, and emerged in an even sorrier state than before. It was finally put out of its misery by the zealous neo-Gothic touch of the Czech Josef Mocker, and the ornate decoration of the façade, and much of the interior, is his work (1875–86).

The sad tower contains two levels. Pay at the first, after negotiating the treacherous spiral staircase. From the viewing gallery, there's a broad panorama over the New Town and a sneak preview of much of this walk.

> *Walk from the Powder Tower into Celetná, named after a medieval sweetmeat—bakers used to loaf around here. The street is one of the oldest in Prague. Behind the Baroque and Rococo façades are the remnants of earlier Gothic buildings; and below them, cellars that were buried along with the rest of the capital during the drastic flood-prevention programme of the late 13th century (see p. 63). However, the first notable building, on your left at the corner of Celetná and Ovocný trh, is a 20th-century Cubist curiosity, the* **Black Mother of God** *(U černé Matky boží).*

Designed by Josef Gočár, and built in 1911–12, the house is recognizable by the caged Virgin suspended above the portals, a 16th-century remnant of an earlier house on the site. Black Madonnas have long been a popular sideline of the Marian cult in Catholic Europe. When the house was built, Cubism was sweeping through Prague's artistic community, and Gočár was one of several Czech architects who hoped to use the principles of Braque and Picasso to restore volume and life to the façades of Prague's buildings without breaking the city's architectural traditions. The experiment sounds shocking, but tradition came out very much the winner; despite the recessed, angular window frames and two-tiered roof, the house slots almost perfectly into its Baroque neighbours.

*Continue along Celetná. Near the end, at No. 8, is an 18th-century
house called* **The Black Sun** *(U černého slunce).*

Prague lore would have you believe that, Madonnas apart, almost all the
black creatures who have adorned the city's houses over the years were
once occult talismans. This house's supposedly dark history goes back to
the 15th century, but the present sign, a sorrowful but splendid Mr Sun
gazing out of a Rococo cartouche, is more curious than furious.

> *Franz Kafka spent some unhappy childhood years living at Celetná
> 2 and 3. The latter is now a vegetarian café, which would have
> intrigued the author, a man who abandoned meat in 1910 and spent
> the rest of his life munching each mouthful of food a dozen times.
> The Old Town Square opens up in front of you, but for now double
> back and walk along Štupartská.*
>
> *At the Hotel Ungelt turn left down Malá Štupartská. To your left
> is the entrance to the* **Týn Court**, *or in German, 'Ungelt'. The
> courtyard looks like a construction site at the time of writing, but
> during weekdays you can snoop among the cement mixers.*

The name 'Týn' comes from the same Germanic root as the English
'town'; this courtyard, dating from the 11th century, was the enclave of
the eastern traders and formed one of the first settlements on the right
bank of the Vltava. It had everything—church, inn, and even a hospice in
which moribund merchants could expire in comfort. Quite why so many
businessmen came to Prague to die is an imponderable question, but
those who survived were a fun-loving crowd. Bohemia's kings knew that
merchants meant money, and after paying their duties (*Ungelt* in old
German), they were allowed to ignore Prague's laws. The consequent
licentiousness apparently led to Týn becoming known as the 'jolly
courtyard', and to at least one legendary murder, by a turbanned Turk
who is still occasionally spotted wandering around the court with his
sweetheart's head in a jewel-box. The fun lasted until the late 1500s,
when the traders upped and went to the Vladislav Hall and the more
abstruse pleasures of Rudolf II's castle; at which point Týn became the
idyllic hideaway that it's been ever since, cement mixers and restoration
notwithstanding.

The court is now a vertical accretion of centuries of building and at
least two years of debris. The Baroque and Renaissance houses are piled
onto Romanesque cellars that have been breached by rubbish chutes;
and paradoxically, while restoration remains incomplete, Týn is one of

the most tangible cross-sections of Prague's architectural history. Many of the buildings will apparently be turned into hotel rooms; but the future of the others is uncertain.

Weave through the machinery to the dignified **Granovský House**, *on the far right, built by the customs officer of Týn in 1560.*

The building is the grandest survival of the Renaissance in Prague other than the palace of Granovský's employer, Emperor Ferdinand I (see p. 216), but the paintings on its first-floor loggia haven't yet been touched by the restorers and are unrecognizable. If you see a Bacchanalian scene, *Justice*, or anything resembling the divine beauty contest of *The Judgment of Paris*, it means that work is under way.

Leave the Týn by the same door you came in. On the other side of the street is the **Church of St James** *(sv. Jakub).*

St James's, founded in 1374, escaped the overkill that turned some of Prague's churches into grotesqueries during the Counter-Reformation. Its interior is now one of the most elegant in the city, but it hasn't escaped the Old Town's stormy history. It was the target of iconoclasts in both 1420 and 1611, and was saved only by the courage and cleavers of the Butchers' Guild, whose history is intertwined with that of their church; while in 1689 it was ravaged by a huge fire, which destroyed about 800 houses in the area covered by this walk. By 1739, the interior and the façade had assumed their present appearance. The church vibrates better than any other in Prague, and its organ concerts are superb; the schedule is pinned up outside.

Above the entrance, rich stucco reliefs of SS Francis of Assisi, James and Antony of Padua crowd out of the wall. The nave is the second longest in Prague after St Vitus's Cathedral. The illusionists in charge of the Baroque reconstruction wanted it even longer, and tapered the galleries in the narrower bays of the chancel.

Although the Gothic proportions of the hall-church keep the 21 Baroque altars firmly under control, the splendid tableau of the **tomb of Count Jan Václav Vratislav of Mitrovice** (1714–16), tries its hardest to break free, at the far end of the northern aisle. Mitrovice was imperial chancellor of Bohemia at a time of strict control from Vienna, when the most important qualifications for the job were dull ambition and knee-jerk reflexes. He may have slipped out of the history books, but when the daunting late Baroque duo of Vienna's J. B. Fischer von Erlach and Prague's F. M. Brokof set to work on this monument, his posthumous fate was clearly seen in more elevated terms. Earthbound Sorrow is left behind as corpulent Jan, double-chins at peace and crucifix slipping from his grip, is tugged heavenwards by a delighted astronomical Muse; hoary Time states the obvious; and an angel, frozen in mid-inscription, has managed to scribble the important details—the name, office and achievements of Count Jan Václav Vratislav of Mitrovice.

None of the other decorations of the church can quite match the tomb. After a brief look at the ceiling frescoes (Life of the Virgin *and* Glorification of the Trinity) *and the* Martyrdom of St James *on the high altar, go to the left of the main doors, where you'll find a less carefully crafted monument to human folly.*

It's a scraggly **human forearm** hanging from a chain. The rag and bone is what's left of a bloodthirsty miracle that took place in 1400, when a thief tried to pilfer the jewels of the Madonna on the high altar. The Virgin would have none of it and grabbed his member, refusing to let go despite the prayers and pleas of church officials (who must have had interesting plans for the luckless villain). The limb eventually had to be lopped off, presumably by one of the congregation's cleavers, and has hung ever since as awesome testimony to Divine Justice. The painting on the wall depicts the memorable scene.

Turn right when you leave the church—next door is the Gothic cloister of the old Minorite friary of St James, with an adjoining Baroque Chapel of St Anne. Turn left at Týnská, which winds through to emerge under the looming chancel of the Týn Church. Crouched in the shadow of the northern façade are the dangling horseshoes and demented springs and attachments of **Mr Čapek's ironmonger's shop**—*one of the stranger sites even of a city in which you come to expect the unexpected.*

Grandfather Čapek founded the shack in 1903. It may look as though his descendants are still shifting the original stock, but the charmed enterprise has been raking in money ever since. For unknown reasons, it was the only family business in Prague to survive 40 years of Communism. Its arched door opens onto a collection of ersatz spare parts for Czechoslovakia's so-called consumer durables, and uncategorizable junk. At the time of writing, there's a comprehensive selection of cuckoo clocks, walking sticks and wooden crocodiles in the side room.

On the arched portal that towers next to the shop is a copy of a Gothic tympanum. The original, by members of Peter Parler's workshop, is in St George's Convent (see p. 127). Follow the northern façade of the church, which runs into the **Old Town Square** *(Staroměstské náměstí); if restoration is not yet over, you can turn left from the shop along Týnská ulička, and then left again along Dlouhá.*

The square is the Brothers Grimm in stone. Gothic towers, a sparkling white church and a pastel wave of pink and blue Baroque rooftops provide the location; and like the Jew-baiting and sadism of central Europe's unexpurgated fairytales, its history is sunk in blood and guts. The merchants of Týn unpacked their wares here from the 12th century onwards, and until the beginning of this century, stalls filled the square. But it was the sideshows that proved its true status. Romping stomping Wenceslas IV threw open-air parties in the square until the Old Townies imprisoned him in 1394; in 1600, scholarly Dr Jessenius (an ancestor of Kafka's epistolary lover, Milena Jesenská) astonished silent crowds of thousands as he fiddled with a corpse during the world's first public dissection; and the square's capacity meant that it played host to all the most significant state killings of Bohemian history. Nowadays, the square—closed to traffic for over a decade—is the strolling intersection of the Old Town, and the perfect spot to soak up rays, history and a beer on a summer's day. (You can pick up a drink to go from the *pivnice* just around the corner of Dlouhá.)

The best place to get an overview is from the steps of the **Monument to Jan Hus**. Heretical Hus was burnt alive in 1415, and his death marked the beginning of decades of war in Bohemia. Two centuries later, his Protestant heirs were eradicated at the Battle of the White Mountain; but although the population reverted in droves, Hus never lost his position as the pre-eminent symbol of Czech nationalism. In 1900, as the Austro-Hungarian empire doddered towards extinction, Prague's authorities commissioned a monument to their man, in preparation for the 500th anniversary of his martyrdom. The artist chosen was Ladislav Šaloun, whose lifelong attachment to Art Nouveau techniques (until 1946) placed him outside both the mainstream and the avant-garde of Czech sculpture; and when this sculpture was unveiled in 1915, it was predictably showered with abuse. It shows Hus flowing from the bronze base, standing tall between two groups representing the crushed and the defiant. Some complained that Šaloun had created a sprawling mess, by letting his fascination with light effects run away with him; others found the very idea of allegory too disrespectful, although it's doubtful that they would have preferred Hus to be portrayed as the bald midget that he is thought to have been. However, the very fact that Šaloun was commissioned shows that the municipal arbiters of Prague taste were slowly coming to terms with the 20th century. Compare the work with the digified pomp of the St Wenceslas Monument (see p. 222), unveiled only three years before.

A bronze line in front of the sculpture marks Prague's former meridian. A Marian column, erected in 1649 to celebrate the Bohemian Counter-Reformation, sent its midday shadow along here until it was toppled by a patriotic mob in 1918. With independence, Prague gave up the increasingly inconvenient tradition of calculating its own time. In the north-east corner of the square is the rinky-dink **Goltz-Kinsky Palace.**

The dainty building dates from 1755–65, by which time Prague's Baroque frenzy had begun to exhaust itself. This is one of the best examples of Rococo architecture in the city, with its frilly stucco garlands and pink and white façade demanding no more than an approving coo from passers-by. Kafka studied here from 1893–1901, and the family connection was resumed some years later when his father, no-nonsense Hermann, moved his haberdashery store into the ground floor. But its moment came in February 1948. A vast crowd gathered here to hear Czechoslovakia's first Communist president, Klement Gottwald, roar from the balcony that the dictatorship of the proletariat had arrived. The masses cheered back and paid the price—every year workers were herded back here to celebrate their emancipation, until Victorious February was thrown into the dustbin of history in 1989.

The palace now houses the National Gallery's collection of 19th- and 20th-century drawings and prints. The permanent exhibition on the first floor is closed for restoration at the time of writing, but temporary exhibitions of graphic art are held on the second floor (open Tues–Sun 10 am–6 pm).

Go to the **Bell House** *(U zvonu), to the right of the palace.*

The creamy façade, stone bell set into the corner, belongs to the oldest intact Gothic house in Prague. It was built in the mid-13th century, and Emperor Charles IV is thought to have lived here as a youth—but you won't find it on any photographs older than a decade. Thorough remodellings after the late-1600s meant that only in the 1960s did restorers realize what lay within the then unremarkable neo-Baroque house. The onion-skins were peeled away, the thousands of fragments pieced together or reconstructed, and the house was opened to the public in 1986. It's now used for concerts, and the city's most consistently excellent exhibitions of contemporary art. It will be closed if there's nothing on, in which case check the notices outside for the dates of the next event.

The Gothic tower, fronting what is now a Renaissance courtyard, is the richest part of the building, but you'll find fragments of murals, pointed doorways and ribbed vaults throughout. The most complete decoration is in the chapel to your right as you walk towards the courtyard, once entirely covered with murals of the Passion (c. 1310). On the first cross-vault are symbols of medieval Christianity, including the bloody pelican, charitably dunking beak into breast to feed her squawking brood. The second chapel, on the first floor, was built some 30 years later. Flanking the former Crucifixion scene of the niche altar are two reliquaries. The first suppliant was quite likely to have been relic-obsessed Charles himself: the date fits, and the sun at the centre of the nearby vault was an especially favoured symbol in the hermetic vocabulary of the future emperor, who mused in his Latin diary (7 July 1339) that 'no body created bears so clearly the traces of the Holy Trinity as the sun'. The cheeky Dionysian orb, wrapped in vine leaves, was also a representation of Jesus in his various alcohol-related personae (true vine, wine press, blood donor, etc.).

Next door is one of the airy halls of the building, with a translucent view of the square from the graceful tracery of the reconstructed windows. After taking in the watery panorama and wandering through the other exhibition rooms, turn left as you leave the house. The next building is the Týn School, its 16th-century façade falling and rising in bulbous imitation of the church that it fronts, the **Church of Our Lady Before Týn** *(Kostel Panny Marie před Týnem)—abbreviated to the Týn Church.*

The multi-steepled towers of Týn bristle like Gothic missile batteries and dominate the square; but they emerge from behind the school, which has given rise to dark tales of Catholic conspiracies. The church was the hub of Hussitism right up to the 1620 rout; and although the Hussites were by then a minority among Bohemia's Protestants, it is said that the Jesuits decided to humiliate Prague by hiding its former parish church behind a house. In fact, the school and its even more obtrusive neighbour were originally Gothic buildings, and appeared around the

147

same time that the church was founded (1385). Their later reconstructions were just par for the course in Prague. Týn created its own problems; it was founded on a self-effacing earlier church and just grew, adding the spires over a century later. The legend may have arisen because of the alterations that the Jesuits really did make. As well as the almost sensible decision to melt down a Hussite statue and transform it into the Madonna that now stands between the towers, the monks melted down the bells because they had been given Hussite nicknames, and then recast them into identical copies. To put the fetishism of the monks into context, it is worth remembering that this was a time when bells couldn't be touched by women or any non-cleric over the age of puberty. The lead spires with their countless golden prongs are an aerial signpost throughout the Old Town, but few ever notice that the tower on the right is significantly broader than its neighbour. That's the result of yet more ancient madness. Medieval rules said that a fat male tower had to protect a slim female tower from the midday sun.

Enter the church (usually open from 4–5 pm) through the passage running from the vaulted arcade. After a fire in 1679 the central vault was rebuilt in Baroque style. The altars and decorations are also largely Baroque, but even more than in St James's, they are swamped by the cavernous Gothic structure of the triple-naved church. At the end of the northern nave, past the 1493 stone baldachin (which now canopies a 19th-century altar) and the tombstone of the dwarf to your left, is a powerful Gothic Calvary of around 1410. From here, cross the central nave. Walk across the high altar, and on the pillar to your left, you'll find the **tomb of Tycho Brahe** *(1546–1601), Emperor Rudolf II's imperial mathematician for two eventful years.*

The red marble relief is relatively flattering. It hardly hints at the gold and silver nosepiece worn by the moustachioed Dane ever since he lost most of the original organ in a duel. Brahe was one of the most colourful men in a court that was hardly dull. He had an unnerving habit of coming up with doom-laden astrological prophecies—he once predicted that Rudolf would share the fate of France's Henry III, murdered by a monk, sending the emperor into terrified isolation for months. His own day-to-day activities were conducted according to the Delphic utterances of Jeppe, a homuncular lunatic whom he placed under the table at mealtimes (no relation to the pygmy whose tomb you've just seen). Nothing became his life so much as his manner of leaving it, the result of over-drinking at a feast when a combination of self-control and a polite reluctance to leave the table caused his bladder to implode. His death, five days later, doesn't really bear thinking about. However, when the aforementioned Dr Jessenius gave the funeral oration, he dwelt at great length on the fate of both bladder and nose—an interesting comment on the mentality of an age, and more particularly, on that of anatomically-minded Jessenius himself.

Near Brahe's tombstone, at the end of the southern nave, is the oldest font in Prague, a tin pot dating from 1414. The Gothic pulpit on the next pillar to the west dates from the 15th century, although the painting and canopy are 19th-century additions. It was from here that rabble-rousing preachers incited generations of congregations to sprees of destruction. Near the pulpit is the rich foliage and drapery of the early-16th century **carving of Christ's baptism** by Master I. P., a Dürer-influenced artist whose work is also exhibited at St George's Convent (see p. 129).

> *There's a smoky coffee shop under the arcade just to your left as you leave the church. At No. 15, on the corner of the square and Celetná is* **The White Unicorn** *(U bílého jednorožce), the site of Prague's one and only true* salon *at the beginning of the century.*

The *saloniste* was one Berta Fanta, an intellectual magpie who led the capital's turn-of-the-century thinkers on a trek that ranged from Nietzsche to the lama-trained theosophist and psychic, Madame Blavatsky. Among those who attended the Tuesday meetings were Albert Einstein, who outlined his theories to the group while he taught in Prague between 1911 and 1912; Max Brod, who nodded in awe and based his novel *Tycho Brahe's Path to God* on questing Albert (although he cast the scientist as a relatively rational Johannes Kepler); and, drumming his fingers on the table, an increasingly impatient Franz Kafka. Kafka chewed, and fretted over his bowel movements endlessly, but he had a mordant appreciation of other people's obsessions. Berta Fanta's philosophical shopping-list eventually became too much for him; but in 1911, he attended a series of talks by anthroposophist Rudolf Steiner, who had come to Prague to speak on 'Awareness of Higher Worlds'. Kafka's extremely limited record of the lectures ran not much further than

> Mrs Fanta: 'I have such a poor memory.'
> Dr Steiner: 'Don't eat eggs.'

> *Cross the square to the tower of the Old Town Hall (see p. 228). The houses that line this side of the square, like those of Celetná, are built*

over older subterranean houses; and at the White Horse (U bílého koníčka), through the Gothic arcade at No. 20, you can writhe in a Romanesque disco from Tues–Sun. As you approach the tower—the interior of which is covered in Walk V—you'll see the sharp oriel window of its chapel, dating from the later 14th century and pieced together after the Nazis reduced it to rubble in 1945. The plaque marked 'DUKLA' contains a pot of earth from a 1944 battle between the Nazis and Soviet/Slovakian forces; and to the right is a memorial to an earlier watershed in Czech history, the executions of 21 June 1621, which took place on the site of the 27 crosses painted on the ground.

After the Battle of the White Mountain, Emperor Ferdinand II wasted no time. The big fish of Bohemian nationalism were put on trial; Viennese judges pondered the evidence and sentenced them to death. A scaffold was set up on this spot, and a grandstand constructed for those nobles lucky enough to find themselves on the right side. The square was shrouded in black and the drums began to roll. The appointed day began portentously—crossed rainbows were seen in the sky—but the executions went like a dream. Dr Jessenius was among those who got their comeuppance, and in a terrible echo of his most celebrated moment, he was virtually dissected himself: tongue extracted, decapitated, then quartered. Mydlář the Axeman was such a virtuoso that Praguers (who have celebrated their national humiliation with gusto ever since) took him to their hearts almost immediately. The hooded hero is still an integral character in the packed universe of Prague childhood. Mydlář plucked and amputated with legendary precision, and according to an English sightseer, the 24 decapitations were performed, 'with great dexterity, not missing one stroake, as if the winde had blowen their heads from their shoulders'. Ten of the unluckiest heads were piked and suspended over the Old Town Bridge Tower for a decade. When Protestant Saxons temporarily occupied Prague in 1631, they piously reburied the grinning ten in the Týn Church, as startled workmen found during restoration in 1766. However, all 27 martyrs apparently still come here on the night of the anniversary, on a rather futile hunt for their many other missing appendages.

Next to the town hall is the burnt-out shell of a pink neo-Gothic stump, which used to stretch across to the bright southern façade of St Nicholas' Church (sv. Mikuláš) in the north-west corner. It was a part of the town hall obliterated by Nazi tanks on 8 May 1945, a week after the suicide of Hitler, and on the same day that western Europe was celebrating VE-Day.

The last fighting on the continent took place in Prague. On 5 May 1945, the city rose up against the Nazis; a week and up to 5000 dead Czechs later, the Soviets arrived in Prague. There seems to have been none of the chicanery that surrounded the Soviet betrayal of the Warsaw Uprising; but US forces—who were within easy reach of the capital—stood idle so as not to breach the terms of the Yalta agreement.

Eight competitions have been held since 1945 to find a way of filling the hole. Endless Stalinist temples and monumental schemes were proposed, but fortunately, even the competition organizers seem to have been unnerved by them, and no one ever won. It's now hard to imagine that anyone would have the nerve to rob the square of its sunbathing green.

Walk towards the **Church of St Nicholas***. Since 1920 it has been used by the Czechoslovakian Hussite Church, re-established as the official creed by early 20th-century patriots.*

The church, backing into the square with its cluttered southern façade, two towers, and the rump of a chancel, is a lop-sided charmer. When built in 1735, it was respectably covered by a very large building and commanded the dim alleyways of the Jewish ghetto. To see it as it was designed to be seen, sidle along about 3 m from the watchful saints and pretend that you're locked in on all sides.

Walk to the end of the southern façade and turn right. The church was stripped of its original decoration when it and its accompanying monastery (now demolished) were turned into storage space by Emperor Joseph II. The most impressive feature is the dome, hovering on a squared-off drum. Walk to the corner of Maislova. The neo-Baroque mansion between church and street stands on the site of the former clergy house of St Nicholas'. The town scribe is said once to have lived here, and suitably enough, it was also **Franz Kafka's birthplace** *in 1883.*

Only the Baroque portal survives from the house that heard baby Franz's first scream. As astute walkers will have begun to suspect, the author spent almost all his life within this square mile. He once stood near here, tracing with his finger while telling a friend, 'This narrow circle ...

encompasses my entire life'; and he wrote his final story as he lay dying in a flat over the Old Town Square, 'the most beautiful setting that has ever been seen on this earth'.

Kafka's bleak and incomprehensible world never fitted neatly into the progressive literary canons of the Communists, i.e. happy endings. Although the small bronze bust of the jug-eared author appeared during the cultural thaw of the 1960s, only since 1989 have his works been freely available again. No one is very sure what is going to happen to this house. It's being remodelled at the time of writing: logic, Prague's cultural heritage, and the profit motive all suggest that it should be transformed into a museum; the capital's uncertain tourist authorities think that it will become office space.

> *Some 10 m to your left on U radnice is a small restaurant called* **The Green Frog** *(U zelené žáby).*

Frogs were once all the rage on this street; two other houses were named after the black and the golden varieties. Mydlář the Executioner used to unwind in this one after a hard day's chopping. Popular as Mydlář was, there were time-honoured taboos surrounding messy jobs, and this was the only hostelry in the Old Town where he could snatch a bite. Even here, he had to slink in through a side-door and sit in a separate room along with the town's animal skinners. If you ask politely you'll be shown the dim chamber in which he used to amuse his fellow pariahs, and the hole in the wall through which he could share anecdotes and pithy observations with the admiring, but respectable, burghers of Prague. You could even make a reservation, and have a meal under the axe-head chandeliers.

> *Take Kaprova, ahead of you veering right, the 20th-century successor of an ancient route which led from the market to the Vltava ford. It leads into* **Jan Palach Square** *(nám. Jana Palacha), opening up onto the river embankment and a view of distant Hradčany Castle lounging across its hillside retreat.*

At the time of writing, the square is being given a thorough facelift. It has been through a lot in recent years. In mid-1945 it served as a temporary burial ground for Soviet soldiers who fell during the liberation of Prague, and was renamed Red Army Square (nám. Krásnoarmějců)—an understandable decision, but not to the thousands who gathered here in January 1969 to mourn Jan Palach. Another generation of the Red Army had invaded Prague, and Palach had just burned himself to death in protest. The crowds tore down the street signs and renamed the square after Palach, who had studied at the grim Philosophy Faculty, facing the river. The change didn't last, but in November 1989, students were again in control of the square, and their strike headquarters were in the faculty building. The street signs were repainted; the huge star-shaped tulip bed in the centre was uprooted and (with rather unfortunate irony) turned into a symbolic grave of Communism; and after a Velvet Revolution, and a polite petition, the square was re-re-re-renamed and Palach was officially honoured for the first time since his death. The young man's handsome profile, made from the death mask secretly cast by the Czech sculptor Olbram Zoubek, was unveiled by Václav Havel in January 1990. It was promptly removed by the redecorators; but if work has finished, you should be able to find both the bust, and the plaque that was simultaneously and generously unveiled to honour the Soviet war dead of 1945.

Turn right along 17. listopadu.

This street—17 November—is one of the few roads in Prague renamed by the Communists which has survived. It commemorates a student demonstration in 1939 during which the Nazis shot dead several protestors. In November 1989, students held an officially sanctioned demonstration to mark the event—and then used the rally to attack the government, in the belief that the authorities wouldn't risk the analogies of using force. They didn't give a damn: the police used batons, and within a month the government had been overthrown. As a result, the street now recalls both 1939 and 1989.

Cross Široká. On your left is the Rudolfinum, home of the Czech Philharmonic Orchestra, and the country's inter-war parliament; on your right, you'll come to the **Museum of Decorative Arts** *(Uměleckoprůmyslové muzeum).*

Open Tues–Sun 10–6, adm. The museum was founded in 1885, inspired by the English Arts and Crafts Movement's dream of elevating public taste in the industrial age. At the time of writing, only the first floor is open, but the collection is a sumptuous one indeed: four rooms of household and palace furnishings from the Renaissance through to the mid-19th century. The work includes escritoires and cabinets inlaid with gemstones, a technique imported from Milan by the Miseroni

153

family, invited to Prague by mineral-mystic Emperor Rudolf II; and timepieces by Erasmus Habermel, who had promised Rudolf the secret of perpetual motion. The rooms also contain Baroque bureaux and chests, pumped into fat curves by the same men who were designing Prague's 18th-century churches, such as K. I. Dienzenhofer and G. Santini (see pp. 69–70). The porcelain—a material which fascinated the 17th-century alchemists of Prague and Europe, according to Bruce Chatwin's *Utz*—includes works from Meissen, the first European factory to unlock the thousand-year old Chinese mystery; and from Munich and Vienna, produced after treacherous Dresden workers swiftly spilled the beans. Pewter pots, cobalt jugs and fussy teacups are scattered throughout, and the tapestries include Gobelins. The collection ends with the stark furniture of 18th-century neo-classicism, rediscovered by the Functionalists of the 1920s, and ornamented neo-Rococo work of the mid-1800s.

On the second floor is one of the largest glass collections in the world. It's closed at the time of writing, but the work begins with 14th-century Bohemian glass (which got off to a flying start under the patronage of Charles IV, another gem-fanatic) and runs through Venetian Renaissance glasswork to Art Nouveau and 20th-century pieces.

The huge holdings of the museum also include over 30,000 posters, as well as collections of photographs and interior design, often the excellent work of the Czech inter-war avant garde. None of that is yet on display, but temporary exhibitions are held, and it is hoped that a permanent space will be found soon.

> *When you leave the museum, turn right, and then right again when you reach U starého hřbitova. Follow the blank grey wall to your right. You're now walking into what remains of the* **Jewish ghetto** *of Prague.*

No one knows when the first Jews came to Prague. Even ghetto legend, which generally had an answer for everything, was unclear about precisely which lost tribe had made their way here. It often set the date at some point between the Exodus (*c.*1300 BC) and AD 33—a period which gave the community a watertight alibi to charges of Christ-killing—but folklorists sometimes settled for about 135, when the Jews had been expelled from Palestine. Even the last date precedes the arrival of the Czechs by about four centuries. Historical sources suggest that the 10th century is closer to the truth; and it's thought that Jews first lived in two separate communities on either side of the river. By the mid-13th century an unhappy set of events had combined to create a single community here. Přemysl Otakar II wanted the left bank for his new town of Malá Strana (see Walk III); the Old Town was fortified; and most importantly, the Church in 1179 had announced that Christians should avoid touching Jews, ideally by building a moat or a wall around them. Another set of walls was accordingly built within the Old Town; and three centuries before the word was coined in Venice, Prague Jews began ghetto life.

The daily routine was much the same as that of Jews elsewhere in central Europe—pogroms, ritual murder allegations, and occasional banishments from the land (on many occasions in the early 16th century, and in 1744–48). By day movement was free, but as the sun set, the portcullis would be lowered. The gates would be locked throughout the Easter/Passover flashpoint. Jews didn't mind, as it kept out the crowds eager to avenge Jesus on Good Friday; but the authorities' concerns were no different from those of the mob. Medieval Christendom generally assumed that the Passover lamb was a cunning codeword for Christ; and that unless the gates were locked, Christian babies and virgins would end up on a Passover plate.

During the 16th century, the ghetto became a vortex of Jewish mysticism, as interest in the cabala grew among both Jews and Christians throughout Europe. The mysterious cabalistic tradition—handed down orally from Adam—was reflected in the intellectual search of Rudolf II's Mannerist court, and the exchange of cryptic data between rabbis and castle scholars became legendary. The period was to inspire a powerful image of the ghetto as a dank universe of miracles and poverty; its 7000 inhabitants living cheek-by-jowl in a shadowy labyrinth of cramped lanes, subterranean passages and hypertrophied buildings. There's more than a little truth to the picture, but although the ghetto was sealed, it wasn't all poor. The richest man in Rudolfine Prague was Jewish.

In 1784, under Emperor Joseph II, the gates were thrown open. Joseph, enlightened despot that he was, was being liberal only in an academic sense. The idea was to wipe the Jews out as an independent community: the use of Hebrew or Yiddish in business was prohibited, and separate schools were banned. That didn't stop him being honoured after 1848, when Jews were finally granted civil rights (Charles IV had made 'imperial serfs' of them in the late-14th century). The former ghetto was formally incorporated into Prague in 1850 and renamed Josefov, as it is still known. Integration proceeded apace—rich Jews moved out, poor Christians moved in. By the end of the 19th century, the district had become a set of 288 stinking slums, brothels and bars, a breeding ground for typhoid and tuberculosis. The authorities could have repaired the buildings, but they chose to destroy them, along with an irreplaceable part of Europe's history. Broad streets, filled with crowds of Art Nouveau buildings, now stand over winding medieval alleys. Of the old ghetto, only six synagogues, the town hall and the cemetery were spared, and still survive thanks to Hitler's macabre decision that they would house a post-war 'Exotic Museum of an Extinct Race'. Of the Jews themselves, some 80,000 of the 90,000 who remained in Bohemia and Moravia in March 1939 were killed.

After the war, the government took over the Nazi collection. It is hard to see what else could have been done, but the Communists proved unworthy custodians. A monument to a destroyed community was loaded with propaganda exalting the role of the Communists during the war, and incredibly inappropriate attacks on Zionism. After 1989, the stooges who had been appointed to run the museum were ousted (the chief rabbi was found to have been on the payroll of the secret police), and the 800–1000-strong Jewish community which remains is taking over the administration of the collections from the state. It's a messy process, and very incomplete at the time of writing; but it should mean that many more of the treasures in the storerooms are eventually put on display.

One ticket lets you in to all the sections of the Jewish Quarter (open April–Oct 9 am–5 pm, Nov–Mar 9 am–4.30 pm, Sun–Fri; last tickets sold 30 minutes before closing). They're sold at the booth which you'll see when you reach the end of the wall, otherwise at the High Synagogue, 100 m down the road. Guided tours are theoretically on request, although there's a reluctance to escort groups of one.

Next to the booth is the entrance to the **Old Jewish Cemetery** *(Starý židovský hřbitov, known in Hebrew as* Beth-Chajim, *or the House of Life).*

The Jewish graveyard, the oldest in Europe since the 1938 destruction of that in Worms, is an astonishing sight—a flash of a lost world that imprints itself on your memory. For over three centuries until 1787, it was the only burial ground permitted the Jews, its elder trees the only patch of green behind the ghetto walls. As space ran out, it was covered with earth, older gravestones were raised, and a new layer of burials was

Jewish Cemetery

begun. Subsidence has turned the graveyard into a forest of some 12,000 madly teetering tombstones. Many are half-interred themselves; many have migrated far from the person they commemorate; and as you walk through, there are thought to be some 20,000 people under your feet, buried in up to 12 subterranean storeys.

The tombs are marked with the name of the deceased and the deceased's father (for women, also that of the husband), usually with verses pointing out some especially good things about the proprietor. The many hieroglyphs include the benedictory hands of the Cohens, the anointing jugs of the Levites, and other respectable symbols born out of the Talmud's rigid division of Israeli labour; but the gravestones are also peppered with figures, and even the occasional portrait. As far as the Talmud was concerned, that was the first step towards the Golden Calf. The freethinking Enlightenment is a partial explanation of the idolatrous experiments, but no one really knows what came over the ghetto Jews.

Descendants, moon-struck lovers and superstitious types leave scribbled wishes, and pebbles, on the graves. Placing stones is a custom unique to this cemetery, and no one knows how it arose. Legend provides the only suggestion: it claims that the tradition dates back to the Exodus from Egypt, when only rocks were available to mark desert graves. The cracked vaults themselves probably contain more desperate prayers; when the Nazis ripped up Jewish cemeteries elsewhere in Europe, their gruesome harvest often included treasures hidden in broken tombs by Jews whose transportation papers had arrived.

*The oldest known plot is that of poet **Avigdor Kara**, dating from 1439. In 1389, Kara lived through and lamented the most vicious pogrom in Prague's history, in which 3000 were massacred—over half of the ghetto's inhabitants. His gravestone is marked on the path running along the eastern wall of the cemetery; it's a copy of the original which has been moved into the Klausen Synagogue.*

*On the southern edge of the cemetery is the **Pinkas Synagogue** (Pinkasova synagóga), which stands over the 11th-century foundations of what may have been the first synagogue in Prague.*

Rabbi Pinkas began the present building on this site in 1479, apparently after a dead monkey stuffed with gold coins had been hurled through his window. A man nicknamed Munka (coincidentally) enlarged the synagogue and constructed the late Gothic vault in 1535; and in about 1625, it was given its present Renaissance façade.

The first Jews of Prague may have worshipped on this spot, and after the war, the synagogue was chosen to house the Czech memorial to the victims of the Holocaust: under the vault are listed the names of each of the 77,297 Czech Jews who died at Nazi hands. The synagogue has been closed for years, but is due to reopen in the late summer of 1991. You'll then be able to check for yourself one of the very few rumours attached to the Communists that is almost unbelievable—that they decided to plaster over the memorial during restoration.

*Follow the western border wall from the synagogue. Just before it turns to the left is the grave of **Rabbi David Oppenheim** (1664–1736), whose 5000-volume library eventually went on a tour across Europe, and made it to Oxford's Bodleian in 1829, where it now forms the Oppenheimer Collection. If you turn right at the path and then right again, you'll find the grand tomb of **Mordechai Maisel** (1528–1601), the mayor of the ghetto during the reign of Rudolf II.*

Maisel had to wear a yellow star like any Jew in Rudolfine Prague (the badge was an intermittent requirement throughout the ghetto's history) but he died one of the wealthiest men in Europe. His will made dispositions amounting to 17 million gulden, at a time when five would buy a fattened ox. Jewish lore claims that young Maisel was an honest urchin who found a gold coin in a ghetto alley, and tracked down the wealthy rabbinical owner. The proud rabbi wasn't pleased, as he had put it there after a trio of goblins had told him that it would be retrieved by his future son-in-law. But prophecies were prophecies, and the ragamuffin moved in; the goblins eventually returned with several treasure chests, and rabbi, daughter and Maisel lived and died happily ever after. Others claim that Maisel made his fortune thanks to the trading monopoly granted him by Rudolf II.

The best-known of all the cemetery's occupants, the subject of tales which are still told to awestruck New York children, is **Rabbi Loew ben Bezalel** *(1512–1609). His tomb, inundated in pebbles, is along the western wall, roughly opposite the entrance gate.*

Loew, born in either Poznań or Worms, was one of the leading scholars of 16th-century Jewry. Most of his life was spent in Prague, and in 1597, he took over as chief rabbi of the ghetto; by the time of his death, he was already a legend. The stories surrounding his life—the most famous of which is his golem, a cabalistic precursor of the Frankenstein monster— are detailed in the Visionary Prague section of this book; but his powers apparently extended even beyond the grave. He's surrounded by 30 faithful disciples, among whom is his grandson Samuel. Solemn Samuel set his heart on being buried next to his grandfather; Loew vowed that he wouldn't be disappointed. Bungling ghetto authorities filled the precious plot with another lucky corpse—but dead though he was, Loew had not forgotten. When Samuel expired, the rabbi and his sepulchre budged a couple of feet. Samuel's grave is the thin one on the left.

After leaving the cemetery, turn left into the neo-Romanesque **Ceremonial House**, *built in 1908.*

The two rooms contain an exhibition of children's artwork and poetry recovered from the Terezín (Theresienstadt) ghetto in 1945 (see Day Trips from Prague). During the earlier years, clandestine classes for the children were organized (often by Jewish Communists), but over 80 per cent of the 140,000 people who passed through were to die. The childhood scenes, disfigured by grimacing figures and black skies, have an eloquence that defies description.

From the exhibition, make your way to the **Klausen Synagogue** *(Klausova synagóga) on the other side of the entrance to the graveyard.*

The late 17th-century synagogue (remodelled in 1884) was built on the site of a mess of schools and prayer halls, supposedly where Emperor Maximilian I began a ghetto walkabout in 1571. Rabbi Loew taught in an older building. As well as initiating Samuel and others into the secrets of the cabala, he practised his new-fangled pedagogical theories on the ghetto children. Loew believed that the familiar was a better starting-point than the unfamiliar, and that the general would be more easily understood than the particular, which in the 16th century would probably have thrown his classes into utter confusion. The synagogue now houses a small museum devoted to the history of printing and literature in the ghetto, which began in 1512 when the world's first printed Hebrew book was published here.

> *Continue along U starého hřbitova until you come to Maislova, and the nose-diving roof of the Old-New Synagogue across the road. Opposite is the wooden clocktower of the* **Jewish Town Hall** *(Židovská radnice). The Town Hall is still used by Prague's dwindling Jewish community, and contains a restaurant (a few metres along Maislova).*

It was donated to the ghetto by rich Mayor Maisel in 1586. Originally Renaissance in style, it was given a Rococo revamp in 1765, when the tower and the clock below it were also added. The lower clock has Hebrew figures; and just as the Jewish alphabet is read from right to left, its hands turn backwards.

> *Cross the road into the narrow alley between the Old-New Synagogue and the Town Hall.*

Next to the Town Hall is the **High Synagogue** (Vysoká synagóga), built in 1586 with a remodelled interior dating from the 19th century. It now contains a small museum of Jewish textiles, some from the 16th century, but most far newer; almost all were confiscated from families and synagogues during the war.

> *From the High Synagogue, enter the* **Old-New Synagogue** *(Staronová synagóga) , one of the oldest to survive in Europe, and still used by Prague's Orthodox Jews.*

There are two explanations for the synagogue's name. One very prosaic offering is that it was coined when the building was newly constructed on an older synagogue; but Jewish legend springs to the rescue with the claim that *Alt-Neu* ('Old-New' in German) is actually a corruption of *Al-Tenai*, or 'with reservation' in Hebrew. Angels and/or outriders of the Diaspora are said to have constructed the synagogue from the rubble of the last Temple in Jerusalem, which they carried over in about AD 135. The name stands as a reminder that when the Messiah finally arrives, Prague's Jews have to take it back.

Unless the legend is true, the synagogue appeared around 1270. The date was about a decade before the level of the Old Town began to be raised; and as you enter, you sink several feet to the level of (not quite) antediluvian Prague. The first chamber is the vestibule, containing two chests for the collection of taxes; and through the door on your left is the section where women are segregated during services. A sign asks men to cover their heads before entering the main hall. There are no temporary coverings available but you can use anything, including this book. The gorgeous Gothic tympanum over the portal, a stylized tree, is a symbol of vitality, but its sections also represent the three continents of the world then known to Europe.

The splayed chinks of light, and the pillar supports, show how much the synagogue owed to Romanesque building techniques; but the vaulted naves, and the slenderness of the octagonal pillars themselves, represent the beginnings of Gothic architecture in Prague. The simplicity of the new features shows the influence of the Cistercians, who like their very different Baroque successors, the Jesuits, were tireless monastic messengers of an austere early Gothic style throughout the continent. The Order had a masonic lodge in Prague, and architectural experts claim that the monks hewed and toiled with the Jews to build this synagogue. It sounds an unlikely scenario, particularly since the fifth rib of the vault, a feature unique in Bohemia, is thought to have been installed specifically to avoid the defiling symbol of the cross.

In the centre is the *almemar* (pulpit), surrounded by a 15th-century wrought-iron grille. Rabbi Loew apparently fought his final and most heroic battle here, when, alerted by a dream, he hurried to the darkened synagogue and found an apparition waving swords, dripping with gore, and ticking off a list of all Prague's Jews. 96-year-old Loew realized that this was Pogrom personified, and lunged for the beast. He ripped the scroll from Death's bloody grip, saved the ghetto from extinction, and missed only a scrap containing his name.

The banner above the *almemar* was a present from Emperor Ferdinand III, after Prague's Jews, preferring the devil they knew, fought off Protestant Swedes in 1648; they had been honoured with flag rights by Charles IV over 200 years earlier. On the eastern wall is a screen covering the Torah (the scrolls containing the Pentateuch, i.e. the first five books of the Old Testament), in front of which are four messy cushions, where the rabbi used to circumcise wailing infants. The Hebrew psalms on the walls date from 1618, and were recovered in the 1960s, after Josef Mocker (see p. 72), had obliterated them during so-called restoration in 1883. Among the other features which ham-fisted Mocker restored to oblivion were the bloodstains of those who barricaded themselves in the synagogue during the 1389 pogrom. For 500 years the unwashed walls had been a memorial to those elegized by Avigdor Kara, 'destroyed in the House of God by the bloody sword of the enemy'.

After leaving the synagogue, make a minor detour to the small adjoining green. It contains Moses (1905) by the Czech sculptor František Bílek, one of the few Baroque-influenced works by the artist; and from here you can contemplate what lies behind the 14th-century bricks of the Old-New Synagogue's roof.

Rabbi Loew's golem (whose full name was Joseph Golem according to Jewish legend) eventually ran amok, as man-made creatures do, and went on a rampage through the synagogue. Loew was holding a service in the synagogue when he heard the news; and after consulting the scriptures to work out whether golems could be deactivated on the Sabbath, he went stalking Joseph and eventually turned him back to clay. Suitably chastened by his dabblings with the laws of creation, he announced that he would never make another golem; lifeless Joseph was taken up to the steep brick roof, and has apparently been there ever since.

Interweaving mysteries still shroud the loft. Several curious rabbis are said to have sneaked up during the 19th-century, all, needless to say, returning white as sheets and dumbstruck; the journalist Egon Erwin Kisch audaciously claimed to have been up and found nothing during the 1920s; and yet synagogue officials now make the mysterious claim that the keys were lost two hundred years ago.

Retrace your steps to Maislova and turn left. For most of the rest of the walk you'll still be in the area of the old ghetto, but little more remains. Under the streets there are reputed to be hundreds of passageways and rooms, silent oubliettes and medieval refuges. The evidence only emerges piecemeal during building-work and is invariably destroyed, but as you walk through the intimidating bourgeois façades, you can't help but hear whispers from the past.

*Cross Široká. On the left is the **Maisel Synagogue**, another of the mayor's gifts to the ghetto, but remodelled in neo-Gothic style at* *the end of the last century. It should contain the museum's silver collection, but has been closed for several years.*

Walk back to Široká and turn right. Art Nouveau-enthusiasts will find plenty to admire throughout this part of town. Walk along until you reach Pařížská. If you look to your left, you should be able to see a massive concrete pedestal on top of Letná Park. In 1955 a 30-m high **statue of Stalin** *was unveiled here, its gaze fixed along Pařížská into the Old Town Square. As you'll notice, it's no longer there; on its fate hangs a tale, which you'll find on p. 102. Cross Pařížská and continue along Široká to the junction of Vězeňská and Dušní. On the corner to your left is the last of the synagogues to survive the great tidying-up of 1897–1917—three were destroyed, along with some 30 smaller prayer halls. It's the the Moorish-tinged* **Spanish Synagogue** *(Španělská synagóga), the last reminder of the Sephardic Jews who settled in this part of the Old Town after their mass expulsion from Spain at the end of the 15th century. They took over an ancient synagogue on this site, but this building dates from the end of the last century, and is now a very closed repository of the Jewish museum.*

Turn left down Dušní. On the corner with U Milosrdných is the Church of SS Simon and Jude. At the time of writing, the interior is closed, but its net-vault sounds to be an example of Prague's tenacious use of Gothic motifs into the early-17th century. Mozart and Haydn played on the organ in its heyday. The Baroque front, along with that of the one-time hospital next door, dates from the 1750s— follow the apricot façade as it sprawls unevenly along the street to your right. As you cross Kozí, you enter one of the loveliest parts of the Old Town. The small houses and cobbled lanes, bathed in a sleepy hush, are a tantalizing glimpse of what a restored Josefov might have become. On your left you'll come to the entrance to **St Agnes's Convent** *(Klášter sv. Anežky), which houses the National Gallery's collection of 19th-century Czech painting.*

Open Tues–Sun 10 am–6 pm, adm. The oldest remaining Gothic building in Prague, the former convent was founded by King Wenceslas I in 1233, on the urging of his sister Agnes (Anežka) who had just signed up with the Order of the Poor Clares. In 1235 she became the first abbess of the new convent; and in 1990, Pope John Paul II told Prague that he had just canonized her (presumably because he didn't want to arrive empty-handed on his first trip to post-Communist Czechoslovakia).

The Poor Clares were a sister-community to the Franciscans; and like bees to a honeypot, the friars arrived next door in about 1240. Nuns and monks cohabited happily for some 500 years, until stern Joseph II demanded that Prague's religious orders show what purpose they served. Poor Clares and Franciscans were mendicants, and as a result entirely useless. They left in 1782, and over the next century, hundreds of stray families moved in, as well as a fair proportion of Prague's tortured-artist community—until in the 1890s, slum clearance loomed. Patriots declared that it was a matter of national pride that the convent be restored, and set up a fund for the purpose. The occupants were swiftly ejected; restoration was completed in 1980.

> *Walk through to the vaulted arcade around what was the convent's cloister. Turn left and walk clockwise. The cloister dates from about 1360. The first arcade is the best preserved, but throughout the convent, the modern restorers have struck a happy balance between architectural non-intervention and confident reconstruction where necessary. After you've walked three sides of the court, turn left through the narrow passage into the oblong nave of the convent's* **Church of the Holy Saviour** *(Kostel sv. Salvátor), dating from 1240.*

King Wenceslas I's wife is buried under the slab, but years of hopeful pottering have as yet failed to unearth Agnes herself. Ahead is the presbytery (1270–80). On the capitals of the arched entrance are miniature heads of Bohemia's Přemysl kings (left) and queens (right). The building was the first in Bohemia to take up the lessons of French Gothic cathedral architecture—on a tiny but sublime scale. Light floods in through tall arched windows with simple tracery, under a high and graceful ribbed vault.

> *Walk back through the arch. To your left is the presbytery of* **St Francis's Church***: it was built some 70 years after the Holy Saviour, but the nuns had no time for the grandeur of late Gothic and stuck with the simple formula of their pocket presbytery. King Wenceslas I (not the Good one) is buried here, and the chamber also contains a plaster model of the National Theatre, for no apparent reason. A door leads to the the old Franciscan monastery, undergoing restoration at the time of writing. The rest of St Francis's is the oldest part of the convent, but now offers little to see; and the adjoining St*

Barbara's Chapel, rebuilt in Baroque style after the 1689 fire, is a cloakroom.

Go back to the arcade of the convent, turn right and take the marked staircase to the first floor, which houses the **National Gallery's collection of 19th-century Czech painting.**

The nationalist revival of the last century produced some terrible art. The subject matter tended to be noble peasants and the more specific myths of Bohemian history; the techniques were those of a country that had been a province for too long. The collection is worth a brief visit; the period is an important one in Czech history, and you've already paid your admission fee.

The first room is devoted to the greatest names of the national revival movement. The Mánes family dominates—as well as lifeless landscapes, father Antonín produced a brood of artistic offspring. Josef Mánes (1820–71) represents the pinnacle of patriotic striving, blending vegetable matter, folksy motifs and the disingenuous simplicity of neo-Gothic art into sub-neo-Raphaelite cartoons that even the most illiterate patriot could feel warm about. While whizzing through the room, look out for the work of Karel Purkyně, which has got a certain tortured realism about it. Rooms 17–20 display the work of the 'National Theatre generation'. These heroes of the movement were firm believers in the unity of art and architecture and many worked on the Municipal House (see above). Mikoláš Aleš (1852–1913), whose cartoons and sketches get a whole room, was particularly active, and his work defaces almost every turn-of-the-century public edifice in Prague. The last rooms contain works of other Czech painters active at the end of the century.

By now, you'll probably need a stiff drink. There's a vinárna *next to the convent's entrance, but the waiters often put up a 'Reserved' or 'Full' sign when they feel like a rest. You could try your luck even if the sign's there; Prague's service industry respects bare-faced cheek. Otherwise there's an excellent restaurant,* U červeného kola *(see p. 279), on Anežská; and if it doesn't have room, you could just wander around the dreamy streets until you find yourself on the way to the hurly-burly of the Old Town Square.*

WALK 3 – MALÁ STRANA

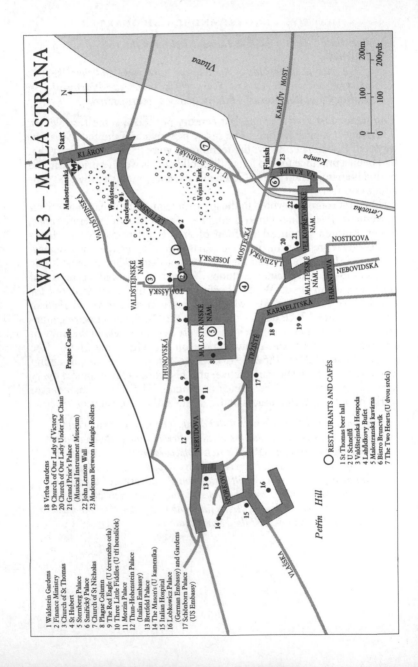

1 Waldstein Gardens
2 Finance Ministry
3 Church of St Thomas
4 St Hubert
5 Sternberg Palace
6 Smiřický Palace
7 Church of St Nicholas
8 Plague Column
9 The Red Eagle (U červeného orla)
10 Three Little Fiddles (U tří housliček)
11 Morzin Palace
12 Thun-Hohenstein Palace (Italian Embassy)
13 Bretfeld Palace
14 The Mason's (U Kamenníka)
15 Italian Hospital
16 Lobkowicz Palace (German Embassy) and Gardens
17 Schönborn Palace (US Embassy)

18 Vrtba Gardens
19 Church of Our Lady of Victory
20 Church of Our Lady Under the Chain
21 Grand Prior's Palace
22 John Lennon Wall
   (Musical Instrument Museum)
23 Madonna Between Mangle Rollers

○ RESTAURANTS AND CAFÉS

1 St Thomas beer hall
2 U Schnellů
3 Valdštejnská Hospoda
4 Lahůdkový Bufet
5 Malostranská kavárna
6 Bistro Bruncvík
7 The Two Hearts (U dvou srdcí)

Walk III

Malá Strana

Waldstein Gardens—Church of St Thomas—Church of St Nicholas—
Nerudova St—Lobkowicz and Schönborn Palaces—Vrtba Gardens—
Church of Our Lady of Victory—Kampa Island

Sloping from the castle to the left bank of the Vltava, Malá Strana's
swirling canopy of orange tiles and chalky-green domes covers one of the
finest Baroque preserves in Europe. The quarter was founded way back
in the 13th century, but a fortuitous fire and the Thirty Years War
cleared out the rotundas and Gothic clutter just in time for the arrival of
the carpetbaggers of the Counter-Reformation. This walk explores their
schemes and dreams: from the Jesuit church of St Nicholas to
the gardens of General Waldstein, all glorious tributes to the power
of money and architecture. You'll follow Catholicism on the march,
tracking down the apparently ceaseless interventions of the Virgin Mary
and the *Bambino di Praga*, a miraculous effigy that's now venerated by
millions in Latin America. The walk takes you through the hills and
gardens of a quarter that can have an almost spooky beauty, with all the
luscious and peculiar flavours that you'd expect of a Baroque chocolate
box.

It's the best of all the walks in this book for a Monday, as it contains
only one museum (of musical instruments), which is facing a very
uncertain future. It **starts** at Malostranská metro station (line A), also

167

accessible by trams 12, 18 and 22, and **ends** at the Charles Bridge.

Walking time: 3 hours, at an average idling pace.

LUNCH/CAFÉS
Some of Prague's most picturesque restaurants are scattered along this route, but most are only open for dinner (see Food & Drink). One idea is to make a reservation and begin this walk in the late afternoon; but by far the best option is to prepare a picnic, which you can unpack in the silent woods behind the Lobkowicz Palace. Otherwise, the recommendations are limited. The best stops are the smoky beer rooms on Nerudova, but at the time of writing, almost all are due to be reclaimed and probably transformed by their pre-war owners. Praguers expect them to become pricey bar-cafés, which may be a mixed curse; the street is worth investigating. Otherwise the following places will keep the wolf from the door.

U sv. Tomáše (St Thomas's), Letenská 12. 5–11 pm. One of Prague's best-known and oldest beer halls, with all that that entails—crooners, the occasional polka, and droves of homesick Germans. The walled garden is open in the summer.

Malostranská kavárna (Malá Strana Coffee Bar), in the middle of Malostranské nám. 7 am–11 pm. Sometimes serves simple cold dishes, i.e. cheese, ham, desserts. The summer terrace is a pleasant spot for a break, which will probably be longer than you expect, given the abysmal standard of service.

U Schnellů, Tomášská 2. 11 am–3 pm and 4.30–11 pm. Pilsner lager and rather dull Czech cooking.

Valdštejnská hospoda (Waldstein Inn), Valdštejnské nám. 7. 11 am–3 pm. Fairly formal restaurant, with a satisfying lunch menu, including poultry and fish. Reservation essential during the summer. Slightly off the route of this walk.

Lahůdkovy Bufet (Snack Buffet), next to Malostranské nám. on Mostecká street. 9 am–8.30 pm. Counter service. Sandwiches, hot meals and soups, beer. Cheap, no frills—but you'll eat something, quickly, which can be a godsend in high season.

U dvou srdci (The Two Hearts), U lužického semináře 38 (opposite the Vojan Park). 3–11 pm. Cheap beer (Smíchov) and sausages.

☆   ☆   ☆   ☆   ☆

The name Malá Strana translates roughly as 'Lesser Quarter' or 'Little

Side', and is a reminder that the district is something of an upstart compared to the rest of town. Until the 13th century, it was little more than a collection of isolated villages, tucked between the Old Town of Prague and the Romanesque castle. A monkish band of the Knights of St John kept themselves to themselves in the area around Prague's stone bridge; further south in Újezd, a Jewish settlement worshipped and buried its dead at a cemetery and synagogue that have long disappeared; and a limpet-like community around a market on the lower reaches of the fortification walls eked out an existence from the wealth of the castle on the hill. A few more centuries of urban sprawl might have given birth to a natural town, but ambitious Přemysl Otakar II didn't have the time to wait. In 1257, he issued a general invitation to German merchants to set up shop in Prague, hoping to strengthen the economy and his claim to the crown of the Holy Roman Empire (see p. 39). With the exception of the monks of St John, the locals were rounded up and expelled, and an entirely new Gothic settlement was built. This 'New Town' became 'Malá Strana' a century later, when Charles IV needed its original name for his new urban development.

The German merchants couldn't avoid the religious shenanigans of their Czech neighbours in the Old and New Towns for long. Malá Strana was almost literally wiped out at the very beginning of the Hussite Wars in 1419; and by the time it had recovered in the next century, it had been drawn squarely into the politicking of central Europe. The Germans got Lutheranism, nobles moved in to be close to the castle, and in 1541, a huge fire raged through the left bank. Property-hunting vultures of every faith descended onto the smoking plots, and Renaissance palaces and houses rose from the ashes.

A century later, Malá Strana's second mass expulsion took place. The Habsburg victors of the Thirty Years War ejected thousands of heretical losers from their new domain, and handed over vast tracts of confiscated land to the soldiers, monks and flunkies who were to complete the Bohemian Counter-Reformation. Fanatics and time-servers turned the winding and hilly streets into one of the most splendid towns of 17th- and 18th-century Europe. For 300 years, Malá Strana was the provincial playground of the Viennese nobility—and then the toffs lost out as the result of another war. The palaces were snatched in the name of the working class by the Communists in 1948, and many were indeed partitioned into apartment blocks; others were turned into embassies (Malá Strana is full of young suits in a hurry). The last twist in the tale was the restitution law passed in 1990. Pre-war merchants and impoverished nobles have been tramping back, statute in hand, to collect 40 years of back-rent and reclaim their properties.

No one really feels for the embassies, and there's considerable sympathy for at least the humbler victims of the thieving Communists, but many fear that the *restituce* will be a death-blow to the community. The Communist housing policy, if not egalitarian, was at least random, and over the years schizophrenic sculptors, war widows and workers have all found themselves allocated crumbling Baroque apartments in Malá Strana. Amidst the tourists and diplomats, children play on the cobbles, corpulent men in string vests gaze out of 18th-century attics, and everyone goes down the local *pivnice* for a beer in the evening. It's all going to change as the yuppy bars and antique shops move in. Rents are rising, privatization is beginning, and the inevitable exodus to the cheaper suburbs is sure to come. However, the eclectic community is one of the tightest-knit in town, and even if it's doomed, the nobles *et al.* will be hard-pressed to transform it by the time you start this walk.

The walk begins in the modern fountain courtyard of Malostranská metro station. At the far end, on the left, is the Riding Hall of the Waldstein Palace, which hosts temporary exhibitions, generally of modern foreign art. Leave the courtyard through the door leading into busy Klárov. Under the weeping willows of the green in front of you are two reminders of the most recent violence to have touched Malá Strana. One is the grave of a fighter who died during the 1945 Prague Uprising, one of thousands of similar memorials dotted around the city. The other marks the spot where an engineering student, Marie Charousková, was shot by a Soviet soldier in 1968 for refusing to open her tool-box. She was one of about 100 Czechoslovakians killed during the Warsaw Pact invasion, but at the time of writing, hers is still the only death to be commemorated.

Walk to Letenská and turn right. About 100 m along, the rumbling street sheers off to the left, diverted by a 10-m high blank wall. The screen is the first hint that you're about to enter what was once a very exclusive place indeed. Through the wooden arch are the **Waldstein Gardens** *(Valdštejnská zahrada), a majestic maze of beech hedges, gravel paths and gurgling fountains lazing under the silhouetted spires and halls of Prague Castle. They're now an idyllic summer retreat from the overheating city, as well as a monument to* **General Albrecht Waldstein** *(1581–1634)—the most epic megalomaniac that Prague has ever produced.*

Open May–Sept 9 am–7 pm. Waldstein belongs to the dubious band of men whose influence on Europe is difficult to exaggerate. Friedrich Schiller turned his life into *Wallenstein*, a three-act tragedy, and the general himself was one of the first to recognize his genius. According to his earliest biographer (1643), from the moment when, at the age of 21, he fell off a window ledge in Innsbruck and found the Virgin Mary swooping to the rescue, he 'made it the study of his life to penetrate the future and to discover the high destiny that awaited him'. At its peak, that destiny took him to the command of the combined Catholic armies of the Thirty Years War; and at its end, it left him bedridden with gout, declared a traitor by the empire he had saved twice, and ignobly dispatched by the dagger of an Irish dragoon.

Waldstein made the most of his opportunities. The first came when he landed the widow Lucretia in 1609. She was so hideous that his hagiographer anxiously had to explain that she had slipped the general a love potion. Although that was a gallant attempt to silence the rakish whispers aroused by the general's lifelong lack of *affaires de cœur*, it seems clear that Waldstein was firmly in control when he popped the question. Lucretia was seriously rich—and when she did what wealthy widows should, and caught the plague five years later, the general buried her in style and scooped up a windfall. A second big break came in 1618. While his countrymen were lobbing Emperor Ferdinand's men out of Prague's windows, Waldstein threw in his lot with the imperial cause. The defenestrators were executed; Waldstein snapped up confiscated lands for a song, and was put in charge of the imperial army, which he led through a decade of almost continuous victories over motley Protestant forces. But he was no employee. He provided the army to Ferdinand under a series of lucrative contracts, and with the help of an inflated currency scheme and manic organizational skills, Waldstein soon became the largest creditor of the Habsburg empire. Without the money to pay his general, Ferdinand had to reward him with other assets. Lands and honours poured through his hands, culminating with a princedom in 1627. To his already formidable powers, only the least of which was the right to legitimize bastards, he could now add the privilege of handing the emperor a napkin after he had used his fingerbowl, and all but unlimited control over a vast fief in northern Bohemia.

Ferdinand's Jesuit advisers already loathed Waldstein for his pragmatic attitude to a war that they saw as a crusade, and to many, the fact that he could now keep his hat on while chatting to the emperor was the last straw. The intrigues intensified, until in 1630 Waldstein was relieved

171

of his command. It was too late—his superbly run army had become indispensable. When Saxon Protestants retook Prague the following year, Ferdinand hastily recalled his champion, and appointed him generalissimo of the imperial forces. An almost omnipotent Waldstein finally decided to slip the leash. He began to negotiate with the enemies of the empire, and in January 1434, launched open mutiny against Ferdinand. Historians have spent the last three centuries discussing his reasons. Few doubt that he wanted to be king of Bohemia, but the riddle is whether he had been a Bohemian nationalist all along, whether he grew into one, or whether he was a power-mad traitor. The nuances didn't really matter to Ferdinand, and the *dénouement* unfurled. As Waldstein crossed northern Bohemia in a crimson litter, looking for the allies who were suddenly and mysteriously fading away, Vienna's churches were put on alert and ordered to pray, for 'a matter of the first importance'. Four days later, placards appeared across the city blaring that the legendary Waldstein was to be taken dead or alive. The noble renegade's game was up, and he and the commanders who remained loyal to him were finally done to death by Scottish and Irish officers in the town of Cheb. Assassination without trial was still considered rather outrageous, and the crocodile emperor did his best to distance himself from his dastardly deed. As Waldstein's Golden Fleece was returned to him, he murmured: 'They painted him blacker than he was'; and the general's name echoed out of history in the 3000 requiems that Vienna's overworked churches were now commanded to say for his errant soul.

Waldstein's character oozes out of both his garden and his palace. When this complex was built between 1623 and 1629, on the site of 23 houses, three gardens and the municipal brick kiln, he supervised every stage of the work. A man who laid down dietary rules for his army's sick chickens wasn't likely to leave his Milanese architects to their own devices.

From the entrance, turn left and then right towards his magnificent terrace, or **sala terrena**, *through the* **avenue of sculpture** *by Adriaen de Vries (1545–1626).*

These green-streaked deities were among the last works to be produced by Netherlands-born de Vries, who died before completing his master's commission. The sculptor studied in Florence under Giovanni Bologna, the master of Mannerist sculpture, and the figures here show the refinement and elegance typical of both men's work. The themes were inspired by the Italian Renaissance's rediscovery of the classics; but the Mannerist fascination with graceful movement appears throughout. It's most evident in de Vries's version of *Laocoön* on the left, which shows the punishment inflicted on the Trojan family by the Greek contingent on Mount Olympus, after Laocoön Snr had threatened to spoil the gods' fun (he had warned that the big wooden horse outside the gates wasn't to be trusted). The work was inspired by a late-Hellenistic antique that had set Europe's artists a-twittering ever since its rediscovery in a vineyard in 1506. The Italian Renaissance had approved of the ineffable grandeur with which those characters had struggled with their snakes, and the Baroque was to seize on the work's emotion and gore—but this sophisticated composition, twisting and straining with a stylized anguish, stands neatly between the two approaches. Waldstein particularly favoured de Vries's work; not only did it give his palace a distinguished touch, but the man who would be king savoured the fact that de Vries's last, and very proprietorial, Prague patron had been Emperor Rudolf II, until his abdication in 1611.

None of the statues are original. Waldstein's former subordinate and fellow turncoat, Hans von Arnim, left the palace untouched when his Saxon army occupied Prague in 1631–32; but the Swedes were less respectful when they took the city 17 years later. The removal men of rapacious Queen Christina carted the sculptures to Drottningholm Palace, where they remain today, and these works are copies, dating from the beginning of the 20th century.

The path of sculptures ends with a fountain of Venus, cast by a Nuremberg sculptor in 1599, beyond which is Waldstein's terrace.

De Vries's sculptures represent the transition between the harmony of the Renaissance and the dynamism of the Baroque. In a very different way, the terrace (1623–30) also shows the beginnings of the new style. Its Milanese architect Giovanni Pieroni followed the 16th-century rules of proportion to the letter; but the sheer size of these gaping arches and doubled Doric pillars left their spirit far behind. Waldstein clearly appreciated the triumphal possibilities of Baroque architecture, but his greatest tribute to his own genius lies under the stucco vault, in the **frescoes of the Trojan Wars** (1629–30) by Baccio Bianco. Apart from Aeneas, staggering off to found Rome with his father on his back, the assembled heroes and damsels are dressed in the contemporary dress and armour of Waldstein's war. The capricious gods lounge around on the cloudy ceiling, but the general had more faith in himself than in any humdrum deity. He is a dead ringer for ginger-haired Achilles, and on the ceiling of the main hall of the palace, he had Bianco paint him as Mars, riding to war under a dark star.

> *In a small salon on the left as you face the* sala terrena, *the general and his second wife (the reputedly less ugly Isabella von Harrach) would dine in the summer, under more heroic frescoes of the Argonauts' quest for the Golden Fleece. It's closed at the time of writing, as is the grotto on the opposite side, which contains a door leading to what was once Waldstein's observatory. The general's astrological obsessions were another part of his fatal flaw, and an essential component of his elevation to tragic hero by Schiller. The best place to contemplate them is at the* **grotesquery** *on the southern wall of the garden. It runs behind a cage containing two* **peacocks**, *which are often claimed to be descendants of proud Waldstein's collection. They're probably a 20th-century introduction, but the aviary is original, and used to house 400 songbirds.*

The general would stare at this wall and listen to the warbles when the pressures of devastating Europe became too much. Grottoes had become popular across the continent during the later 1500s, and this pendulous foliage, growing tumour-like into a mass of hidden faces and shapes, reflects Waldstein's mystical pursuits. He had spent some years studying in Padua, a hotbed of the quasi-sciences of the day, and his unorthodox interests were well known even during his lifetime. He had converted from tepid Lutheranism to lukewarm Catholicism, a fairly conventional step for the social climbers of the day, but many of his enemies muttered darkly that he had long since pawned his soul to the devil—a rumour fuelled by the black hound that he was apparently seen to consult prior to major military manoeuvres. The general took any diabolical secrets he may have had to the grave, but his astrological mania was public knowledge. He had mundane stargazers scattered across his dominions, and seemed to have hit the jackpot in 1628, when Ferdinand asked him to look after the imperial mathematician, Johannes Kepler (see p. 98). The emperor had little use for the Lutheran son-of-a-witch, to whom he owed 11 years' back pay and who had fled his proto-Counter-Reformation in Styria back in 1600; but Waldstein hoped that the scientist would be a particularly reliable source of inside information as he planned his future. Unfortunately, it wasn't to be. Kepler had long been nagged by doubts as to how powerful planetary aspects really were, and his only comprehensive analysis of the general's fate was something of a deconstruction of astrology. It contained the news that 'the applicant is full of superstition' and warnings that to act on a horoscope was 'arrant nonsense', even though all that the general wanted to know was whether he would die of apoplexy and the star-signs of any enemies that he might have. However, the imperial mathematician was still sufficiently impressed by something that he saw to mention that March 1634 boded ill; the comment turned out to be a very veiled reference to Waldstein's murder in February of that year.

> *At the opposite end of the garden is the Riding School (see p. 249) and a pool around a sculpture of Hercules, another copy of a work by de Vries. When you leave the gardens, turn right down Letenská, past the Finance Ministry on your left, home of Thatcherite minister Václav Klaus. The suitably granite façade is an extension of a complex which belonged first to the Barefooted Carmelites and then to the Order of the English Virgins. On the right is U sv. Tomáše (St Thomas's), once owned by the beer-drinking hermits of the friary that you are about to see, and still serving the descendant of the dark concoction that they first brewed in 1358. After the road bores through a building, turn right and you'll come to the entrance of the* **Church of St Thomas** *(Kostel sv. Tomáše), built for the friary of Prague's Augustinian hermits, whose one-time* **cloister** *is next door.*
>
> *The friars arrived in 1285, and left five centuries later when Joseph II purged the empire of its 'unproductive' elements, which included most religious orders and all hermits. The entrance to their hidden cloister is on the left as you face the church. It's now an old people's home, but non-geriatrics are welcome. The door is usually open during the day, but if not, have a word with the porter, through the window on the left of the vestibule.*

The present courtyard was built in the later 1600s, but several of the tombstones that line the first arcades date from the reign of Emperor Rudolf II, a century earlier. St Thomas's was the favourite church of the thinkers and drop-outs who hovered around his court, although the emperor himself steered clear of the friary, having developed a general fear of cowls ever since stargazing Tycho Brahe warned him that Death would come in the form of a knife-wielding monk. Among those buried here is an Englishwoman, Elizabeth Jane Weston, whose slab is at the end of the first arcade. She was just one of the more permanent of the colourful English contingent who drifted through Rudolfine Prague. Weston had personal contacts with most of the ex-pat community, and was apparently educated by Elizabethan England's most outlandish contribution to the city, the earless necromancer and alchemist Edward Kelley (see pp. 95–7). Little Elizabeth seems to have escaped his more baleful aspects, and by the time of her early death in 1612, at the age of 30, she was widely regarded as one of the most talented humanist poets in central Europe. Her fame has withered since, perhaps because she wrote all her verse in Latin. A better remembered English visitor was the poet Sir Philip Sidney, who returned to warn the Virgin Queen that Rudolf was 'few of wordes, sullein of disposition & extreemely Spaniolated'; and the most spectacular was Sir Anthony Sherley, swashbuckling emissary of Shah Abbas. His camel train rolled into an awestruck Prague three times, giving rise to folk legends that would last for generations, as Rudolf mulled over his proposal for a Habsburg-Persian alliance.

The two Renaissance portals (1596) in the next arcade lead into a Gothic hall that was once part of the friary, but they're closed to the public. Return to the street and take a brief look at the late Baroque façade. It looms over the tiny cul-de-sac, demanding a level of respect that the humble alley can't muster. The church's architect, K. I. Dienzenhofer, had begun to think in epic terms, and both its front and interior are grandiose trial runs for his later works. If the church is closed, try sweet-talking the sacrist; the bell is near Weston's tombstone.

The powerful nave of the church, its stucco arches driving towards a sunlit chancel, is decorated with frescoes (1728–30) by Václav Reiner. They show Reiner's typical use of blocks of colour and monumental figures, and depict the life of St Augustine, formerly Bishop of Hippo, from his late baptism to his ascension. The hermits' hero made important contributions to early Christian thought, notably that Original Sin was transmitted through sexual intercourse. (He had the benefit of hindsight, having had a son by a mistress of 15 years' standing.)

Stern Augustine once said that 'beauty cannot be beheld in any bodily matter'. It's something that even confirmed hedonists might stop to contemplate under the third set of piers, where you'll find the skeletons of St Just and the Blessed Boniface crammed into glass cabinets, topped with two happy cherubs, and gripping the Augustinian emblem of a flaming heart (religious passion).

The brighter side of Prague Baroque returns under the **dome**. It dates from the late 1720s, just before Kilian Dienzenhofer was to start work on the eastern end of the Church of St Nicholas (see below). Light floods through the hidden windows around the dome and down from the cupola, illuminating more frescoes by Reiner. Produced later than his frescoes of St Augustine, they show a deliberate attempt to limit the exaggerated proportions of his earlier work. The fresco inside the dome seems to be of the *Resurrection*, and at the base are the *Four Corners of the World*: dark Africa, censer-waving and sensual Asia, crowned and learned Europe, and a shimmering, savage America with her then-traditional severed head and reptilian cayman. The easternmost frescoes are of St Thomas, whose legend culminates with the painting of his murder by savage Madrasis above the high altar. That, and *St Augustine* above, are copies of works by Rubens; the originals are in the National Gallery (see pp. 209–10).

> *A small vaulted passage from the northern aisle is a remnant of the Gothic basilica that was replaced by the present church. It contains some delicate Gothic frescoes, and leads to the sacristy (which is closed to the public). From the church, return to Letenská and turn right. The next street on the right (Tomášská) is haunted by the best-known of Malá Strana's many ghosts, the skeleton of a cuck-olded ironmonger who is still looking for someone to remove the nail that his wife drove into his head one night. At No. 4 is an example of Prague's Baroque sculpture at its most melodramatic, F. M. Brokof's* St Hubert, *kneeling above the doorway.*

Hubert was a huntsman before he became a saint, and converted when he spotted a crucifix between the antlers of a deer that he was stalking. The passion of the legend sounds difficult to convey, but Brokof was undaunted, and has invested the eyeball-to-eyeball meeting of man and stag with an emotion that's almost unseemly.

> *Retrace your steps the short distance to Malostranské nám. (Malá Strana Square).*

This area has been at the centre of left-bank life for a millennium. Prague's first market is thought to have stretched from here in the direction of Tomášská street to the outer bailey of the castle, and when the Jewish merchant Ibrahim Ibn-Jakub sang the praises of the bargains to be found in Prague in 965, it was the stalls here that he had seen. A rotunda in the middle of the square confirmed its growing importance, and with the foundation of Malá Strana in 1257, the square assumed full municipal functions. A parish church (consecrated to St Nicholas) and a town hall joined the rotunda, and for three hundred years the most exciting things to happen in the square were ritual humiliation (the pillory stood on this corner) and strangulation (gallows on the next one up the hill). However, its history hotted up, quite literally, after 1541. The fire that destroyed most of Malá Strana and Hradčany in that year began in the **Sternberg Palace**, the second building over the arcade rising up the hill; and less than a century later, an even more far-reaching conflagration was sparked off in the **Smiřický Palace**, next along. On 22 May 1618, Albrecht Smiřický invited his noble friends around to discuss what to do with Ferdinand II's hated Catholic governors. They plumped for a defenestration, carried it out the next day, and the Thirty Years War began. Albrecht himself died in the same year, and in a good example of the convolutions of Malá Strana title deeds, the eventual recipient of the traitor's estates was traitor-to-be General Waldstein, whose grandfather was a Smiřický. The generalissimo is recorded as having said that the worst mistake that the nationalists ever made was to throw the governors out of a window instead of stabbing them. It's a mysterious comment, but it is interesting to note that he had survived one of these fates, and was to perish by the other.

> *On the corner of Letenská is a Renaissance building over an arcade, now known as the* **Beseda** *('Meeting Place'). It's now a rather sorry music club, the haunt of hairy guitarists and lost trendies; but between the late 1400s and 1784, it was Malá Strana's town hall. Towering over the square is the Baroque mass of the* **Church of St Nicholas** *(Kostel sv. Mikuláš) and adjoining one-time* **Jesuit College**. *All of Malá Strana now revolves around the odd couple of the tower and dome of the church. The Jesuits would have appreciated the compliment, but their enjoyment of their masterpiece was sullied by endless problems, of which their conflict with the town hall over the* **tower** *is a case in point.*

The Jesuits were given the old church of St Nicholas in 1623 by fanatical Ferdinand II, who was dishing out newly-vacated places of Protestant worship to almost any monkish zealot who was prepared to fight the good fight, and with particular alacrity when it came to the Spaniards, who infested his Viennese court. The Order planned to build a new church and college from the outset, but this complex took years to get off the ground. The first problem was that the overstretched Order was impecunious. With the long-term vision of good monomaniacs they clung to their dreams, until in 1653 they were able to present the town hall with firm plans. Serious dispute then arose about who owned precisely which pieces of the architectural jungle in the centre of the square. The crucial stumbling block was an old Gothic tower, standing roughly where the present one is today. The monks hoped to turn it into a belfry, but the councillors angrily claimed that it was Malá Strana's venerable fire post (and a useless one, judging from the blaze that had started a few feet away in 1541). Work stalled for another 20 years, until in 1673 the cunning monks promised to build the town an even better watchtower if they could start work on their church. The council agreed and the monks swiftly set about destroying the tower, school, vicarage, former town hall, two churches and street full of cobblers that had occupied their land. Eighty years later, this tower rose almost as an afterthought to the completed church—and the mendacious monks connected it to the church and planted saints on it. The sculptures briefly stood on the now-empty pedestals on the corners of the tower. An aggrieved citizenry removed them, locked the door, and until 20 years ago, the tower—which looks to be part-and-parcel of the church—was one of the most unusual flats in the capital.

The Jesuits' tribulations didn't end there. They put the finishing touches to their church in the 1750s, and had hardly settled in when their Order was placed under a worldwide ban by the pope in 1773. It had served its purpose, and was becoming a little too powerful for the European establishment's liking. The monks found a refuge in Catherine the Great's Russia, but although the Holy See let them start up again in 1814, they were never to return to Prague. In a neat little turn, St Nicholas' then became the parish church of Malá Strana.

Make your way to the church, which exudes the confidence and ideology of Prague Jesuitry at its height. Cross the square and turn right just past the Malostranská kavárna. The front door of the tower is at No. 29 (556 according to the older system of numbering), and is marked by the crest of the jealous town. Walk along the southern side of the church, and then cross over to see the façade. The Jesuits put so much thought into this, the pinnacle of Prague's religious Baroque architecture, that it deserves a moment.

The Order had a glacial appreciation of human psychology, which you can begin to appreciate by comparing the grim west front of the former Jesuit College (and now maths faculty of the Charles University) on the left, with the seductive face of the church itself. Although there was a 20-year gap between the two façades, and a church might be expected to be grander than a school, the contrast also had a deliberate purpose. The

General of the Order, Father Oliva, warned the architects in 1673 that the lay house mustn't have the sumptuousness of the west front of the Clementinum (see pp. 239–42). With their own building the Jesuits thrust their humility and austerity into the face of the heathens; the richness of the later church façade was all the more inviting as a result.

But the Jesuits were no aesthetic puritans. Following the example of their fervent Spanish founder, Ignatius of Loyola, each monk had to go through a month of 'spiritual exercises', during which he progressed from contemplation of sin and damnation to, *inter alia*, a mental munching of 'the loaves and the fishes with which Jesus feeds the multitude'. Ignatius' teaching that God was to be known through all five senses was instrumental in the development of later Baroque architecture, which was given an added punch in Bohemia, where the Jesuits had to seduce a population which had fought Catholicism for 200 years.

The façade was the work of Munich-born Kristof Dienzenhofer, and was completed around 1710. It's a development of the undulating rhythm used by Borromini in 1667 for his church of S. Carlo alle Quatro Fontane in Rome. But it is when you enter the church that the mobility of Prague's late Baroque architecture finally overwhelms you.

Open Nov–Feb 9 am–4 pm, Mar–April 9 am–5 pm, May–Sept 9 am–6 pm, Oct 10 am–5 pm. All of the city's churches built during this period sought to capture hearts and minds for the Church Militant; but none other has the potency of this Jesuit cocktail of illusion, threat and promise. Even hardened cynics are momentarily stopped in their tracks; and it's relevant that this was one of the few churches to be given a full restoration in 1955, at a time when the Communist government's policies of Scientific Atheism were at their height. Inspired by the work of Guarino Guarini, who carried the idea of expressing movement through curves to an extraordinary degree, the decoration and structure create a space that pulls you in every direction. The nave's piers jut out at a diagonal, dragging your attention upwards; while the balconies sway forwards from pier to pier, over vast saints urging you onwards to the high altar. The vault adds to the intoxicating confusion, flowing almost imperceptibly from the pillars into three central bays, while the *trompe l'œil* extravaganza of the 1500-sq m **fresco** (1760) makes it almost impossible to say where construction ends and illusion begins. The fresco was the work of Johann Lukas Kracker, an Austrian who is thought to have trained under Franz Maulpertsch (see p. 71), and wasn't intended to be viewed from any single point, adding even more to the church's fluidity. It opens the vault into the dark drama of the life of St. Nicholas. Better known to pagans as Father Christmas, Nicholas was a 4th-century bishop from Asia Minor and the patron saint of perfumers, pawnbrokers and sailors in distress.

> *The east of the church, from the third vault onwards, is the work of Kristof's son, Kilian Ignaz Dienzenhofer, home-grown and educated by the Jesuits themselves in the Clementinum.*

From the nave, the choir and altar seem almost irrelevant, a result not of an unsuccessful union between the work of father and son, but of the overpowering effect of the church as a whole. But by the time you're standing under the diffuse light of the painted dome, it is the nave that has become an appendage. The size of the dome caused terror; no one would enter the church until a commission of experts certified in 1750 that it wouldn't collapse. The painting, by Franz Xavier Palko, is the *Celebration of the Holiest Trinity* (1752–53).

God moves in mysterious ways while you keep your eyes heavenward—but there's little room for doubt when you notice the colossal statues (1755–57) stationed above and around you. The venerable Doctors of the Church standing at each corner of the stunted transepts have physiques more often associated with steroid abuse than religious devotion. Their brutality was no accident. SS Basil, John Chrysostom, Gregory of Nazianzus and Cyril of Alexandria are all associated with the early Christian struggle against heterodoxy in the East, and the Jesuits were drawing a parallel with their own cause in Bohemia. There are equally gargantuan statues of the Order's heroes, SS Ignatius and Francis Xavier, flanking the copper St Nicholas on the high altar. The analogy was clear but the Jesuits hammered the point home: Ignatius and Cyril are each coolly plunging a crozier into the throats of jug-eared heretics.

After the initial shock of the church, as you walk back, the trickery reveals itself. As in almost all Prague's churches, the marble is actually *scagliola*, a painted mixture of plaster and glue; the intimidating saints are plaster casts; and the chapels contain little decoration that stands up to a brief examination. The Jesuits knew that by the time their prey had got as far as the entrance, they were willing victims—and all eyes would soon have been on the equally fake, but splendid, **pulpit** at the end of the nave. It dates from 1765, and is decorated with reliefs of John the Baptist. The shell on which it stands was one of the favourite motifs of the Rococo, but this swirling mass of cream and pink still belongs in spirit to the Baroque.

As you leave, take a look at the last chapel on your left, the **Chapel of the Dead**.

It was the first to be completed and, with its oval plan, it is the only one to stand outside the scheme of the church. The fresco is *The Last Judgment*, and the chapel contains one of the church's better paintings, a *Crucifixion* by the Czech Karel Škréta (1646).

Turn right past the plague column, one of Prague's many tributes to the saints who called off Bohemia's epidemic in 1715, and then left into **Nerudova**. *The street is named after Jan Neruda (1834–91), a 19th-century Czech poet and journalist who lived here. His name was later filched by the Chilean writer and 1971 Nobel Laureate, Pablo Neruda, who apparently chose it at random, although he deposited flowers outside Jan's birthplace after finding out who he was. More a chasm than a street, its Baroque and Renaissance façades cling onto the incline. As you grapple with it, spare a thought for the assorted beasts and heralds who once had to lug the paraphernalia of the coronation procession along here,* en route *to the castle.*

The street has more **house signs** than any other in Prague—multicoloured beasts, birds and apparently random objects which sometimes date back 600 years. They originally followed, in a lowly way, the strict rules of heraldry, but matters slipped out of control as the city grew. House-owners, desperate for an original name, resorted to zoological monstrosities (a house in the Old Town used to be called the 'Stag with Two Heads'); people adopted their property's name and took it with them when they moved; and streets were sometimes consumed by a counter-productive craze for a particular sign. Another grave problem was that people began to forget their significance altogether. Golden geese became white swans, Magi were transformed into musketeers, until in 1770 city fathers called a halt to the collective madness by introducing numbers. At No. 6 on the right is the narrow 18th-century façade of the **Red Eagle** (U červeného orla), one of the innumerable variations of the 26 avian species which adorned Prague's houses. The sign, surrounded by an intertwining Rococo cartouche, may have begun life as a vulture, which was the only creature allowed to perch on rocks by the heraldic guilds. The plaster decoration swirls into two less apparent images, sinister faces with dark tadpole eyes gazing out from the stucco above the first-floor windows. There's another sign at the **Three Little Fiddles** (U tří housliček) at No. 12. Three generations of violin-makers lived in the house, but legend insists that the sign has more to do with satanic fiddlers who gather here when the moon is full. It's also a cosy wine bar (see p. 283). Other signs to decipher as you walk up the street include a golden goblet (No. 16) and a golden key (No. 27), both from the 17th century, when castle goldsmiths used to heat and beat their metals along Nerudova; and a golden horseshoe (No. 34), recalling the days when steep Nerudova used to be the site of several humbler smithies. No. 34 is now marked only by a painted sign of a staid St Wenceslas on a bridling stud, but until the 1950s a large shoe used to hang under the picture, which some said had fallen off the hoof of the saint's white horse.

On the left at No. 5 is the Baroque **Morzin Palace** *(1713–14), now the Romanian Embassy, and the first of several embassies on this walk.*

The palace is an example of the inventiveness of Giovanni Santini, another of the greats of Prague's late Baroque (see p. 70). It was an adaptation of three older houses, and rather than go to the trouble of putting an entrance through the middle building, Santini put a balcony in the centre and had both sides of the façade thrust outwards towards it, making the asymmetry almost unnoticeable at first glance. The tension is thrown into even higher gear by the two atlantes, sombre Moors (the Morzin family emblem) who carry the balcony with ease and make a good job of supporting the rest of the façade. The other sculptures (all by F. M. Brokof) reinforce the illusory balance, both by their position and theme. The balcony is flanked by sunny Day and starry Night, and up on the roof, the Four Corners of the World are back to hold the building under their feet.

Atlantes became fashionable during the 18th century, but if you look at the portal of the Italian Embassy (Thun-Hohenstein Palace) across the road at No. 20, you'll see that they didn't always work. It was built in 1721–26 for the Kolovrats, very soon after the Morzins had moved into No. 5. The newcomers liked the idea of having the family emblem supporting the portal. Unfortunately, the Kolovrats' was an eagle, and Matthias Braun duly sculpted these two preposterous creatures. Jupiter and Juno are left to perch above.
Next to the embassy a set of stairs burrow up the hill to the New

Castle Steps (see Walk I). Continue the climb up Nerudova, until you reach another set of steps to the left. The house to the left as you face the staircase is said to conceal the walled-up Kuzmack Tunnel, built by an imperial stooge in the 18th century to provide an escape route from the castle in case of siege. On the opposite side is the Rococo façade of the former **Bretfeld Palace** *(1765), now a greying and blue-rinsed set of private apartments, but a centre of merriment in its youth.*

The first Count Bretfeld threw balls that were renowned across central Europe, one of which Mozart attended in 1787. He wrote to a friend in Vienna that 'the cream of the beauties of Prague flew about in sheer delight to my *Figaro*', which was played repeatedly in his honour; and according to legend, he also rubbed shoulders with Giacomo Casanova on the dance-floor. The story sounds a little too neat, given that Wolfgang was in town to conduct the premiere of *Don Giovanni*—but it's not impossible. The ageing lover had been invited by one of General Waldstein's descendants to pen his kiss-and-tell memoirs in the family castle in 1785, and he lived in Bohemia until his death in 1798.

If you have the energy, a detour to the top of the street will take you past the remnants of two mutant signs (the Red Lion at No. 39 and the now very peeled and not-at-all Green Lobster at No. 43) to Jan Neruda's birthplace at No. 47, itself marked by two very sorrowful suns. There's also a serene and very normal white swan at No. 49. A final climb up the lane to the castle leads to a postcard view across the roofs of Malá Strana. As you retrace your steps, you'll walk past *Toileta* opposite Jan Neruda's house. It's a charming sculpture by the Czech Jan Štursa, whose work was marked by a particular affection for the female form until he blew his brains out during a burst of creative angst in 1925; but generations of snapshooters have predictably been more impressed by the fact that its name is plastered across the base.

Return to Mozart's ballroom, walk down the adjoining stairs, and turn right into the sudden hush of Šporkova. The lane narrows and then opens into a junction. At the end of the cul-de-sac on the right is **The Mason's** *(U kameníka), remodelled with rich stucco decoration in the late 1720s. The mason himself, one Ondřej Kranner, used to stand on the empty pedestal over the door. The statue has mysteriously disappeared, but he was responsible for the façade, the theme of which is the Holy Trinity. Conspiracy-theorists could*

184

ponder the gable's eye in a triangle, which is both an old Trinitarian symbol and a sign of the strange-handshake society. It also appears on the mid-18th-century façade of the Sporck Palace, at the foot of the cul-de-sac. Coincidentally—perhaps—both Mozart and Casanova were active masons.

Continue along Šporkova to the left. On the right is the one-time **Italian Hospital***. It's now the cultural centre of the Italian Embassy; film-screenings and an excellent library continue the work begun four centuries ago, when north Italian craftsmen settled around here to look for jobs during Prague's half-hearted foray into the Renaissance. The street drops you into a quiet square in front of the* **Lobkowicz Palace***, now the German Embassy. The building dates from the early 18th century, and the stately aspect that it presents to the street conceals a beautiful garden and a much more charming façade at the rear of the palace. Turn right past the ravaged* Good Samaritan *(c. 1710) painted onto the Italian Hospital, and walk towards the whitewashed walls of the route leading up to the Strahov Monastery (see pp. 196–9). Turn left opposite the medical school-cum-church, and left again along the leafy path that runs behind the palace. The wood that appears out of nowhere is the foot of Petřín Hill. (You can clamber all the way to the summit from here, but you'd be kissing this walk goodbye if you did—and in any case, it's more fun to take the funicular railway to the top and zig-zag down here instead. See pp. 266–7.) On the left are the* **Lobkowicz Gardens** *and the rear façade of the palace.*

The top floors of the side wings were added in the later 18th century, and have disrupted the scale originally intended for the building. The elliptical plan, inspired by the work of Fischer von Erlach, originally bore a close resemblance to a 1665 project by Borromini for the rebuilding of the Louvre in Paris. Louis XIV rejected the design in favour of the grandiose colonnade that survives today, and if you imagine this prior to the alterations, you'll see why Borromini's plans lacked the required pomposity. The English layout of the gardens dates from the late 1700s, but they're still recuperating from the most momentous event in their sheltered history. In September 1989, thousands of East Germans arrived in Prague, dumped their Trabants, and clambered over these railings in the hope of being allowed to go west. They lived on the flower beds for a fortnight until permission was granted—and the rumble of their sealed trains, which President Honecker strangely insisted should pass through East Germany, were the final tremors before Europe's revolutions of 1989.

Retrace your steps back to the front of the palace, and continue along Vlašská. Next to the embassy is a restaurant originally opened by the Lobkowiczes to sell wine from their estates in Mělník, and now a favourite among the capital's diplomatic and journalistic corps. The **Schönborn Palace** *is on your right, just past a police station which the thoughtful Communists installed after the palace became the United States Embassy.*

The palace was built in 1643–56 and remodelled by Santini at the beginning of the 18th century, but its most glorious feature is its garden. The sight of Old Glory, fluttering from the tiny summerhouse half-way up Petřín, will bring a catch to the throat and a hand to the heart of any red-blooded American. You can't see it from here, and US citizens should head for Hradčany Square. During the 19th century, the palace crumbled into disrepair, and, no longer fit for noble habitation, it was rented out. Among the tenants was Franz Kafka, for a few months in 1917. The location made him uncharacteristically and dangerously jolly. He told his fiancée that it was 'the most marvellous apartment I could dream of', but his priorities were unfortunate in view of his weak constitution. 'I have electric light, though no bathroom, no tub, but I can do without that', he claimed; five months later, he suffered a massive haemorrhage that heralded terminal tuberculosis. A modern cultural hero of a different stamp now lives here. Ambassador Temple-Black is older, and almost certainly wiser, but still the same Shirley who told the world about the Good Ship Lollipop.

Walk to the end of Tržiště and turn right into Karmelitská. On the right at No. 25 are the **Vrtba Gardens**, *laid out in 1720. The observation terrace at the top of the gardens, lined with lonely Baroque gods sculpted by M. B. Braun, is one of the most still and secluded parts of Prague. It has been closed for years, but see if there's been any change—the entrance is through the gate at the end of the courtyard.*

From the gardens, continue along Karmelitská to the **Church of Our Lady of Victory** *(Kostel Panny Marie vítězně) on the right, which sits on the site of Prague's first Baroque church (1611). That was built by German Lutherans—a paradoxical start to religious Baroque architecture in Prague. After the Battle of the White*

Mountain in 1620, Ferdinand II gave their church to the Order of Barefooted Carmelites, who had trudged into the city as part of the Catholic squad. The friars, who actually wore sandals, renamed it in honour of the Virgin (their protectress) and, more specifically, in commemoration of her role at the White Mountain where she had rained down destruction and smites on the enemy. The discalced crew took to their heels again when Saxon troops looted the church in 1631, and the present edifice is a rebuilt version dating from 1640. The Carmelites were finally expelled in 1784 as a result of Joseph II's anti-clerical policies; and the church was taken over by the Knights of Malta, whose base was near by and whose cross now adorns the façade. The Knights were themselves expelled in turn by the Communists.

Open 8.30 am–4 pm. The structure is unimpressive—an ugly development of the façade of the 1568 Gésu in Rome (only the portal on the right remains from the Lutheran church) and an interior that retains much of the Lutherans' rigidity and austerity. The striking late Baroque gold-on-black decoration is denied the play of light and motion that it deserves, since the church's few windows are obstructed by altars. These weren't planned for when rebuilding began, and were only made possible as a result of the miraculous financial assistance of the *Bambino di Praga*, in the illuminated altar on your right.

Rome's Barefooted Carmelites put Bernini's *Ecstasy of St Teresa* in their church. The showpiece of the Prague friars was this 1-foot high wax effigy of the Infant Jesus. It's hardly less famous. Italians gave it the name by which it is best known, and the Bambino is venerated throughout the Hispanic world. In Central America, there's said to be a tribe which worships it as a god, and has very confused notions about what *Praga* involves. Intercessory prayers are now provided in 15 languages, and during high season coach-loads of more-or-less credulous pilgrims arrive daily.

The Bambino's rise to stardom began when Polyxena of Lobkowicz, one of many Spanish brides taken by Czech Catholics during this period, gave the figure to the friars in 1628. It had belonged to Polyxena's Habsburg mother, and had been known to work the occasional wonder in the old country, but its big break came in 1637. The new abbot, picking through the debris of the church (which had remained untouched since the Saxons had swept through) found that the trinket had been tossed behind the high altar, and was missing only its arms. He declared it a miracle. Equally incredible was the discovery, made while the Carmelites were drumming up funds for a new church, that the Bambino would do anything in return for a small sum. After Countess Kolovrat touched it and had her sight and hearing restored, there was no looking back. Cripples and imbeciles poured in, and in 1741 enough money had been made to buy the doll its silver altar; during the early 1700s, it was granted the rights of a Count Palatine; while the most mysterious (some say miraculous) tribute came in 1958, when an official delegation from Communist North Vietnam stepped off the plane with a set of silk clothes for the Bambino. To this day, no one knows why. It's been bought and given scores of other costumes; after the Carmelites were expelled, the Order of English Virgins was allowed to continue dressing it, and even through the Communist era, a prelate of St Vitus's Cathedral continued changing the Bambino regularly. Look out for outfit No. 5, an apple-green number with gold embroidery, which was handed over personally by Queen Maria Theresa in 1754.

Above the altar, there's a dim celebration of the Battle of the White Mountain, but the church's other main attraction is now inaccessible. The power of the Bambino meant that few friars wanted to stray too far during the interval between death and resurrection, and the most fortunate had their corpses put into a catacomb, where they were blow-dried into mummies over the years. Privileged benefactors were also let in. Everyone's still there, but a spot of putrefaction has set in and the smelly chamber is now closed.

From the church, continue along Karmelitská, and then turn left down Harantova. You emerge in front of the imposing Baroque façade of the Nostitz Palace, now the Embassy of the Netherlands. Turn left. The dainty Turba Palace on your left is the Rococo home of the Japanese diplomatic corps. Over the sunken arcade on your right is the Prague Conservatoire, and during term-time, a walk past the building can be accompanied by anything from a sublime recital to a series of threatening groans and squeals. At the end of the street is a group of saints around John the Baptist—another example of Malá Strana's gratitude for having been only partly eradicated by the plague. The 16th-century restaurant on the corner (U malířů, or The Painter's) is one of Malá Strana's best-known. Until it was taken over by a gang of French gastronomes in early 1991, it was even popular with the locals. Nowadays, the nearest most Praguers get to a

*meal is a wry glance at the menu by the door and the calculation that
it would take them a week to earn the turtle soup.*

*The square that you're in is Maltézské nám. (Maltese Square),
named after the title adopted in the 16th century by the crusading
Knights of the Order of St John. They set up a self-governing
enclave here in 1169 and were allowed to stay when everyone else
was expelled in 1257. Turn right, and you'll see the two much-
restored 14th-century Gothic towers of their* **Church of Our
Lady Under the Chain** *(Kostel Panny Marie pod řetězem).*

The Virgin has performed innumerable functions in Malá Strana over
the years, and here she helped the knights guard the first bridge across
the Vltava. That bridge has gone, but the chains still hang over Karel
Škréta's painting on the high altar. The church is almost always closed,
but that's no great loss. The monks knocked down their first Romanesque basilica in the 14th century, and only had time to replace the
towers and chancel before they were chased out of town by anti-clerical
Hussites. The chancel was remodelled in Baroque style in the 17th
century, but as with Our Lady of the Snows (see pp. 224–5), no one ever
got round to building a nave. The open forecourt is where it should have
been; if the gate is open, you can see remnants of the first church in the
wall on your right.

*Turn right. The Grand Priors of the Order lived through the gate
next door, marked by their Maltese Cross and dating in its present
form from the early 18th century. After the monks were expelled by
the Communists, the palace was turned into Prague's* **Musical
Instrument Museum** *(open April–Oct Tues–Sun 10 am–5 pm).*

The opening times given are those that have applied for the last few
decades, but in post-revolutionary Prague that doesn't always mean very
much. At the time of writing it looks as though the Grand Prior will
return to his palace, evicting the instruments in the process. In any case,
the management is being very cagey as to whether the museum will ever
continue in the present premises; someone made off with five priceless
Amati violins and a viola in 1990, and security arrangements are being
reviewed. If it does re-open, the elegant chapter hall on the first floor
contains carved Baroque furniture and a panoply of instruments, including several pianos tinkled by visiting composers. In the summer,
concerts and plays are traditionally held in the walled garden, which
contains what is claimed to be the oldest plane tree in Prague,

carried back from Jerusalem by the gallant monks. They planted many more, but none of the others are thought to have survived a frenzied tree-slaughter which occurred in 1420, when Malá Strana's inhabitants were apparently seized by the fear that Emperor Sigismund's invading army would otherwise hide in them.

Turn left into the leafy shade of Velkopřevorské nám. (Grand Prior's Square). Opposite the very proper charm of the apricot and white French Embassy (the Buquoy Palace), the musical theme continues with the polyglot scrawl of the **John Lennon Wall**, *a colourful tribute to the Beatle-saint.*

The singer was a powerful symbol of nonconformity throughout Communist-ruled Europe after his murder in 1980, and this wall became the site of a surreal struggle between Prague's youth and the police. The former would daub it with pictures and slogans; the VB responded with regular pots of whitewash and, at the height of the subversion, video-surveillance equipment. When a fair proportion of Prague's hippies became government officials after December 1989, it was expected that moody adolescents would be able to doodle at will, but in 1990 battle was rejoined against new meanies (probably no more sinister than the Musical Instrument Museum, which owns the wall). At the time of writing, the messages are returning in force. If you're around on 8 December come and join the punk-rockers and dreamy types who spend much of the night imagining no possessions, greed or hunger. Brush up on your Lennon lyrics and try to lay your hands on a musical instrument.

Follow the wall onto the bridge over the **Čertovka** *(Devil's Stream), an arm of the Vltava which is either named after a sprite who lives in it, or as a commemoration of the diabolical temper of a washer-woman who lived nearby. At the time of writing, the stream has been turned off while the crumbling cellars which line it are repaired. When the work is over, the mill-wheel which has stood by the bridge since the late 1500s will also be returned. Adjoining the other side of the stream is a sky-blue 18th-century summerhouse which is generally agreed to be the most desirable residence in Prague. From the bridge, walk over onto* **Kampa Island** *(from the Latin* campus, *i.e. field).*

Like most of Prague's romantic spots, the island has had its ups and downs. A long-standing border dispute with the Vltava river saw its shape change regularly, and despite being strengthened by imported debris from the 1541 fire, the deluges continued until the damming of the river in 1954. The abundant supplies of water meant that Kampa was particularly favoured by Prague's washer-women, who are commemorated both by the stream and by the small early Gothic church of St John at the Laundry, just off the southern tip of the island on Říční.

Walk through the narrow passage ahead of you and just to the right. It takes you into a beautiful tree-filled square, crossed at one end by the rough Gothic arches of the Charles Bridge and lined with quietly decaying Baroque houses. It's one of the gentlest patches of Prague, and a spot in which to meander as you contemplate two final house signs. On your right at No. 1 is a sweet blue fox chomping a twig, under the Bambino di Praga. *The juxtaposition is puzzling, but nothing compared to the* **balcony** *of No. 9, overlooking the Charles Bridge.*

The assemblage of objects here makes up one of the best-known signs in Prague, and a perfect example of a Prague myth which is still in the making. It comprises a Madonna between carved mangle rollers fronted by a lantern. An old-timer who lives in the house claimed that the painting floated past during a flood, and was recovered by a Mr Rott, who installed the lantern after the Virgin saved the life of his daughter. The icon proceeded to perform sundry other miracles, including the healing of a pair of hands which had been mangled by the rollers of the house laundry. The rollers were then piously removed and placed alongside. The tenant claimed to know all the parties concerned, and added the convincing details that Mr Rott was murdered across the road in 1945, and that the mangle was used as a barricade across the Charles Bridge in 1968; but she was mysteriously silent when asked why the rollers are stylized carvings. Another mildly suspicious circumstance was the fact that she was only 82 years old, while a 1911 guidebook could already state that the lantern (now electric, and apt to go out) was an eternal flame for all those in the throes of death.

To end this walk, you could pick up a drink from the tiny Bistro Bruncvík across the square and take it to one of the two remaining gardens of Malá Strana. The first stretches across the south of the island, with a shady embankment over the swan-filled Vltava which is a favourite spot for canoodling couples. Equally secluded is the **Vojan Park** *(Vojanovy sady), which was owned by the Carmelites, then the English Virgins, and now backs onto the Finance Ministry,* *which you saw at the beginning of this walk. It's on the way back to Malostranská metro station. Walk under the Charles Bridge, and then along U lužického semináře; the entrance is on your left.*

Open 8 am–7 pm (summer) and 8 am–5 pm (winter). The park has a few notable curiosities, including a grotto-chapel to the Old Testament prophet Elijah (who, the Carmelites insisted, had founded their Order), and just to the left of the entrance, an impassioned late 18th-century sculpture of St John Nepomuk standing on a fish.

Walk IV

Hradčany

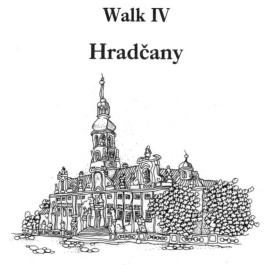

Loretto

*Strahov Monastery—Loretto—Nový svět—Hradčany Square—National
Gallery of European Art—Royal Garden*

The shadow of the castle has always fallen between Hradčany and the
city below. The district was founded in 1320 as a set of hovels in which
the royal serfs could sleep and breed—and although it slipped out of the
castellan's personal control in 1598, it never grew into a normal town.
Locked into a slowly turning backwater, monks and nobles indulged
their peccadilloes here for centuries; today, its cobbles and courtyards
are a silent suburb of the castle that many visitors never see. This short
walk takes you through the magnificent libraries of the Strahov Monastery, Prague's collection of six centuries of European art, and tours the
Baroque miracles of Prague's Loretto shrine. It skims across the castle
and ends in the royal gardens, where the Habsburgs grew their tulips and
built the most splendid Renaissance palace north of the Alps.

Any day except Monday (closing day for most attractions) is fine for
this serene stroll, and you can take regular shelter if it's raining. It ends
near the castle; you could combine it with Walk I if you were up bright
and early.

There's only one convenient way to **start** the walk if you're staying in
the centre—luckily it's the ubiquitous 22 tram, which slithers all over
town. Two easy points to pick it up are Malostranské nám., and Národní

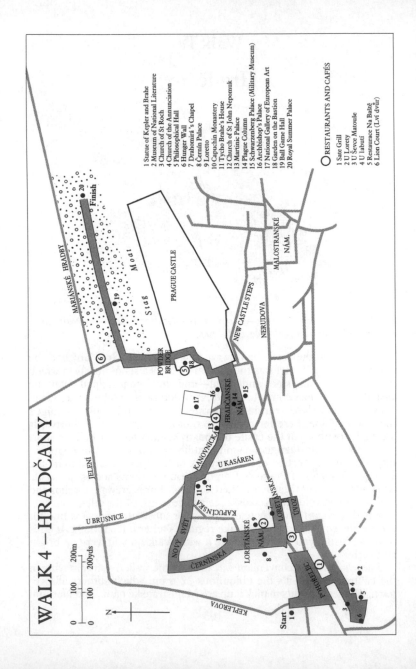

WALK 4 – HRADČANY

1 Statue of Kepler and Brahe
2 Museum of National Literature
3 Church of St Roch
4 Church of the Annunciation
5 Philosophical Hall
6 Hunger Wall
7 Drahomíra's Chapel
8 Černín Palace
9 Loretto
10 Capuchin Monastery
11 Tycho Brahe's House
12 Church of St John Nepomuk
13 Martinic Palace
14 Plague Column
15 Schwarzenberg Palace (Military Museum)
16 Archbishop's Palace
17 National Gallery of European Art
18 Garden on the Bastion
19 Ball Game Hall
20 Royal Summer Palace

○ RESTAURANTS AND CAFÉS

1 Sate Grill
2 U Lorety
3 U Ševce Matouše
4 U labutí
5 Restaurace Na Baště
6 Lion Court (Lví dvůr)

street. You can take the 22 again at the **end** of the walk; alternatively, Malá Strana isn't far if you retrace your steps to Hradčany Square.
Walking time: 3 hours—although the National Gallery of European Art could extend that considerably.

LUNCH/CAFÉS

This district is a cornucopia for Prague, and all the more inviting because many of the tourists who make it up the hill come in coaches, and are spirited away at lunchtime to their mass-reservations in the Old Town. Don't expect wonders, but you're unlikely to go hungry.

Sate Grill, Pohořelec 12, 10 am–7.30 pm. A mixture of dishes, served quickly. Purportedly Indonesian in inspiration. Soya sauce seems to be the only thing on the spice rack, but the food's still tasty and filling. The cook is usually happy to mix up a veggie dish.

U Ševce Matouše (roughly, Matthew the Cobbler), under the arcades in Loretánské nám. (Look for the copper boot outside.) Tues–Sat 12 noon–10 pm , Sun 12 noon–6 pm. Several dishes (including one for vegetarians), but the long list of steaks deceptive—try telling them apart.

U Lorety, next to Loretto, 11 am–3 pm (lunch). Tranquil summer terrace with lunch snacks. Free entertainment provided by the strained strains of the bell-tower next door.

U labutí (The Swan), Hradčanské nám. (north side). Supposedly open 10 am–9 pm, Sat–Sun 10 am–7 pm, but there's neither rhyme nor reason to when this place opens and closes. The crummy sister of one of Prague's most exclusive restaurants (next door)—perhaps it's psychological but the steaks are sometimes a notch above average.

Restaurace Na Baště (Restaurant on the Bastion), in the castle courtyard to the left of the main gates. Tues–Sun 9 am–7 pm (summer), 10 am–6 pm (winter). Unexceptional food, but a good view over the castle ravine.

Lví dvůr (Lion Court), next to the Royal Gardens at the end of the walk. Tues–Sun, 10 am–11 pm. Once the home of the Habsburgs' cats. There's nothing wilder on the menu than beefsteak these days, but the courtyard's a relaxing spot to finish the walk.

☆   ☆   ☆   ☆   ☆

The tram snakes through hairpin bends to the top of the castle hill. Get off when you see the statue of stargazing Tycho Brahe and Johannes Kepler, a 1983 sculpture which invests the squabbling duo with a calm that neither would ever have shown in the other's

*company during their lives (see pp. 216–7). Cross over into Pohořelec, a
Baroque square nestled high over the glistening city. It earned its
name—which roughly translates as 'afterburn'—after being razed
to the ground for the third time in 1741. Cross over to No. 8, where
you'll find a stone portal in the peach façade. The arched staircase
carries you into the wooded forecourt of the* **Strahov Monastery**
(Strahovský klášter), part of which houses the **Museum of
National Literature** *(Památník národního písemnictví).*

Open Tues–Sun, 9 am–4.30 pm, adm. Cling on to your ticket, as it
admits you to two separate parts of the monastery. The name Strahov
comes from *stráž* ('guard'), and dates from the mid-14th century, when
the western gateway of Charles IV's new fortifications around the left
bank of Prague was built here. It's an unsuitably militaristic name for the
monastery. When founded in 1140, it was called Mount Sion; although
fires and armed mobs stormed through with monotonous regularity until
the later 18th century, in spirit the monastery has always been a world
apart from the bloodshed and religious tomfoolery of the city below. The
Premonstratensian canons were an austere order—their insistence on
celibacy didn't make them popular among the licentious monks of the
day—but they were also an honest and hardworking crew. On their
hilltop retreat, they assembled a library which, despite sacks at the hands
of Hussite swarms in 1420 and oafish Finns in 1648, became the finest in
Bohemia. The books came in useful in 1782, when Joseph II announced
the dissolution of almost all the monasteries and convents of the empire.
While nuns and monks everywhere were being clapped in jail or told to
find honest work, Strahov's wily abbot, Václav Mayer, saved the day by
turning the monastery into a research institute for scholars. Strahov was
one of very few monasteries to survive in Bohemia. The Communists
were tough cookies—in 1951 they expelled the monks and turned their
cloisters into the national literary museum—but the Premonstratensians
proved themselves even tougher. Since the revolution of 1989 they have
been shuffling back, and Strahov is once again a functioning monastery.

*The canons like their privacy; the complex is now divided into
sections open and closed to the public, and you're unlikely to glimpse
even the flash of a white cowl. The architectural history of the
monastery is Prague's usual* mélange—*18th-century Baroque on
top of hardy little Romanesque and Gothic details. The cerebral
monks also had an evident fascination for illusionistic art, and along
the cloister are several two-dimensional altars to St Norbert (who*

*founded the order and whose body the monks acquired in 1627),
and one particularly curious green door, painted for unknown
reasons onto a corner of the far wall. On the same side is a
Romanesque flight of steps creeping between the walls of the Romanesque heart of the monastery, which contains the museum itself.*

A museum devoted to Czech literature won't appeal to many English-
speakers, but the gloomy chambers are worth a quick visit. Highlights
include two ancient tomes of Glagolitic scrawls, and a set of rather more
accessible illuminated manuscripts. They include the *Kunigunde Passional* and the *Kunhuta Passional*, mystical prayer books produced for the
delectation of well-heeled nuns (who generally did much to advance
Bohemian art and literature during the 14th century); and examples of
Hussite illumination, glorifying the chalice and the rebel himself. The
museum has a more modern second floor which is devoted to the
19th-century national revival of Czech literature—but you might want to
go directly to the highlight of Strahov, its magnificent **libraries**.

*Work your way back to where you bought your ticket, turning left into
the main courtyard. To your right, you'll see the **Church of St
Roch** (Kostel sv. Rocha).*

The church was built after Rudolf II had promised the plague-resistant
saint a church if he protected Prague from the approaching pestilence.
Roch accepted the offer—the bacilli screeched to a halt a few kilometres
from the city walls—and although Rudolf took no chances and moved to
Plzeň for the duration, he was as good as his word. The peculiar church
dates from 1603–12. Gothic architecture lingered late in Bohemia, and
the Renaissance influence of the blank niches and pedimented door is
almost lost among the tenacious buttresses and tall, tracery-topped
windows climbing the façade. St Roch didn't share the luck of the rest of
the monastery; once the Strahov parish church, it was abolished by
Joseph II in 1784, and now hosts sporadic exhibitions.

*Turn left past the Church of the Annunciation (Kostel Nanebezvetí
Panny Marie), a Baroque edifice built over hidden layers going back
to the Romanesque origins of the monastery, and face the neo-
classical façade of the **Philosophical Hall**.*

The library was built frantically between 1780 and 1782, after Abbot
Mayer got wind of the new Emperor Joseph's plans. Designed to provide

room for a wider range of books and readers, it was intended to persuade the emperor of the quarter-truth that there was no conflict between rationalism and what the monks had been up to for centuries. Mayer also resorted to a prudent cringe: the haughty figure in gold above the stark façade is the scourge of the monasteries himself.

The entrance is below. Breeze through if you can, knock on the door if you can't, but you may have to wait for the officious door-opening ceremony every quarter-hour.

The anteroom contains a few illuminated manuscripts and monkish doodles, but you'll find it hard to resist being dragged into the opulence of the hall beyond. Walnut bookcases, strung with overripe gilt Rococo decoration, push through two levels. Any sensible library would stop at the gallery, but here the tomes march on, climbing 15 m in all to the ceiling. When the cabinets arrived, the plan for the half-built room had to be changed to accommodate them. There are over 40,000 books, comprising works that Strahov had picked up from benefactors and less fortunate monasteries than itself, all lined up to prove to Joseph that the monastery was providing a useful social service. The emperor seems to have been convinced—he bought the shelves for the monastery, after driving down their market value by abolishing the previous owner. Non-religious scholars were now allowed in in greater numbers than ever before, and at the organ-grinder desks, they could make up for lost time by spinning through four books at once.

The ceiling fresco, rising from the sombre stacks into a celestial blue, was the last work of the Viennese Franz Maulpertsch, and dates from 1794. It's called *The Struggle of Mankind to Know Real Wisdom*, but there's also another struggle going on, between the sacred and the profane, which owes as much to Joseph II's threat as to the rationalist bent of the Strahov monks. Christianity gets an honourable mention at both ends, but the woman in the cherubic supernova is not the Virgin, but Providence; and along both sides Antiquity's truth-seeking heroes hog the stage. Alexander the Great and pensive Aristotle on the left face Plato on the right; Socrates welcomes his hemlock on the far right; and even Diogenes the Cynic has moved in, barrel and all, on the far left. Five years after the French Revolution, neither emperor nor monks had any sympathy for the troublesome Encyclopaedists—Diderot *et al.* are tumbling into an abyss next to the pillar on the right—but the nefarious Rational Dictionary still found its way onto the stacks, filed under AA.1.

*Strahov's monks didn't just bury their heads in books. They also
stared at their collection of curiosities, now in the cabinets outside the
hall: monstrous creatures of the deep, a sad crocodile, and cases of
shining beetles and butterflies. Walk past the musty, dusty leather-
bound books along the corridor. The display case at the end contains
a replica of the oldest manuscript in the library, a 10th-century New
Testament bound in fussy 17th-century encrustations, and on the
right is the* **Theological Hall.**

This library was built in 1671, during the restoration of the monastery
after the damage it suffered at the end of the Thirty Years War. It doesn't
quite have the solemn majesty of the later Philosophical Hall, but its
stucco-laden barrel vault is, if anything, even more sumptuous. It is
decorated with ceiling frescoes, extolling the virtues of True Wisdom.
They were painted by one of the monks in 1723–27, and although
Grecian philosophers don't crowd out the scenes, the secular nature of
the allegories shows that the Enlightenment hadn't passed Strahov by.
Favoured lay-scholars could work here along with the monks—all were
prodded along by the frescoes' Latin inscriptions, dully insistent reminders that 'it is better to acquire knowledge than to make money',
'knowledge is difficult but fruitful' *et cetera ad nauseam.*

The monks were liberal—but to a degree. They observed the prohibitions of the Vatican's Index, but kept choice selections dangling tanta-
lizingly in the cabinet above the far door. If a prurient monk wanted to
flick through one of Galileo's potboilers or a diabolical Hussite tract,
he'd have to explain his reasons in detail to the abbot—a cumbersome
process which was swept away during the perestroika and glasnost of the
1780s, when the books were removed into the profanity of the Philosophical Hall.

*When you leave the libraries, take a look at the heavy fortifications
around the gate to your left as you re-enter the courtyard. They make
up the end of the* **Hunger Wall** *(Hladová zed'), which was built by
Charles IV in about 1360 to enclose the entire left bank of Prague,
and which still crawls unevenly across the length of Petřín Hill (see
pp. 266–7). The name comes from a legend that Charles didn't
really need a new wall and built it to create jobs for peckish Praguers
after a failed harvest (although this project seems neither more nor
less functional than all the other walls, churches, castles, bridges,
cathedrals and towns then being built by the emperor). Near where
you bought your ticket is a door leading into the Strahov gardens. To*

your right is Petřín—walk along the path on the left until you come to Úvoz. The view of Prague from here is one of the best in the city. The unmistakable dome of St Nicholas' dominates the foreground; across the river on the right are the twin towers of the Týn Church; and the Soyuz launch pad on the horizon is Prague's modern television tower, the emissions from which were apparently so powerful that alarmed residents, fearful of mutating, forced it to close within months.

When you get to Úvoz, turn right. The steep street careers down to Malá Strana, but jump off when you see a set of stairs to your left. Turn left at the top—to your right is a curious cubby-hole on the pavement looking like the stranded remnant of a little-lamented church. In fact it's a chapel celebrating the spot where Good King Wenceslas' bad old mother, Drahomirá—a pagan, and a murderer to boot—was dragged into Hell. In front of you is Loretánská nám., with the thirty Doric half-columns of the 500-foot long **Černín Palace** *ranged like riot police against the boisterous mob of cherubs and green onion-domes of Loretto (Loreta) to your right.*

The palace is the largest in Prague, and it's a beast: in form, its façade is still Renaissance; in its scale and deliberate repetition it belongs to the Baroque; and with its awesome pomp it has the timeless stamp of distant power. Humprecht Černín was one of the wealthiest of the *arrivistes* who moved into the jobs and properties left vacant by Protestant exiles after the Catholic victory at the Battle of the White Mountain in 1620. From his sojourn in Venice as imperial ambassador, he returned in 1664 with money to burn, a handful of half-baked architectural ideas, and several thousand paintings looking for a home—and this behemoth was the monstrous offspring of his appetites. He tried out plans by Rome's Bernini and rejected them; he tirelessly argued with his Prague architects who tried to endow his baby with some human features; and when he died in 1682 the palace remained unfinished. The family frittered away their fortune to complete it; and they had barely moved in the furniture before they decided to sell it in 1779, only to find there were no takers. In the end, the government moved in. It became a barracks in 1851, and since 1932 the bureaucrats of the Ministry of Foreign Affairs have stalked its desolate corridors. In 1948, Prague's fourth (and so far, last) defenestration occurred here, when the Foreign Minister, Jan Masaryk, fell from his office window. No one knows whether he jumped or was pushed. On the one hand, he was the popular son of

Czechoslovakia's first president, and the Communists had good reason to bump him off; on the other, he was a manic depressive—but it's always a useful subject to bring up in Prague if the conversation starts to flag.

Černín's builders excavated a mysterious pagan cemetery full of headless skeletons, and hundreds of tons of earth. The fate of the bones is unknown, but the earth lay around in the centre of the square for a couple of centuries, and was only properly patted down this century to form the embankment that divides the square into two levels. Turn left towards the bell tower of **Loretto.**

Open Tues–Sun, 9 am–1 pm, 1.30 pm–4 pm, adm. The original Loretto in Italy was a medieval Lourdes, one of the most visited shrines in Europe. It was the house where the Archangel Gabriel told Mary the good news, rescued from pagan hands and flown over from Nazareth by a flock of angels in about 1291. The cult was wildly popular, and hundreds of imitations appeared across the continent in the following centuries. After the Battle of the White Mountain, 50 were built in Bohemia as part of the miracle-culture being constructed to re-Catholicize the country. The Prague Loretto wasn't the first, but it became the grandest. The shrine was begun in 1626, only six years after the Catholic victory, and three generations of architects spent a century perfecting it.

The façade (1716–23) was the work of both Kristof Dienzenhofer and his son Kilian (see p. 000) and it's a charmer: bouncy cherubs and dinky tower cheerfully taunting the armed might of the Černín palace opposite. The atmosphere inside is altogether less sunny. The Loretto was established by Benigna Kateřina of Lobkowicz, one of the minor relatives of the Spanish Habsburgs who found their way to Prague; it was owned and run by an order founded by a Spanish warrior-saint; and it speaks the unearthly language of Spain's Counter-Reformation, the mixture of fanatical cruelty and sensual mysticism that spawned both an Inquisition and the art of El Greco. Pleasure and pain are part and parcel of any shrine, but in Prague the new cult was being thrust onto a people who had fought against Catholicism for two centuries: it worked, but only by tapping a morbid superstition and voyeurism that permeate it still.

First, walk around the cloisters, built in 1661 to protect the hundreds of homeless pilgrims from heavenly deluges. They're lined with rows of painted saints in recently renovated pine cabinets. The Capuchins knew their audience—suffering and penitence were out, *and the cloister is a department store of useful intercessors. Under this one roof, suppliants could get rid of toothaches (Apollonia), sore throats (Blaise) and gallstones (Liborius); if they'd lost something, Antony of Padua would find it for them; and Sebastian inoculated them against the plague. You'll find plenty of others here, with their specialities helpfully inscribed underneath.*

Half-way around the cloister, you're led into the **Santa Casa,** a replica of the Nazarene hovel itself, complete with rich Baroque stucco reliefs. As you walk through the pedimented portal, you may feel that it's all slightly at odds with your understanding of the Gospels, but have faith—the exterior is the work of mid-17th-century Italians, but inside is what it *really* looked like. The brick room is something of an anti-climax: a sombre box, with a cedar Virgin on the altar, surrounded by smiling silver cherubs who look as though they were put together with tin foil. On the left are two beams and a brick from the original Loretto.

*Walk from the Santa Casa to the **Church of the Nativity**, taking a look at the relief on the back, which shows the story of the angelic transportation. Christians are slaughtered below—but there's room on the house for two. Madonna and child sit elegantly on the roof, before being whisked to safety over a rolling Tuscan landscape.*

The church fits the cruel and surreal spirit of the shrine well. On the far right is a painting of the tortured martyr St Agatha—the patron saint of women with breast complaints—handing her own severed breasts on a dish to a welcoming angel. Even more macabre are the dummies in the glass cases on either side of the altar. The wax masks and dusty costumes shroud the skeletons of SS Felicissimus and Marcia, another Spanish addition to Loretto's box of tricks.

The most preposterous Iberian introduction to the shrine is yet to come—continue round the cloister, to the chapel on the corner before the entrance.

The figure with the Castro beard, on the cross to your left, isn't Christ (as you'll probably realize from the sky-blue dress with silver brocade) but the unfortunate Portuguese **St Wilgefortis**. She prayed on the eve of her wedding to be saved from her heathen suitor, and God in His mysterious way decided that the best remedy was facial hair, which she sprouted overnight. The prospective groom was suitably awed, and hastily withdrew from the wedding. Her father was less impressed—he crucified her. She's the patron saint of unhappily-married women, and it sounds like the kind of story that should have done a roaring trade in Loretto, but apparently it was a flop. According to one of the workers here, 'a woman with a beard was alien to the traditions of Bohemia'.

From the chapel, walk back to the entrance and go up the stairs to the **Loretto Treasury**, *a priceless collection of glittering monstrances and reliquaries.*

Most of the jewels behind the reinforced-glass cases were gifts from the quislings and newly rich who now made up Bohemia's aristocracy, and they smell less of pious duty than anxiety that the propaganda machine of Loretto should remain solvent. The Vatican understood the shrine's importance: in 1683 Emperor Leopold I received permission to sell off the precious metals of the empire's churches to finance his war with the Turks, but the Prague Loretto was granted a blanket exemption. There's some superb silver filigree work, but the most impressive bauble is at the far end—the **diamond monstrance**, over 6200 of the stones sprayed out like the quills of a horror-struck hedgehog. It was designed by Fischer von Erlach in 1699, and formed part of the gift of Ludmilla Eva Franziska of Kolovrat, who left her entire estate to the Madonna of the Santa Casa.

Walking around the shrine, you may have heard the appealing but cacophonous chimes of Loretto's carillon, 27 mechanical bells which have been urgently trying to learn a recognizable tune every hour for three centuries. They were among the few to survive a central European bell holocaust in the First World War, when the Austro-Hungarians turned most of the metal they could find into cannons (Prague's 267 bells were all rung for the last time on St Wenceslas' Eve in 1916). They're synchronized, for want of a better term, by grooved cylinders; their current effort is apparently called 'We Greet Thee a Thousand Times'.

From Loretto, turn right and walk diagonally across the square. The compact tiled roofs to the north cover the low-lying **Capuchin Monastery**, *founded in Prague in 1600 by the Spaniard St Laurence of Brindisi, who had been sent here from Rome. Laurence had the honest virtues of a fanatic: at Rudolf II's request, he took time out while in Prague to rally the empire's anti-Turkish troops, and ended up leading them into battle armed only with a crucifix. He survived; the Turks were massacred. But Prague's Capuchins were a sneaky bunch. As well as maintaining the perverted pleasure palace* *of Loretto, the monks let General Waldstein's Catholic army clamber over their garden wall in 1632. The Saxons then occupying Prague were caught napping, and the balance of the Thirty Years War was swung. Follow the perfidious wall into Černínská.*

The little mess of cottages sinking into a dell of grassy cobbles is ridiculously dreamy. In any town with a spot of commercial acumen it would have been turned into a warren of wine-bars and poster shops long ago. It's not a good idea to say anything vaguely favourable about the Communists in Prague these days, but at least here, you can be grateful for the rigor mortis of their iron grip.

*Turn right down **Nový svět**, which is also the name of the whole hamlet.*

It means 'New World'; Dvořák's symphony has a certain appropriateness, although it is Hovis commercials rather than the Land of the Free that come to mind. The quarter grew up during the 1500s as a set of ramshackle hovels for workers to trudge back to after a hard day's work at the castle. The Capuchins cleaned them up after moving in, and they're 17th-century cottages at heart, despite modifications made over the next two hundred years.

As you wander along the street, you'll pass a notorious studio to your right, containing piles of air-brushed spacescapes which make up what several Praguers feel to be one of the most atrocious art collections to be found in the capital. The last house on the right was the **home of Tycho Brahe** during his stay in Prague as imperial mathematician to Rudolf II (1599–1601). Brahe was never really at ease in the house, and had incessant problems with his Capuchin neighbours. He complained that the monks had begun to ring their bells in a manner calculated to unnerve him—which sounds like the kind of thing that the Spaniards would do, but Brahe was little better. The Dane had the ear of the emperor throughout 1600, a year in which the rest of Rudolf was plumbing new depths of mental instability, and it's thought that it was he who convinced the monarch to expel the Capuchins a few months after he had invited them in. As the monks packed their bags, Rudolf had another turn and commanded them to remain; and the see-saw of intrigue continued for another year until Brahe set off from this house on the fateful journey to the banquet at which his bladder would implode (see p. 147).

Turn right at the end of the street. On the right is the **Church of St
John Nepomuk** *(Kostel sv. Jana Nepomuckého), the first of K. I.
Dienzenhofer's works in Prague to be built independently of his
father. It dates from 1720–28, roughly the same time that he was
finishing the more elegant façade of the Loretto. Follow Kanovnická
to your left, with luck avoiding the crazed drivers who occasionally
swerve around at death-embracing speed, until you emerge into*
Hradčanské nám. *or Hradčany Square.*

When a part of Prague can be described as tranquil, it often means that
its history is steeped in gore or grinding poverty, but this square has got
less to hide than most. Many of the grand buildings that line it predate
the Battle of the White Mountain; and although it had the standard
pillory and gallows, the most impressive judicial murders took place in
the Old Town Square where a larger audience could be guaranteed. It
never even really had the hurly-burly of a marketplace—a few groceries
and trinkets were sold here over the centuries, but the kings and nobles
preferred to do their shopping downtown.

On the corner of the square is the façade of the **Martinic Palace**,
plastered with cream-on-brown scratchings.

The palace was built by the count of the same name in 1620, two years
after his defenestrated descent into a dungheap had plunged him into the
footnotes of history as one of the minor causes of the Thirty Years War
(see p. 51). The *sgraffito* decoration was rediscovered during restoration
in 1971. It's a merry Renaissance retelling of Old Testament stories. On
the front is Joseph (of Technicolor Dreamcoat fame). The wife of his
master Potiphar is eagerly trying to lie with him, but he doesn't want to
know her. The artist seems to have had a penchant for men wronged by
the treachery of the fairer sex—in the courtyard, there are fragments
from the story of Samson, wrestling with his lion and tossing a Philistine
pillar. Tucked away on the opposite side of this corner of the square is a
house which cinema buffs might recognize. Miloš Forman chose it as
Mozart's house for *Amadeus*, which was largely filmed in Prague.

On the opposite side of the square is the eye-catching façade of the
Schwarzenberg Palace, *endless* sgraffito *triangles crawling in
diagonal formations across its Renaissance splendour. Walk towards
it—you'll pass a* **Plague Column** *in the woody centre of the
square; F. M. Brokof sculpted it in 1726. Unlike Rudolf's gift to St*

Roch, this was an ex post facto *offering to appease the fickle saints, who had just done nothing as the pest had stormed through for the second time in 50 years. The palace was built by a member of the ubiquitous Lobkowicz family, who took advantage of the slump in property prices after the 1541 fire to buy up the site. It now houses a* **Military Museum** *(Vojenské muzeum).*

Open May–Oct, 9.30 am–4.30 pm, adm. Those of a bloodthirsty bent will find plenty to enjoy here; and even pinko peaceniks should take a look, out of respect for Bohemia's savage history. A language which has given little else to the world provided it with the word 'pistol' (from the Czech word *píšt'ala*, meaning flute), and the Bren machine-gun, named after Brno where it was originally made. You'll find a millennium's worth of global warfare represented here: merciless corkscrew daggers, crescent scimitars and pencil rapiers, terrifying wind-up crossbows, and more artillery than you can shake a stick at. The fraternal peace-loving propaganda of the old regime that used to be in the last room has been cleared out and surprises are promised for 1991. Keep your eyes open for any mention of Semtex, Czechoslavakia's most recent contribution to mass-destruction.

Walk across the square from the museum. Just next to the castle gate is the **Archbishop's Palace** *(Arcibiskupský palac), built in Renaissance style but given the present Rococo façade in 1763–64 to keep up with Queen Maria Theresa's revamp of the castle. The interior contains a magnificent staircase and furnishings. It's only opened to the public once a year, on Maundy Thursday, but if you are around then, get in line. Next to the palace is an arch, through which a lane winds down to the* **Sternberk Palace***, housing the* **National Gallery of European Art***.*

Open Tues–Sun, 10 am–6 pm, adm. The collection is divided into three parts. The first floor contains icons and Italian art up to the 14th century, but it's been closed for over a year at the time of writing, and is likely to move rather than reopen. Ask at the cash desk for further information. On the second floor, you'll find European art up to the 20th century; and across the central courtyard is the gallery's collection of 19th- and 20th-century French art.

Walk up to the second floor, and enter through the door on your right.

The first rooms contain work by German artists of the 14th–16th centuries. To the left of the second room is a collection of work by Lucas Cranach the Elder. At the beginning of his career, Cranach was an important representative of the so-called 'Danube School', the first European artists to paint landscape for its own sake, but the works here come from his comfortable stint as court painter to Saxony's Frederick the Wise. There's barely a shrub to be seen, although the deciduous twig covering the pudenda of *Adam and Eve* (*c.* 1538) has a certain Danubian feel about it. That work is an example of the way that Cranach (and others working in the stern atmosphere of proto-Lutheran towns) used religious themes to conceal his Renaissance-minded experimentation with nudity. As it and several other works show, the Gothic traditions of northern European art had some way to go before the proportions of the human form would be mastered, but despite some excessive deformations, most notably, the rather tragic *Christ Child—Emanuel* (*c.* 1530), the work here also shows the artist's characteristic realism and refusal to idealize beauty. Despite his humanist leanings, Cranach, who was living in Wittenberg while Martin Luther nailed his theses to the door and became a close friend of the man himself, produced endless propaganda for the new religion. His *Suffer the Little Children to Come Unto Me* (*c.* 1540) represents a theme that left his studio in many versions and became one of the most popular in early-16th-century northern European art. The Gospel gobbet was apparently seized upon to bolster the dour reformer in his bitter struggle with the even grimmer Anabaptists, who insisted that until voluntarily dunked, infants were damned. However, commercially-minded Cranach had no objections to lucrative Catholic commissions, represented here by *SS Catherine and Barbara* and *St Christina* (1520–25) (the Calvinist iconoclasts of a century later were rather more strict, and both are fragments from a destroyed altarpiece painted for St Vitus's Cathedral).

In the next room is Albrecht Dürer's **Feast of the Rose Garlands** (1506), regarded as one of the most important paintings of the northern Renaissance. It represents Dürer's deliberate attempt to marry his country's late Gothic art with the technical tricks and new visions of the south, and this work—with its shimmering colour, noble proportions and beauty, and use of perspective—was an attempt to beat the Venetians at their own game (Dürer painted it on a visit to the city). It shows Virgin, Child and St Dominic handing out rosy honours to kneeling worthies, and is also one of the first group portraits in northern art. Those attending the outdoor ceremony (any excuse to stick in a landscape) include Pope Julian II and Maximilian I, plenty of bourgeois bigwigs, and, humbly hopeful on the far right, hairy Dürer himself, clutching a small C.V. Rudolf II was obsessed by the artist's work, and had a special yearning for this painting—his father is the character being crowned by the Virgin. When the emperor eventually procured this, 'four stout men' were hired to carry it by hand over the Alps. In 1782, no-nonsense Joseph II put it under the hammer; luckily for Prague, bargain-hunting monks from Strahov were at the auction, and although it's been restored and re-restored far too often, it's still the National Gallery's pride and joy.

In the room on the right, you make a sudden hop in time and place to the brooding *Portrait of Don Miguel de Lardizábal* (1815) by Goya, whose recent experiences of the French invasion of his country were to explode into some savage work over the next decade; and a handful of 17th- and 18th-century French works including a portrait by Pierre Mignard, which combines the intensity and restraint of a man who was never really able to paint the anti-classicist art that he theorized.

The next wing begins with Prague's collection of Italian Renaissance art. The biggest names disappeared when the Swedes pilfered Rudolf II's massive collection in 1648, but a few delights have found their way here over later years. Lorenzo Lotto's *Portrait of a Musician* (pre-1530) may be one of the few works in the gallery to remain from the emperor's collection. It's a typical portrait by the Venetian, who dug deep into the individuality of his subjects and imbued them with a sense of transience and melancholy more often encountered in the art of the north than in the art of his less troubled home. The effect here is achieved with characteristic sense of detail—a sideward glance, a hand hanging list-lessly over a (16th-century) musical score. (An interesting detail is that contemplative Lotto went off to die in Italy's Loretto.) Sebastiano del Piombo's *Madonna with Veil* (1520) is of an altogether more heroic nature, produced after he had moved from Venice to Rome, and exuding the statuesque grandeur developed through years of studying antiques and chatting with Michelangelo. The room also contains two portraits by Agnolo Bronzino, *Cosimo de Medici* (1560) and *Eleanor of Toledo* (1540–43), both of which are among many similar works painted by the artist for his Florentine patron. The relentless accuracy which Bronzino brought to his portraits was often a cruel unveiling of the weaknesses of his subjects, but at least here, Eleanor is more than a match for his piercing eye. The painting commemorates the birth of one of four little Medicis that she produced during the three-year period, and she exudes a cool but almost sensual triumph. Bronzino was to have richer pickings in later portraits, capturing her pain as she spent 12 years dying of tuberculosis.

Prague's Mannerist collection was unmatched in northern Europe until the Swedish heist of 1648, but it's thought to have contained few if any works by El Greco. However, the gallery has one recent acquisition by him, a *Head of Christ* (1595–7), in which the artist's fervour is reflected in the damp eyes of the Messiah, gazing at a light that only the lucky few are likely ever to see. As usual, El Greco plays havoc with the artistic conventions of an age. Christ the Man, somehow combining humility with an almost superhuman nobility, is framed by a flaming rhomboid, taken from the figure of Christ the Judge in the rigid iconography of Byzantine art. The painting is one of the most unforgettable in the gallery.

Baroque light effects fill the next few rooms. The works include the scrawny and *chiaroscuro*-lit frame of *St Jerome* (1646) by Lo Spagnoletto (Jusepe de Ribera), much influenced by the realism of Caravaggio; the no less harsh but far more polished classicist tinge of Simon Vouet's *Suicide of Lucretia* (1625–26); and Domenico Fetti's *Christ on the Mount of Olives* (1615), convulsed by rippling movement and illumination. Take a look also at the tempestuous and faintly macabre *Penance of Mary Magdalene in the Wilderness* (1710) by Il Lissandrino (Alessandro Magnasco), the flickering light and nervous brush strokes of whose work make it instantly recognizable. The gallery's Italian collection ends with Canaletto's *View of London from the Thames* (1746), painted from the balcony of Lambeth Palace at the beginning of his ten-year stint in England. The artist had painted too many of his gay Venetian waterscapes to change his ways by then, and this work transforms the Thames into a festive lagoon, with barques and rowboats messing about on the river while the launch of the Lord Mayor-cum-Doge cruises past. The unfinished Westminster Bridge stretches across in all its pristine glory. The painting is placed next to a painted snapshot by Francesco Guardi (*Palace Courtyard*). It's a rather minute example of Guardi's work, but his almost Impressionistic views of Venice are often contrasted with the detailed deliberation of Canaletto.

The next few rooms contain the gallery's collection of Flemish and Dutch art. All is from the 17th and 18th centuries, save the first painting to your left, Pieter Bruegel the Elder's *Haymaking* (1565). The happy landscape of rural harmony originally formed part of a cycle, though seven of the 12 months have gone missing over the years. There are several works by Rubens here and in the following rooms, including the superb *Expulsion from Paradise* (1620), a preliminary sketch for one of 39 scenes commissioned by the Jesuits for their church in Antwerp. The Jesuits didn't use it (they decided to celebrate their foundation instead), but even in its stillborn form, this study shows the swirling brushwork and the ability to conjure up an instant of dramatic movement that set Rubens apart from every other European artist of his day. The room also contains the exquisite *Bunch of Flowers with Tulips* (1607–08), by Jan Brueghel, flower-painter *extraordinaire*; and a set of the clammy oysters with which part-time cork-seller Osias Beert made his name.

In the next room are some notable minor works (as well as works by Rembrandt and the Dutch landscapist Salomon van Ruysdael). There's an oddly spooky *Parliament of Animals* by Cornelis Saftleven, who spent his life perfecting such satires in the days before they became the stuff of wrapping-paper. Look out also for *Raising of Lazarus* (1640) by Leonaert Bramer, a powerful work sunk in darkness by an artist who is thought to have been the teacher of Vermeer. There are some fine still lifes, notably that by Jan Jansz den Uyl (1632), and the *Shelves with Bunch of Flowers and Fruit* (1600s), which the Frankfurt artist Georg Flegel filled with as many contrasting vegetables and minerals as he could muster, in a clear attempt to show that no texture was beyond his skills.

The oval heart of the palace that you enter next contains some of the grandest Dutch and Flemish painting in the gallery. Rubens holds centre stage with his *Martyrdom of St Thomas* (1637–38), showing the dramatic skills of the artist at their larger-than-life best. The Madras saint-killers are caught in mid-hatchet job, while the speared apostle heroically stretches for a palm of martyrdom being proferred by a squadron of exhilarated cherubs hovering overhead. Frans Hals is represented by a masterful *Portrait of Jasper Schade van Westrum* (1645). Like Rubens, the Dutchman didn't waste a brushstroke, and he's captured the brashness of his 22-year-old subject with a typical economy of expression that's made him a perennial favourite among artists (and rich American buyers) in the hurried 20th century. The very different portraiture of Rembrandt, kneaded from the palate and laboriously formed on the canvas, is reflected in his *Scholar in his Study* (1634)—an unknown character painted early in the artist's career, but showing the quizzical mystery of facial expression that was to obsess him in later life.

The art of the Low Countries ends in the next room which contains some minor gems, including the eerie monochrome of *Lighthouse in the Estuary* (1646) by Jan van Goyen, whose lifelong fascination with moody clouds placed him (along with Salomon van Ruysdael) at the forefront of

Dutch landscape painting of the 17th century. Jan van de Velde's *Still Life with Smokers' Effects* (1647) is a strikingly simple example of Dutch still life, lighter glowing and beer unfinished to bring to mind the absent presence of the puffer concerned; while Jan Davidsz de Heem's *Still Life with Fruit* (1652) exemplifies the more opulent Flemish still life tradition, dripping with moisture and very active life forms.

The corridor has landscapes by various Romantics, including Caspar David Friedrich's *North Sea by Moonlight*, and a small collection of late-19th-century Russian realist painters, including several works by Ilya Repin. The gallery's compendium of central European art from the first half of this century comes next and starts with a dreamy *Water Castle* (1909) by Gustav Klimt, next to his luscious *Virgin* (1913). Klimt's celebration of feminine fecundity is perversely reflected in Egon Schiele's nightmarish *Pregnant Woman & Death* (1911), the cadaverous couple dolefully contemplating life's bloody terror. Schiele visited Bohemia the same year, but the trip didn't lift his spirits judging from his holiday snap: in *Town (Český Krumlov)*, he transformed one of its more beautiful spots into a Pittsburgh of the soul. Another tortured spirit, Edvard Munch, is represented by three paintings. His lyrical *Dancing on the Shore* (*c.* 1900) dates from the height of his creative powers, and is one of the works that was probably intended for his loosely-planned 'Frieze of Life', an utterly beautiful piece of what he called his 'poem of life, love and death'.

German Impressionism is represented by a couple of earlier works by Lovis Corinth, including his *Self Portrait with Glass* (1907), apparently snatched with an urgency unusual even for Impressionism, in a state of undress and half-way through a drink. However, it's the social concerns of Expressionism which take over, with two rather unnerving portrayals of the powers-that-be. Wilhelm Thöny's *Verdict* (pre-1929) is Kafka in monochrome, while Max Oppenheimer's *Operation* (1912) takes the form of an indictment of the medical profession—a turbulent sea of white coats surround the all-but-hidden patient, fingers grasping for the jagged wound, and Mephistophelian doctors fascinate themselves with everything other than their charge's wellbeing. The late works by Max Pechstein (*Bridge in Labe*—1922) and Karl Schmidt-Rottluff (*Village Green*—*c.* 1920) turn German rural landscapes into tropical outposts of thunderous colour, reflecting the primitivism of which they were so fond. The deliberate restraint more typical of German Expressionism in the 1920s is shown by Karl Hofer's *Boy with Ball* (1925), as well as the Flemish Constant Permeke's *Peasant Woman with Bared Breast* (1942).

Oskar Kokoschka is represented by several works, most painted during his stay in Prague between 1934 and 1938. Over the previous decade, he had painted a series of city views, always surging away from an elevated viewpoint, and *Charles Bridge and the Hradčany Castle in Prague* (1935) is one of the finest examples of such works. Imbued with the powerful subjectivism of all the artist's work and with the affection that he felt for Prague (his father's birthplace), they're visions of a magical island of peace in a continent that was slipping into insanity. The idyll didn't last—the Nazis put Kokoschka on their aesthetic blacklist, and he left shortly before they rolled into town. He spent the war years in London, and his *Red Egg* (1941) is a powerful attack on the common enemy, with a doubtlessly Czech-influenced stab at appeasement and the Munich sell-out.

The rest of this floor contains an interesting set of work from pre-revolutionary and 1920s Russia, spanning the spatial methods of Cézanne and Cubism, the velocity of Futurism and the themes of German Expressionism. The final stretch of corridor contains the most modern work acquired by the Gallery, a strangely restrained collection which can't all be put down to limited funds. Politics played an important role—the most recent work is Renato Guttoso's vast *News* (1971), a bloodcurdling catalogue of the West's ills by an honest anti-fascist.

Walk back down to the ground floor and cross the courtyard to the collection of 19th- and 20th-century French art. Prague discovered Impressionism, Post-Impressionism and Cubism within a few years of each other during the first decade of this century, and has taken France's culture very seriously ever since. The collection is a small one, but you've got to give credit to the city's taste. At the time of writing, the gallery has recently been reorganized and begins at the end—close your eyes and work your way back into the main hall if you want to see the work in order.

The gallery contains several sculptures by Rodin, who attended an exhibition of his work in Prague in 1902. He called Prague 'the Rome of the north', but the city didn't mind, and bought his seminal *Age of Bronze*, which stands in the centre of the main room. Critics accused him of using a live model to make the original cast in 1875, paradoxically affronted by the fact that the work was so realistic that it lacked the idealism they still required in a nude. Rodin was undaunted, and ten years later, those detractors that remained were confronted with the open sensuality of *Martyr*. The far end of the room contains a patchy collection of early-19th-century work, a portrait by Manet (of Proust) and Degas, and a summery set of hazy Impressionism. The last group includes works by Camille Pissarro—*Countryside at Eragny* (1880) and *In the Greengrocer's Garden* (1881); the idyllic *Lovers* (1875) by Auguste Renoir; and a verdant *Ladies in Flowers* (1875) by Claude Monet.

Cézanne's small but juicy *Fruit* (1882) and his *House in Aix-en-Provence* (1885–87) show the beginnings of a preoccupation with volume that was to consume his career (and soon much of Europe). Although the artist was generally less concerned with the mood than with the spatial location of his human subjects, his *Portrait of Joachym Gasquet* (1897) creates a rare intensity of expression with the studied and extraordinary use of colour and tone on the subject's face. The two romantic heroes of Post-Impressionism come next. Gauguin's lifetime preoccupation with colour is reflected in his *Bonjour, Monsieur Gauguin* (1889), as well as the hopefully-named *Escape*, dating from 1902, by which time he'd settled in Dominica and left everything behind except the syphilis that killed him the following year. Next come the swirling undercurrents of *Green Rye* (1889) by Gauguin's erstwhile friend, Van Gogh—created from the lunatic asylum that he entered after his failed knife attack on Gauguin and his notoriously more successful assault on his ear. A gay *Moulin Rouge* (1892) by Toulouse-Lautrec, and two nautical pieces of pointillism by Seurat and Signac, are followed by Maurice Vlaminck's *Landscape* and *Grey House* (1914), sets of wonky buildings *à la* Cézanne. Pierre Bonnard was having none of the fancy experiments of his contemporaries, and his *Conversation in Provence* (1912–13) is a serene memory of Impressionism. The small *Joaquina* (1910) by Henri Matisse is rather stunning.

The representation of artists in the gallery is generally limited to one or two paintings, but thanks to the obsessions (and generosity) of one Vincenc Kramář, it has a sizeable Cubist collection. André Derain's *Cadaques* (1910) and *Montreuil-sur-Mer* (1910) show the influence of the new style, but as with *Still Life with Jug* (1913), it's still the influence of Cézanne which predominates. However, the works by Georges Braque show Synthetic Cubism in all its confusing glory, tearing apart its subjects and then reconstituting them in an entirely new visual language. No one's ever been quite sure whether you're meant to reconstruct the puzzles (which would slightly defeat the point of the exercise), but the paintings' English titles are probably more useful here than in most other sections of the gallery (*Still Life with Violin and Glass* (1910–11), *Still Life with Clarinet and Violin* (1913), *Still Life with Guitar II (Hearth-Quartet)*

(1921), *Still Life with Guitar I (Hearth-Waltz)* (1920–21) and *Still Life with Pipe* (1919–20). There's a large selection of work by the co-creator of Cubism, **Pablo Picasso**, including the artist's *Self-Portrait* (1907), painted while Picasso was still thinking his way out of the world of appearances. It dates from the same year as his *Desmoiselles d'Avignon*, and like some of those well-known characters, the black-rimmed eyes and stylized features of the painting borrow heavily from the primitive sculpture then being studied by the artist. The room also contains a copy of his *Woman's Head* (1909), the first ever Cubist sculpture (followed closely by the work of the Czech Otto Gutfreund—see p. 75), and another long line of ever-more mysterious visions from the period of Synthetic Cubism. The titles might again provide some useful hints: *Harlequin* (1908), *Toreador Playing the Guitar* (1911), *Woman in a Coach* (1910), *Clarinet* (1911), *Woman with Guitar at the Piano* (1911), *Boxer* (1912), *Guitar and Gas Ring* (1912–13) and *Violin, Glass, Pipe and Anchor—Memories of Le Havre* (1912).

Prague's museums have been steadily decimated by thefts since the Velvet Revolution, and in May 1991 four other works by Picasso—worth about $30m—were spirited away by a cat-burglar early one morning. However, at the time of writing there are still three more works by the artist in the next room, fairly representative snapshots of his career separated by 20-year intervals: a statuesque *Standing Woman* from the period of married tranquility and the aforementioned fat women phase (1921); the grim *Woman's Head (Head in Grey)* from the war years of bulls and horses (1941); and *Abduction of the Sabines* from the years when the artist had finally reached uncategorizable status (1962).

As well as the Gallic charm of Henri Rousseau's *Moi-même, portrait paysage* (1890), the room contains an early *Bathing* (1908) by André Derain and a copy of one of Rodin's best-known works—*Balzac* (1898). As Rodin mulled over the meaning of genius, he transformed the novelist into this epic, which he called 'the sum of my whole life'; when it was unveiled, others called it a 'toad in a sack'. With one-liners like that, the scoffers have predictably joined the ranks of the fall-guys of art history. It has to be said that on the purely visual level, the work bears a more than passing resemblance to a toad in a sack, but the psychological mystery and almost Expressionistic power of the work make it perhaps the most original sculpture ever produced by the artist. Rodin's *Iris* (1890–91) is an interesting example of erotica.

The collection ends in the next room, but there's no great burst of Surrealism, nor even much evidence that French art survived the

Second World War. Price had something to do with it; more important were the cultural shutters that were drawn down over Czechoslovakia. There are four paintings by Maurice Utrillo, and a pretty *Flowers* by Suzanne Valadon, mother of Utrillo and active lover of plenty, including 'Teapot' Toulouse-Lautrec. The room also contains works by Raoul Dufy (including *Still Life with Sea in Background* (*c.* 1926)), Georges Rouault (*In the Bar* and *Three Naked Women*—both 1914), and an example of would-be proletarian art by Fernand Léger (*Two Lovers in the Country*). There's a song in the heart of Marc Chagall's *Circus (Equestrienne)* (1927), which makes for a rather joyful end to the collection.

Turn left when you leave the gallery and enter the gate to the left of the castle's main entrance. Continue through the **Garden on the Bastion** *(Zahrada na baště). Now a peaceful little spot, it was once a defensive ditch and later an artillery emplacement. Walk through the arch in front of you to the second courtyard of the castle, and turn left through the arch. In front of you is the* **Powder Bridge** *(Prašný most). If you look over the sides, you'll see that it's now firmly supported on a solid bank of earth, but until the rebuilding of the castle in the 18th century, it was a wooden bridge over the ravine below. Ferdinand I built the first bridge, and in his weirdo Habsburg way, included a not-very-secret tunnel underneath, so that he could sneak off to his newly-built Royal Summer Palace without anyone seeing him. (His grandson Rudolf II liked the idea and built an entire warren under the castle.)*

Far below to your right is the **Stag Moat** *(Jelení příkop)—at first, it was a useful natural ditch, but with the invention of artillery, Vladislav II of Jagellon sensibly decided to rely instead on the powerful fortifications that you can see on the right. The Habsburgs filled the fissure with stags, who multiplied and gambolled here until 1743. They actually had a rather rough time—not only did Rudolf II occasionally include his pet lions and tigers in the hunting parties, but they also suffered regular epidemics from the slop poured over them by the residents of the Golden Lane (see pp. 132–3). Over the bridge, to your left is the Riding School of Prague Castle (Jízdárna Pražského hradu). At the time of writing, it houses the National Gallery's collection of 20th-century Czechoslovakian art, but that's another collection due to be moved very soon (see p. 249). On the opposite side of the path is the* **Royal Garden** *(Královská zahrada).*

Open Sat–Sun, May–Sept. The garden was founded by Ferdinand I in the mid-16th century, and until the Habsburgs left for Vienna after the Thirty Years War, it was their Prague playground as well as a laboratory for their explorations of the natural world. Shrubs and plants were grown in greenhouses (tulips stopped off for several years on their way from Turkey to Amsterdam, obtained thanks to the untiring efforts of Ferdinand I's ambassador to Constantinople) and on the slope down to the Stag Moat, Rudolf II grew figs and oranges. The park was laid out as an English garden in the 19th century, after having been devastated during the 17th and 18th centuries; the Swedes and Saxons bombarded the figs, and the rest of the blooms were blown up by the Prussians in 1757. Only the French showed some refinement—they occupied the garden in 1743, but agreed not to obliterate it after the head gardener offered them 30 pineapples.

> To your right as you walk through the garden is the sgraffiti-*covered* **Ball Game Hall** *(Míčovna), dating from 1567–69, which resounded with the rackets of the Habsburgs and favoured guests for the next 50 years, until the family deserted troublesome Prague for good. The sculpture in front is an* Allegory of Night *by Antonín Braun. The one-time* **Orangerie** *stretches along the slope below the garden, which is closed by the graceful splendour of the* **Royal Summer Palace** *(Královský letohrádek). At the time of writing, the interior is being restored, but you can get a clear view through the railings at the end of the garden.*

The palace was built between 1538 and 1564 for Ferdinand I, and is the purest example of Italian Renaissance architecture in Prague. Slender Ionic columns swing up and down in happy harmony along the arcade running around the palace, and there are none of the alien Mannerist growths that infected the city's later explorations of the Renaissance (although its roof, an upside-down ship's hull of sea-green copper sheets, defies categorization). The **Singing Fountain** in front of the palace dates from 1568 and is said to tinkle when the water's on. Ferdinand and his entourage would trot through his tunnel to the palace when life at the castle became just too dreary, perhaps to have a ball in the room upstairs. His grandson Rudolf II was less given to revelry; according to Prague's papal nuncio he smiled once during his 26-year reign, when confronted by a diplomatic delegation from Persia scurrying towards him on all fours to kiss his feet. In 1600, he installed an observatory for Tycho Brahe inside the palace. Johannes Kepler also worked here, but his short-lived collaboration with Tycho was fraught with difficulties. He had accepted the Dane's offer of a menial assistant's post only after he and his fellow Lutherans in Styria had been given 45 days' notice to quit by Catholic Archduke Ferdinand; and despite his respect for Tycho's mathematical wizardry, he had already begun to doubt the latter's necessarily ever-more complex model of the universe, in which five planets circled the sun in a flotilla that hurtled around the earth at different speeds. From the moment that Kepler arrived, he tried to double-check Brahe's evidence. In a series of unhappy letters he reported that the tetchy astronomer would only mention the occasional apogee or planetary orbit over dinner, that he had had to promise to keep all the morsels to himself, and more generally that 'Tycho philosophizes rather queerly'. Brahe's unfortunate death was a stroke of luck for the German astronomer. Although his heirs guarded his work with equal jealousy (the notation of observable facts was widely regarded as a creative invention) Kepler managed to weasel them out through disingenuous flattery, and was appointed Brahe's successor as imperial mathematician. As the title suggests, Kepler was subject to Rudolf's occasional quirk, but he got on well with the tolerant emperor, who was correspondingly fascinated by his astronomer's outlandish vision of a heliocentric universe. It all bore fruit in 1609, when he published his first two Laws of Planetary Motion based on the work he did here, with an effusive dedication to the emperor.

> *Animals were another important part of the life of any self-respecting Renaissance monarch. If you leave the garden and turn right, you'll see the* **Lion Court** *(Lví Dvůr)—now a restaurant, it was once the Habsburg zoo.*

Lions were kept here as early as the 14th century, simply as a heraldic emblem, but when Rudolf moved the imperial court to Prague in 1576, they were joined by wolves, leopards, lynxes and a host of other beasts. Ivan the Terrible's son brought three leopards for the emperor on his visit in 1585. The cats were often taken a-hunting, and would line up like kittens behind the horses, ripping the stags apart only on command. The court favourite was Muhammad the Lion, and Tycho Brahe once cast his horoscope. He solemnly announced that the beast and emperor Rudolf were bound by the same fate. Rudolf died a day after Muhammad—a mystery to chew over while eating your steak.

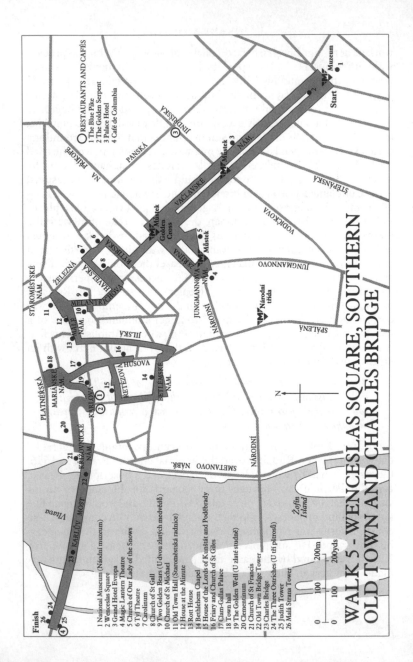

RESTAURANTS AND CAFÉS
1 The Blue Pike
2 The Golden Serpent
3 Palace Hotel
4 Café de Columbia

WALK 5 - WENCESLAS SQUARE, SOUTHERN OLD TOWN AND CHARLES BRIDGE

1 National Museum (Náodní muzeum)
2 Wenceslas Square
3 Grand Hotel Evropa
4 Magic Lantern Theatre
5 Church of Our Lady of the Snows
6 Tyl Theatre
7 Carolinum
8 Church of St Gall
9 Two Golden Bears (U dvou zlatých medvědů)
10 Church of St Michael
11 Old Town Hall (Staroměstská radnice)
12 House at the Minute
13 Rott House
14 Bethlehem Chapel
15 House of the Lords of Kunštát and Poděbrady
16 Friary and Church of St Giles
17 Clam-Gallas Palace
18 Town hall
19 The Golden Well (U zlaté studně)
20 Clementinum
21 Church of St Francis
22 Old Town Bridge Tower
23 Charles Bridge
24 The Three Ostriches (U tří pštrosů)
25 Judith Tower
26 Malá Strana Tower

Walk V

Wenceslas Square, the Southern Old Town and the Charles Bridge

The Charles Bridge

Wenceslas Square—Church of Our Lady of the Snows—Tyl Theatre—Carolinum—Old Town Hall—Bethlehem Chapel—House of the Lords of Kunštát and Poděbrady—Clam-Gallas Palace—Clementinum—Charles Bridge

This walk is a whistle-stop tour back through the centuries. It begins in Wenceslas Square, the clamorous boulevard where four decades of Communism died in November 1989; and ends on the Charles Bridge, the vortex of the capital for 600 years. On the way, it passes the mechanical marionettes of the ancient Astronomical Clock, descends to the level of Romanesque Prague, and stalks the royal coronation route through the labyrinth of the Old Town. Its streets, fading into a peeled and pastel charm, are swamped by tourists, but as you explore its silent back-alleys and cloisters, you'll encounter the evidence of a past that most never see.

Start this walk by lunchtime at the latest. Although the museums on the walk have no more than curiosity value, there are several galleries, courtyards and interiors that tend to close by 6 pm. Choose a clear day. You could hop from café to café in the rain, but you'd miss most of what's on offer. The sprawling Old Town is divided between this walk and Walk II, and you may want to explore the Old Town Square as you skim across its edge. On a warm summer evening, you could cross the few hundred yards that separate the Charles Bridge and Walk III, and begin a twilight exploration of Malá Strana.

The walk **starts** at the top of Wenceslas Square. You may be staying near by; otherwise, take the metro to Muzeum (lines A and C). It **ends** on the Charles Bridge. There are metro stations flanking both sides of the next bridge northwards (Malostranská and Staroměstská, both line A); trams 12 and 22 stop at Malostranské nám. just beyond the end of the walk; and trams 17 and 18 follow the embankment on the Old Town side of the river.

Walking time: about 3 hours.

LUNCH/CAFÉS

There are plenty of cafés and restaurants along this route, but most offer Prague's traditional fare of identical menus and abysmal service, slowly. The following is a list of some of the more interesting stops; but in high season you'll probably find yourself grabbing a seat wherever you can.

Evropa Café, Václavské nám. 25. 7 am–11 pm. Service can be terrible, only cheesey and hammy dishes are available at rather random intervals (try before 2), but the Art Nouveau decor almost makes up for everything. At least stop for a coffee.

Palace Hotel, on the corner of Panská and Jindřišská. 10 am–10 pm. The soulless salad-bar of one of Prague's smarter hotels. Self-service. Not a place for a leisurely meal, but it's healthy, dependable, and quick. It's slightly off the route of this walk.

U modré štiky (The Blue Pike), on the corner of Karlova and Liliová. 9 am–11 pm. Once Prague's first cinema; now a fish restaurant. Pilsner on tap.

U zlaté konvice (The Golden Tankard), Melantrichova 20. 5 pm–midnight. Gipsy music and bottles of wine in subterranean chambers several metres under Old Town Square, Great fun, but be sure to make a reservation in advance.

U zlatého hada (The Golden Serpent), other corner of Karlova and Liliová. 11 am–midnight. A beer-less alternative to the Blue Pike; steaks dominate the menu. The adjoining bar sometimes serves food if the restaurant has no space.

Café de Columbia, Mostecká 3, next to the Judith Tower. 10 am–11 pm. Owned by the Colombian Embassy—the ambassador sometimes makes surprise visits. Cakes, coffee, vodka and a tiny courtyard at the back.

☆　　☆　　☆　　☆　　☆

There's an odd connection between the beginning and end of this walk: both Wenceslas Square and the Charles Bridge were founded almost simultaneously by Emperor Charles IV in the mid-14th century. The square, actually a half-mile boulevard, was the horse market that Charles needed for his New Town (see p. 000), and you could have followed the route of this walk 600 years ago. It's not something that's apparent any more: Wenceslas Square itself is now the commercial centre of the city and significant for its recent political history rather than for any lingering remains of its horse-trading days. But as you leave the square, you sink ever deeper into streets that are simultaneously an accretion and detrition of centuries of architecture, and petrified testimony to the history that has raged through the Old Town.

The walk begins at the head of Wenceslas Square. Whether you're walking or emerging from Muzeum metro station, you'll have no problems finding the first stop. It's the grandiloquent **National Museum** *(Národní muzeum), which now seals Prague's central avenue with all the half-pillars, pilasters and pomp that the brown and solemn architecture of the Czech national revival was able to muster.*

A museum of Bohemian history was a dream of early 19th-century patriots. They launched an appeal for objects, but as the domestic appliances and folk art poured in, it became apparent that Bohemia's traditions needed a home more glorious than the temporary accommodation that was so far available. In the 1870s Prague's council stepped in with this rent-free site. The grandeur of the neo-Renaissance building (1885–90) was meant to express the confidence of the Czech national revival movement; the effect was to shatter the balance of old Wenceslas Square. It encouraged the almost complete renewal of the street's architecture over this century; and paradoxically, the symmetry of the museum, its bulk set off by a golden central dome, now makes it an almost elegant point on the 20th-century exclamation mark that Wenceslas Square has become.

Open Mon and Fri 9am–4 pm, Wed–Thurs and Sat–Sun 9 am–5 pm, adm. The museum is worth a visit just for the open staircase that greets you beyond the entrance—three floors of veined marble pillars and banisters, globular lamps and swaying palm fronds. Under the glassy dome, on the first floor, is a **sculptural pantheon** of some 60 national

PRAGUE

heroes gazing down from the walls and plinths: an eclectic and eerie collection of work by most of Prague's leading early 20th-century sculptors. Wait for a very, very rainy day before exploring the rest of the building, which houses a stupefying collection of stuffed animals and anthropological knick-knacks. Even the mammoth is fake.

As you leave the museum, you'll be faced with a view of the former horse market, rolling towards the hidden Old Town. The image is one that you may recognize: in November 1989, this was the site of one of the hardest-fought battles of the Velvet Revolution, between the cameramen of the world's press. Silhouetted against the panorama is the rump of one of the symbols of Prague, the **equestrian figure of St Wenceslas**. *Make your way to the figure, crossing the main road by the subway around the corner on your right.*

Although a familiar name to English carol singers since the 1850s, Good King Wenceslas ruled as a prince rather than a king, until murdered by his notoriously cruel brother, Boleslav the Cruel, in 935. Just to confuse matters, there were eventually four *King* Wenceslases; and the country is now ruled by another (Václav=Wenceslas). The saint's reputation for goodness arose from an obsessive and harmless Christianity, but over the years, Wenceslas has metamorphosed from religious to national hero. The legends have followed him; and this figure will apparently gallop into life at Bohemia's moment of greatest need.

The symbolic importance of the statue came to obsess its designer J. V. Myslbek. The grand old man of 19th-century Czech sculpture, Myslbek began work in 1887 with the idea of Wenceslas as a shaggy Slav; but as the reality of a national state grew closer, he transformed the Dark Age prince into the serene and noble leader you see today. Ardo the stallion had to take weeks off his military duties to pose in the sculptor's studio; and when his work was finally unveiled in 1912, Myslbek sighed, 'Now I see it could have been still bigger.' Perhaps—but he needn't have worried. Ever since it was unveiled, it has been a public rallying point: in 1918, Czechoslovakian independence was announced at Wenceslas' feet; after 1948, Communist May Day parades goose-stepped along the square; and after the Soviet-led invasion of August 1968 the monument was the focus for Prague's desperation. In that month, an 11-year-old boy was shot dead as he stood on the steps and pushed a Czech flag down the barrel of a Soviet tank; and on 16 January 1969, next to the fountain of the National Museum, **Jan Palach** burned himself alive. A week later, 800,000 Czechs followed his coffin past the statue. The happiest moment of the monument's recent history came in November 1989, when Wenceslas and Ardo made it onto millions of television sets across the world, at the head of the demonstrations which finally saw off the shoddy dictatorship.

Directly in front of the statue is a round pedestal which became an impromptu memorial to victims of Communist oppression after the revolution.

Among those commemorated by the candles and pictures is Jan Palach. Every year on the anniversary of his death, police would come out in force to protect public order; in February 1989, Václav Havel was sentenced to nine months in jail for having attempted to place flowers here. Another of those honoured is Professor Jan Patočka, a 70-year old spokesman for the Charter 77 movement (see p. 59), who died of a brain haemorrhage while being questioned by the police. The authorities paid their respects by sending a helicopter to the funeral, which hovered a few metres above the open grave as the oration was read.

Stroll on down the street—you'll probably run a gauntlet of mous-tachioed chaps whispering 'Cambio?' or 'Moneychange?'. You respond at your peril (see Practical A–Z). Men should also beware of women in tight leather skirts. On the right just before the central crossroads is the glorious Art Nouveau façade of the **Grand Hotel Evropa** *(1903–06).*

The hotel café is a favourite spot for the same prostitutes and money-changers to compare notes, and a subtle variation on a clichéd theme of central European elegance. The interior looks the part—revolving doors spin you into a shabby and beautiful room of mirrors and mahogany, crystal chandeliers and carriage lamps—but the clientele is a motley crew indeed. The living legends who swan past oblivious tourists include one of the city's most confident transvestites, a gipsy king, and an ageing-Bette Davis-lookalike who was, according to informed rumour, the most popular call-girl of Nazi-occupied Prague. During the winter, one table is often occupied by an extremely animated deaf and dumb discussion group. Come back in the evening, when the house trio add their cacophonous touch to the ambience.

As you leave the Evropa, turn right. The next half of Wenceslas Square is a hotch-potch of Prague's early 20th-century architecture;

223

while between the Functionalist Alfa and Tatran buildings on your left is the Hotel Adria, one of the last Baroque façades on the square. The Air India offices on the right (No. 13) used to house Aeroflot; some older Praguers still fondly remember the night in 1969 when Czechoslovakia beat the Soviet Union at ice-hockey and they made a bonfire of the furniture.

As you gaze at the façades, you can now safely consider one of the more surreal rumours of the November revolution: that after July 1989, the jittery authorities had a cardboard copy of the entire square constructed somewhere in Slovakia, in which their troops could practise Tienanmen-inspired crowd-control techniques. It has never been found.

*Walk to the foot of the square, the so-called **Golden Cross**, a junction of shoppers and idle youth which is curiously regarded by the tourist authorities as the hub of swinging Prague. Turn left along 28. října, which takes you past a series of reminders of the 1989 revolution. On the left is an exhibition centre belonging to Civic Forum (*Občanské fórum *or OF), the now very broken umbrella movement that sprang up after the first demonstrations. At the end of the paved precinct, you'll see the bizarre crenellations and turrets of the **Magic Lantern Theatre** (Laterna Magika) to your left across the street, which was the organization's press centre during the hectic first weeks.*

The building is a striking example of the Rondocubist architecture that Pavel Janák, the designer, was trying to develop into a Czechoslovakian national style fit for the 20th century (see p. 79). Modern Prague would have been an architectural curiosity of titanic proportions had he succeeded, but this urban citadel (1923–25) is one of only a few examples that got off the ground. For the last 30 years, the theatre has been occupied by a tourist-trap extravaganza that's a favourite among package-tour organizers with other people's time to kill (see p. 303).

*The street running on from 28. října is Národní třída (National Avenue), the scene of the clash between police and students on 17 November that sparked off an action-packed month. There's a memorial a few hundred metres down the road on the left, but save that for another day. Make a U-turn to your left, and in the wall ahead of you is a doorway leading into the forecourt of the **Church of Our Lady of the Snows** (Kostel Panny Marie Sněžné), one of the last survivors of Emperor Charles IV's New Town.*

Charles founded the church in 1347, five years before the 1000th anniversary of its Roman namesake, better known as Santa Maria Maggiore. The latter was built after the Virgin appeared in a wintry flurry one August afternoon and showed Pope Liberius a snowy model of what was required. Construction of Prague's version proved less straightforward. The open courtyard was to be the body of a vast triple-naved church, but the Hussite Wars and lack of money put paid to that idea, and the blank wall in front of you closes the only part of the project to be completed. It's the cavernous Gothic chancel (1397), which at about 33 m matches the height of St Vitus's Cathedral. The buttresses and narrow arches of the stump towered over the left bank of Prague until the redevelopment of the New Town locked it behind a wall of modern architecture and turned it into the best-concealed church in the capital. The interior is dominated by a splendid early Baroque high altar, climbing in three black-and-gold storeys to an aerial Crucifixion scene; Christ is pinned to a net-vault which dates from the 17th century, built after its predecessor found the weight too much and collapsed.

Leave the forecourt of the church through the door to the right. Walk towards the lamp post to the right, a curious piece of Cubo-Expressionism dating from 1912 with a built-in seat, and then continue through the passageway which takes you back to the Golden Cross (it's temporarily closed at the time of writing, and you may have to retrace your steps). The broad street opposite is **Na příkopě**—*the name means 'on the moat', and true enough, it was a muddy ditch separating the Old and New Towns until 1760. Following the example of its Viennese namesake, Der Graben, Prague's Germans turned it into their weekend promenade during the 19th century; and by the early 1900s, when duelling scars were the latest thing, it had become the scene of regular Sunday afternoon battles between proud German thugs and their Czech counterparts.*

Take Můstek, the narrow route to your left, running on from Wenceslas Square and beginning the journey into the heart of the Old Town. The stone bridge over the moat used to stand here; a chunk of arches was unearthed when the metro was built, and now sits sadly in the vestibule wall of Můstek (Little Bridge) metro station. Turn right at Rytířská. The neo-Renaissance lump across the road used to celebrate the life and times of Klement Gottwald, the loathed post-war leader of the Communist Party, and was the dismal destination of generations of school outings. It's now a savings bank, installed in another theatrical late 19th-century interior. When you reach the corner of Železná, on your left, you'll see the pale green and white façade of the **Tyl Theatre** *(Tylovo divadlo).*

Its pediment and pillars flow from the body of the building in concave curves, with all the elegance of neo-classical architecture at its best. It's now named after the composer of the Czech national anthem, but it was a bastion of German opera for 150 years until 1945, and its early history has made it a minor place of pilgrimage among Mozart-groupies for two centuries. With two tiers of boxes and a capacity for over 1000 opera-buffs, the theatre was already the finest in central Europe when its curtain first rose in 1783. In 1786, it saw the performance of Mozart's *The Marriage of Figaro.* The opera was panned by the snooty Viennese, but Prague's critics couldn't praise it too highly. Wolfgang came to town and had a ball, literally (see p. 184) and metaphorically. Fêted by the city's bourgeoisie and nobility, he merrily wrote back to Vienna that 'Nothing is played, sung or whistled like Figaro. No opera is drawing like Figaro. Nothing, nothing but Figaro.'

The management knew a box-office success when it heard one and collared the composer. Commissioned to write another opera, he returned with the score of *Don Giovanni* (minus the overture—see p. 252), which he conducted here for the first time in October 1787. The theatre's place in the minutiae of musical history was assured.

The building next to the theatre, the **Carolinum**, *is the core of the Charles University, founded by Emperor Charles IV in 1348. It was the first university in central Europe, as Prague's guidebooks proudly state, and the 35th in the rest of the continent, as they generally forget.*

Charles had high hopes for his college. Like any good imperialist, he knew the subtle advantages of educating potential enemies, and in its early years, budding prelates and princes enrolled from across Europe. But Prague soon showed that it wasn't ready for the hurly-burly of medieval contemplation. As the city's politics polarized in the later 14th century, the melting pot boiled over. The heretic-to-be Jan Hus (see p. 44) became rector in 1402 and declared his support for the writings of the Oxford reformer John Wycliffe; the university's German Catholics rallied to the defence of their rotten Church. A noisy stalemate ended in

1409, when the Czech Hussites persuaded feeble Wenceslas IV to triple their voting power, and 5000 Germans packed their bags and left to found Leipzig University. For the next two centuries the Carolinum was a think-tank of anti-Catholicism, and when Bohemian Protestantism was trounced at the Battle of the White Mountain in 1620, its fate hung in the balance. The cruel Spanish generals on the Habsburg team murmured that the building should be obliterated; but the cunning Jesuits, who understood the power of education, persuaded Ferdinand II to give it to them instead. To keep the Spaniards happy, the notoriously eloquent tongue of ex-rector Jessenius was sliced off before he was quartered in 1621.

The building was gutted by retreating Nazis in 1945, and its front almost entirely destroyed—but through the large windows, arched by restorers to retain a Gothic touch, you can see the vaulted arcade of the original building provided by Wenceslas IV in 1383. The cloister and rooms are sometimes opened for exhibitions, but otherwise the only reminder of the Carolinum's former glory is in the lane next to the Tyl Theatre, where you'll find an oriel window (1370), decorated with crests, pinnacles and a small but beastly set of Gothic nightmares. Retrace your steps, and turn left down Havelská, the street facing the entrance to the Carolinum, which takes you past the green onions and quivering Baroque façade of St Gall's Church (sv. Havel).

Like so many of Prague's churches, St Gall's is built on layers of earlier buildings. It dates from the 13th century when it was founded as the parish church of St Gall's Town, a German community invited to set up their laws and markets in an enclave of the Old Town. The church was reconstructed in the late 1600s and the present façade, plastered on in 1723, is a *tour de force* of Prague's late Baroque architecture. The architect was Giovanni Santini (see p. 70), who, like contemporaries across northern Europe, fell under the spell of Borromini's undulating works in Rome. With the asymmetry and interweaving elements of this work, he created the most energetic exterior of all the churches in central Prague (with the extremely honourable exception of St Nicholas' in Malá Strana—see pp. 178–82). The façade shimmies across the street, with sculptured saints, reproachful and violent, glaring at you from the rollercoaster roof.

Walk along until you get back to Melantrichova. Havelská continues across the road with a picturesque set of Renaissance and Baroque façades, veering distantly over a broad stone arcade left behind from Gothic days. St Gall's Germans were a business-minded bunch, and their markets (trh) filled their entire town, stretching in a still recognizable bow around the church. The stalls in Havelská (and the parallel street), with their herbs, flowers and acrylic sweaters are the lacklustre survivors of a tradition that half pulled through Communism and stretches back 700 years.

Turn right down Melantrichova. On your left is a spindly green neon sign for the **Vinárna Narcis** *running down the outside of No. 5. If you are with a Praguer, tell him or her that your guidebook recommends the bar, and watch the reaction. It's the dodgiest dive in central Prague: only off-duty police officers and hardened criminals are treated with respect, and any customer without friends in very low places is likely to suffer at least a spot of battery (see Entertainment and Nightlife).*

Continue down Melantrichova, past the plaque of rumbustious Jan Marek Marci, until you come to Kožná on your right. On the corner are two brutes padding through the arched entrance to **The Two Golden Bears** *(U dvou zlatých medvědů). The Renaissance doorway (1590), saturated with the twirling vegetation more characteristic of late Gothic art, is one of the most sumptuous portals in Prague, and was understandably kept in place when the rest of the house was rebuilt in around 1800. The corridor through the door winds into a tiny arcaded court. On the other side of Melantrichova is a tunnel leading through to the shattered Baroque* **Church of St Michael** *(c. 1740) (Kostel sv. Michal). Deconsecrated in 1786, once used as a warehouse, and now utterly ruined, the crumbling masonry is beginning to yield up a 15th-century archway from the Gothic church it cannibalized when built.*

Go back to Melantrichova, and continue to the left until it spits you out from a buttressed bottleneck into the Old Town Square in front of the **Old Town Hall** *(Staroměstská radnice).*

The privileges attached to town life in medieval Europe were immense. Peaceful coexistence and fortifications had always been a way for decent folk to protect themselves against rapine and pillage; but a town charter also gave them a degree of political power that was potentially more or less independent of the monarch. The dilemma for a king was that to declare war on uppity subjects could strain resources (although it was still often judged worth while); and when a community had reached critical mass, monarchs tended to cut their losses and hand over a town charter. The Old Town got fortifications and a royal charter in the mid-13th century, and Wenceslas II grudgingly let Praguers have a clerk in 1296; but he put his foot down when they asked for a town hall to put him in. The townspeople had to wait until 1338, when they were able to take advantage of blind King John of Luxemburg. The errant king was too busy being gallant to fret over the trivia of municipal affairs, and waved the plans through—but commanded that the town hall be funded from a new tax on wine. That threw the thrifty burghers; but they were able to make a humble start later that year when they bought a house and turned it into the **tower** in front of you. As the receipts poured in, they were slowly able to add all the buildings on your left. It was a piecemeal process, involving the destruction of spinners' sheds and the roofing-over of the lane to the goose market, but the maroon and white 18th-century façades—encrusted with Gothic and Renaissance survivals from earlier days—now house a single interior, stretching from the tower to the end of the block.

On the tower is the town hall's pride and joy, its **Astronomical Clock***, or horologe* (orloj).

Prague woke up late to the idea of clocks—by the time this one was installed in 1410, every other major city in Europe had one—but they were still exotic devices, and the city's burghers were apparently concerned that things should stay that way. Legend has it that when it was remodelled by a certain Master Hanuš in 1490, the Municipal Council took the precaution of blinding him to protect their copyright. A peeved Master Hanuš scaled the building, tossed a medieval spanner in the works, and promptly died. Prague's timepiece was out of joint for almost a century; but since 1572, it has ticked away without interruption, the occasional fire and artillery blitz notwithstanding.

The arcane clock is a reminder of an age when such machines were regarded as very powerful creatures indeed. Only in the 19th century did the industrial world really begin to operate on the assumption that clocks simply recorded the hours—as far as medieval thought was concerned, it was just as plausible that they created them, and even into the 17th century, the connected notions of clocks, clockwork and perpetual motion were imbued with a mystery that is hard to imagine today. This one purports to tell the time, but that's only the beginning. Its astronomical symbols, pointers, and interlocking circles also register the

229

phases of the moon and sun, the length of the day, the equinoxes, the rising and setting of the stars, and the dates of innumerable mobile feasts; and all the cogs and wheels whirr with added complication, according to the orbit of the heavens around the earth. Mechanical magic also treated awestruck spectators to a morality play, all but unchanged for 500 years. Every hour two cuckoo-clock windows open and statues of the 12 Apostles mince past while bony Death tinkles his bell. The great leveller is pooh-poohed by preening Vanity, and those bugbears of 15th-century Europe, the Turk and the Jew. The latter now lacks his beard and horns, and is politely referred to as Greed, having been sanitized following the town hall's bombardment in 1945. The post-Holocaust decision was understandable; but the paradoxical effect was to whitewash the bloody feature of central Europe's history that had just reached its culmination. A cock, and delighted children, screech when the ceremony is all over.

The temporal theme is taken up by the painted calendar below the clock showing the monthly labours of rural folk. It's by Josef Mánes, a prolific artist of the 19th-century Czech national revival movement. Bucolic subjects were favoured by Romantics everywhere, and especially so in Bohemia where popular imagination tended to see Germans as an unhealthy brood of urban lounge lizards. Again, the stereotype had connotations that stretched back to darker times; by the early 20th century, 85 per cent of the German-speakers in Prague were Jewish.

The Gothic arch on the left, engulfed in foliage and 16th-century cats, is the formal entrance to the Town Hall. If it's Saturday, you'll probably stumble across a marriage here, as this is a popular spot for tying the knot—look out for shifty men in brown suits. Behind it is some more patriotic work by one of the most ubiquitous of the 19th-century patriotic artists, Mikoláš Aleš: cartoon-like mosaics of Libuše founding Prague *(see p. 37) and an all-purpose* Bohemia, *showing the noble personification herself, enthroned between various symbols and architectural pinnacles of 19th-century nationalism. Walk to the modern entrance of the town hall, under the Renaissance window (1520). The Latin phrase means 'Prague, head of the kingdom', and was a motto extracted by the burghers from devil-may-care John of Luxemburg. You pay separately for the chapel and the tower, and a guided tour (just after the clock strikes) takes you around the rest of the building.*

The small Gothic **chapel** (kaple) on the first floor dates from 1381 (open

8 am–6 pm, adm). Nazi tanks shelled it to smithereens at the height of the Prague Uprising, but it has been restored well, using as much of the original rubble as could be identified. The delicate cross-ribs of the far vault frame 19th-century paintings of the Evangelists; the 15th-century crests on the walls belong to once-privileged families and trade guilds. Under the stained glass of the oriel (now a serene modern design from 1987), kneeling unfortunates would take their leave of life before being done to death next door (see below) or in front of the hoi polloi in the square.

*From the chapel, go up the stairs again to the **tower** (open 8 am–6 pm, adm). If you've timed this well, you can take in the view, scoot downstairs to watch the clock, and then go on the **guided tour of the town hall's rooms**.*

Open 8 am–6 pm (just after the hour), adm. The tour starts in the third house of the town hall, at the end of the ground floor gallery, which now hosts temporary exhibitions of modern Czech art. At the foot of the steps is a **memorial cross** made from two charred wooden beams, commemorating the anti-Nazi fighters who died here in 1945. The tour takes you under painted Renaissance joists on the first floor; on the second, faded Gothic murals and a turn-of-the-century drawing of Prague from Petřín Hill, minus the housing estates on today's horizon. The next two rooms contain four works by Václav Brožík (1851–1901), whose speciality was portraying crucial moments of Bohemian history with a turgid solemnity. Until 1526, the country's king was chosen in the town hall, and *The Election of King George of Poděbrady* shows Hussite George being given the nod by the country's nobles in 1458. The equally monumental *Jan Hus's Trial at Constance* is one of several versions churned out by Brožík for the nationalist movement. Among those watching Hus's doomed attempts to present a defence to charges which included the allegation that he believed himself to be a fourth member of the Holy Trinity are the great men of 19th-century Bohemia, including Smetana, Dvořák and none other than Václav Brožík himself. The two canvases in the next room are *Charles IV Founding Prague University* and *Comenius in Exile in Amsterdam*.

The **Old Council Chamber**, dating from about 1470, does most to conjure up the years when municipal powers were at their height. Councillors would hammer out policy at the broad table, supervised by the solemn Gothic sculptures. The haunting figure of Christ (*c.* 1410) implores them in Latin to 'Judge Justly, Sons of Man'—a fair plea, since it is here that Master Hanuš's fate would have been decided; summary execution was the norm in politically sensitive cases, when last rites would be swiftly administered in the neighbouring chapel. The councillors found themselves at the receiving end of some rough justice in 1483, when a Hussite mob threw the Catholic mayor and several cronies out of the window in the second of Prague's four defenestrations. The reformers then continued the good work with a pogrom in the Jewish Quarter—eradicating Judaism was widely thought to be a precondition of the Messiah's expected return in 1500. The scene of the first crime is no longer known; the Renaissance window through which light now trickles into the chamber was installed 40 years later.

> *Turn right from the Town Hall. In front of you is the striking cream and brown façade of the* **House at the Minute** *(Dům U minuty), one of Franz Kafka's many childhood homes in Prague (1889–96).*

No one knows how the house got its name—the only explanation that's been offered is that 'minute' doesn't refer to time, but to the apparently very small bric-a-brac that was once sold here. The scenes that cover the building date from around 1610. The direct influence of the Italian Renaissance on the city was limited, but *sgraffito* decoration was a remarkably popular Italian import to the capital. The rediscovery of classical myth was another Italian innovation that found its way to Prague, and here centaurs and assembled deities brush shoulders with Biblical worthies. The more coquettish of the Seven Virtues who adorn the lowest set of windows, swathed in diaphanous *sgraffiti* and displaying pounds of statuesque flesh, would have raised eyebrows in the puritan Old Town even when the plaster was first peeled away in 1610; and they disappeared after the arrival of the Counter-Reformation, only to be uncovered again by accident during the 1920s.

> *Continue into Malé nám. (Small Square), no more square than any of Prague's misnamed náměstís. The triangular junction, the historical haunt of French merchants and fruit-sellers, is dominated by more Aleš-inspired paintings, on the proud 1890 neo-Renaissance house of connoisseur, patriot and ironmonger, Mr Rott. Tatra and Škoda exhaust pipes have done their best, but the façade, entirely swamped by organic growths and rustic heroes, is still a smoky blaze of crimsons, oranges and greens. On your left is a quaint pharmacy (open Mon–Fri 8 am–3 pm), full of empty mahogany drawers and phial-filled shelves.*

232

The noble torsos at the door are the classical friends of apothecaries everywhere: ancient Asclepius, Greek myth's first physician, eventually struck off by Zeus for resurrecting a corpse; and his youthful father, Apollo. The American Hospitality Centre next door appeared within months of the 1989 revolution: curious Czechs used to come here to find out about freedom, but it's now full of ex-pats looking for popcorn. Sky TV is another of the attractions.

> *Walk down Karlova. You're now entering the riddled core of the Old Town, with lanes and passageways crawling through the gaps left by the architectural undergrowth of centuries. Follow the road as it turns to the left. The solemn drummers, carriages and grinning yokels that made up the royal coronation procession used to advance precariously around this corner and then lunge to the right, where Karlova continues its tortuous progress to the Charles Bridge. The road ahead of you forks around a* sgraffito-*laden art gallery. Continue along the left prong (Jilská). The street uncurls between huddled Baroque and Renaissance houses and the backside of a monastery that you'll see soon. Continue past the Esperanto society on your left. The Street opens into a square, and then narrows and twists again. You'll suddenly emerge into a grim 20th-century junction. U-turn to the right into Husova, and then take the first road to your left. This leads into Betlémské nám. where, on the right, you'll find the reconstructed twin peaks of the* **Bethlehem Chapel** *(Betlémská kaple).*

True to Prague form, this calm square has had a tumultuous history. The trouble began in the mid-14th century, when Prague's spellbinding ascetic and resident fanatic, Jan Milíč, stumbled upon the peaceful hive of prostitution that existed here. One of the leading chiliasts of his century, his personal way of preparing for Heaven on Earth was to take the harlots under his wing and rename the brothels Jerusalem. Milíč himself fell foul of his apocalyptic visions before long, clapped in jail by Emperor Charles IV after he warned the monarch that he was the Beast, but Jerusalem became established as sanctified turf. In 1391, reformers chose to build a church here in which services could be held in the vernacular. The idea was never popular in the medieval Church, which only approved a chapel and began to monitor events closely. Bohemians rose to the challenge and built the largest chapel in the land; with panache, they centred it around the pulpit rather than the altar; and with a healthy disregard for miraculous saints, they, like Milíč, turned to the scriptures to find a name. Jan Hus began to preach in the Bethlehem Chapel in 1402, the same year that he became rector of the Carolinum. His sermons filled the 3000-capacity chapel, which set alarm bells ringing in the Church. Prague's archbishop warned him to pipe down; Hus was excommunicated; and an exasperated pope finally had to have him roasted in 1415. The second Vatican Council retrospectively voided the sentence in 1965.

The ribbed tent-like roofs of the austere chapel now stand over a small museum devoted to the reformer; but apart from the sermons daubed on three walls, the building is a modern copy of the original, which was all but demolished in 1786. Its historical significance had little to do with the destruction; rational despot Emperor Joseph II rarely saw the point of religious organizations. Neither did his ideological heirs, the Communists, but in 1949, they began faithfully to rebuild the chapel according to the original plans. President Gottwald, a stalwart of Scientific Atheism, was asked why. He patiently explained that '500 years ago, the people of Prague were already fighting for Communism.' At the time of writing, Hus's museum is closed; the curators are still purging the exhibits of their Gottwaldian commentaries.

> Continue past the chapel. If you're in the mood, you could pop into the museum at No. 1, a monument to the ever-wider obsessions of a Mr Náprstek—intended as a tribute to Europe's machine age, but now full of tomahawks, boomerangs and didgeridoos (see p. 225). Otherwise, turn right at Liliová, and right again at Řetězová. The narrow cobbled alley, with its cast-iron green lanterns and line of Prague brownstones (i.e. 18th-century cottages) is a short but sweet plunge into the picturesque days of rats and slums, and—like the similar streets around nearby Anenské nám.—has been a favourite location for foreign film-makers for years. After about 20 m, you'll find, on your left, the **House of the Lords of Kunštát and Poděbrady** (Dům pánů z Kunštátu a Poděbrad).

This Renaissance building stands over a cross-section of an even older Prague. The cellar dates from around 1200—about a century before the burghers buried the town under 3 m of earth, in protest at the incessant floods of the Vltava river. It was an extreme step, and not one that was tried again (although the river didn't give up); most of the city's Romanesque architecture disappeared for centuries.

Open May–Oct, Tues–Sun 10 am–6 pm, adm. Pay at the room to the left, which houses temporary exhibitions, usually of broken pottery. Retreat to the other door. The ground floor (the first floor of the Romanesque building) has a permanent display devoted to George of Poděbrady, who lived here until promoted to king in 1458. Most of the exhibits chart his entirely unsuccessful attempts to create a League of Princes to fight the Turks. The little-known scheme was a favourite historical detail in Communist Czechoslovakia: it was said to show the deep-seated desire for peace and international co-operation of the Czechs, while George's infidel-smashing organization was ominously presented as a still-born model of the United Nations.

At the end of the main room, a staircase descends to the damp odours and street level of 13th-century Prague. The sepulchral chambers, with the cracks of their windows peering into the emptiness of a buried outside world, were built several decades before even the hints of Gothic architecture had begun to arrive in the city. Later centuries would use ribs to carry weight to the walls—here, central pillars have to support the massive roof, and the rough curves of the vaults and portals are a world apart from the arches then leaping skyward in the cathedrals of Paris. The house is still one of the grandest of the period to have been found in Prague, but no one knows who the first owner was; it lurked in damp subterranean isolation for 600 years, until the beginning of this century.

On leaving the house continue along Řetězová, and turn right along Husova. A small door to your left at No. 8 leads into the **Dominican Friary and Church of St Giles** *(Konvent řádu bratři kazatelů Dominikanů u sv. Jiljí), founded in the mid-17th century.*

Open Mon–Fri until about 6 pm. Irreligious Communists turned the friary into a technical institute in 1954, but the brethren are back. Their small cloister is ethereal, filled with rambling rose bushes and creepers, and occasionally the song of the Prague and Czech Philharmonic Choirs, whose rehearsal rooms are next door. The friars have shown a worrying tendency towards neatness, and you should try to see this before they tidy their jungle out of existence. The southern arcade is connected to the Order's adjoining Church of St Giles. Friars wander through, but you have to use the street entrance.

Apart from the northern tower, stunted by fire in 1432 and never the same again, the triple-naved church has retained its 14th-century structure. However, the gloomy Baroque interior is caged off and is only worth a brief visit to see the ceiling frescoes. The church vault has three, all by the Czech Václav Reiner (1733–34). On the left is *The Legend of St*

Thomas Aquinas; on the right *The Legend of St Giles*, a sympathetic character who patronizes lepers, cripples and, most helpfully, anyone who needs forgiveness but won't tell him what they did wrong; but the most exciting, in the centre, shows *The Foundation of the Dominican Order*. Here, Rome's Lateran Church is on the verge of collapse and being stabilized only thanks to Dominic himself. Pope Innocent III woke up from this nightmare scene while Dominic was in town hoping to get papal sanction for his Order; he hurried the papers through the next day. Innocent was a worried man; the dream apparently recurred eight years later, when Francis of Assisi had just arrived with another monkish scheme.

> *Retrace your footsteps along Husova. On the left is a well-known beer hall,* **The Golden Tiger** *(U zlatého tygra). Among those who regularly quaff Pilsners here is Bohumil Hrabal, one of Czechoslovakia's best writers, whose respect for alcohol is legendary. The street on your right, and that further to your left are the zig-zagging Karlova again—another traumatic intersection for the royal procession to conquer. Just beyond the bustling junction is a flood-marker, showing what the Vltava was getting up to in 1845, and next to it are the colossal atlantes of the* **Clam-Gallas Palace** *(Clam-Gallasův Palac), built in 1713–19 and designed by one of the masters of Austrian Baroque, J. B. Fischer von Erlach.*

The tense powerhouses, straining to hold the balcony, are one of the most characteristic motifs of Austrian and Bohemian Baroque architecture. They're the work of Prague's Matthias Braun, who, showing both humour and the Baroque love of illusion, gave one of the giants a loincloth which turns into a lion's head if you stare shamelessly enough. The rough sandstone figures were intended to set off the cool façade of the palace; as it is, they command the little junction, and manage to overwhelm the palace itself. Fischer von Erlach's design is extremely impressive on paper, structured around a triangular pediment with a sense of proportion and balance that is almost neo-classical, but it's easy to walk along the narrow alleyway without really registering the palace's existence. That wouldn't have surprised either the Austrian or Count Gallas. Both assumed that the entire block opposite would be knocked down and turned into a square, a plan which was only scuppered by residents' protests when Gallas let the occupants know.

Under the sculptures are two more heroic scenes: Hercules astride the Nemean lion, and clubbing an unidentified centaur. The interior of the palace contains a magnificent four-flighted staircase, crowned with an illusionistic fresco (*The Triumph of Apollo* by Carlo Carlone 1727–30); and two small archivists' rooms (the *Badatelna*), filled with scholars, two peeling ceiling frescoes, and Baroque stoves and wallpaper. If you're curious, you can usually get past the porter and librarian (open Mon, Tues, Thurs 9 am–4 pm, Wed 9 am–6 pm; closed for lunch 12–1).

Otherwise, continue along the façade—you'll pass a second set of atlantes and Herculean reliefs, and emerge into Mariánské nám. On your right is a niche containing a fountain. It's the neo-classical Vltava (1812: copy), a jug-bearing nymph popularly known as **Terezka**.

Terezka has been a Prague talking-point ever since the turn of the century, when a pensioned dragoon made her the sole beneficiary of his will. He was upset that she had been painted green by unknown assailants. His greedy relatives were no less perturbed, and had him posthumously declared of unsound mind. Fortunately, the city authorities took up the case, and she's been dribbling ever since.

On the eastern side of the square is Prague's modern Town Hall. The façade and roof are decorated with relaxed nudes peering down the street, and reliefs representing various virtues, the most rarely honoured of which have to be Control and Accounting on the right-hand cornice. On the corners of the building are sculptures to two of Prague's legendary figures. Go first to the one on the right, a 1910 **statue of Rabbi Loew**, *the Jewish mystic of 16th-century Prague (see pp. 108–10).*

The sculptor, Ladislav Šaloun, also sculpted the Monument to Jan Hus in the Old Town Square (see p. 145); and he intended this to be no less solemn a tribute to a man who represented 'everything noble which was produced from the ghetto'. In fact, the hook-nosed and slovenly figure, grasping his robes with gnarled fingers, looks rather like an extra from that classic of the Nazi screen, *Jud Süss*. (The Nazis themselves didn't think so, and removed the figure during the war.) The lion to the left represents Loew's name in German; the rest of the work portrays one of the legends surrounding his demise. Death shied away from a direct confrontation with the fearsome rabbi, and pounced on the 96-year-old after hiding in a rose being given to him by his granddaughter; Šaloun's freestyle adaptation omitted the rose, and transformed the granddaughter into a voluptuous nude flinging herself at his cloak (which may have been what the sex-obsessed fascists objected to most).

To the left of the Town Hall is a **stone knight**, Šaloun's tribute to an iron knight who hung outside Prague's armourers' guild until 1908. The original is now in the Museum of the City of Prague. Legend has it that he was flesh and blood until cursed for murdering his lover, and now clanks these streets once a century, trying to kiss a virgin and break the ferrifying spell.

> *Opposite the Town Hall is the eastern entrance of the Clementinum, which you'll see soon. Walk along Semínářská, to the left. The street winds into Karlova. The junction is filled by* **The Golden Well** *(U zlaté studně), its bow windows and angled façades ploughing through the block like an icebreaker.*

This Renaissance building is covered with Baroque decoration. The lower figures are St Roch, with his faithful canine provider (looking rather like a pig here), and St Sebastian, punctured with his traditional arrows. Both characters are guardians against the plague: Roch, because he helped victims, eventually succumbed, and recovered thanks to prayer and the loaves of bread brought daily by his worried dog; Sebastian, only because his arrows reminded the symbol-minded of Apollo's poison-tipped weaponry (the god caused as well as cured disease). The saints appear incessantly in monuments around Prague and Bohemia, almost all built around 1715, when the pest had just paid one of its periodic visits.

> *Continue along Karlova. On the corner with Liliová is* **The Golden Serpent** *(U zlatého hada), marked with a sign of its hissing, glistening namesake, and once the home of an Armenian named Deomatus Damajan, who opened Prague's first café here in 1708.*

The deed has ensured him an honourable place in Prague folklore, but he actually left the city under something of a cloud. Damajan had the odd habit of distributing calumnious tracts with his cups of coffee, and once went too far by accusing a leading Prague Jew of embezzling charitable moneys. His victim sued, Damajan fled, and returned only very briefly to collect the 130 gold pieces that he was awarded by an extremely generous pardon granted by Emperor Charles VI (the troublesome Jewish community had to come up with the cash). The house has now become a modern restaurant and wine bar, a reminder of the sorry pass to which

Prague's once-legendary café society has come. That society, and probably Damajan himself, inspired Kafka to write one of his many unpublished stories. Lonely Franz explained to a friend that it centred around a man who wanted somehow to 'make it possible for people just to see others, to talk to them, observe them without getting involved in any close relationships, without any hypocrisy'. It all sounds rather too high-flown for Damajan, who was only looking for a captive audience, but Kafka's hero did solve his riddle by inventing the coffee house.

Opposite The Golden Serpent are two porches, built to follow the bend in the road, and nestling under the domes, tiles and steeples that hang over the final stretch of Karlova. They form the entrance to two chapels associated with immigrant communities: in front of you is the oval Italian Chapel (Vlašská kaple), built by and for the Renaissance Gästarbeiter *of the 1590s; and to your right, embedded within the sheer wall, is the 18th-century* **Church of St Clement's** *(sv. Kliment). The second is now used by Prague's small Greek Orthodox community, refugees from the colonels' coup in 1967, and is worth a very discreet visit when priests clad in green mumble services according to the Old Slavonic liturgy.*

Retrace your steps and go through the doorway on your left, which leads into the **Clementinum** *(Klementinum), the first Jesuit college in Bohemia and the nerve-centre of the country's Counter-Reformation.*

The Society of Jesus was founded in 1540 by St Ignatius of Loyola. Waved off by Pope Paul III, the monks scattered across Europe to confront the Antichrist of reform. Organized on military lines and headed by a general elected for life, the Order made up the advance platoons of the Counter-Reformation. Setting up Baroque base camps and barracks as they moved, the monks penetrated deep into Protestant Europe; and during the uneasy peace which preceded the Thirty Years War (1618–48), the Clementinum relit the Catholic flame in a city that had become 90 per cent Protestant.

One of the most successful weapons in the Order's armoury was education. While the monks themselves lived on an austere diet of mysticism and martyrdom fantasies, their schools became known throughout Europe as solid centres of excellence. Jesuit pedagogues showed an ever greater open-mindedness as the scale of their task became apparent. The extremely useful and excellently-named theory of Probabilism was developed (nothing heretical unless manifestly absurd);

239

many went the whole hog and subscribed to Laxism (absurdities not to be condemned out of hand); and the monks would also lead their charges in singing and dancing lessons to hone their sensual skills, and thus, their ability to feel God.

Prague's Jesuit college took shape after 1556, when a squad of 40 monks was invited into Bohemia by Emperor Ferdinand I. The Jesuits' rivals watched hamstrung as the singing, dancing monks seduced their pupils away and even let them titter at the occasional heresy; all that Prague's dour quasi-Calvinism had to offer curious boys was a sound thrashing. The Clementinum's success was such that, by the 17th century, non-Catholic families were queuing up to enroll their little ones; and after a short-lived expulsion on the eve of war, the Society returned in force in 1620 to supervise a century of militant reconversion. The Clementinum swallowed up its arch-rival, the Protestants' Carolinum, two years later, and only in 1773 did it lose its religious nature. It's now the Czechoslovakian State Library.

> *The Jesuits took their architecture seriously. They moved into this site in 1556, but the present complex was built in protracted stages between 1653 and 1723, on the site of 30-odd houses, three churches, ten courtyards and several gardens. The central tower, topped with a Baroque Atlas, was the last part to be built (1721–3, and remodelled in 1749); it was the monks' observatory, and as late as 1918, a flag would be waved from the balcony when its sundial struck noon, and a cannon would thunder across the city from distant Letná Park. The once graceful plan of the whole isn't easy to appreciate any more, paved in asphalt and disrupted by the chunk of modern concrete on the left, but its rooms and walkways are filled with surprises. Turn left, and walk through the door marked 'Národní knihovna' (National Library). Turn right down the corridor. Stride past the porter's lodge silently and without flinching, and bear in mind that the building is crawling with sensitive scholars.*

About half-way along, the passage becomes what was once the vaulted cloister of the monks. The sides have been glazed but the drowsy courtyard to your left has remained untouched. The ivy-drenched enclave is a stunner, with its spurting fountain and painted solar clocks, flowing under the gables in undulating sections that are hardly any more comprehensible than the Astronomical Clock. Just opposite the entrance to the court is the way into the main reading room. Under the crisp stucco decoration and dangling putti of what used to be the Jesuits' refectory, you'll find what some claim to be the largest Rococo stove in Europe. The swirling reliefs are filled with Jesuit motifs, including their device—IHS, the abbreviation of the name Jesus in Greek—and the conventionally-balding head of Ignatius himself. The monolith kept the monks warm for only 11 cosy years until their abolition in 1773.

Return to the corridor and turn left at the end. Go up the staircase (along on the right), and turn right at the top. You'll be led to the beginning of a 100-m long barrel-vaulted passage, a lonely tunnel lined with 34 stucco cartouches containing scenes from the hectic life of St Francis Xavier.

Francis, proto-Jesuit and the Order's second saint, spent the last ten years of his life in Asia on a one-man baptism drive. His achievements were considerable. On his first stop, he curbed the activities of Goa's syphilis-spreading Portuguese settlers; and in 1549, he gave the Mikado a clock and a music-box and swiftly immersed Japan's first 2000 Christians, which proved to be something of a mixed blessing when later and less liberal Mikados gave the country its first several hundred martyrs. He died on the way to fresh pastures in China and now lies incorrupt back in Goa, minus an arm (nabbed by the Vatican in 1615) and a toe (swallowed by an ecstatic pilgrim some years before). The scenes here were painted by an unknown monk. They're of no artistic merit, but—in this case at least—the Order clearly believed that subject-matter alone would be enough to inspire and prepare the hopeful novices. Those who mastered their spiritual exercises could aspire to levitation and resurrections; disasters, savages and lonely death were what all should prepare themselves for in heretical Bohemia.

Ignatius's life-story is in the corridor immediately below. Unfortunately, it's been sliced down the middle by prefabricated offices: they're called temporary; at the time of writing, they look increasingly permanent. There's one more stop to complete your Jesuit experience. Follow the corridor running off the centre of Francis's parade. At the end, you'll see a sign marked 'Hudební Oddělení' (Music Library) on your right—walk through the door and head right around the passage. The small reading room, with its cherub-topped Rococo bookshelves, contains the Jesuits' fascinating tribute to astronomy: models of the universe, diagrams of eclipses, and on the vault, a Baroque parade of approved thinkers.

Open Mon and Thurs 2 am–7 pm; Tues and Fri 9 am–7 pm. The Jesuits did their best to keep abreast of new learning, but as the Enlightenment advanced, astronomy became very tricky territory. The pantheistic philosophy of Giordano Bruno had shown where outlandish speculations could end: in his own case, frying on a Roman stake in 1600, and more importantly for the monks, to a nasty question mark over the first line of the Bible. They soon accepted that there was more to the heavens than met the eye, but although they were among the more intellectually honest monks of their day, they never stopped looking for a compromise.

Prague's Jesuits built their observatory in 1721, and the fresco was painted at some point between then and the tower's remodelling in 1749, as shown by the fact that the original building is part of the background. On the left are seven pretty Mathematical Disciplines including Gnomonics, the once-popular spirit of sundial construction; and under the Latin inscription 'God Gave the World to be Comprehended by Discussion', astronomy's heroes are gathered. Aristotle, doodling in the sand, is in front of Appolonius of Perga, Hipparchus and Ptolemy; on the far right Tycho Brahe, wearing his false nose (see p. 148) is holding full and frank discussions with Giambaptista Riccioli (1598–1671), the Jesuits' black-robed representative. Riccioli's last-ditch attempt to keep the earth at the centre of the universe is on the right of the wall in front of you. A century after Galileo and Johannes Kepler had suggested alternative proposals, the Clementinum's scientists still regarded it as the pinnacle of astronomical achievement.

Walk down the stairs at the entrance to the room. You'll emerge back at the porter's lodge. As you leave the building, turn right and then right again. The dapper student in the next courtyard, sporting goatee and banner, is Josef Max's 1847 tribute to the pupils who dashed across the road in 1648 to fight the last battle of the Thirty Years War (see below). As you leave the complex, on your right is the western wing of the Clementinum, the section containing the paintings of SS Francis and Ignatius and the oldest part of the college (1653).

The almost martial façade, with its relentless alternation of pilasters and windows, was one of the trailblazers of the Baroque in Prague. Pollution and erosion have taken their toll, and it now takes some imagination to picture it in its prime—but it certainly impressed General Oliva, the then head of the Order in Rome, who let it be known that it was too ostentatious. Coming from a Jesuit, that's saying something.

Turn left. The Church of the Holy Saviour (Kostel sv. Salvátor) next door was the first church built by the Jesuits in Prague (1593–1601). Take a brief look back up Karlova—Kepler lived behind the ill-maintained sgraffiti of No. 4 between 1607 and 1612, five fertile years during which he produced inter alia the principles of planetary motion and Somnium, a short description of life on the moon. In the courtyard is a tower-like construction which was allegedly the site of his observatory.

Walk back to the main street and cross over. The oval-domed St Francis's (sv. František) (1679–89) on your right is Prague's only church to make extensive use of real marble; everyone else had to make do with scagliola, but the rich Knights of the Cross owned a quarry. Follow the tide of people flowing towards the **Old Town Bridge Tower** *(Staroměstská mostecká věž), designed by Peter Parler (see below), and completed in the 1390s during the reign of Wenceslas IV.*

As part of the fortification walls, this titan has had both symbolic and practical functions. After the execution of Bohemian nationalists in 1620, ten heads putrefied from its first floor for a decade; and in 1648 the final hours of the Thirty Years War raged around the tower, when Sweden's army went on a last-minute looting spree and the Old Town was saved by a motley alliance of bearded students and Prague Jews. A Europe-wide peace had already been negotiated, but another truce was clearly necessary. It was signed on the middle of the bridge, in a cabin specially partitioned to keep the opposing factions from each others' throats.

The battle destroyed most of the decoration on the western façade of the tower. The east still has its original 14th-century decoration, with sculptures of SS Adalbert and Procopius at the top, Charles IV and Wenceslas IV enthroned below, and St Vitus in the centre. More intriguing are the minor details, which show the whimsical spirit that was abroad in the late Gothic art of Wenceslas' court. On the corner to your left is a figure running his hand up a nun's habit, a scene which is sadly eroding into non-indecency; and one of Wenceslas' dalliances is directly commemorated by the birds and scantily-clad woman who appear all over the sides, and golden-ribbed vault, of the tower. The birds are probably kingfishers, but possibly halcyon birds (creatures of yore who were said to calm waves and wind in order to copulate more comfortably), both of which are symbols of bathkeepers. According to legend, it's all in honour of one Zuzana. In 1394, the feckless king was temporarily locked up by disgruntled nobles in the Old Town, and she rowed him to the safety of Malá Strana after he persuaded his captors to let him have a bath. She was only a bathkeeper's daughter, but the king's gratitude knew no bounds—not only did he bed her, but he also raised her hitherto-shady profession to the status of a guild. The situation seems to have got out of hand by 1561, when male bath-attendants were reminded, on pain of death, of the need to wear loin-cloths when attending female customers.

The tower is closed at the time of writing. If it reopens, take a look at the Latin phrases on the roof of the second floor: *Signatesignatemeremetangisetangis* and *Romatibisubitomotibusibitamor*. They seem to mean, respectively, 'Take note, take note, you are touching and torturing me' and 'Rome, love overcomes you with sudden force', and were intended to guard the bridge from evil spirits. It is unlikely that anyone expected them to take fright at the substance of the first message; and almost impossible in the case of the second one. The plan was far more subtle. Demons were known to read every inscription in case it contained a curse, and with a burst of lateral thinking, these palindromes were drawn up. With luck, the fiends would never be able to tear themselves away. If the scheme worked, there's now an entire confused colony in the tower, urgently scanning the text—back and forth—just one more time.

Through the vault of the tower lies the **Charles Bridge** *(Karlův most), a curving, swerving ley line through Prague. For centuries the city's energy has squeezed through this narrow channel; and the coronation processions and fairs of yesteryear find their modern equivalent in the scores of musicians who turn every evening into a fiesta during the summer.*

There was a wooden way over the river over 1000 years ago, if Cosmas the chronicler is to be believed; an incidental detail of his account of the murder of St Wenceslas is that the bridge was damaged in 932, requiring a spot of Divine Intervention to fly the pallbearers across. Nothing is left of that structure, but remnants of the Judith Bridge, built in 1158 and Europe's second stone bridge after Regensburg, survive in the piers of the present work. The Judith Bridge was destroyed by floods in 1342, but the civic pride of Charles IV, who ascended the throne four years later, ensured that Prague didn't remain bridgeless for long. Astrologers were asked to find a suitably auspicious celestial configuration, and in 1357 Charles's architect, 27-year-old Peter Parler, got to work. No expense was spared—when the masons asked for eggs to strengthen the mortar, an egg tax was imposed on every hamlet in the land—and in the early 1400s, construction was complete. For over 400 years, the bridge was Prague's only river crossing. This feat of medieval engineering has survived centuries of deluges and, until 1950, the trundle of motor traffic.

The stark structure of the bridge is perfectly complemented by the 30 sculptures that now line it. The 14th century, in its unostentatious way, saw a simple wooden crucifix placed on the bridge; the Counter-Reformation knew a propaganda opportunity when it saw one, and during the late 1600s and early 1700s an entire avenue of Baroque saints was added to the bridge, inspired by Bernini's 1688 work on the Ponte Sant'Angelo in Rome. The hapless commuters of Prague were a captive audience to what would then have been an awesome array of swooning and gesticulating saints. According to the autobiography of a Prague old-timer, even into the early years of this century, pious souls would doff their caps 30 times as they made the crossing. Many of the works have now been replaced by copies, and there is some lifeless neo-Gothic statuary from the 19th century, but the overall effect of the sculpture is still superb.

The oldest work is the bronze **Crucifixion** (1657), third on your right, flanked by 19th-century work. The figure hasn't met with universal approval: the Hebrew inscription on the statue was the compulsory contribution of an outspoken Jew, who apparently wandered past in 1695 muttering blasphemies; while English-born Queen Elizabeth is said to have been horrified by the sinuous manliness that she glimpsed somewhere in the Messiah on her arrival in Prague in 1618. The fifth statue to your left shows Francis Xavier being borne aloft by grateful coolies. It's a copy of a 1711 work by F. M. Brokof which was swept away by a flood in 1890. The river also destroyed three arches around where you're standing, and was dammed, not before time, in 1954. Ignatius used to stand on the opposite side of the bridge; after sinking in 1890, he was replaced by the youngest statue here, Karel Dvořák's 1938 sculpture of SS Cyril and Methodius.

About halfway across on the right is a small bronze Lorraine Cross embedded in the wall, marking the spot where **St John Nepomuk** was hurled into the river. Put your hand on it, make a wish and then go to his statue, the eighth on the right. John was a Vicar-General of Prague who was put in a sack and dropped into the Vltava in 1383 by Wenceslas IV. Two explanations for the king's act exist: the boring truth is that John appointed an abbot against the king's wishes; far better is the jolly tale put about three centuries later by the Jesuits when they were casting around for a wholesome Catholic rival to Jan Hus. The story is that Wenceslas, never a reasonable man, asked John what the queen had told him during confession. Honest John supposedly replied from the rack that he'd forgotten, and wouldn't tell even if he could remember. Five stars appeared above the bobbing corpse (hence the unusual headgear that you'll see on all the saint's monuments in Prague). The Jesuits erected the statue in 1683; but John's canonization had to wait until 1729, after the monks had exhumed his coffin and claimed to find his tongue (see p. 120). A chapel used to stand around the the saint, and the rubbing of a million fingers has meant that tumbling John is still a glittering dot on the oxidized reliefs at the base of the figure. He'll get you across any bridge safely, despite his own misfortune; and he's the saint to turn to if someone suspects you of doing something that you just didn't do. He also gets women pregnant.

SS Vincent Ferrer and Procopius on the left deserve a mention; among the feats noted on their statue are the salvation of 100,000 souls, the conversion of 2500 Jews, 70 exorcisms and 40 resurrections. A downcast devil, Turk and Jew support the saints. If you look over the bridge here, you'll see the statue of **Bruncvík**, a chivalrous character linked to the legend of Roland. The latter was a sanguinary epic of crusading Christianity, but Bruncvík has become enmeshed in a *pot-pourri* of mythological motifs and Prague legend. Various versions exist, but the most complex is that his invincible sword, buried in the Charles Bridge, will be unearthed in Bohemia's moment of greatest need by a stumbling white horse belonging to St Wenceslas; the saint will be at the head of the lost Hussite heroes who fell asleep in Blaník Mountain in 1434.

Of the petrified melodramas that remain, take a look at Matthias Braun's **St Luitgard**, fourth from the end on your left. Generally agreed to be the best-crafted sculpture on the bridge, it shows Christ letting the blind saint nuzzle His wounds, a vision she enjoyed late one night. Two statues along is F. M. Brokof's pantomime-like tribute to the **Trinitarian Order**, established for the now unfashionable purpose of ransoming Christian hostages from infidel clutches. The founders of the order stand above a little grotto full of captives, guarded by a pot-bellied pasha and a mad dog.

The Baroque hubbub subsides as you near the end of the bridge.
A slow arm of the Vltava separates the island of Kampa (see
pp. 190–91).

from the mainland, although at the time of writing, it has been dammed to prevent all 13 houses of Prague's so-called 'Little Venice' from collapsing. The end of the bridge is punctuated by the **Malá Strana Bridge Tower** *on the right, which was built in the early 1400s (open April and Oct 10 am–5 pm, May–Sept 10 am–6 pm; adm), and the stumpy* **Judith Tower***—which despite the Renaissance decoration, belonged to the 12th-century predecessor of the Charles Bridge. The inseparable duo, wearing tiled top hats and forming the parapet and arch into Malá Strana, frame St Nicholas's Church and one of the most tempting photo-opportunities in Prague.*

Just to your right is **The Three Ostriches** *(U tří pštrosů), a Renaissance house (the scrolled top-floor is a later Baroque addition) with paintings of the creatures on the façade. Jan Fux, purveyor of novelty plumage, bred and plucked the beasts here at the end of the 16th century; unconfirmed reports also suggest that it was here, rather than at the Golden Serpent, that Deomatus Damajan brewed Prague's first coffee. It has since been turned into a hotel and overrated restaurant, and isn't the place to end this walk. If you're feeling energetic, you could go on a final burst of tower-climbing; if you're not, people-watching is a respected sport on the bridge, which is a favourite stage for the capital's youthful* poseurs.

Museums

The National Museum in Wenceslas Square

The biggest museum and art gallery in Prague is the city itself, and many visitors never set foot inside the collections scattered across the capital. However, there are some curious and beautiful things behind its doors, and this section will help you decide what may be worth a visit. Prices aren't listed below (or anywhere else in this book) simply because inflation will probably make the figures redundant within months, but admission fees are minuscule (at the time of writing, from 2–15kcs, i.e. 4–30p or 8–54¢), and there are 50 per cent reductions for students, children, pensioners and disabled people. The standard closing day is Monday, with a couple of maverick collections shutting down on Tuesday instead; you can never count on being allowed into *any* building in Prague if its advertised closing time is less than half an hour away. Otherwise there's really no best or worst time to pay your choice a visit. In some cities you almost have to queue to see each painting or exhibit, but you'll find boundless space to roam in Prague's museums and exhibitions; on occasion your very arrival at the box-office will represent the largest crowd of the day. However, there's one minor obstacle to free movement that you'll face in all the city's art galleries, without exception. It's the dreaded and legendary *babička* posted in each room, whose veins tense the moment you trespass on her turf, and who is always ready to snap or spring at you if you move to within a very vaguely-defined security zone around the paintings. Particularly suspicious-looking coves may find themselves being stalked, and passed from *babička* to *babička* like a relay baton as they walk through a gallery.

One final point is that certain museums have recently ceased to exist. You probably won't need to be told, but no matter how tempted you are by the offerings which still linger in some Czech tourist brochures, there's little point in trying to find the V. I. Lenin Museum or the Klement Gottwald Museum.

PAINTING

The first four collections in this group all belong to the National Gallery. There's still no permanent venue for its huge collection of 20th-century Czechoslovakian art. At the time of writing, some work is being displayed in the **Riding School of Prague Castle** on U Prašného mostu, but the bulk of the collection will almost certainly move to the Tradefair Palace next to the Park Hotel (see p. 299) before long. You should also be warned that an even more general shake-up of the organization of the galleries is being contemplated, and if you don't find what you're looking for, contact the Šternberk Palace on the number below.

European Art to the 20th century, Šternberk Palace, Hradčanské nám. 15, tel 53 23 79. Tues–Sun 10 am–6 pm. The first floor, with its collection of 14th- and 15th-century icons, has been closed for over a year. The rest of this excellent gallery achieves the impossible, and takes you through six centuries of European art, almost ignoring the High Renaissance and often having artists represented by only one work, and yet leaving you momentarily at a loss to think of anything that you missed. Its acknowledged masterpieces are few (Dürer's *Feast of the Rose Garlands* and Bruegel's *Haymaking*), but the works here by Cranach, El Greco, Goya, Rubens, Rembrandt and a host of others leave few disappointed. The 20th century is represented by Klimt, Schiele, Munch, Kokoschka and others; and another section of the museum runs through French art from Impressionism through to Chagall, including 15 Picassos. (See pp. 206–15.)

18th- and 19th-century Czech Art, St Agnes' Convent, tel 231 42 51. The convent itself is a tranquil retreat on the edge of the Old Town, and one of the first examples of Gothic architecture in Bohemia, but the romantic collection of nationalist-minded art on display here is highly mediocre. (See p. 165.)

Czech Gothic and Baroque Art, St George's Convent, tel 53 52 46, ext (*linka*) 11. Tues–Sun 10 am–6 pm. The Gothic painting of this collection represents a unique period of Bohemia's artistic history. Some of the extraordinary panels by Master Theodoric (see p. 64) are on display, and even those who generally shudder at the thought of endless Crucifixion scenes and Madonnas with Children will find some of the painting and sculpture here sublime. The same can't really be said for the Baroque collection, but the statues lose none of their power to fascinate when seen at close quarters; and there's a small selection of work from Emperor Rudolf II's court. (See pp. 66–68.)

Graphic Art Collection, Goltz-Kinsky Palace, Staroměstské nám. 12, tel 231 51 35. This collection has been under wraps for over two years, but regular temporary exhibitions of Czech and foreign artists occur on the second floor. Recent displays have ranged from the entries to a door-designing competition to the scratchy lithographs of the first artist to illustrate Kafka.

Picture Gallery of Prague Castle (Obrazárna Pražského hradu), Second Courtyard of Prague Castle. Tues–Sun 9 am–5 pm (April–Sept) 9 am–4 pm (Oct–Mar). A small collection of art from Renaissance to Rococo, which lay around unrecognized for some 200 years. Contains paintings by Tintoretto, Titian, Veronese and Rubens, but although the gallery is worth a brief visit, it's less exciting than the hit-list might make it sound. (See pp. 111–14.)

Troja Chateau, U trojského zámku. Tues–Sun 10 am–6 pm. This Baroque palace to the north of central Prague houses a collection of 19th-century Czech art, but it's the decoration of Troja itself that makes the journey here worth while. It was built in the 1600s by an ambitious Czech nobleman, who was so anxious to please Bohemia's new masters that he submerged his main hall in an apotheosis of the Habsburgs. Painted by the Flemish-born and Roman-trained Abraham Godyn from 1691–97, it is the richest illusionistic painting in the capital. Austrian triumphalism is the order of the day, and as well as innumerable scenes showing the wisdom, prudence and bravery of the kooky clan, the gaudy masterpiece heaps scorn on the Turks, who had just overplayed their hand for the last time. With the relief of Vienna in 1683, the Sublime Porte had begun its relentless metamorphosis into Sick Man of Europe, and there are cringing infidels dotted throughout, and one particularly impressive turbanned loser, with *trompe l'œil* shadow, tumbling from the wall. The simple theme returns as allegory in the chateau's small grounds, littered with scenes from a Baroque battle of the Gods and giants, and including a series of sculptures cascading down both sides of a stone staircase.

SCULPTURE

Collection of 19th- and 20th-century Czech sculpture, Zbraslav Monastery. May–Oct Tues–Sun 10 am–6 pm. This gallery is a 30-minute journey from the city centre, and as a result, although it is among the capital's finest collections, it is only visited by a determined and well-informed minority of visitors. If you have the time, you should try to be one of them. To get there, take any of the following buses from the terminus outside Smíchovské nádraží (metro line B)—129, 241, 243, 255. Get off at Zbraslavské nám., a quiet suburban square just past the second bridge you cross, and the grounds of the low Baroque monastery are to your right.

The ground floor is dominated by the work of J. V. Myslbek, the country's most influential 19th-century sculptor. His work teeters between classicist restraint and the sweeping Romanticism demanded by his patriotic times, a conflict evident in his early studies for the *St Wenceslas Monument*. In the finished version at the head of Wenceslas Square (see p. 222), Myslbek synthesized the struggling tendencies. There are many more of his later works here, including the startling larger-than-life *Crucifixion*, wrapped in an almost Art Nouveau arrangement of thorns and hair.

The mainstream of Czech Art Nouveau is represented by Ladislav Šaloun, and a gentle series of small copper and bronze reliefs by Stanislav Sucharda. Upstairs, the belated influence of Rodin, who exhibited in Prague in 1902, is reflected in the earlier works of Josef Mařatka and Bohumil Kafka, both of whom spent a couple of years working in the great man's studio. Kafka's sculpture pays the less heavy-handed debt, with the spontaneous and dark Impressionism of *Mummies*, inspired by the sight of desiccated Peruvians whom he had seen on show in Paris. There's a broad selection of the exceptional work of Otto Gutfreund, which begins with some of the first and most original Cubist sculpture in the world, and ends with the beautiful simplicity of the painted wood and terracotta figures he produced in the 1920s. The social realism of Gutfreund's later work (see p. 75) influenced the whole of next generation of Czechoslovakian sculptors, including Karel Pokorný, Jan Lauda, Karel Dvořák and Karel Kotrba; and their tributes to the humble and the meek pepper the gallery. There's also a small selection of post-war work, which will probably grow considerably larger now that the Communists are no longer in charge of purchasing policy.

Bílek Villa (Bílkova vila), Mickiewiczova 1. April–Sept Tues–Sun 10 am–6 pm. Filled with the work of František Bílek, one of the most isolated and extraordinary sculptors in modern Czech history (see p. 74), in the house that he designed for himself. It apparently represents a cornfield.

MUSIC

Mozart Museum (Bertramka), Mozartova 169, tel 54 38 93. Wed–Mon 10 am–5 pm. This charming villa is one of the few houses of the suburban gentry to survive the dark advance of industry into Smíchov during the 19th century. Mozart stayed here on three of his visits to Prague, as a guest of the musically-minded Dušeks; and he allegedly polished off the overture to *Don Giovanni* in one of its rooms in 1787, having been locked in by Mrs Dušek in the hope of loosening his composer's block. (The drastic measure worked, and he conducted the completed opera at Prague's Tyl Theatre.) The building was seriously damaged by fire in 1871, giving the exhibits a certain speculative feel; no one's *quite* sure whether Wolfgang really slept, studied or was incarcerated in any of the rooms that escaped. If you ask sweetly, the cashier can usually be persuaded to play the English taped guide as you walk through the rooms. The rapid-fire commentary is interspersed with snatches of the composer's greatest hits. Cult-followers might appreciate the collection of 13 hairs belonging to Mozart, a rare relic of the body that notoriously got lost somewhere under Vienna's St Mark's cemetery. Evening concerts are held in the summer on the outdoor terrace, where there's also a stone table at which the composer is said to have mused.
Musical Instruments Museum (Muzeum hudebních nástrojů, Lázeňská 2, tel 53 08 43. This is said to be the second-largest collection of musical instruments in the world. It's housed in the Baroque palace formerly owned by the Grand Prior of the Maltese Knights, but thefts and returning monks mean that it's unlikely to last at the present address. Call the above number and either a monk or a curator will give you the latest news. (See p. 189.)

Prague also has two small museums devoted to its two great 19th-century composers (although none to the Moravian-born Leoš Janáček). Both have small collections of scores, photographs, diaries and the like, and again they lay on greatest-hits tapes for the benefit of visitors.

Antonín Dvořák Museum, Ke Karlovu 20, tel 29 82 14. Tues–Sun 10 am–5 pm. This museum is housed in a charming Baroque villa designed by K. I. Dienzenhofer, and the surrounding streets are one of the least visited but most tranquil parts of the New Town. (See p. 261.) **Bedřich Smetana Museum**, Novotného lávka 1, tel 26 53 71. Wed–Sun 10 am–5 pm. Set in an adapted water-tower very close to the Charles Bridge. Very unreliable opening hours.

GENERAL MUSEUMS

Alois Jirásek and Mikoláš Aleš Museum (Muzeum Aloise Jiráska a Mikoláše Alše), Letohrádek Hvězda, tel 36 79 38. Tues–Sat 9 am–4 pm, Sun 10 am–5 pm. The exhibits, minutiae from the lives of two very patriotic Bohemians (writer and artist respectively), are self-explanatory and dull—but their home, in the Hvězda (Star) Summer Palace, is another location that merits a visit in itself if you find yourself near by. The six-pointed Renaissance palace was designed in 1555–56 by the son of Bohemia's first Habsburg emperor, Ferdinand I, and the ground floor of his folly is entirely covered with some superb Italian stucco work. The crisp decoration is centred around the piggy-back duo of Aeneas and Anchises, off to found Rome (and, as Habsburg lore would have it, the empire that the family had taken over), and scores of other deities, satyrs and crazy chimeras dance across the rest of the ceilings. The cellar of the palace has a small exhibition on the Battle of the White Mountain. Although Czechs commemorate their mammoth defeat with peculiar zeal in every historical museum in the country, it has a special relevance here: the White Mountain is about a kilometre from Hvězda; the sanguinary last stand occurred about half that distance away; and when it was all over, the tired but happy Catholics came to the palace to celebrate.

Museum of Decorative Arts (Uměleckoprůmyslové muzeum), 17. listopadu 2, tel 232 00 51. Tues–Sun 10 am–6 pm. A colourful display of the decorative arts from the late 16th century onwards, and the custodian of tens of thousands of modern posters and photographs (only occasionally and very partially displayed). (See p. 153.)

Lobkowicz Palace National History Museum, Jiřská, tel 53 73 06. Tues–Sun 9 am–5 pm. Rather too small to encapsulate Bohemia's history, but it neatly wraps up a trip to the castle, and is covered at the end of Walk I (see p. 135.)

Military Museum (Vojenské muzeum), Hradčanské nám. 2. May–Oct 9.30 am–4.30 pm. The joy of warfare, from flails to cannons. (See p. 206.)

Museum of the City of Prague (Muzeum hlavního města Prahy), Sady

Jana Švermy 1554, tel 236 24 50. Tues–Sun 9 am–12 noon and 1–5 pm. The box-office has an English catalogue, but the museum's highlight is almost self-explanatory. It's a 1 : 480 model of most of Prague minus the New Town, the work of an obsessed amateur artist who spent some ten years completing it (almost), before his death in 1837. It answers those questions that begin to niggle once you've been in Prague for a while— what the Jewish ghetto once looked like, how many spires the City of One Hundred has really got, and so on. The rest of the exhibits form an interesting collection of Romanesque and Gothic decorations rescued from the attentions of rapacious bulldozers over the years.

National Museum (Národní muzeum), Václavské nám. 68, tel 26 94 51–7. Mon and Fri 9 am–4 pm, Wed–Thurs and Sat–Sun 9 am–5 pm. The splendid neo-Renaissance interior is worth seeing, and the exterior is unavoidable, but otherwise this is a natural history museum with few of the features that generally make such places tolerable. The skeletons are of small and humdrum creatures, and it's hard to be impressed by the museum's claim to own every mineral known to man. It apparently contains a collection of very rare meteorites. (See pp. 221–2.)

State Jewish Museum (Státní židovské muzeum), Jachýmova 3, tel 231 06 81. Sun–Fri April–Oct 9 am–5 pm, Nov–Mar 9 am–4.30 pm. This covers what remains of the Prague ghetto, and includes several synagogues, the 12-layer Jewish cemetery, and collections of thousands of Jewish artefacts (textiles, books and silver) from across Europe. The latter were assembled by the Nazis, who planned to transform the quarter into an 'exotic museum of an extinct race'; another memorial to the Holocaust is an almost unbearably painful exhibition of drawings and paintings by children from the Terezín ghetto. (See pp. 337–41.)

Physical Training and Sports Museum (Muzeum tělezné výchovy a sportu), Újezd 40, tel 53 45 51. Tues–Sat 9 am–5 pm, Sun 10 am–5 pm. Physical culture has assumed mass proportions in the nation's past, but this is a very low-key celebration of the temple of the body. Highlights are limited to three boneshakers and an eight-person sled.

Postage Stamp Museum (Muzeum poštovní známky), Nové mlýny 2, tel 231 20 06. Tues–Sun 9 am–5 pm. A very small museum in one of the New Town's oldest houses, next to an early 17th-century water tower. The staff are shocked if someone stops by, and all the more friendly as a result. Philatelists can choose from 300 pull-out displays from the international world of stamps, and the ignorant can have a quick stare at the Penny Blues and Blacks in the UK section; while upstairs, there are some pretty 19th-century lithographs concentrating on the pleasures and perils of a postman's life, and a series of wall paintings, entirely unrelated to postage, by the 19th-century Czech artist Josef Navrátil.

Náprstek Museum of Asian, African and American Cultures (Náprstkovo muzeum), Betlémské nám. 1, tel 22 76 91. Tues–Sun 9 am–12 noon and 12.45–5 pm. Mid-19th century Mr Náprstek apparently intended to set up a museum devoted to the wonders of industry, but assembled so many primitive objects while pondering the superiority of technology, that his wife persuaded him to put them on display as well. In the end, his machines were hived off to form the beginnings of the National Technical Museum, and there's no longer a flywheel or spring to be found here. Náprstek's first artefacts came from Milwaukee, but the museum now contains shaking sticks, boomerangs, ponchos and peace-pipes from the entire non-technical world.

National Literature Museum (Památník národního písemnictví), Strahov Monastery, tel 53 88 41. Tues–Sun 10 am–5 pm. A perusal of Bohemian literature from Cyrillic bibles through to the literary efforts of the 19th-century national revival movement. However, it's the opulent libraries that make a visit to Strahov essential. Be quick—the Premonstratensian canons have returned and are making grumbling sounds about the number of visitors.

National Technical Museum (Národní technické muzeum), Kostelní 42, tel 37 36 51. Tues–Sun 9 am–5 pm. Tremendous fun. The colossal main hall is a Grand Central Station of transport, with infernal steam engines, Bugattis and Mercedes, and long lines of motorbikes dating from 1887. The first car Karl Benz ever sold (in 1893) is here; there's also a 1900 railway carriage, whose mahogany trimmings and upholstered sofas were designed for the comfort of Habsburg monarchs on the move. Sailing over everything are 12 aircraft (13 if you include the balloon that's apparently rising through the roof), an impressive assortment of translucent dragonflies and vintage biplanes. The history of chronography is recorded in one of the other rooms. Some of the devices are calm enough (look out for the Renaissance pocket sundial), but most of the dropping balls and swinging pendulums tick mercilessly throughout, and erupt into pandemonium around the turn of the hour. Another room is filled with hundreds of still and movie cameras, including some of the earliest doomed attempts at stereoscopic photography; and upstairs you'll find a room devoted to the cutting edge of Czech technology, filled with junk, and a small astronomical collection which includes sextants and astrolabes used by Tycho Brahe and Johannes Kepler in

Prague. If you arrive at 11 am, 1 pm or 3 pm, you can follow a guided tour into the belly of the building, a tremendous mock-up coal mine far underground.

Peripheral Attractions

Cubist house in Vyšehrad

New Town—Vinohrady—Vyšehrad—Smíchov—Petřín—Letná Park—Holešovice and Troja

The few square miles covering Hradčany, Malá Strana and the Old Town contain more than enough to keep most visitors busy, but there's a ragbag of more or less interesting attractions further from the beaten track. Explorers and romantics should all find something to their tastes in the sights listed below, and there are particularly rich pickings for cemetery ghouls. All are easily accessible by public transport, and are included in the clockwise order in which they circle the Old Town.

Nové Město/New Town

The New Town rises in a crescent from the south-west to the north-east of the Old Town, which it locks into the river-bend. It's actually not very new, having got its name back in 1348, when Emperor Charles IV established it to cater for the monks and merchants flooding into his new capital. Charles was also worried that the cacophony of Prague's cobblers, wheelwrights, smithies and the like would disturb the repose of his new university in the Old Town, and over the next century the quarter came to have a higher concentration of workers than any other section of the city. They, and the vagabonds and riff-raff who joined them, turned the New Town into one of the most radical Hussite centres. In the early

257

1400s they vied for supremacy with the relatively moderate wing of the movement in the Old Town, but lost, and for several centuries the quarter was little more than an appendage of Prague proper.

Over the last century, however, the New Town has become the commercial and administrative centre of the capital. It's only listed as a 'peripheral' attraction because its sights are scattered over too wide an area to be covered elsewhere in this book. The New Town was the most careful and grandiose piece of town-planning in Europe for over a millennium. With the help of only a handful of modern roads, the broad boulevards, squares and streets have carried Prague's traffic unchanged for over 600 years. Paradoxically, the area's ability to adapt has meant that it's suffered from the 19th and 20th centuries to an incomparably greater extent than the other three districts of medieval Prague. Most of its buildings are sooty blocks of every neo-variety possible, with an uncoordinated mess of modernist architecture scattered throughout. However, if you have the time and muscle to spare, a trek unearths the occasional gem, and takes you through a part of living Prague that most visitors never find.

Wenceslas Square is covered in Walk IV, and most of the other sites worth seeing are near **Karlovo nám.** (Charles Square), which you can reach by metro (line B) or trams 4, 6, 16, 21, 22 and 24. The square was laid out as a park during the last century, but it was originally the hub of the New Town. As well as serving as the capital's cattle market, it was the spot that Charles IV used for his annual relic displays (see p. 43) and in the north-east corner is the **New Town Hall** (Novoměstská radnice). It was founded in the mid-1300s, but only the tower (1425–26) has any look of age about it; the rest of the building was completely rebuilt during the 19th and early 20th centuries. In 1419 its former windows were the venue for **Prague's first defenestration**. Jan Želivský, a Hussite firebrand of a priest, led a rabble to the building to demand the release of some heretics, and the Catholic councillors apparently lobbed stones at his monstrance. This pointless provocation proved a serious misjudgement. The crowd turned ugly, stormed the building, hurled the councillors from the windows, and then bludgeoned to death anyone who survived the fall. The times were violent ones, and Jan himself didn't escape: in 1421 the genteel burghers of the Old Town invited him to their place for full and frank discussions, and beheaded him. The Communists always had a soft spot for radical John, and there's a monument to him on the door here dating from 1960.

Halfway down the square, at the junction with Ječná, is the **Church of**

St Ignatius (sv. Ignác), which along with the neighbouring college (now a hospital) formed the Jesuit encampment in the New Town. The powerful arches of the chapels and broad nave are laden with half-immured cherubs and angels, and the gold and creamy-pink interior give it the predictable ostentation of Jesuit architecture. It was built in 1665–70, too early for it to display the fluidity and seductive power of later Jesuit churches such as St Nicholas's in Malá Strana (see pp. 179–82).

In Resslova, the main street leading off the opposite side of the square, is another notable Baroque church, **SS Cyril and Methodius** (sv. Cyril a Metoděj). It is recognizable by a pock-marked section of wall that commemorates one of the most dramatic events to occur in Prague during the Second World War. After the killing of Reinhard Heydrich (see p. 56), seven members of the group responsible holed themselves up in the church's crypt, along with almost 120 other members of the Czech resistance. All were betrayed, and in the late evening of 18 June 1942 over 300 SS and Gestapo soldiers took up positions around the building. Through the night, wave upon wave of machine-gun fire poured into the crypt. As dawn broke, the Nazis managed to push a high-pressure hose into the building, and as the water rose, those inside who still survived blasted each other with their remaining bullets. It's usually thought that the ferocity of the Nazi attack was inspired by the fact that the assassins of Hangman Heydrich were among the prey—but testimony at Nuremberg suggests that the Nazis had no idea that that was the case, and were just being themselves.

At the southern end of the square is the Baroque **Faust House** (Faustův dům). The name was conjured up during the 19th century and is only very tangentially related to Goethe's tragic diabolist. A student tenant left without having paid the rent, there was a hole in the roof, and Prague's overworked fabulists oddly concluded that he had been abducted by the devil. However, the house's history is not entirely without mystery. One of Emperor Rudolf II's pseudo-scientists, the necromancer and would-be wife-swapper Edward Kelley (see pp. 105–107) lived in the original Renaissance building, and in the 18th century it was occupied by Ferdinand Mladota, another mystical trickster. Today the building is occupied by chemists rather than alchemists, and unless you've got a prescription there's no point venturing within.

To the south of the square, on Vyšehradská, is the Baroque **Church of St John Nepomuk on the Rock** (Kostel sv. Jana Nepomuckého Na skalce). Effortlessly perched on a craggy curve, it's one of the most elegant of all K. I. Dienzenhofer's churches in Prague. The twin towers of the narrow façade are echoed by the bizarre peaks of the **Emmaus Monastery** (Klášter Emauzy) across the street. The roof of the Gothic monastery was obliterated during an Allied bombing run in February 1945, and the 1960s replacement, flowing into two spires, is one of the most distinctive pieces of post-war architecture in the capital. The monastery was founded by Charles IV in 1347 for Croatian Benedictine monks, who (thanks to a spot of pressure on the pope) were granted the rare privilege of being allowed to chant their dirges and liturgies in Old Slavonic here. Pope and emperor each hoped that their respective spheres of influence would thereby be extended eastwards, but the clever Croats played their own game. When the Hussites popped round to storm the monastery, the monks told the mob that they fully sympathized with the anti-clerical cause. It was an outrageous gamble, but the confused crowd eventually slunk off, and the monks were left to intone in peace. In 1446 they consolidated their position by re-establishing themselves as the only Hussite Order in the world. The Spanish Benedictines recovered Emmaus from their wayward brothers after the Battle of the White Mountain in 1620, and the Order has ebbed and flowed through ever since. It was last evicted by the Communists in the early 1950s, and reinstated in 1990. The monastery's cloisters contain a (somewhat battered) cycle of Gothic mural paintings, commissioned by Charles himself. The scenes juxtapose incidents from the Old Testament with those that they allegedly prefigured in the new world order of Christianity. Their astrological and alchemical symbolism (as well as a healthy dose of sun-worship) provides a fascinating glimpse into arcane depths of religious belief in 14th-century Prague. The inconvenient return of the monks means that long and occasionally futile arguments with the Benedictine bouncer are now necessary before you can get in to see them. Try at the door to your left as you enter the monastery grounds. Just further along the street, where it rolls into Na slupi, are Prague's **botanical gardens** (Botanická zahrada), a sloping retreat of roses, rhododendrons and azaleas. They're open all year round from 7 am–7 pm.

Although the New Town is riddled with some particularly thunderous streets, life slows to a standstill in the small island of hills, cobbles and educational institutes behind the gardens. On Viničná 7 you'll find part of the science faculty of the Charles University, where Albert Einstein lived between 1911 and 1912, when he taught as Professor of Theoretical Physics in Prague. The blank wall across the road conceals the gardens of the Neurological Institute—and fun-loving Einstein apparently once told a visitor, while gazing down at the pottering lunatics, that you'd have to be mad not to understand quantum theory. There are two worthwhile stops further up the hill on Ke Karlovu street. At No. 20 is the **Dvořák Museum** in the **Vila Amerika**. If restoration has finished, it's open from Tues–Sun 10 am–5 pm, and the gorgeous Baroque summer-house, designed by K. I. Dienzenhofer and set among sculptures by Antonín Braun, is worth seeing in itself. The crimson dome of the **Church of Our Lady and Charlemagne** (Kostel Panny Marie a Karla Velikého) stands at the far end of the road. The church was founded by Charles IV in 1358, this time for French Augustinians. Its unusual octagonal plan was loosely modelled on the Aachen burial church of Charlemagne, one of the many patron saints adopted by Charles to bolster his political credentials. Like several other new churches in the area, it was deliberately sited to command the horizon of the New Town, and towers over the vast Nusle valley.

The most awe-inspiring feature of the church is its remodelled interior, shaped like a single star, 24 m in diameter. Legend has it that the architect was a novice who built it with the devil's help; others claim that it was designed in about 1575 by Bonifaz Wohlmut, court architect to Ferdinand I—but either way it's one of the grandest flourishes of (extremely) late Gothic architecture in Prague. The church is only open from 2–5.15 pm on Sundays and holidays.

The neighbouring monastery used to house the splendid propaganda of the Museum of the National Security Corps and the Army of the Interior Ministry (see p. 113). It was always a worthwhile stop for some light relief, and one can only hope that Prague's post-revolutionary authorities can now be humorous in victory and reopen it. Otherwise, there's little left to see in this part of town, other than the 14th-century fortification walls stretching down from the church. You could meander back to the main road along the grassy stone steps of Albertov street, which was the starting point of the candle-lit demonstration on 17 November 1989 that went to Národní street to meet the batons and last stand of a rotten government (see p. 60). Alternatively, contemplate the gargantuan **Nusle Bridge** (Nuselský most), leaping half a kilometre across the Nusle valley. Some Praguers still suspect that the bridge, which carries six lanes of scooting traffic and two tracks of tunnelling metros, was intended to facilitate any urban military manoeuvres that the government or their fraternal foreign allies might deem necessary. It's probably not true, since construction of the trunk road began during the relatively liberal mid-1960s, but it's hard to believe that someone somewhere didn't check that a line of tanks could safely trundle across. The bridge used to be named after Klement Gottwald, Czechoslovakia's first Communist president, and has long been the most popular spot for public suicides in Czechoslovakia. The former regime never got round to releasing the annual figures, but a worker under the bridge made the surreal, and fortunately rather unbelievable, assertion that for several years, at least one body a month had plummeted to a halt outside her shop.

Vinohrady

This district, sprawling away to the south-east of Wenceslas Square, is so close to the New Town in feel and architecture as to be almost indistinguishable. However, you'll find almost no houses older than 150 years here. While Charles IV was drawing up the plans of his Prague extension, this site was being planted with vineyards (*vinohrady*), and it remained more of a field than a suburb until well into the last century. Only in 1920 was it incorporated into the capital, and it's now a busy residential district crowded with neo-Renaissance and Art Nouveau mansions.

Although a trip through the district's streets and bars is an interesting way of finding out what Praguers get up to when tourists aren't around, the sights are limited. However, at Nám. Jiřího z Poděbrad, you'll find the 1933 **Church of the Sacred Heart** (Kostel Srdce Páně), perhaps the most extraordinary piece of modern architecture in Prague. The monochrome church, the eastern façade of which combines the pediments of classicism, the ornamentation of Art Nouveau, and a mammoth glass clock, defies any form of categorization. It's the work of Jože Plečnik (1872–1957), a Slovenian who studied in turn-of-the-century Vienna and spent most of his life teaching and designing in Ljubljana. Plečnik's use of historical motifs was a deliberate attempt to preserve the aesthetics and spirituality of architecture, for which his work was heartily derided by the cube-lovers of the day. After the dubious triumph of the concrete block, this church has come back into its own and now looks not only more human, but also far more new-fangled than the Constructivist and Functionalist designs of Plečnik's contemporaries.

The second attraction in this part of town is the necropolis that stretches from Flora to Želivského stations on line A of the metro. It's less spooky than Malá Strana cemetery (see below) but more suited to a lazy graveyard stroll. The **Olšany cemeteries** (Olšanské hřbitovy) began life in 1680 as a repository for plague victims, but since 1784 they have made up Prague's main cemetery, and the 500,000 sq m are still being filled (open Nov–Feb 9 am–4 pm; Mar–April 8 am–6 pm; May–Sept 8 am–7 pm; Oct 8 am–6 pm). The complex comprises 13 different sections, and its tombs range from the stoic neo-classicism of Prague's golden age of tombstone design to the bourgeois wealth of marble obelisks and granite sarcophagi. Rows of white crosses mark the dead of central Europe's endless wars, and there's an entire plot filled with the odd crucifixes of the Russian Orthodox Church. The eastern wall is lined with thousands of urns, arranged in stone display cabinets and counters which look rather like a line of quaint chemist shops. The grounds become a fearsome sight between All Saints' Eve (31 October) and All Souls' Day (2 November), ablaze with candles and filled with silent mourners.

Just to the right of the main entrance on Vinohradská is the **grave of Jan Palach**, the young man who burnt himself alive following the Warsaw Pact invasion in 1968 (see p. 59). Some 800,000 people followed his coffin here from the Old Town in January 1969, and Alexander Dubček, still clinging to power, ordered that black flags be flown from every public building in the capital. One of the most sordid acts of the profoundly shabby regime that followed was to disinter Palach in 1973 and rebury him outside Prague. He was replaced by an unknown woman, Marie Jedličková, but for 16 years determined mourners decorated her tomb with flowers and candles on the anniversary of his death (19 January). In 1990, Palach was returned to his original resting place.

Near the Olšany cemeteries, on the other side of Jana Želivského street is the **New Jewish Cemetery** (Sun–Thurs Sept–Mar 8 am–4 pm, Apr–Aug 8 am–5 pm; men are asked to cover their heads). Unfortunately, this doesn't carry on from Prague's Old Jewish Cemetery; the ground used between 1787 and 1891 was in Fibichova street, and was unbelievably destroyed and turned into a park less than 20 years ago. You'll find the **grave of Franz Kafka** here, at plot 21 14 33, a couple of hundred metres along the path to your right. The writer spent the last months of his life in Berlin and then in a Viennese hospital, but as he once claimed, his home town had claws. Dr Kafka—he had studied law—is buried with his mother, and the father he reviled. All his novels remained unpublished (and incomplete) at his death, and he was mourned only by some close friends. There's no adequate obituary on the gravestone, but the notice penned two days after his death by his former lover Milena Jesenská is suitably dramatic food for thought as you stand in front of the tomb:

'He wrote the most significant works of modern German literature, [which] reflect the irony and prophetic vision of a man condemned to see the world with such blinding clarity that he found it unbearable and went to his death.'

The halo of martyrdom nowadays settles rather too easily over artists who die young, particularly those cut down by tuberculosis, but uncompromising and screwed-up Kafka, who wrote his last story on his deathbed, probably merits it as much as any cult hero of modern times. The cemetery, a riot of dandelions and buttercups and ivy, is the loneliest in the capital. No old women tend the tombs; few come any more to mourn; and as the number of professing Jews in Prague sinks into the hundreds, the graves still being dug mark the protracted conclusion to a story that lasted a thousand years.

Vyšehrad

This ancient crag over the Vltava has spawned a thick web of nationalistic lore and legend. Most Praguers will still be able to reel off the myths, but its romantic heyday was a century ago, when it was infested with poets and painters in search of patriotic inspiration. It's now little more than a pleasant retreat on a lazy afternoon. The easiest way to get here is on line C of the metro to Vyšehrad station—walk away from the Hotel Forum. Alternatively, you can scale the rock from the stone steps on the embankment (Podolské nábř.), linked to the centre of town by trams 3, 17 and 21. There's a superb view over the river, but huffers and puffers might appreciate it more on the way down.

The area was probably settled way back in the 9th century, and according to the city's oldest legend, soothsaying Princess Libuše was standing here when she came over all funny and prophesied Prague (see p. 37). In the later 11th century, Vratislav II moved to the rock, prompted by dislike of his brother, who insisted on living in the castle; the change of royal address lasted almost a century, but the only remaining evidence is the heavily-restored Romanesque **Rotunda of St Martin** (Rotunda sv. Martina). Near it are more remains of the fortification walls built by Charles IV around the New Town in the mid-14th century. The area's landmarks are the twin towers of the **Church of SS Peter and Paul** (Kostel sv. Petra a Pavla), founded in the late 11th century but entirely rebuilt in dull neo-Gothic style a hundred years ago. To the north of the church is the **Vyšehrad Cemetery** (Vyšehradský hřbitov). Established at the end of the last century to accommodate the cultural heroes of the Czech national revival, it forms an impressive gallery of modern Czech sculpture. Among the 600-odd corpses of the great and good are those of Smetana and Dvořák. At the far end is a **pantheon** (slavín), a mass grave of 50 artists (at the last count) and still the final destination of the *crème de la crème*.

On the other side of the church are the **Vyšehrad Gardens** (Vyšhradské sady), small but peppered with a selection of strapping sculptures from Czech myth. They're all 19th-century works by J. V. Myslbek (who also sculpted the St Wenceslas monument—see p. 251). Enraptured Libuše is here, next to moody Přemysl the Ploughman; along with *Ctirad and Šárka*, another duo from the prehistoric battle of the sexes that informs early Czech folklore. Faithless Šárka belonged to a bunch of Bohemian Amazons, and tied herself to a tree to catch Ctirad off-guard; the gallant prince stopped to woo her, came to a sticky end when he blew his horn to show off and Šárka's lady friends charged to the rescue. There's also a strange old column, which is thought to have kept track of the solstice in the days when Vyšehrad was still a glorified pagan mound.

Before leaving the area, be sure to see the **Cubist houses** designed by Josef Chochol (see p. 75) between 1911 and 1913. There's a little triplet on the embankment below Vyšehrad (Podolské nábř. 6–10), one on Libušina 3, and most impressively, the prismatic apartment block jutting outwards and upwards from the corner of Přemyslova and Neklanova.

Smíchov

This is Prague's most intriguing suburb, minutes from the centre but a world apart from the golden city. In the 19th century it became the capital's industrial powerhouse and brewery, traditions which continue today. Factories and traffic seem to belch out more greenhouse gases than the rest of the city combined, but the uniqueness of the atmosphere now owes more to the large concentration of gipsies living here. You won't find tinkers' stalls or caravans, but on warm evenings the streets can have the liveliness of an extremely tranquil and central European New York. Gangs loaf, music blares from apartments, and no-good kids yell obscenities or invitations (or both) from their tenement windows. If you want action, pop into one of the lively bars around here (see p. 308). You won't get blown away, but leave your credit cards at home.

The best streets are those around the macabre **Malá Strana Cemetery** (Malostranský hřbitov), open from May–Sept 9 am–7 pm. Trams 4, 7 and 9 will get you there. Founded during the 1680 plague epidemic, it's been disused for over a century, and the only evidence of many of its tombs is the rise and fall of the ivy sheet that has inundated it. It has one of the most impressive concentrations of late Baroque and neo-classical sculpture in Prague, centred around the monumental cast-iron tomb of Bishop Leopold von Thun-Hohenstein; but it's the ruin and disrepair that somehow makes this one of the most extraordinary cemeteries in Europe. Decapitated angels teeter from pillars; crucifixes lie in pieces on the ground; and yawning tombs leave you in little doubt that everything here is slowly crumbling into nothingness.

The cemetery is eerie, but tucked between two (very) main roads. If you need a break from the rumble of traffic, even the tone-deaf will appreciate the tranquility of the **Mozart Museum at Bertramka** on Mozartova (Wed–Mon 10 am–5 pm—see p. 252). Finally, you could check whether **T23** is still squatting on its pedestal in nám. Sovětských tankistů, which roughly translates as **Soviet Tank Personnel Square**. The tank was almost the first to rumble into Prague in May 1945, but although liberation from the Nazis was no bad thing, the dubious role of Soviet tanks in the city's subsequent history has meant that T23's fate has been in the balance ever since the 1989 revolution. On the 22nd anniversary of the 1968 invasion, an upside-down tank appeared overnight in Wenceslas Square, and was widely presumed to be this one. To the relief of a surprisingly large number of people, it wasn't, and it now seems safe for the foreseeable future. As a result, although the flags and flowers have disappeared, this is one of the few spots in central Europe where Soviet weaponry is still publicly honoured.

Petřín

Petřín is the green and wooded hump on the left as you cross the Charles Bridge from the Old Town. The forest that once used to stretch for miles to the south has disappeared, and vineyards no longer clamber up the hill, but its collection of gardens still makes for a perfect retreat as temperatures rise in the hazy city below. The best way of getting there is the funicular railway which slides up and down between about 5 am–midnight. It leaves from a station just above Újezd street, about 100 m north of the junction with Vítězná. Alternatively, the Strahov gardens (see pp. 199–200) are linked by paths to Petřín; there's a gate into the Kinský gardens on nám. Sovětských tankistů (see above); and one of the loveliest walks in Prague is along the path to the north of Nebozízek restaurant, which turns from asphalt to forest as it slowly sinks into Malá Strana's sea of olive domes and orange tiles.

The first stop on the funicular is Nebozízek, marked by a terrace restaurant standing on what used to be a vintner's cottage (see p. 283). In the woods to the south is a monument to the Romantic poet Karel Mácha near which generations of wistful Praguers claim to have necked and spooned for the first time. At the summit is a rose garden and a series of minor spectacles. On the left is the Baroque St Lawrence's Church, and the Prague Observatory and Planetarium (open Tues–Sun, but the hours vary wildly from month to month—call 53 55 51/3 if you're set on a visit). Across the lawns to the right is a **model of the Eiffel Tower**, built in 1891 (two years after the original) by the Club of Czech Tourists, and now used as a TV transmitting station. The globetrotting club was apparently very proud of its tower, but at 60 metres it falls rather laughably short of the Gallic symbol. 1891 was the year of Prague's Jubilee Exhibition, and the Czech Tourists also contributed the nearby **maze** (bludiště), full of mirrors and a diorama showing the Swedish attack on the Charles Bridge in 1648. It sounds no less potty than the tower, but it's hard to tell as it's been closed for many a year now. Finally, look out for the remnants of the 14th-century **Hunger Wall** (Hladová zed') (see p. 199), the crenellations and battlements of which crawl unevenly across Petřín as far as Strahov.

Letná Park

This second expanse of greenery stands over the bend of the Vltava, and separates central Prague from its northern flank. It was landscaped in the mid-19th century, and though it doesn't have the rolling splendour of Petřín, its several curiosities make for an enjoyable stroll. One way of entering the park is by climbing the set of stone steps opposite the Svatopluk Čech Bridge (most Svatopluka Čecha), which fork and then rejoin at the graffiti-covered **plinth of the former Stalin statue**. Uncle Joe was blown up in 1962, but some of his rocky remains are still in the chambers below, which were also used to store potatoes for many years. By the time you're reading this they may well have been turned into a nightclub (see p. 306). There's a more conventional dance-floor in the

267

nearby **Hanava Pavilion** (Hanavský pavilón) to the west, an Art Nouveau exhibition piece which was moved here in 1898. To the north is the
barren expanse of **Letná Plain**—which is entirely devoid of interest,
save that it used to host the speech days of the Communists (1 May), and
that on 25 November 1989, it was the site of the demonstration that
marked the death of the old régime, when a million people watched
Václav Havel shake hands with Alexander Dubček. The nearby
National Technical Museum on Kostelní is filled with venerable
one-time miracles of modern technology and is great fun (Tues–Sun 9
am–5 pm—see pp. 225–6).

Holešovice and Troja

These two areas of northern Prague contain the city's largest and wildest
park, a series of minor spectacles, and next to the tragic city zoo is Troja
Chateau (see p. 250). The two districts are separated by the Vltava, an
island and a railway line, but it's possible to make your way from one to
the other along a route that runs from Stromovka Park to Troja. To get to
the area, go to Holešovice nádraží, on line C of the metro. Holešovice
Park and Stromovka are a short walk from the station (or a stop away on
trams 5, 12, and 17); and bus 112 will take you to Troja.

Holešovice Park used to be named after the Communist journalist
Julius Fučík (see p. 89) and the name given it here is a guess at what it will
probably be called one day. It was the site of Prague's 1891 Jubilee
Industrial Exhibition, and its neo-Baroque iron and glass structures have
the cranky charm of seaside piers and crystal palaces. The architectural
contraptions are being polished up at the time of writing, and great
exhibitions are promised to commemorate the centenary of the original
show. The nature of the novelties is as yet undecided, but the permanent
attractions include a small funfair (12 noon–10 pm) and another kooky
diorama, dating from 1898 and this time celebrating the Battle of Lipany
with 1000 sq m of three-dimensional drama (open May–Sept 10 am–5
pm). The curious entertainment complex also contains a circular
cinema, a planetarium, and a mini-golf course.

You couldn't get much further from the quirky spirit of the industrial
park than in the wooded wilderness of neighbouring **Stromovka**, which
dates back to the 14th century, when it was founded as a royal enclosure
by King John of Luxemburg. However, its lake is the product of an
earlier age's fascination with mechanics. Rudolf II had it created in 1593,
and it's fed by an underwater canal running from the Vltava river nearly

1 km to the south. The entrance to the tunnel is near the lake, but Rudolf's chateau has disappeared, as have the 4000 creatures with which he stocked the park. It's still Prague's finest spot for an urban ramble.

Troja is north of the Vltava, and opposite the Baroque chateau on U trojského zámku, you'll find **Prague zoo** (Oct–Mar 9 am–4 pm, April 9 am–5 pm, May 9 am–6 pm, June–Sept 9 am–7 pm, adm). The attractions here are extremely limited. Some of the 2000 beasts are apparently extinct in the wild, but judging from these often insane specimens, it might have been preferable to let them all die out in peace. The zoo's two mitigating features have nothing to do with its *raison d'être*: the first is a wonderful hilltop location (it was once a vineyard); and the other a stupendous chairlift which scoops you up as you stand on a platform, and carries you hundreds of metres over an aviary far below. The seat harness is optional and useless—perfect for children, horrifying for anyone beyond the age of reason.

Food and Drink

Eating out can sometimes be an unforgettable experience in Prague, in the very worst sense. Stodgy food, almost identical menus, and abysmal service still characterize most of the city's restaurants, and it can be next to impossible to find a free table during high season. There has historically been little connection between what the public wanted and what the restaurants provided. Private restaurants were unknown during 40 years of Communist rule, and while monolithic bureaucracies issued menus from above, the establishments became little fiefdoms, with waiters and waitresses often paying large bribes for the privilege of cast-iron job security. To the delight of many Praguers, mass dismissals are imminent at the time of writing as the spectre of privatization haunts the city. The changes will be a mixed blessing, as prices increase and Euro-wine-bars replace atmospheric dives, but they'll make for a much happier and healthier stay. Problems will remain—but although you should be prepared for difficulties, the information at the end of this section should ensure that Prague doesn't leave a bitter taste in your mouth.

Food

The specialities of Czech cuisine represent the culmination of centuries of serfdom and peasant experimentation. Favoured vegetables tend to be the turnip and potato; and although meat of every description finds its way onto the table, offal is treated with unusual respect. There's a robust suspicion of most herbs other than marjoram and all spices save garlic which is only mitigated by the influence of the hot-blooded Slovaks and their Hungarian neighbours.

The most distinctive delicacy of the Czech kitchen is the *knedlík*, or ubiquitous dumpling. Praguers treat them as the highest expression of the country's cuisine—and if you say that you recently ate an unexciting one, you're almost certain to be told that *you have to know where to go*. Unfortunately, only the most discriminating foreign palate can truly tell the difference in most cases. The main distinction is between the flour *mouka knedlík* and the *bramborova knedlík*, made of mushy potato. Both are usually served with a lump of flesh in a thick gravy, and are staple fare in beer halls. *Špekové knedlíky* are marginally more interesting, mixed with bacon; while *kynuté knedlíky* are downright wild in comparison, centred around lumps of stewed fruit.

You're on tastier ground when it comes to cold meats. Prague ham (*šunka*) is of high quality, but it's generally agreed that the best salamis are the harder Hungarian-tinged varieties, particularly the flat *lovecký salám*, and both *Oherský salám* and *salám alékum*. Sausages are much loved, and you can pick up a *párek* (two long porkers) in stands across the city. The frankfurter-like *Liberecký parky* and the paprika-flavoured *čabajka* are the best varieties; and if you avoid pork, you can safely eat *hovězi parky* and *drubeží parky*, made of beef and chicken respectively.

Soups (*polévky*) are often delicious, and in cheaper beer halls and cafés they're among the most likely winners on the menu—but among the standard meats and vegetables, there are a few Czech favourites of which you should be aware. *Dršt'ková* is one of the most popular soups and comprises floating pieces of a cow's stomach; while *zabijačková polevka* is a pungent concoction made largely of pigs' blood. The name, roughly translated, means 'slaughter soup', although it's also known by the mildly obscene term *perdelačka*.

There are a few other snacks that you'll probably encounter. *Vafle* (waffles) are everywhere, and to find one of the squashy pieces of sponge and cream, you generally need do no more than follow your nose. There are also stalls across the city selling *bramborák*, a garlicky potato pancake that is delicious if not greasy. *Ďábelský toust* is a fiercely tasty mixture of meat (usually beef) on toast. *Svážeby sýr* is fried cheese, which is more appetizing but no less unhealthy than it sounds. The most common cheeses are bland copies of Edam (*eidam*) or Brie (*Hermelín*), but native creations are usually of the most malodorous kind. If you can stand the whiff, they go well with the rich wine. One of the most fetid is *olomoucké sýrečky*; and if you're drinking beer, ask the barman if they have *pivní*. It isn't designed to be eaten by itself—pour some of your drink onto the plate, knead gently, and offer the rank concoction around. In the summer, you'll also see hawkers selling bags of Slovakian sheep cheese (*gorbáč*), which looks like stringy pieces of fresh pasta. Prague's sweet-meats are fairly unremarkable, although cream cakes are making a comeback as German tourists return. Sweet teeth may enjoy *koláče*, tasty tidbits topped with curd, and *palačinky*, pancakes which can be atrocious or scrumptious depending on the tosser.

Drinks

Czech food may often be nothing to write home about, but the beer is world famous. Plzeň is the home of Pilsner Urquell, while the town of Budweis (České Budějovice) has become part of the American dream; although the American brewers Busch actually borrowed little more than the name, and the potent brew produced in Czechoslovakia puts the US slop to shame. Both beers are chock-full of alcohol (and sugar which is all natural, unlike western imitators). You may already like sweet beers, and if not you should develop the taste in Prague—look out for beer-halls and bottles marked *Plzeňske prazdroj* and *Budvar*. Prague produces beers of its own (*Staropramen* and *Smíchov*), which are slightly more bitter. They taste fine to most people, but some of the capital's own beer bores disavow them, and you may hear it claimed that the Vltava is pumped directly through the brewery. Most beer is 12° proof (i.e. 6 per cent alcohol), but 10° beer is also sold in shops and the cheapest dives. A dark alcoholic treacle is served at the beer halls U Fleků (14°) and U sv. Tomáše. When you have your first draught in a *pivnice*, Praguers claim that you should stick a matchstick into the head to test the quality. The only danger is that if it doesn't stay erect for at least ten seconds, you may be accosted by a staggering drunk who'll suggest that you all go elsewhere.

Wine connoisseurship is a game that is played by waiters in the swankier restaurants in Prague, but it is even less merited than usual in the case of Czech wine. Moravia has the best grapes, but you'd have to have your tongue embedded in your cheek before you could describe any of the wines as cheeky, playful or vintage. Most of the whites tend to be as sweet and thick as a bottle of red plonk. The driest is probably *Rulandské*, but in most cases, robust reds slip easier down the throat, and *Frankovka* and *Sv. Vavřinec* are two of the better labels. Bohemia's only worthwhile wines come from the Mělník vineyards, and have a rather pleasant woody fragrance–try *Sv. Ludmila*. A glass of Czech wine is twice the size of a regular measure in the UK and US, and if you're a moderate sort you should ask for a *deci*. The quality of the wine makes it particularly suitable for mulling, and during the winter most cafés have a permanently bubbling pot of wine, cloves and cinnamon—ask for *svařené vino*. One other speciality is *burčák*, which is sold and drunk across the capital from late August onwards. It is the first wine of the year, Prague's semi-fermented Beaujolais Nouveau—and it's an impudent little rascal which masquerades as a soft drink until it knocks you senseless. Bohemia also produces sparkling wine (*sekt*), which is good for popping and conspicuously wasting, but it seems to make many people feel very queasy if they drink much of it. Soviet *sekt* is marginally less sickly, and widely available.

Czechoslovakia produces no vodka worth the name. However, Soviet *Stolichnaya* and *Moskovskaya* can be found everywhere for a fraction of the price in the UK or US, and they're both rather excellent when cooled to semi-viscosity. Czech rums and whiskies are little better than hogwash, but on your alcoholic reveries through the city, you should look out for three native liquors. The first is *Becherovka*, the 20-herb recipe of which is one of the world's many distilling secrets supposedly known only to two men. The mystique surrounding the ingredients, along with the manufacturers' only-too-garrulous bumph about every other stage of the drink's creation, sells about 10 million of the flat green bottles worldwide, and you'll find it sold in every single bar and pub in Prague. It comes from the spa town of Karlovy Vary (see pp. 330–35) and is said to calm an upset stomach, as Prague's dipsos are fond of telling foreigners as they drink their way into double figures. Two other spirits, eclipsed by the fame of their big brother but nevertheless popular are *Slivovice* (plum brandy) and *Borovička*, a native form of mother's ruin made from juniper berries. Finally, couples dining in the more expensive restaurants may want to relish a cognac, which is usually provided in huge glasses, sometimes bigger than your face. Men usually get balloon-shaped ones, and women are given tall and curvaceous vessels. The waiters love the ceremony, and may come to your table with a selection of glasses before warming your choices over a portable stove.

Eating Out

There are five main types of eating and drinking establishment in Prague, although the distinctions often overlap. Draught beers are served in a *pivnice*, *hostinec* or a *hospoda*—any of which may serve simple Czech dishes and wine as well. A *vinárna* only has wine or spirits to drink, and the food on offer varies from cold plates of ham and cheese to what passes in Prague for a full menu. A *kavárna* is a café, serving non-alcoholic beverages, probably wine and spirits and possibly snacks. Anything goes in a *restaurace*.

Reservations: If your visit is during high season (especially July and August), you should *always* try to make reservations as far in advance as posible, even if the thought would never occur to you at home. Many of the central restaurants are booked for up to a week and long queues often develop outside even ordinary cafés. Summertime Prague is filled with roving bands of lean and hungry tourists, crossing and recrossing on the Charles Bridge as dinnertime runs out. It's a sorry fate, and one that you can avoid with just a few phone calls. Someone who speaks English is usually around, and you could even sort out your meals before leaving home. If you don't make prior bookings, the list of restaurants below will tell you which are more likely to have space. But, if autocannibalization begins to set in, there are a few emergency steps which you can take.

* Be creative with your meal schedules, e.g. lunch at 4 pm, dinner at 5 pm. Restaurants are more likely to have space at bizarre times, although most close their kitchens by 10.

* The streets just behind the National Museum and around nám. Republiky are dotted with (admittedly unexceptional) cafés and restaurants. They're within walking distance of the centre, but are overlooked by most visitors.

* Most of Prague's beer joints will have something on the menu, generally sausages and dumplings. There are sausage and kebab stalls on Wenceslas Square, and the town is full of cheap and chrome-plated stand-up dining halls (*bufet*).

* Picnics solve all problems. See pp. 313–14 for Prague's best food shops.

Dress and other codes: In the smartest restaurants, men are expected to wrap a tie around their throats, and women should make the appropriate equivalent gestures. Most places also insist that jackets be either worn or handed in at the cloakroom, and some of the surlier waiters and waitresses studiously ignore you if you have anything draped over the back of your chair. Otherwise there are no major dining quirks in Prague. Traditionally, Czechs say nothing while eating a meal, but although you should still think twice about accepting an invitation to a village dinner party, the custom has thankfully all but died out in urban Czechoslovakia.

The standard of service can actually be wonderful in the best restaurants; informal, friendly and conscientious. In such places, your neighbours are often far more offensive—Czech émigrés talking loudly and proudly in English, or power-dressers from the west urgently discussing how to clinch the Deal before the beano is over. However, in most of the cafés and bars that you're likely to find yourself in, handling Prague's waiters and waitresses demands exhausting skills. Most important is a willingness to give as good as you get. Don't wait to be seated unless there's a physical obstruction in the way, and never be afraid to accost a member of staff who has walked past you twice. If your course doesn't arrive for some time, always assume that you've been forgotten. Leaving a restaurant can take as long as getting in. The first stage is to say *za platím* (may I pay?) to someone. He or she will probably nod, mumble *koleg* (colleague), and walk away, never to return. What that means is that the man with the purse has to be tackled. He'll often be hiding in the kitchens or sharing a joke with friends, and although he can get fairly upset if interrupted, the best thing to do is to present him with your bill and cash. Alternatively, you could make as if to do a leisurely runner, which may or may not draw some attention in your direction. A final possibility is to leave your money on the table, and walk out—which usually causes consternation, and may lead the man with the purse to deliver a mini-lecture on the fact that they do things differently in Prague.

Tipping: In the most expensive restaurants, a tip of 10–15 per cent is expected; in others, anything over a couple of crowns is OK and 10 per cent will startle your waiter or waitress. In most places, your bill is totted up in front of you, and you're expected to tell the waiter how much you want to pay in total, rather than the amount of change you want returned. How much you actually leave depends on your theory of the tip, but given the often pitiful standard of service, you'll be doing your bit for future generations of visitors by strictly linking the amount to your level of satisfaction.

Vegetarians: Vegetarians have a rough time in Prague. You'll be confronted with slabs of meat and internal organs everywhere you go, and the city's one nominally vegetarian restaurant (Vegetarka—see below) has a habit of sneaking fish, fowl and flesh into the day's menu—and if you complain, you're usually regarded as an unhealthy obsessive. However, restaurants are slowly adapting to the new-fangled fads of western stomachs, and to ask whether there are meatless dishes, say *máte bezmasé jídlo?*.

Breakfast: There are few places in Prague which serve anything like a healthy breakfast. The word exists in Czech (*snídaně*), but the concept is little understood and toast doesn't exist. However, you can occasionally find *hemenex*, the Czech version of the English 'ham and eggs'; the café behind the Paris-Praha on Jindřišská 7 does them, and its breakfast menu also includes the rarely-found scrambled egg (Mon–Sat 8.30–11 am). The Evropa Café at Václavské nám. serves a leisurely brunchy affair between 7 am and 2 pm every day, although the copies of the *Morning Star* that used to be available for perusal have been removed, with no English replacement provided. You can buy the *Guardian*, *FT* or *Herald Tribune* just outside the hotel after about 11 am.

The following restaurants offer some of the most unusual, tasty and/or available meals in Prague, but be warned— you'll come across the same dishes time after time. The same menus, almost identical and usually carbon-copied into illegibility, can be found in hundreds of the capital's eateries, and offer either basic Czech food, or a ubiquitous set of steaks often glorified with the term *mezinárodní* (international). You'll find menu terms in the Language section of this book. The capital's restaurants are officially divided into four price categories (*skupiny*), but the divisions have completely lost touch with what passes for reality in Prague, and the selections below are divided into three categories— expensive, moderate and cheap. At the time of writing, a welter of increases in the cost of food is imminent, and the prices can only be very rough, but you should expect to pay the following for a **complete dinner for two, including a bottle of Czech wine**:

Expensive—£14–24 ($26–43).
Moderate—£8–14 ($15–26).
Cheap—up to £8 ($15).

Several of the places below don't serve full three-course meals, but they've been put into whichever category they would probably be in if they did. Most foreign visitors will find even the most fantastically lavish meal a snip, but even if crowns sometimes seem like Monopoly money, remember that most Czechs would think of eating out at even the top end

276

of the 'cheap' category as something of a luxury. If you've asked a friend to join you, you can avoid a lot of embarrassment by asking him or her to choose a place, or insisting that you pay. *Dobrou chut!*

Credit Cards
AE = American Express, DC = Diners Club, MC = Mastercard and Access, V = Visa. Few restaurants yet take credit cards.

Nové Město

EXPENSIVE
Indická restaurace, Štěpánská 61, tel 236 99 22. Mon–Sat 12 noon–4 pm and 6–11 pm. Limited vegetarian choice, but the seekh kebabs and tandoori chicken can occasionally lift you far from the world of *knedlíky*. However, Czech handiwork is unmistakeable in the watery dals. Very polite service. Reservation essential. There's also an **Indian snack bar** next door (Sat–Fri 11 am–11 pm), which serves some of the same food and often has a table free if you can wait.

MODERATE
Dům Slovenské kultury (House of Slovakian Culture), Purkyňova 4, tel 29 19 16. 11am–11pm. One of the best places to try Slovakian food in Prague. Try the *Živáňska ihla*, a spicy shashlik of beef and pork. (AE)
Klášterní vinárna, Národní 8, tel 29 05 96. 11 am–3.30 pm and 5.30 pm–midnight. Fairly stiff and gloomy restaurant set in a former monastery. Useful if you're going on to the National Theatre next door. Fairly standard menu.
Palace Hotel, Panská 12. 10 am–10 pm. A salad bar made out of wood, plastic and mirrors that's useful for vegetarians and anyone in a hurry. Introduced the 'as-much-as-you-can-eat' principle to Prague but cheats by providing saucers, so you should cheat back by piling the red and greenery high. Also has school-dinner type hot dishes. You'll always find a meal here.
Peking, Legerova 64, tel 29 35 31. Mon–Sat 11.30 am–3 pm, 5.30–8 pm and 8.30–11 pm. Apparently spells its name backwards on the door—but although authenticity isn't at a premium, the restaurant is useful for a change and may improve as imported ingredients become more widely available.
U kalicha (The Chalice), Na Bojišti 12, tel 29 07 01. 11 am–3 pm and

5–11 pm. Only mentioned because you might hear of this beer hall and think that it sounds interesting. It was mentioned in *The Good Soldier Švejk*, and it's milked the fact dry.

U šuterů, Palackého 4. Mon–Fri 11 am–midnight, Sat 4–midnight. Very lively and cosy tunnel-like restaurant. Popular with Czechs, and worth trying if you're stuck, as it doesn't usually take advance reservations. Cheapest end of this category.

Viola Trattoria, Národní 7, tel 26 67 32. Small and very red Italian restaurant, filled with empty gourds and usually booked for several days in advance. Relatively broad range of dishes, and even Italians have been known to appreciate the food. (AE)

Jizera, Václavské nám. 48. Mon–Sat 9 am–10 pm, Sun 2–10 pm. Dark arched cellar in Wenceslas Square. Steaks and/or dumpling-type dishes, with service that's fairly rough and rarely ready. The food's no worse than many other more expensive spots, and if you have reasons for wanting to stick around Wenceslas Square, this is one of the places that's more likely to have space free. The *bufet* upstairs, where you can always pick up a beer and a chunk of chicken, is even cheaper.

Slovanská hospoda (Slavonic Inn), Na příkopě 22, 11 am–11 pm. Beer, dumplings and sausages in a modern but ivy-drenched courtyard popular among Praguers. Occasional music, and sufficiently hidden to guarantee a meal if you arrive before the kitchen decides to close. This address is filled with eateries, and on the ground floor, you can often have a steak until 4 am.

U Fleků, Křemencova 11, tel 29 32 45/6. 8.30–11 pm. Prague's most legendary beer hall, founded in 1459. The 1000 seats are largely filled by Germans. Simple Czech food. Permeated by unfortunate smell of vomit—escape to shady garden.

Baltic Grill, Václavské nám 43. Sun–Fri 10 am–11.30 pm. The best of a fishy complex in an arcade off Wenceslas Square. If this is full, you can pick up a trout in the bright and starchy **Rybárna** opposite (Mon–Sat 11 am–10 pm), and next to the street is the cheap **Rybí bufet** (Mon–Sat 8.30 am–8.30 pm, Sun 9 am–8 pm), with herring and carp a-plenty.

Šumická vinárna, Mikulandská 12, tel 29 15 68. 5 pm–midnight. Steaks again, but this is an extremely popular and lively spot, with red-jacketed gipsies wandering among the tables each night from 7. Often turns into quite a party.

Staré Město

EXPENSIVE

Diplomatic Club, Karlova 21, tel 26 57 01. 7.30 pm–1 am. Food and service is said to be impeccable, but you could hardly cut the stiff atmosphere with a knife. Although women and blacks are apparently allowed in, Czechs have to be accompanied by a foreigner.

Moskva, Na příkopě 29, tel 26 27 74. 11 am–5 pm and 6 pm–1 am. Russian again. Useful for late-night food if you don't object to sitting in what feels like a very expensive McDonald's. You'll usually find space, you'll eat lightly but well (salads, caviare, lobster cocktail), but you'll pay through the nose.

Opera, Karolíny Světlé 35, tel 26 55 08. Mon–Fri 7pm–2am. Pianist and Baroque furniture; intimacy and exclusivity to match.

U červeného kola (The Red Wheel), Anežská 2, tel 231 89 41. 10 am–10 pm. Long list of steaks, almost always among the best-cooked in Prague, and excellent service. Tucked away in a sublime corner of the Old Town near St Agnes's Convent.

U Plebána, Betlémské nám. 10, tel 26 52 23. Mon–Sat 11 am–11 pm. *Knedlíky* are inescapable here, but this is one of the tastiest spots to try Czech cooking. Only two soups, but the lovely cream-and-dill *kulajda* is one of them. An occasional haunt of Václav Havel.

MODERATE

Berjozka, Rytířská 31, tel 22 38 22. Mon–Sat 11 am–11 pm. Russian food—including several dishes flambéed in Stolichnaya. The staff seem to make a habit of fobbing off diners with dubious 'recommendations', and you may have to insist on getting a menu. May have space for the same evening.

Blatnice, Michalská 8, tel 22 47 51. Sun–Fri 11 am–11 pm. Serves the standard set of steaks, but usually has an alternative of a packed cold plate. The inside isn't worth reserving unless you're desperate—but the outdoor tables are part of the liveliest (wine) drinking street in Prague during the summer.

Kosher Restaurant, Maislova 18, tel 231 09 09. 11.30 am–2 pm and 6–9 pm. Prague's last Jewish restaurant in the former town hall of the ghetto. Strange atmosphere, which veers from clattering liveliness when the locals are around to all-foreign evenings with piano music. Increasingly developing its tourist-trap potential, and non-Czechs are now surcharged several hundred per cent. Worth a lunchtime stop, but the food rarely makes dinner worth while.

Obecní dům (Municipal House), nám. Republiky. 11 am–11 pm. Service with a snarl. However, the Art Nouveau interior and the availability of seats (and eventually steaks) make this a useful emergency destination.

Restaurace 'Praha', Rašínovo nábř, tel 20 58 93. 11 am–10 pm. A moored boat that regularly lifts its anchor in the evenings. Standard menu, centred around the usual list of steaks, but special orders are entertained. Reservations essential for floating dinners. Rooftop terrace in summer.

Slavie, Národní 1, tel 26 57 60. 11 am–3 pm and 5–11 pm. No atmosphere at all, but a useful place to eat after a visit to the well-known but almost foodless café next door.

U modré štiky (The Golden Pike), Karlova 20, tel 26 30 65. 9 am–11 pm. Serves fish (almost invariably over-cooked trout) and the standard menu, along with Pilsner lager. Unexceptional, but accessible if you're prepared to queue.

U pavouka (The Spider), Celetná 17, tel 231 87 14. Mon–Sat 11.30 am–3 pm and 6–11.30 pm. Very friendly service and a tasty menu revolving around duck and veal, in one of Prague's best subterranean eateries. The comfy and cosy rooms used to have a pianist in the evenings, and although he's moved on, mood music will probably return. (AE, DC, MC and V—but may not take cards for much longer.)

U Rudolfa, Maislova 5, tel 232 26 71. 10 am–10 pm. A tiny modern restaurant filled with sizzling smells from the stove behind the bar, in the heart of the old Jewish ghetto. The menu is even more minuscule, but no one ever complains about a meal here. Hams, cheeses and steaks. Reserve at least a day in advance (AE, DC, MC, V). If you're out of luck, you could try Rudolf's ungainly larger twin, **U Golema** (The Golem), on the opposite side of the road, which serves the standard dishes and is (just about) more likely to have room. It takes all credit cards and is open Mon–Fri 11 am–10 pm, Sat 5–11 pm, tel 232 81 65.

U sedmi andělů (The Seven Angels), Jilská 20, tel 26 63 55. Mon–Sat 12 noon–3 pm and 6–midnight. Pleasant little Czech restaurant in a winding thoroughfare of the Old Town. Favoured by tour parties, which can be fun if you and they are in the mood for a spot of dancing (violins and twirling every evening). Dinnertime often kicks off with a rather bizarre ceremony in which the catering staff and manager light the chandelier's candles in silence and bow.

U zelené žáby (The Green Frog), U radnice 8, tel 26 28 15. 3–11 pm. A gloomy vault dripping with history, thanks to the fact that Prague's executioner ate here in the 17th century (see p. 150). Book yourself into his alcove, and sink your teeth into the bloody roast beef, with garlic toast. (AE).

U zlaté konvice (The Golden Tankard), Melantrichova 20, tel 26 21 28. 5pm–midnight. Excellent service and one of the most unique locations in Prague, stretching through 600-year-old chambers and cellars running a fair way into the Old Town Square. Used to serve only wine and snacks, but a hot food menu is currently in the final stages of preparation. Gipsy musicians serenade your table from Tues–Sat until you bribe them to leave. Drunken dancing is possible. Advance reservation essential, in every sense. (AE, DC, MC, V).

U zlaté studny (The Golden Well), Karlova 5, tel 26 33 02. 11 am–3 pm and 5 pm–midnight. The lamb dishes that are the speciality of the chef are often fairly bland concoctions, but the Romanesque basement seems to have space late in the evening, after 10 pm.

U zlatého hada (The Golden Serpent), Karlova 18, tel 235 87 78. 11 am–midnight. Another set of steaks, but this rather odd set of high-backed chairs and cosy cubby-holes is one of the few spots on the beaten track where you stand a good chance of finding a space in high season. The bar next door is a good place to meet Finns, and also serves food until about 8 pm.

U zlatého jelena (The Golden Stag), Celetná 11, tel 26 85 95. Mon–Fri noon–midnight, Sat–Sun 6–midnight. Set in the oldest Gothic banqueting hall in Prague, this is one of the cosiest spots to pick up a tasty steak. The waiters are particularly proud of their Moravian wines, and will think long and hard on the best one for your dish. You can find several of them in the meanest Prague supermarket, but let the boys earn their keep.

Železné dveře (The Iron Door) Michalská 19, tel 26 27 31. 1–4 pm and 5 pm–1 am. The electric organ won't appeal to all tastes, but this underground restaurant has a broad menu and is very friendly if you get a table. Specializes in Mělník wines.

CHEAP

Arbat, Na příkopě 29. 7.30–11 pm. The Soviet Union's contribution to fast food culture. Greasy shashliks, tobacco chicken and french fries in slovenly plastic surroundings, but a speedy and guaranteed anti-hunger stop.

U dvou koček (The Two Cats), Uhelný trh. 10 am–10 pm. Lively spot for Pilsner and Czech food.

U medvidku (The Little Bear), Na Perštýně 10, tel 235 89 04. 9 am–11 pm. Popular beer hall (Smíchov) with plenty of Czech dishes on the menu.

U supa (The Vulture), Celetná 22, tel 22 30 42. 11 am–10 pm. This large and airy beer hall is for anyone who enjoys drinking but not the compulsory smoking that comes with it in most of Prague. You'll always get a space if you wait, followed by regular supplies of beer and sausages. A small adjoining restaurant also serves steak, but the waiters are often reluctant and occasionally abusive if you ask for one. Persistence usually pays off. Serves Braník beer, another Prague brand.

Vegetarka, Celetná 3. Mon–Fri 11 am–2.30 pm. As mentioned above, vegetarians should beware being slipped a sausage here, but otherwise this can be a swift and convenient lunchtime stop. The queue is often long, but there's counter service at the end of it. Simple, mass-produced food.

Malá Strana

EXPENSIVE

Lobkovická vinárna, Vlašská 17, tel 53 01 85. 6.30 pm–1 am. Small and unexciting steak menu in one of the favoured haunts of Malá Strana's diplomatic community. The restaurant was set up by the Lobkowiczes in the 18th century to sell their Mělník wines, and the done thing here is to splash out on the sparkling variety.

U Malířů (The Painter's), Maltézské nám. 11, tel 53 18 83. Mon–Sat (occasionally closed Wednesday) 11.30 am–3 pm and 7.30 pm–midnight. It's difficult to know what to say about this place. Ever since being taken over by French gastronomes in late 1990, the food and service have been getting rave reviews, but its price explodes off the scale of this book. Not a place to go Dutch with a Praguer (the American lobster costs £50 ($90), or almost a month's salary), but if you can afford it, you probably won't be disappointed. Very pretty interior—the wall paintings aren't old, but this has been a restaurant ever since the original 'painter' moved here in 1541.

U mecenáše (Maecenas'), Malostranské nám. 10, tel 53 38 81. Sun–Fri 5 pm –1 am. An interior structurally unchanged for almost 400 years and filled with pieces of gallows, firearms and swords amassed over the centuries. Reserve a place either in the comfortable back room or underground cellar, and ask to see the 1626 signature of Mydlář the Executioner, who regularly popped over from the Green Frog. The food is unexceptional, but the service and conversation-piece furnishings make this one of the most comfortable restaurants in town to pursue a romance.

U tří pštrosů (The Three Ostriches), Dražického nám. 12, tel 53 61 51. Part of the beautiful Renaissance hotel at the end of the Charles Bridge—but the fairly gloomy interior and mediocre standards of the restaurant have got some way to go before they catch up with its reputation. Reserve well in advance.

MODERATE

Nebozízek, Petřínské sady, tel 53 79 05. 11 am–6 pm and 7 pm–midnight (closed on Mondays in winter). Nothing special about the food, but a meal here is pure romance from the moment you step into the funicular railway up Petřín Hill (get off at the first stop). The outdoor terrace in the summer is unreservable, and you should be able to nab a table before long. Be sure to walk back down, to catch the winking city at its heartmelting best, and try to avoid the canoodlers who congregate on the hillside as the sun sets.

U tří housliček, Nerudova 12, tel 53 50 11. Tues–Sat 3.30–11.30 pm. One of the best of the small wine bars running up Nerudova street. The menu's limited to snacks, but they're a tasty selection and include salty *losos* (salmon), almonds and caviare.

U tří zlatých hvězd (The Three Golden Stars), Malostranské nám. 8, tel 53 96 60. 5 pm–1 am. Only cold dishes, but this wine bar under the arcade next to St Nicholas's Church is a useful pause during the early evening and one of the cosiest spots for a nightcap. Tables still need to be reserved until about 11 during the summer, although groups of up to three can eventually insinuate themselves onto the bar seats.

Valdštejnská Hospoda (Waldstein Inn), Valdštejnské nám. 7, tel 53 61 95. 11 am–3 pm and 6–11 pm. Varied menu stretching from venison to trout, in smart surroundings.

CHEAP

Olympia, Vítězná 7, tel 53 27 61. 11 am–11 pm. A complex of three eateries, ranging from beer and dumplings, to quick steaks in the video bar. Almost always has space, and is a 10-minute walk from the Charles

Bridge. Despite the advertised opening hours, the kitchen usually closes by 9.30.

U kocoura, Nerudova 2. A place where the Plzeň beer flows and Malá Stranites gather. A Prague favourite, and sausages are available.

Hradčany

EXPENSIVE

U labutí (The Swan), Hradčanské nam. 11, tel 53 94 76. 7 pm–1 am. One of Prague's most exclusive spots, set in a former stable with intact watertroughs. It's divided into two sections—if you're dining to impress, make sure your reservation is for the 'Club'. Intimate; service is very attentive, but leisurely to downright slow. The food is average, but there's nothing quite as beautiful as the wending descent back into Malá Strana after you've downed your cognac here.

U Sevce Matouše, Loretánská nám. 4, tel 53 35 97. Jan–Apr Mon–Sat 12 noon–10 pm, Sun 12 noon–6 pm; May–Dec 11 am–11 pm. Recognizable by the golden boot that hangs in the vaulted arcade outside the restaurant. Service varies (which sometimes can't be said for the sauces on the steaks), but this is one of the few spots where the waiters at least enquire whether you would prefer a brown crisp or beef tartare. Cobbling was once the trade here, and from Mon–Sat, there's a while-you-eat repair service available. Bottom end of this price category.

U zlaté hrušky (The Golden Pear), Nový svět 3, tel 53 11 33. 6.30 pm–12.30 am. Excellent service in perhaps the most secluded and romantic lane in Prague. Reserve at least a couple of days in advance, even in winter.

MODERATE

U Lorety, Loretánské nám. 8, tel 53 13 95. 12 noon–11 pm. Outdoor eaters should head for the terrace here in the summer: apart from a splendid location next to the Loretto shrine, the menu is often more varied than usual; and if you're prepared to wait a while, it can be a lifesaver when all else is full. The expensive interior is always reserved well in advance, and serves a broad range of Czech and Slovak dishes.

Vikárka, Vikářská 7, tel 53 51 50/8. May–Sept 11 am–10 pm, Oct–April 11 am–8 pm. Steeped in the shadow of St Vitus's Cathedral and heir to a long tradition of hostelries on Vicars Lane. Could make a commercial killing from its location, but the service and food are never more than ordinary. Its lack of atmosphere is typified by the fact that the walls of its wine cellar were once signed by most of Prague's early 20th-century artists, until the management decided to repaint them. Still the only place to have dinner within the castle grounds.

CHEAP

Sate Gril, Pohořelec 12. 10 am–7.30 pm. No frills, but this is a quick and guaranteed place to pick up a set of very, very vaguely Indonesian dishes. The staff can cater for vegetarians by removing the few scraps of meat from the noodle dishes.

U cerného vola (The Black Ox), Loretánské nám. 1. 9.30 am–9 pm. Serves its own beer, brewed just outside Prague and highly popular among the locals. Basic food.

Outside the centre

The following restaurants are a few of the best outside the four central districts of Prague. None are more than a short metro or tram ride away, but advance reservations of at least a couple of days are necessary for all of them.

EXPENSIVE

Chang-Čou, Janáčkovo nábř. 1, tel 54 91 64. Mon–Sat 11.30 am–midnight (closed 3–5 pm). Two Cantonese chefs make for Prague's newest and tastiest Chinese restaurant.

Thang Long, Dukelských hrdinů 48, tel 80 65 41. 12 noon–3 pm, 5–7 pm. Czechoslovakia has a population of some 30,000 Vietnamese, but thanks to the rigidities of Communism none opened a restaurant, and this plush set of screens and fans run by Czechs is still the best place to try Vietnamese cuisine. The chef has gone home, but he's said to have taught his Czech protégés everything he knew.

MODERATE

Kalypso, Slezská 134, tel 73 91 94. Tues–Sun 5 pm–midnight. Prague's Greek restaurant. There's no plate-smashing behind the net curtains of the dinky blue and white interior; Beach Boys but no bazoukis; but there really are olives, fetta and retsina on the menu. Popular among the Greeks who fled the colonels in the late 1960s, and now make up one of Prague's most interesting subcultures. Has some useful vegetarian dishes.

Myslivna, Jagellonská 21, tel 27 22 11. 11 am–11 pm. Prague's best spot to bag some game. Half-hearted hunting decor, but the food can be excellent, the mood is often jolly, and service is friendly without being fawning.

Orient, Otakarova 1, tel 43 09 13. 11 am–3 pm, 5–7.30 and 8–11 pm. A Czech chef's idea of what non-Europeans might eat. The Chinese/Indian/Arabic dishes are generally unrecognizable, but they're a tasty alternative to dumplings if you're in the area.

U pastýřky (The Shepherdess's), Bělehradská 15, tel 43 40 93. Mon–Sat 5 pm–1 am. Charcoal-grilled steaks in a suburban Slovakian shepherd's hut. Resident quasi-gipsy band, and the smoky atmosphere swirls into drunken and raucous life as the relentless carafes of wine take hold.

Where to Stay

The Evropa Hotel

Prague's hotel industry is in an utterly pitiful state. An annual influx of visitors which is crawling into the millions is greeted by a total of some 60 hotels; and the city which can boast one of the most extraordinary architectural preserves in Europe has no more than a handful of hotels which can honourably claim to be a century old, and only one with the charm to meet honeymoon specifications—and even that only moved into its Renaissance address in 1976. Until the outbreak of war in 1938, the city was peppered with genteel palaces and pensions serving the needs of young men who had strayed off their grand tours. Neither they nor private property were favoured by the Communists who took over in 1948. The hotels were confiscated wholesale, and most were given plywood partitions and turned into educational institutes or cramped collective housing. A few fleapits were preserved for the bands of fellow-travellers who passed through over the next decade. The late 1970s saw the creation of some five-star palaces for those who had come to pump some serious money into the economy; but until 1989, arriving in Prague without guaranteed accommodation was a recipe for at least adventure, and potentially disaster. Stultification has now been replaced by chaos. *Restituce* and *privatisace* are the buzz-words of the moment—disposessed owners are re-emerging to claim their woodwork, and as of mid-1991 almost all the other hotels are going under the auctioneer's hammer, with no guarantees whatsoever as to their future.

Accommodation Agencies *(Int. dialing 42-2)*

You'll find more details of booking a hotel below, but unless your reservation is confirmed, you're almost certainly better off relying on one of the private agencies that have sprung up since 1989. All of the following have a broad range of properties on their books, often slightly outside the centre of town but with a few gems in the heart of the Old Town and Malá Strana. The offerings stretch from student dorm rooms (cheap, comfortable and available between July and September) to spacious self-contained apartments. All offer plenty of rooms in Czech family houses, which is rarely as constricting as it sounds, although your hosts may insist on waking you up with coffee and cakes and asking endless questions about home. Most of the agencies will have somewhere free even if you pull in on a warm August evening, but during high season, it's best to send a fax in advance. At the time of writing, few are in practice willing to accept very specific orders (e.g. first floor flat on the Old Town Square), but that may change as credit-card machinery and telephone payments become more widespread in Czechoslovakia. The price ranges given are approximate, **per person per night**. The lower price is almost invariably for a shared double room in student lodgings or living with a family. At the time of writing, many of the agencies (all of which are based in central Prague) still require payment in hard currency. Breakfast can usually be provided for a small additional charge.

City of Prague Accommodation Service, Haštalské nám. 13, tel 231 02 02 (fax 231 40 76). Oct–Mar 9 am–5 pm; April–Sept 9 am–9 pm. 600 beds. The owner here can sometimes help out after hours (he has a telephone extension in his own flat). £8–25 ($15–45).

Agentura B & B, 28. října 9, tel 26 82 20 (fax 26 69 79). Dec–Mar 9 am–6 pm; April–Nov 8 am–7 pm. Can be chaotic, but offers some of the cheapest lodgings, generally shared doubles in pensions and colleges. £7–14 ($13–25).

AR Tour, Karolíny Světlé 9, Praha 1, tel and fax 235 83 89. April–Sept 9 am–9 pm; Oct–Mar Mon–Fri 9.30 am–6 pm, Sat 1–6 pm. Well-run and friendly. Advance booking of the better hotels (10–20 per cent commission); some very attractive flats in centre (£8–30 ($15–54). Approx 500 properties.

AVE, Hlavní nádraží, tel 236 25 60, 236 25 41, 236 30 75, fax 236 29 56 (May–Sept 6.30 am–2 am, Oct–April 6.30 am–10.30 pm). The most convenient spot for recent arrivals, although the queue outside the small office can reach a daunting length in high season. £10–28 ($18–51).

CAK Agentour, Široká 10, tel 231 00 36 (Mon–Fri 9 am–8.30 pm). Well-run and sometimes more expensive than the other agencies. Has rooms in flats, pensions and boarding houses from £10–100 ($18–180).

CKM, Žitná 10, 121 05 Praha 2, tel 236 27 98, (fax 235 12 97). Mon–Fri 9 am–12 noon 1.30–6 pm. Youth-orientated but open to all. Cheap hotels and student dorms from £5–12 ($9–22). Approx 200 beds. Youth hostellers enjoy discounts and priority in high season.

Toptour, Rybná 3, Praha 1, tel 229 65 26, 232 10 77 (fax 232 08 60). Mon–Fri 9 am–8 pm and Sat–Sun 11 am–7 pm. Helpful and efficient with a broad range of about 450 properties. Prices for a self-contained flat range from £18–32 ($33–58) in winter to £24–48 ($44–87) in high season.

Uniset, 28. října 9, tel 26 69 79. Mon–Fri 9 am–7 pm. Very cheap dorm rooms in summer; and usefully shares an office with Agentura B & B. £5–14 ($9–26).

UVD Tour, Václavské nám. 38, tel 22 19 29, 236 3365/6 (fax 236 33 65). April–Sept 10 am–8 pm; Oct–Mar 9 am–6 pm. Hotel bookings to dorm beds, from £9 ($16) in private accommodation to £15 ($27) in a small lodging house.

Hotel Booking

If you're determined to book yourself into a hotel, be prepared for disappointment. Almost all of Prague's mid-range hotels have long-term contracts with Čedok and private foreign tour organizers, and are often booked up for months in advance. Your local branch of Čedok (see p. 1) may be able to make the arrangements, for a price, in which case you should check what they're giving you against the information below. However, if it tells you that there are no hotel beds left in Prague for months ahead, as it has been known to do, you can now take your custom elsewhere. **Arstour** will make bookings at the hotels Intercontinental, Forum, Panorama and Paříž, but you're then committed to one of a variety of cultural tours which spare neither expense nor much time (Arstour Praha, Na švihance 6, Praha 2, tel 275 82 94). The above accommodation agencies may also be able to find you a room in a hotel; and last of all, it's just possible that you'll be able to make a reservation yourself, by fax or telephone. As a general rule, you should try on around the 15th of the month preceding your arrival, which is when most hotels find out exactly how large is the tour group which is about to inundate them. **None of the hotels below category B take credit cards unless**

otherwise stated, but if they accept your reservation, they generally honour it even without prior payment.

If you arrive in Prague without a hotel, and still harbour hopes of finding one, go to the Čedok office at Panská 5 (tel 22 56 57) which can tell you if any places have rooms available on that day. It's open from Mon–Fri 8 am–9 pm, Sat–Sun 8 am–4 pm (April–Oct); Mon–Fri 8 am–8 pm, Sat–Sun 8 am–4 pm (Nov–Mar). It also has a range of private accommodation available, in case the news is bad. However, as there's a certain inevitability that it will be in high season, when you find yourself at the wrong end of a 20-person queue you could cut your losses and take up the private accommodation offers of one of the milling band of Praguers outside the office. Look up the address on a map, and if it's central, take the plunge—many of the renters are houseproud types who'll provide you with more room and a better standard of service than most of Prague's hotels.

The hotels below are divided into four price categories:

A—£100–140 ($180–252)
B—£50–100 ($90–180)
C—£30–50 ($54–90)
D—£10–30 ($18–54)

Several of those listed aren't recommendations, but are mentioned simply because you may find yourself offered one by Čedok; after reading about it below, you may consider making alternative arrangements. On the other hand, none of the hotels are any worse than dilapidated, and at times of crisis, their telephone numbers may come in useful.

Czechoslovakia's hotels have historically divided themselves into a convoluted A/B/C/* division, which has become too out of touch with observable facts to be worth repeating. However, those hotels which are classed **** and above are marked as such below. None of the others provide room service, but all have adjoining dining rooms or restaurants which serve meals from breakfast onwards. Many of the cheap hotels have no rooms with bath or shower. Every room will have a basin, and at least one bathroom and toilet per floor. Finally, although all the information is up to date as of March 1991, the wind of change that's billowing through Prague is unlikely to leave any of its hotels quite the same. You'll have an inkling of improvements if you find that your choice has leapt three price categories; but otherwise expect the worst, and you just may be pleasantly surprised.

Nové Město

This area actually dates back to the 14th century, but very few of its buildings survived large-scale redevelopment over the last 100 years. The majority of Prague's hotels are now situated here, and range across the scale of noise and comfort. Expect shuddering and dirty streets, but you won't be more than a 15-minute journey from the peace of the Old Town Square.

CLASS A

*******Esplanade**, Washingtonova 19, tel 22 25 52, 22 60 56/9 (fax 26 58 97). More mixed-up chintzy decoration than any other hotel in Prague creates an elegance that's strained; but food can be excellent and the stiff-necked staff try hard to please and live up to their five stars. Close to main railway station and head of Wenceslas Square. 95 beds.

*******Jalta**, Václavské nám. 45, tel 26 55 41 (fax 26 53 47). Comfortable, central and unexceptional. 121 beds.

*******Palace**, Panská 12, Praha 1, tel 236 00 08, 235 93 94 (fax 235 93 73). 250 beds. Modern, central, comfortable, and the only hotel in Prague where the porter wears a topper and a turquoise cloak. Conference facilities and casino. The former Art Nouveau hotel has been completely remodelled, and apart from a whiplash bar and some crazy-paned glass there's no reminder of its past. Guests enjoy an unctuous level of service and pay more than anywhere else in Prague. Has special rooms 'designed for lady travellers', which are pink, have more mirrors than usual, and come with a red rose.

CLASS B ·

******Ambassador**, Václavské nám. 5, tel 214 31 11. Elegant neo-classical furniture in comfortable rooms and a lobby that's a lively extension of Wenceslas Square at most hours. Booked for months in advance. 281 beds.

******Atlantic**, Na poříčí 9, tel 231 85 12. Modern, airy and pleasant, and close to the bottom of this category. One of the best hotels for wheelchairs and their occupants; but parking can be a problem. 118 beds.

Tatran, Václavské nám. 22, tel 235 28 85. Central—but otherwise shabby, unfriendly and overpriced. No cards. 100 beds.

CLASS C

Albatros, nábř. Ludvíka Svobody, tel 231 36 00/34/81. One of Prague's 'boatels', permanently (and stably) moored on the Vltava. Closer to the Old Town Square than Wenceslas Square, but the view as you wake up is just too far from the Charles Bridge to be dreamy. Two long corridors of clean cabins (all doubles, save for a few four-bedders), all with showers. Largely young crowd and an on-board nightclub, a minuscule dance-floor open until 3 am. Perfect for fervent teenybop-pers, but anyone's allowed to check in. 158 beds

Družba, Václavské nám. 16, tel 235 12 32. Unpleasant staff, stark rooms. Not worth the effort of a phone call unless you hear that it's been privatized. 86 beds.

Evropa, Václavské nám. 25, tel 236 52 74. This legendary Art Nouveau hotel in the centre of Wenceslas Square is the closest that you'll get to faded elegance in Prague. Although the rooms completely fail to match up to the promise held out by the glorious façade and ground floor, there are sinuous decorations and rickety banisters throughout. The open lobby on the second floor, under a skylight three floors above, is the perfect place to carry on night-time conversations with fellow guests (although outsiders can't come up after midnight, and even you might have trouble with the sleepy doorman if you arrive any later). Make a reservation while you still can—reconstruction is imminent, and the Evropa that emerges from the rubble will almost certainly be unrecognizable. 166 beds.

Koruna, Opatovická 16, tel 29 39 33. Set in a slumbering corner of the New Town; and no more than a crawl away from the oldest beer hall in Prague. Clean rooms (all doubles), but pervasive smell of Czech cooking from the restaurant below. Try booking with a fortnight's notice. 40 beds.

Meteor, Hybernská 6, tel 235 85 17, fax 22 47 15. Currently undergoing a thorough rebuilding at the government's expense—and the recently discovered former owner is about to be handed a windfall. Parts of the hotel will remain open throughout; and although a sojourn is rather chaotic at the moment, this could be one of the better mid-range hotels in the centre by the time work is done. Its place in this category is highly speculative; could well hop up one. Prior booking is still a problem, but try 14 days before departure. 138 beds.

Opera, Těšnov 13, tel 231 56 09, 231 57 35. A stately neo-Renaissance mansion left out on a limb by the construction of a flyover next door. Most of the rumble is kept out of the rooms, and if you're not a light sleeper, this isn't a bad choice. It's at the very bottom of this price category; and the bright dining room below serves a breakfast menu that includes porridge and cornflakes—a rare treat in Prague. 93 beds.

CLASS D

Adria, Václavské nám. 26, tel 236 04 72, is a set of sparse boxes behind a Baroque façade. No dining facilities. Only creeps into this price category because none of the rooms have baths or showers—and you pay extra for use of the common facilities. No advance bookings are taken and it's usually packed with Russian, Korean and Afghani tour groups. 75 beds.

Axa, Na poříčí 40, tel 232 44 67. The cheap favourite of weary students, and a time-honoured spot for exchanging horror stories and back-packing tips. The rooms are plywood-and-orange, but there are 154 of them. Can be noisy. 248 beds.

Centrum, Na poříčí 31, tel 231 00 09. A sooty block on a grimy corner of the New Town, which is in such a state that the owner won't let it be seen pending reconstruction.

Hybernia, Hybernská 24, tel 22 04 31. Grim, and facing a very uncertain future. Will either have been demolished or remodelled into something worth investigating by the time you read this.

Juniorhotel, Žitná 12, tel 29 29 84. Clean, cheap and well worth the price. All rooms are doubles or triples, with showers and fuzzy TVs. Long-term contracts with the national youth travel agency, but if there's a gap, any age is welcome. Small and lively cocktail bar downstairs. 54 beds.

Kriváň, nám. I. P. Pavlova 5, tel 29 33 41. A peeling neo-Gothic palace that deserves to be more than the jagged and clattering mess of brown corridors that it has become. A likely candidate for elegant restructuring, but until then absolutely no frills—but cheap and near the centre.

Merkur, Těšnov 9, tel 231 68 40, 231 69 51. Hard beds, no rooms have baths or showers. May have space, but try the nearby Opera first—and if you don't get a room there, at least use its café for breakfast.

Moráň, Na Moráni 5, tel 29 42 51. Has very few rooms with either bath or shower. Noisy, bare and cheap.

Old Town

This area is perhaps the most convenient location of them all, but only the Ungelt is actually part of its history (see p. 142).

CLASS A

*****Intercontinental, nám. Curieovych 5, tel 280 01 11, 231 18 12 (fax 231 97 91). An ugly piece of concrete Lego on the bank of the Vltava. Five-star rooms, restaurants and supercilious staff, but the management proudly lets it be known that if you're an individual you should book at least a year in advance. 730 beds.

Paříž, U Obecního domu 1, tel 236 08 20, 236 83 84, fax 236 59 48. The extraordinary Art Nouveau façade, turned into a fortress by neo-Gothic turrets and arches, lets you down with very ordinary, if comfortable rooms. Expensive and popular. Lackadaisical staff. 162 beds.

Hotel Ungelt, Štupartská 1, tel 232 04 71. Only has six suites (with ten more to be added), but if you manage to bag one, you'll be sitting prettier than almost any other hotel-dweller in the city. A modern reconstruction of a once Gothic house, its tiled floors and airy corridors are on the edge of the Old Town Square. Feels more like a chalet camp than a Prague hotel; no room service, but as you glance at the handful of fellow guests over breakfast in the courtyard, you'll find it hard not to exchange gently victorious smiles at having triumphed over the odds. No lift. Travellers' cheques, but not credit cards, are accepted.

CLASS C

Centrál, Rybná 8, tel 232 43 51. Dingy and forlorn, but the grim corridors open into small clean rooms and its name does not lie.

Malá Strana and Hradčany

As with the Old Town, it's incredible how few hotels there are in this picturesque quarter, filled with orange pantiled roofs and smoking chimneys. If you're offered lodgings here by one of the accommodation agencies, count yourself very lucky indeed.

CLASS B

U tří pštrosů, Dražického nám. 12, tel 53 61 51. A 16th-century house that's everyone's dream of their stay in Prague. Waking up under the painted Renaissance joists and throwing open your windows over the Charles Bridge looks to be an unbeatable yawn. Has 18 rooms, and if you nab one, many, many congratulations. No cards.

Pension U raka, Černínská 10, tel 35 14 53 (fax 35 30 74). Tucked into one of the drowsiest streets of Prague, this offers another of the capital's most memorable stays. The log cabin itself is a fairly offensive extension, but it's probably warmer and more comfortable than the mess of ancient cottages that surrounds it. Only five rooms, and no meals—but the owner of this moneyspinner is an efficient sort with a mobile telephone, and he claims fairly credibly that he'll sort everything out once you arrive. No cards.

Dům rekreace Pyramida, Bílohorská 24, tel 311 32 41/96. A vast glass temple with clean if unexciting rooms, all with showers. Fitness centre below, and a short walk from Prague Castle, albeit one along a dusty main road. The poor man's Forum (see p. 297). 7–14 days' prior booking. No cards as yet. 600 beds.

CLASS D

Savoy, Keplerova 6, tel 53 74 50. The ravaged Art Nouveau façade on a busy road conceals no hidden personality. Some large rooms, the doors of which can be extremely rickety, but if you have nothing worth stealing and don't mind showering in the corridors, this is a stone's throw from some of the loveliest streets in Prague.

Smíchov

This area is industrial, but it's a hop away from Malá Strana, and has some of the liveliest pubs in town.

CLASS C

Admirál, Hořejší nábř. tel 54 74 45–9. Another boatel. All details are as for the Albatros above, except that it has 180 beds.

U Blaženky, U Blaženky 1, tel 53 82 66, 53 80 75. One of the best-value hotels in Prague, a spotless neo-Renaissance villa in a quiet residential street. The friendly couple who run it will provide a TV, fridge and even English breakfast if you need it. Looks out onto a patch of scrub, but the terrace is still a languid spot to start or end your day. Long climb; but ample parking. 13 doubles, 1 apartment.

CLASS D

Balkán, Svornosti 28, tel 54 01 96. Set on a busy street, this looks like a crumbling brothel. A place to dump your rucksack and run. Has occasional single beds for £4 ($7).

Praga, Plzeňská 29, tel 54 87 41. Rock-bottom prices, with fairly spacious and clean rooms. 120-capacity, and often has space. No lift, and only three rooms have more than a basin. Very basic, but friendly cleaning ladies, and a restaurant that's better than its price category would suggest. Good for emergencies—particularly financial ones.

Vinohrady and Žižkov

These residential districts range from hilly cobbled streets to busy Art Nouveau thoroughfares. Many of the hotels are crummy, but many are also a convenient walk from Wenceslas Square.

CLASS B

Flora, Vinohradská 121, tel 27 42 41. Potentially worth booking in advance. Within easy reach of the centre, and large and well-appointed even before reconstruction began in February 1991. No further information; category speculative.

CLASS C

Bílý lev (White Lion), Cimburkova 20, tel 27 11 26, (fax 27 32 71). Spanking new pine and white hotel in a very quiet street. Small rooms, but all have showers and are spotless. Best time to reserve a room is on the 10th of the month preceding your arrival. 50 beds.

Vitkov, Koněvova 114, tel 27 93 41. A curving Functionalist block, some distance from the centre, but the trundling trams which meet at the crossroads outside will get you into town. Comfortable rooms, all with bath or shower. No advance bookings; and very popular with tour companies. Takes American Express.

CLASS D

Ametyst, Jana Masaryka 11, tel 691 17 74. Forlorn and fading in a quiet avenue of neo-Renaissance institutes, which hasn't quite been touched by a wave of reconstruction in nearby streets. Dingy, and no rooms have baths or showers. 139 beds.

Beránek, Bělehradská 110, tel 25 45 44. Cramped set of cells, but they're close to Wenceslas Square and 200 in number. The old owner has been found; with luck he'll sack the unfriendly staff and make this a half-decent place to sleep. No advance bookings; more likely to have space on the day than many other hotels. 287 beds.

Juventus, Blanická 10, tel 25 51 51. Rooms with no frills, no baths, but the central location makes them worth the low price. Popular among the young, despite the fact that the doors lock at midnight (ring and the night porter will come to the door, albeit without too much enthusiasm). Street-side rooms can be very noisy when the trams start to run (5 am). 32 beds.

Lunik, Londýnská 50, tel 25 27 01. Undergoing reconstruction in summer 1991, which may just render this chunk of concrete fit for human habitation once again. A stone's throw from Wenceslas Square. It's worth trying to see what the new owner has done. 110 beds.

Národní dům, Bořivojova 53, tel 27 53 65. Peeling Art Nouveau mansion winding round the corner of a side street. The tragic hotel is in one plywood wing, and your neighbours' conversations may prove distracting at times. Has a certain character: the small bar overlooks the theatre of the locals' community centre, and polkas are held twice-weekly. Can be enjoyable, but don't count on it. 48 beds.

Ostaš, Orebitská 8, tel 27 28 60. Quiet street, very functional rooms. New management as of April 1990. 65 beds.

Tichy, Seifertova 65, tel 27 30 79. Triple-bedrooms only, and the price is still (deservedly) well within this category. Dark and fairly distant, but inexplicably popular among tour groups. Weekend entertainments laid on for tourists; the Czechs themselves prefer the Sex-Kino on Tuesdays. Mired in the slough of despond, but if you're even lower, it may have a very cheap bed (tel 27 85 16 for reservations). 36 beds.

Nusle and Michle

Heavily damaged towards the end of the war, and not a place that you'll want to explore too much, but has two of Prague's smartest modern hotels.

CLASS A

****Forum**, Kongresová 1, tel 41 02 38/9 (fax 49 94 80, 42 06 84). Reservations can also be made abroad—try London (071) 741 9000. Over 1000 comfortable beds, and well-equipped aerial fitness centre. Tremendous views over a very long bridge and a dull suburban valley; 50 yards from the metro platform; and a five-minute whizz along the motorway into the centre. Every facility imaginable; and the place to come if you're rich and fear risk.

****Panorama, Milevská 7, tel 41 61 11, (fax 42 62 25/63). A swanky tower block which has about 80 per cent of everything that the Forum has got, except bowling and squash. Slightly further from the centre, but just as convenient for cars and metro. 860 beds.

CLASS D
Union, Jaromírova 1, tel 43 78 58/9. A very brown hotel with equally murky rooms. None have baths or showers; but it's a cheap and fairly quiet choice for penny-watchers. Often has space. 126 beds.

Dejvice, Letná and Holešovice

These areas to the north of the Vltava stretch from the heartland of Prague's (ex-)Communist chattering classes, across a bustling residential district to the the city's best park (Stromovka) and the sad zoo.

CLASS A
Hotel Praha, Sušická 20, tel 333 81 11, (fax 312 17 57). A curving ribbon of glass and concrete that's become one of the most talked-about hotels in Prague. It was owned by the Central Committee of the Communist Party until retrieved for the international travelling class in early 1990. The Party built itself unembellished but extraordinarily comfortable rooms, and half come with terraces that look out over rolling lawns and the best panorama of Prague that you'll ever see. If you have about £350 ($630) to spare, you can even book into one of the four presidential suites (365 sq m) and unwind in the jacuzzis that may or may not have been used by Mikhail Gorbachev and/or Eduard Schevardnadze. Otherwise, there's a small pool, bowling lane, jogging tracks; and ever-expanding business facilities as capitalism moves in. This will almost certainly leap into ***** category very soon; Hyatt-Regency is drawing up contracts. Full and fairly prompt room service already. Offers one of the quietest and most relaxing stays in the city.

*****Hotel Atrium, near Vltavská metro (line C). Will presumably be luxurious, but is still under construction at the time of writing.

****Hotel Diplomat, Leninova 15 (a.k.a. Dr Benešova 15), tel 331 41 11, (fax 34 17 31). Newly-built Austrian-owned hotel—the staff are still learning the ropes and the languages, but otherwise an unsurprising island of international comfort. Yuppy globetrotters will find this a good place to hold a conference.

CLASS B

******Parkhotel**, Veletržní 20, tel 38 15 26, (fax 38 10 20). One of Prague's more venerable glass and concrete hotels, dating from 1968, and not quite as plush as the next generation. However, the staff are experienced and professional, and you'll have few problems with a stay here. 383 beds.

Splendid, Ovenecká 33, tel 37 33 51–9. Comfortable and very clean rooms in a tranquil avenue of Art Nouveau buildings. Nothing exceptional, but a hassle-free stay is almost guaranteed. 69 beds.

CLASS C

Belvedere, Milady Horákové 19, tel and fax 37 03 51. All the rooms are doubles with showers, but although they're comfortable enough that's about the extent of this soulless spot's attractions. 219 beds.

******International**, Koulova 15, tel 33 19 91, 331 91 11, fax 311 60 31. The most perfectly preserved example of Stalinist architecture in Prague, a granite tower covered with friezes honouring the onward march of labour. The rooms are comfortable but unexceptional, and it's something of a mystery how it ever earned its four stars—it certainly wasn't for the chaotic service, and it's unlikely to have been for the facilities, which extend not much further than a dire nightclub and a mini-golf course. Good for anyone who misses Communism.

Peripheries

Although the following hotels are situated away from the centre of town, none are beyond the municipal transport system.

CLASS B

******Club Hotel Průhonice**, on the E50 and E55 motorway, tel 72 32 41–9 (first and last numbers are also faxes). A newly built sporty paradise: ten tennis courts, two squash courts, bowling, pool, gym, and even caters for horsey types. Conference facilities. Lurks low on the edge of a motorway, and although the rooms are as well-appointed as you'd expect, atmosphere isn't its strong point.

****Olympik, Sokolovská 138, tel 684 55 01. Small and pleasant rooms in another tower block. Room service cuts out towards the end of the morning. Friendly fellow guests, and popular among coach parties. Try reserving a week in advance—tel 82 86 25.

CLASS C

Golf, Plzeňská 215a, tel 52 32 51 (fax 52 21 53). All rooms with showers. A dull modern motel in the suburbs, named for the one facility that makes it unique in Prague. You'd have to be an obsessive putter to spend much time here. 299 beds.

Olympik II, U sluncové 14, tel 68 30 19. Next door to its namesake, and inexplicably considerably cheaper. The rooms are slightly shabbier, and no token room service is provided, but otherwise this is a perfectly acceptable alternative. Telephone reservations at the number above.

Solidarita, Soudružská 14, tel 77 80 41. A vast tower block of 630 beds, filled with singing, dancing and mattress-hopping teenagers from across the continent. A non-stop party—not a place for light sleepers, but fun if you're young and enjoy hotel nightlife. A long tram-journey into town, but every taxi driver in Prague knows where this place is. Fairly likely to have space, and mature types can check in.

Student/Youth

There are no hotels or agencies offering discounts to ISIC-card holders, but CKM (see p. 289) tends to offer some of the cheapest deals. Prague has one youth hostel, not too far from the town centre in U skolské zahrady. Forty dorm beds are available, for about £4 ($7) a night including breakfast; and to get one, you'll need to be at the reception desk of the Juniorhotel (Žitná 12) at midday, armed with a Youth Hostel Card (for British citizens) or an IYHF card for anyone else.

Camping

The following are among the least isolated and best appointed sites in Prague. All are closed during the winter.

Caravancamp, Plzeňská, tel 52 16 32.

Na Vlachovce, Rudé armády, tel 84 12 90 (provides chalets inside large Budvar beer kegs).
Sportcamp, V podhájí, tel 52 18 02.
Kotva Braník, U ledáren 55, tel 46 17 12.

Entertainment and Nightlife

Organized entertainment in Prague was almost a contradiction in terms before 1989. The wicked witches of the bureaucracy often insisted on not just being invited to the ball, but on drawing up the programme. Spontaneity was discouraged and occasionally criminalized, while the work of the country's best playwrights, directors and singers was regularly banned. Since 1989, it's been legal to have fun again, and trendy President Havel has set his compatriots an impressive example. As well as turning up to performances of his plays, he went clubbing through Prague with Frank Zappa and Lou Reed in 1990, and in the heat of the moment, appointed Zappa the Czechoslovakian cultural envoy at large (a decision that was hastily reversed). The re-emergence of a public culture has been slow, hampered by lack of facilities and the caution instilled by four decades of official frowns; but at the time of writing, independent initiatives are beginning to mushroom across the capital. Details of information and booking services are on pp. 34–5.

Concerts, Ballet and Opera

Even the paranoid Communists couldn't find a political threat in classical music, although modern musicians and conductors were occasionally banned. There are performances in the city throughout the week, often including Sunday. The two most time-honoured venues are the **Smeta-**

novo divadlo (Smetana Theatre) on Wilsonova 8 and the Národní divadlo (National Theatre) on Národní 2. The Smetanova sín Obecního domu (Smetana Hall of the Municipal House) on nám. Republiky is equally grand but the lack of a full stage means that only concerts are held there. The last two buildings owe their existence to the 19th-century national revival, and their programmes are heavily weighted in favour of Czech composers, although Mozart is a favourite thanks to Prague's insistence that his connection to Salzburg was no more than an accident of birth. Another important venue is the soulless *Palác kultury* (Palace of Culture), an unimaginative block built in the late 1970s which you'll have no problems finding if you take the metro (line C) to Vyšehrad. There are also regular concerts and recitals in most of the churches in central Prague—their noticeboards provide details, as do the sources on p. 35. The best acoustics are generally agreed to be in St James's (sv. Jakub), but the all-encompassing splendour of the Prague Symphony Orchestra in St Vitus's Cathedral leaves most people feeling very small and rather overjoyed. It happens during the Prague Spring music festival, details of bookings for which are on p. 35.

Theatres

The Big Three are the National Theatre again, the neighbouring Nova Scena (New Scene), looking rather like a very large piece of plastic bubble wrap, and the Laterna Magika on Národní 40, tel 26 00 33. The first generally shows suitable unadventurous performances of Shakespeare, Molière, Karel Čapek (see p. 87) and the like; while the second is more daring, stretching to Chekhov and Strindberg. The Laterna Magika combines film, theatre and mime. The granddaddy of Prague's tourist traps, it has degenerated from its radical beginnings and international plaudits at the Brussels Expo '58 to a candyfloss multi-mediocrity. The first wave of dramatists to work at the theatre, who included Miloš Forman of cuckoo's nest fame, were forced out when it was given its permanent home, and although it's perfectly inoffensive it's hardly changed since.

With a playwright in the presidential office, it may come as no surprise that the capital's smaller theatres have been experiencing a renaissance since 1989. It's difficult to do any specific preparatory reading before coming out, as the repertoire is so wide, but you may want to pack a couple of Havel plays, and the frequently-dramatized work of Bohumil Hrabal is an excellent read. Two of the most consistently interesting

303

small theatres are the **Divadlo na zábradlí** in Anenské nám., tel 236 04 49, and the **Realistické divadlo** on Štefánikova 57, tel 54 50 27. The first was where Václav Havel worked his way from stage-hand to literary adviser in the early 1960s, and had his first play premiered; the second saw the very beginning of the Velvet Revolution in 1989, when the theatre's actors apparently suggested the general strike that rang the death knell of the old regime. Its radicalism continues with the performance of once unthinkable plays such as Tabori's *Mein Kampf*. The **Činoherní Klub** on Ve Smečkách 26 (tel 235 23 70) is also very highly regarded, and is run by the Czech filmmaker Jiří Menzel (see pp. 83–4).

There are scores of avant-garde theatre companies bubbling under the surface, and they often stage art and photographic exhibitions as well as plays. They're not in the tourist-orientated listings magazines, and if you're interested, you should scan *Přehled kulturních pořadů v Praze* (see p. 35). Prague also has a small and smoky poetry club, **Viola** on Národní 7, tel 235 87 79, tucked at the end of an Art Nouveau corridor, which is sometimes worth a visit (Mon–Sat, 8 pm–midnight). The atmosphere varies, but among the not-very-angry young men and women who use the club as their local wine bar, there's usually a smattering of ageing poets with shabby jackets and beards, and gently nodding women with long hair and longer skirts. The events include talent competitions, one-man plays and sometimes very beautiful recitals of Czech lyrical poetry. The box-office for advance tickets is open from Mon–Sat 4–8.15 pm.

Cinema

None of Prague's cinemas specialize, and if you scan listings, you'll find a hotch-potch of films Czech and foreign, old and new. At the time of writing, soft-porn is popular and *Emanuelle* is belatedly taking the capital by storm. All foreign films are dubbed unless they're marked *Film v původním znění*, in which case they're subtitled. The Ponrepo at Veletřní 61 is the closest that Prague yet has to an art cinema, and has been known to show anything from Tarkovsky to James Dean. It uses the quaint technique of reading out a simultanous translation, which can have very interesting effects—on one memorable occasion, the female translator read through all the voices of *Last Tango in Paris*, and retained her composure even while husky Marlon Brando warmed up for the Butter Scene.

304

Jazz

The only regular venues are **Reduta** on Národní 20, tel 20 38 25 (Mon–Sat 9.30 pm–12 midnight), and the **Press Jazz Club** on the first floor at Pařížská 9, tel 232 62 82 (Mon–Sat 9 pm–2 am). Both provide a cosy, if oddly parochial, evening's entertainment. Czech musicians and foreign audiences predominate, and everyone whoops a little louder if a visiting black musician appears on the stage. The second club has a high ceiling that swallows up all the best notes. One of the newest spots to hear Czech jazz is Viola (see above) on Saturday evenings, although the music usually ends by 10 pm.

Live Pop, Nightclubs and Discotheques

Visiting foreign musicians, even those with only a cult following in their home countries, tend to be treated as conquering heroes in Prague, so get a ticket in advance. There are several potential venues; the Rolling Stones played at the 200,000-seat Strahov stadium (bus 176 from the western end of Karlovo nám.), but lesser mortals are usually assigned the Obecní dům, the Palace of Culture, or the Lucerna, a huge hall designed by Václav Havel's uncle on Vodičkova 36.

The clubbing scene isn't a patch on nearby Berlin, but the comparison is in the minds of many, and new clubs have been springing up since the revolution. At weekends, a succession of rock bands thrash the night away at **Újezd** on Újezd 18 (Fri–Sat 8 pm–6 am). It's cheap, tearfully smoky and looks like a crummy squat, albeit one with a 14th-century cellar. The mood of the largely young crowd varies from sullen ennui to extraordinary friendliness, and in the summer, long pleading is sometimes necessary before you're allowed in. Swingers of all sorts tend to enjoy it, and adventurous funlovers should persevere at the door. Another favourite of Prague trendies is the **Rock-Café** on Národní 20 (Mon–Sat 8 pm–3 am), where a broad and noisy selection of bands play most nights. There's more space and less atmosphere than Újezd, but it's still an important spot for Prague's hipsters to see and be seen. You could also try **Julek**, Prague's newest club, in a cellar at Staroměstské nám. 15 (Mon–Sat 9 pm–2 am). Occasional concerts are held at **007** (near Chaloupeckého among the student dormitories at Strahov), for which extreme youth and tone-deafness are essential. The **Beseda** at Malostranské nám. 21, tel 53 90 24, often has live music, although it can be stone dead even on a Saturday evening.

During the summer, you could also keep your eyes open for **acid house parties**. Bellbottoms and headbands hit Prague in the summer of 1990 (some say they never left), and the capital's first, rather subdued, rave was organized. Lastly, two more clubs may or may not exist by the time you're reading this. The first is under the plinth of the former monument to Stalin (see p. 267) and is called variously 'Totality Zone', 'Stalin' and 'Suicide'. At the time of writing, it's been closed for safety reasons (too many inviting tunnels leading off into the hillside), but it's widely expected to reopen soon. The most intriguing of the planned new clubs is due to open in early 1992 at Lodecká 2. The provisional name is 'Bunker'—its subterranean premises were apparently built as the bolt-hole of the Czechoslovakian Communist Party, in preparation for the Big One.

Discotheques are concentrated in and around Wenceslas Square, and aren't worth the effort in most cases. They're prohibitively expensive for most Czechs, and as a result they're teeming with lonely businessmen planning to be unfaithful and Czech prostitutes eager to help. If you're still tempted, try to get in early (by 9 pm) and be prepared to be told insistently that there's no room, or that the entire disco has been re-served. It's sometimes true, and making a reservation is generally advisable everywhere in the summer, but what the bouncer often means is that he wants to be bribed, or doesn't like your clothes/face/attitude. Never believe the line that the disco round the corner definitely has space—Wenceslas Square in the early hours is full of gullible fools bouncing up and down like ping-pong balls. Many of the hotel discos also have officious dress codes—no jeans in the Yalta, no denim of any description in the Ambassador. As for trainers...

Far more enjoyable is the tremendous dank Romanesque cellar of U **bilého koníčka** (Tues–Sun 9 pm–1 am), through the passage at Staroměstské nám. 20, tel 235 89 27. U Holubů is popular among Praguers in the know (Tues–Sat 9 pm–1.30 am). It's slightly outside the centre at Stefánikova 7, tel 54 23 48/9 (Anděl metro—line B). There are also two gay clubs in Prague: U **Petra Voka z Rožmberka** on Na bělidle 40, tel 53 75 31 (Tues–Sat 9 pm–4 am); and the **T-Club** on Jungmannovo nám. 17, tel 236 98 77. The first is the jollier (you may be served by waiters in pink skirts), but in both clubs, straights and lesbians are often treated with curiosity if not contempt. Although all the above spots are often far more fun than the expensive holes in Wenceslas Square, attempting entry can be no more pleasant, and you should always make a reservation in the morning.

Café Society

The notion was always more of a German (and particularly Jewish) one in Prague, and since the war the trail has grown rather cold; there are plenty of places to snatch a wine or coffee, but legendary hangouts are few. The **Café Arco** still survives at Hybernská 12. In its heyday, it was an oasis for central Europe's literary and artistic élite, a favourite of Kafka, Max Brod and the other 'Arconauts', but now it's a waiting room for sad couples and drunken boors (7 am–11 pm). Still, you never know—by the time you're reading this, an enterprising German might have taken over and filled it with faded armchairs, a rack of art journals and a collection of Kafka souvenirs. The **Evropa Café** on Wenceslas Square was a favourite among Prague's long-lost bourgeoisie. The clientele has changed, but it's immeasurably livelier than the Arco. Louche Czechs, loud fellow tourists, and an Art Nouveau interior combine to make this a surreal variation on everyone's idea of central European elegance. The service is generally so appalling that it's charming; and the same is true of the caterwauling trio who torture their instruments through an unchanging repertoire of tragic Slovakian folk melodies, symphonic poems and the occasional polka. If you ensconce yourself by 5.30 you'll avoid admission charges and queues, and may even be able to lay your hands on a waiter before the music starts half an hour later.

The best-known of Prague's cafés has to be the **Slavia**, on Národní opposite the National Theatre. In the inter-war years, it and the now-destroyed Café Union were the main Czech cafés in Prague; and until 1989 it was where Prague's unofficial opposition would come to exchange ideas and *samizdat* manuscripts. They've since moved on to greater things, although Václav Havel returns occasionally. Once you risked being punched if you spoke German here; now you're in danger of not being served if you don't. Despite a large foreign contingent, it's still popular with young Czechs; and among the regular clientele are several legendary old women with as many stories under their bonnets as they have hours to kill. The last of Prague's great pre-war cafés was the Café Continental, known affectionately as the Conti amongst the duelling Junkers, Nazis and generally proud Germans who patronized it. *Untermenschen* entered at their peril. The Czechs got the last laugh, linguistically speaking—since the war, it's been called **Slovanský dům** (Slavonic House), and it's been transformed into a labyrinth of eating and drinking establishments, including the Arcádia cocktail bar (see below).

Beer Halls

Prague takes its beer as seriously as most other cities in central Europe, but to enjoy it as it should be enjoyed, your best bet is to scan the information on p. 272 and then launch yourself on a *pivnice* crawl without too many preliminaries. Trial, error, and dubious drinking partners will soon help you assemble your own list of favourite watering holes. However, it's only too easy to get mired in the first stop—your glass is replaced and a notch added to your bill before you can say *už nepiju* (roughly, 'Enough drinking, already'), which soon becomes far too difficult anyway. The procedure reaches almost industrial scale and efficiency at **U Fleků**, where hundreds of people are intoxicated nightly by trained waiters who coast around with huge tin trays of brimming black beers. The only problem with the inn is that it's long been ceded to Germany by Praguers; if it's Czech company that you want, go down the local *pivnice* or head for **U černého vola** (The Black Ox) and **U kocoura** (The Tomcat). You'll find addresses and further details in the Food and Drink section.

One of the best areas for an adventurous stagger is Smíchov, where the pubs are full of raucous gipsies, and occasionally erupt into fistfights and/or song. You're unlikely to have any problems, but don't pack any valuables, and think carefully before accepting invitations to move on, especially to the Vinárna Narcis (see below). Try the **Hospoda na čečeličce**, on the junction of Na Čečeličce and Plzeňská. If you ask politely, the barman will give you a set of well-fingered cards (*karty*). They look rather like the tarot, and you can often find someone who's happy to break you into the game, so long as you're prepared to bet on winning each lesson. The rules change quite often. The pub is officially open until 8.30 pm, and sometimes until 11 or later. Nearby is **U černím vechem** (The Black Mountain), on the corner of Vrchlického and Erbenova, which is usually open from 2–11 pm, although the precise times vary on the owner's mood. The same applies to the availability of the 'country music' that may or may not be heard here from Tues–Thur. Both pubs edge onto Prague's most macabre and beautiful cemetery (see p. 266), and the temptation to scale the walls on moonless nights has been known to overcome heavy drinkers, but sadly that's illegal.

Wine Bars

The best wine bars (*vinárny*) are also restaurants and are listed in the Food and Drink section. Outdoor drinking on summer evenings, preferably from a bottle on the slowly-cooling cobbles of the Charles Bridge, provides an unbeatable vision of Prague. The string of wine houses along winding Michalská is another traditional spot to have a glass *al fresco*—neighbours and weather permitting, scores of young drinkers spill out onto the street to compare the day's suntans and interrelate. U **Kafku** (a.k.a. U tří zlatých lvů), under the arcade and through the corridor of nearby Uhelný trh 1, is a lively wine bar favoured by the slightly alternative tendency among Prague's youth (Mon–Fri 3 pm–midnight, Sat 5 pm–midnight).

Late-night Drinking

Beer taps close at 11 at the latest, and wine bars usually go on no later than 1 am. Most working Praguers are already tucked up in bed, ready for their 5 am alarm clocks, but the young and sleepless emerge onto the streets looking for action, and several more for the road. The capital's nightlife used to be dire, but with the opening of new clubs (see above) the situation is improving. Late-night bars as such are still few and far between. U **Františkánů** is a reliable spot for a drink until 1 am. It's remarkably well hidden in the courtyard next to the church of Our Lady of the Snows, and if you look for long enough you'll find either the *vinárna* or the police station (which is used to drunks staggering in by accident, and is usually happy to point you in the right direction). At **Arcádia**, on the third floor of the Slovanský dům (Na příkopě 22), you can usually find a seat in the corridor bar or roof terrace and begin to work through the list of cocktails until 1 am (it serves eight, which is extraordinary for Prague). The ground floor of the same building is usually open until 4 am, although prices are high and atmosphere is low. Skinheads and punk-rockers get drunk at **Orlík**, on Masarykovo nábř (10 pm–2 am); gentler types could try **A-Scena**, at the end of Novotného lávka, where thespian types and tourists mingle until the same time. It also sells late beers. Most of the other late-night haunts, such as the **Gril** on Vodičkova (open until 4 am), are unsavoury even at midday, and the **Vinárna Narcis** at Melantrichova 5 deserves a special mention, having become a byword in Prague for robbery and violence. It closes at 5 am—but expect worse than the worst if you enter, and you probably won't be surprised.

Shopping

Bohemian crystal

Prague's retail industry represents the dubious culmination of 40 years of Five-Year Plans. Until 1989, some 97 per cent of Czechoslovakia's shops (and approximately 100 per cent of those in the capital) were owned by the state, and privatization is only beginning to change them. Most are part of chains called things like 'Tobacco', 'Fashion' and 'Meat', and across the country each branch will offer virtually identical sets of goods. The lack of choice can come as a blissful relief if you're fed up with the demands of capitalism, but it's been no fun for Praguers. Shelves are generally full, albeit with fairly dull produce, but centralized production has led to some catastrophic shortages over the years. In late 1989, when the Velvet Revolution was at its height, most of the country's toilet paper factories suddenly seized up—leading, according to legend, to the largest-ever sales of the Communist Party daily, *Rudé Právo*. The unpredictability of supplies has meant that queuing has become an ingrained habit among many citizens, and it's frighteningly common to find a line outside a shop where no one is quite sure what's on offer. The self-defeating theory is that so many people can't be wrong, and the ridiculous practice actually becomes contagious after you've been in the city for a while. You're best advised to ignore any queue that you see—the prize in the past has usually been a pineapple or a bottle of olive oil, at best. At the time of writing, things have begun noticeably to improve for the better-off, with the lifting of price controls and the

310

legalization of private shops. The result is that most Praguers have now had to add the previously unknown knack of bargain-hunting to their repository of shopping skills, but prices are still far cheaper than those in the west.

There are certain strange rules which can perplex visitors. In many shops, particularly supermarkets, you aren't allowed to pass a set of turnstiles without a basket—for which there's usually a queue. The worry isn't that you might pocket a pot of yoghurt, but that the number of people in the store would otherwise reach critical mass. Another time-honoured tradition is that you often order your goods in one place, pay in another, and pick your goods up at a third. There are generally queues at all three spots.

Given the hurdles to be overcome, you should avoid Prague's shops as much as possible, but the stores listed below are among the best that Prague has got to offer for souvenirs and food. One good place to get a general idea of what Czechoslovakia itself has got to offer is at **Kotva** on nám. Republiky: five floors packed with Comecon castoffs and charmless detritus, as well as an extraordinary variety of consumer goods up to and including cars and motorbikes. Another of Prague's consumer palaces is **Máj**, at the junction of Národní and Spálená (Mon–Wed and Fri 8 am–7 pm, Thurs 8 am–8 pm, Sat 8 am–4 pm).

Shopping Hours

Most shops are open from 9 am–6 pm on weekdays, and until 1 pm on Saturdays. Food stores reflect the early working day of many Praguers and usually open at 6am. Some make up for it by closing at 5 pm, but in the centre they often stay open until 7 pm. Many shops take a break for lunch at any time between noon and 2 pm. Very little is open on Saturday afternoon or Sunday. If you're stuck for food, you can pick up staple foods in the vestibule of Můstek station (Tues–Fri 6 am–10 pm, Sat and Sun 2–10 pm); and there's a non-stop food shop on Roháčova.

Markets

There are always hawkers at Můstek and on the Charles Bridge, but their wares often consist of devotional literature or the discarded togs of departed Soviet soldiers. Communism never fully wiped out free-marketeers, but the tradition will take some time to revive properly. On Havelská you can buy fruit and veg, and flowers; one street along on V kotcích is a set of stalls selling cheap clothes and prints. The biggest market in the city is on Bubenské nábřeží (Vltavská metro—line C). At the time of writing, most of the stalls still sell crummy rags, digital watches and pornographic videos, while Romanian and Russian emigrants walk around forlornly with a couple of pots of Beluga caviare. But as capitalism marches in, it's likely to develop into Prague's best, if saddest, market, as heirlooms and history are sold off to the highest bidder.

Books

Praguers are avid readers, especially since the revolution of 1989, and the official publication of decades of suppressed work. Their bibliophiles can look downright obsessive on Thursdays, when the state publishing house issues the week's new books and long queues form outside most of the city's *knihkupectví*. The following are the most interesting shops for foreigners:

Melantrich, Na příkopě 5. Mon–Fri 8.30 am–8 pm, Sat–Sun 8.30 am–6 pm. Fairly large map collection; foreign newspapers.

Zahranicní literatura, Vodičkova 41, Mon–Fri 9.30 am–6 pm. Prague's only English-language bookstore, stocking a selection of remaindered pulp, and exorbitantly-priced paperbacks in a branch of Collets upstairs. Staff may not speak English.

The Charles Bridge Bookstore and Gallery, Karlova 2. Mon–Fri 10 am–6 pm, Sat 11 am–4 pm. The first privatized antiquarian bookstore. Well-stocked, but definite bias towards rich Germans who collect old Baedekers.

There are also a number of anonymous second-hand stores (*antikvariat*), where you can often find cheap prints and English pre-war curiosities, as well as piles of junky potboilers. You can find them at:

Ječná 36
Milady Horákové 66
Skořepka 2
Újezd 13
28. října 13.

Music

Classical records and compact discs are usually well recorded and extremely cheap. They're available from any **Supraphon** store, and you'll find one of the widest selections at the branch on Jungmannova 20. There are more records to be found at the Polish and Hungarian cultural centres (Jindřišská 1 and Národní 22 respectively). If pop music is your bag, Czechoslovakia's first independent label, *Bonton*, has a shop at Malostranské nám. 21 (10 am–8.30 pm), and there's a shop in the Rock-Café nightclub on Narodní 20 (Mon–Sat 8 pm–3 am). You can always try before you buy.

Crystal and Porcelain

Bohemian crystal is said to be among the finest in the world by those who know. Praguers capitalize on its reputation by producing huge amounts of cut glass. The following two shops sell some of the most splendid and some of the most tasteless trinkets in town:

Sklo—Porcelán, Pařížská 2. Mon–Fri 9 am–7 pm, Sat–Sun 9 am–1 pm. The grandest of them all, and the place to pick up a chandelier. Be sure to keep any receipts, as purchases here are duty-free.
Dana, Národní 43. Mon–Fri 9 am–6 pm, Sat–Sun 9am –1 pm. Two shops in an arcade. Less choice, considerably less cost.

For some pretty glasses and an array of puppets, go to the shop with no name at Nerudova 37. Mon–Fri 10 am–noon and 1–6 pm, Sat 10 am–1 pm.

Food and Drink

Truffles and quails' eggs are still unavailable in Prague, but these shops offer the widest range of consumables available in the capital. A shopping spree here will add life to a picnic; and if you're in the city for a while, they'll help stave off culinary doldrums.

Dům potravin, Václavské nám. 1. Mon–Fri 8 am–9 pm, Sat 8 am–2 pm. Two floors of food counters, with cooked meats, cheeses, drinks, sandwiches and salads—and longer opening hours than most stores.
Václavská pékárna, Václavské nám. 35. Mon–Fri 6 am–7 pm, Sat 9 am–2 pm. Various breads and doughy sweetmeats.
Mostecká pekárna, Mostecká 18. Mon–Fri 8 am–6 pm. Fresh bread, and *bochánky*, succulent almond-topped currant buns.
Paris-Praha, Jindřišská 7. Mon–Fri 8.30 am–7 pm, Sat 8.30 am–1 pm. French cuisine *à la Prague*. No Bollinger as yet, but you can find mustards, oils, vinegars and even the odd *appellation contrôlée* here.

Casa Pascual, Národní 27. Mon–Fri 7 am–7 pm, Sat 8 am–1 pm. This used to be the undisputed fruit and vegetable centre of Prague. It's slowly losing its monopoly, but if you thirst for a mango or star fruit you're still most likely to find it here.

Jídelna, Václavské nám 36. Mon–Fri 7.30 am–7 pm, Sat 7.30 am–6 pm. Sells a huge variety of salamis, sausages and unidentifiable organs.

Frionor, Vodičkova 34. Mon–Wed and Fri 8 am–6 pm, Thurs 8 am–7 pm, Sat 8 am–noon. Fairly unremarkable freezer store, but has more fishy dishes and TV dinners than any other spot in Prague.

Sports and Activities

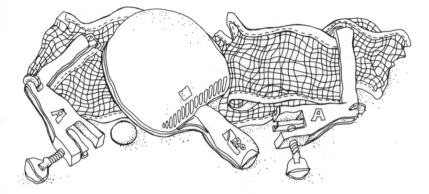

Over the last century, Praguers have shown a rather unhealthy attachment to mass-mobilization in the name of sport. Until very recently the quinquennial highlight of the sporting calendar was a celebration of beauty and youth organized by the Communists, and known as the *Spartakiáda*. Every five years, 160,000 identical gymnasts would perform feats of co-ordinated kitsch in the capital's Strahov stadium, watched by 220,000 awe-struck spectators. Very few Praguers will admit it now, but being selected as a cog in the machine was regarded by many as a great honour, and the festival was only the successor to the even more popular *Sokol* movement, founded in 1862 and devoted to celebrating the physical glory of the Czech race. However, the capital may have finally lost its fascination with sporting crowds and power. The plug was pulled on the June 1990 *Spartakiáda*, and any lingering traces of beauty and youth evaporated two months later when Mick Jagger and Keith Richards strutted the Strahov stage.

Propaganda rallies apart, Praguers have rather sedate sporting habits. There are no queer games to speak of, and although a Sparta v. Slavia soccer match will arouse the passions of the man on the Žižkov omnibus, the interests of most reasonable-minded folk stretch not much further than ice-hockey and tennis. Most Czechs have some knowledge of the latest fortunes of Martina Navrátilová, Hana Mandlíková and Ivan

Lendl, although relations are tinged with the peculiar mixture of love and hate that successful émigrés inspire in Czechoslovakia.

Prague is dotted with community leisure centres and sporting complexes, and several of the facilities below form only part of extensive palaces of physical culture. Many of the capital's modern hotels have particularly plush 'fitness centres', but they're only mentioned if they offer something that's unique rather than simply expensive. However, there are two conveniently-located sports halls that are considerably cheaper. The **Fit Centrum Dlabačov** on Bílohorská 24 has a 25-m pool, gym, ping-pong tables and a sauna (Sun–Fri 1–9 pm. The sauna is open to women only from 1–2.30 pm, to men from 2.30–4 pm and you can mix it between 4 and 8.30 pm. The **YMCA** has just muscled into premises in the heart of town at Na poříčí 12. The Communist former owners are still packing their bags, and the facilities are so far limited to a pool, weight machines, and overhead running track, but the newcomers plan to expand. Non-members and women welcome.

If you forget your tools, or are bitten by the bug while in Prague, sports goods can be bought at the **Dům sportu** on Jungmannova 28 (Mon–Fri 8.30 am–7 pm, Sat 8.30 am–1 pm). The department store sells Czech-made equipment from skis to sweatbands, as well as an increasing range of imports. There's a repair service at **Temposervis** on Rybná 3 in case your skis crack or your strings snap (Mon 2–5 pm, Tues–Thurs 10 am–1 pm and 2–5 pm, Fri 10 am–3 pm).

Boating

Rowboats can be hired during the summer from Žofín (a.k.a. Slovanský ostrov), the island near the National Theatre. The Vltava's sluices and gurgling rapids lock you into a small section of the river, but floating in the sun is a rather matchless way of whiling away a dog day in Prague. A passport is required as a deposit, although the attendant can sometimes be hoodwinked with a library card. During the summer, boat parties regularly set sail from the quay near Palackého most (Palacký Bridge), but be clear about what you're embarking upon before buying a ticket. Lambada cruises have become a perennial favourite, and they can last up to seven hours, which is usually enough to tame even the wildest party animal. On the other hand, if you fancy the idea of an entire holiday on the river, contact Mr Vojta, whose motley crew and pleasure steamer (*Kamenice*, or 'The Mason') will be happy to take you as far along the

Vltava/Moldau as Dresden, depending on your wishes and wealth (tel 854 19 20, 80 52 16).

Bowling

The best place to have a bowl in Prague is the Hotel Forum, but the fun's limited. The alley appeals to Prague's strangely off-the-mark *jeunesse d'orée*, and also attracts gangs of bored businessmen letting their cuff-links down for an evening. It sells ten types of beer, which is over twice the number of lanes.

Golf

If you've come to Prague to putt, you're probably already booked into the capital's only green, at the Motel Golf (see p. 300).

Horsey Sports

The city's racecourse is at Velká Chuchle, a 15-minute bus journey from Smíchovské nádraží metro station on line B (Nos. 129, 172, 241, 243 or 245). Steeplechases and hurdle-races hammer the turf on Sunday after-noons from May–Oct; and there are trots all year round on Thursdays. The gambling culture is fairly alien to Praguers, but if you fancy a flutter, you can take limited advice and then stick a pin in the card at CAK Agentour on Široká 10 (Mon–Fri 9 am–8.30 pm). More active canterers will find information about riding excursions at friendly Mrs Bureškova's leather shop on Maislova 7, where you can also pick up hand-crafted boots, bits and bridles (Tues–Fri 10 am–6 pm, Sat 10 am–4 pm).

Skating

There are ice-skating rinks in Holešovice park and Štvanice island, both in Prague 7.

Skiing

It's fashionable to head out of Prague with your skis in the winter, but you'd be breaking new ground (and possibly much more) if you tried cross-country skiing in the capital itself. However, hundreds of tobog-gans emerge from Prague's cupboards with the year's first snowfall, and if you're small you'll be able to find one in Dům sportu. A warm and safe alternative is to avoid the slush altogether, and go to the artificial slope at Na Máchalce, tel 83 47 31.

Squash

Prague's only squash courts are at the Hotel Forum and the Club-Hotel Průhonice (see pp. 297 and 299).

Swimming

As well as the pools in the sports centres noted above, there's a 50-m indoor pool at Podolská 74. Atmosphere, and even more suspicious effluents than usual, are provided by Prague's oldest swimming pool (1840), on the Malá Strana side of most Svatopluka Čecha (Svatopluk Čech Bridge). It has a small paddling pool, and a slightly larger stretch of the foul Vltava, in which you're still allowed to take a dip. It's only open in the summer, as is the less central but cleaner Šeberák lake (in Prague 4, near K Šeberáku), where you'll be expected to take all your clothes off.

Tennis

There are courts peppered across Prague's suburbs, but you'll cause a commotion if you try to get onto one and don't speak Czech. To avoid problems, call 231 12 70 and book one of the tourist courts on Štvanice island in Prague 7. There are also courts on Letná, which you can sometimes reserve (tel 37 36 83).

Children's Prague

If you are looking to abandon your child, you couldn't pick a better city than Prague. Musicians, puppet-shows and jugglers turn the streets into a perpetual playground during the summer; it's still remarkably safe; and should you succumb to remorse, the city's inexplicable way of engineering unexpected meetings would quickly throw you back into each other's arms. Even if you're the responsible type, there are still endless ways to keep the brats from insisting that life was more fun at home.

Maps and (Czechoslovakian) money are useful ways of drumming up interest before you leave; Good King Wenceslas is another limited way of introducing the country to younger children. Unfortunately there are no books of Czech children's stories, or even legends, currently in print in English, but the country has produced an impressive body of childrens' cartoons (which are sometimes shown at London's National Film Theatre).

All ages will appreciate the funfair and dinky seaside-pier architecture of the Park of Culture, which is filled with a mass of pleasure-inducing marvels including a planetarium and a circular cinema. Similarly there's no age bar to enjoying the National Technical Museum: there should be many more buttons to press, but your infant would have to be a dullard indeed not to enjoy its collection of clocks and cameras, and the hundreds of wings and wheels in its transport exhibition. An added bonus for younger children is the carousel just outside the museum (open all year round, weather permitting); and if there's a circus in town, it will almost certainly have pitched up on nearby Letná Plain. You or your offspring would have to be beastly to go to Prague's cruel zoo; but there's another set of attractions on Petřín Hill. The funicular to the top is a thrill in itself, and at the summit is a planetarium and a mirror maze.

In the centre of town, the hourly mechanics of the Astronomical Clock are a thing of endless fascination to most children, and tower-climbing is a game that the city caters for well. You can even have fun on the move. Trams can be mightily impressive to someone small who's never seen the beasts before; horse-drawn buggies and rowboats on the river are less useful as means of transport, but just as good if your child has learnt to walk and had enough already.

Many of the city's theatres cater for children. There are occasional plays and puppet shows for them at the **Divadlo Jiřího Wolkra** on Dlouhá 39, and marionettes take the stage on most days at the **Divadlo U věže** on nám. Maxima Gorkého 28. There's an entire entertainment complex at Albatros, on the corner of Na Perštýně and Národní, tel 22 52 52. As well as a bookshop, it has a theatre and cinema with activities every day of the week (Mon–Fri 9.15 and 10.30 am, Sat 10.30 am and 2.30 pm, Sun 2.30 pm). The listings magazines usually have a children's section—the best is in *Přehled kulturnich pořadů v Praze*, although it's in Czech (under the heading 'Našim dětem' (Our Children). Finally, the **Dům československých dětí** (Czechoslovakian Children's House) on Jiřská in Prague Castle is a godsend if you want to dump your little ones for a few hours. The friendly staff are happy to look after anyone above ga-ga age and below 15 while you go romping around the castle or further afield; it's open from Tues–Sun 10 am–5 pm, it's free, and the amusements provided include toys, computer games and plays. There are regular theatre performances every weekend and Wednesday, usually at 3 pm; and the helpful staff can tell you about plenty of other kiddy-oriented entertainments that are going on in the capital.

Living and Working in Prague

Setting up a second home in Prague is a prospect that flits through the minds of most visitors. If even a fraction of the dreams came true, the city would now probably have the largest concentration of jazz cafés and bookshop diners in the world. Hassle and obstruction are the lot of anyone who tries to make a go of it. But all the problems can eventually be overcome, and the city is filling with an ever-growing population of semi-permanent foreigners.

Form-filling: Since the collapse of the totalitarian house of cards in 1989, a largely benign anarchy has swept through Czechoslovakia's official institutions; and trying to glean information about the law can be even more perplexing than before. Few can be sure about which directives have been overruled, which amended and which clarified, and you should expect a long haul through the labyrinth before you become legal. However, the pleasant flipside is that no one really cares what you get up to; and most police stations will regard you with amazement and confusion if you turn yourself in at the required times. At the time of writing, the only vaguely defined rules for British and US citizens are that you should register with the local police within a month if you intend to stay in Czechoslovakia for longer; and if you're working, that you should pop in after three months with six passport photos to get a work permit and let someone know how you're getting along. If you're a glutton for punishment, contact the Interior Ministry for further information.

Finding a Job: Several million Czechs are likely to be getting on their bikes over the next few years, and the situations vacant will be limited. Catering work and the like are going to remain all but impossible to find in a country unused to a fluid labour market let alone an international one; and foreign companies that have opened up have shown a marked preference to hire and train eager Czechs rather than potentially irksome and almost certainly transient westerners. Your biggest asset is less likely to be your CV than your mother tongue, and **teaching jobs** are currently all the rage among the growing contingent of foreign hobos settling in Prague. The monthly pay is currently on a par with the national average (about 3000kcs/£60/$100), and likely to rise above it; and you don't need any experience, let alone TEFL qualifications. However, Praguers pay a lot for private courses, and are quick to spot a charlatan. There are a number of new schools in Prague, but to get the latest information (and possibly a job) head for the longest-established college, the Jazykova škola at Národní 20.

Once you've found work, your employer will tell you his or her theories about what forms you need to complete. For your part, you should demand a certificate from the school/firm which states that you earn only Czech crowns. The form grants you the right to certain benefits generally available to Czechs only (e.g. cheap travel, hotel accommodation). Taxes are deducted at source, and theoretically you should automatically be eligible for the whole gamut of entitlements paid out by the state. The problems rarely work out so easily in practice, as you soon find out when you state your case and your accent is heard; but again, your employer can be a powerful ally.

Finding a Flat: Accommodation in Prague was about 90 per cent state-owned before the revolution. Although the property market was entirely freed for about a month in early 1990, any sale to a foreigner is now invalid, as a fairly orderly privatization is put into effect. Despite the capital's housing shortage, there have been sublet properties available ever since 1989, and you should have few problems finding a flat of some description, although the competition is stiffer if you arrive during high season, July and August. At the time of writing, foreigners are often expected to pay at least a proportion of their rent in hard currency. That will change as the *koruna* learns to float, but if you're planning on staying for some months, a larger than usual stack of western cash will come in useful.

The best place to begin a flat hunt is in the 'Podnájmy' section of *Annonce*, the capital's largest and best magazine of classified ads (published thrice-weekly on Monday, Wednesday and Friday). There are usually plenty of offers, but don't jump at the first; among the honest brokers are swarms of would-be property tycoons who try to dump dives on foreign greenhorns for exorbitant sums. Also ask around among your friends—most Praguers know of someone who knows someone. You'll probably begin with your sights fixed on an *atelier* in Malá Strana, but so too will many others, and most foreigners eventually find a place somewhere slightly outside the centre. Prague's neighbourhoods are so heterogenous that the only way of finding your dream pad is to trudge along and have a look. The areas you might consider are Smíchov (central, smoky, dirty, lively and gipsy), Vinohrady and Žižkov (pretty similar but slightly less of an atmosphere, at least in the social sense), and Dejvice/Letná (stretching from the detached residences of the Communist dinner-party circuit to another bustling district with some large parks). If you want a telephone, make sure that the flat comes with one, as an application generally takes several years to come to the point of decision, let alone success. You can find self-contained flats for less than £30/$54 a month, excluding bills, and you should try to agree a fairly firm price before moving in. Praguers, confronted with spiralling costs in every direction, are understandably reluctant to fix long-term rents; but if you're earning a Czech wage, you're going to face similar difficulties. If you're not, you may as well accede to their every demand.

Business in Prague: Most Czechs balk before a dotted line, having long adopted the sensible view that unwanted responsibilities carry few advantages and plenty of dangers. The habit, along with industrial and managerial overmanning, lives on even in the brave new world of private enterprise; and western wheeler-dealers almost invariably find that the Czech business world turns slower than their own. What you need is a good lawyer. The largest of the newly-legal private firms is a band of 13 shysters (no innuendo intended) who operate out of Národní 32/110 00 Praha-1. They may or may not be specialists in private international law, but in any case, they should be able to put you in touch with someone who can draft your plaint. If you need yuppy gizmos, contact the Hotel Diplomat (see pp. 298–99) which can rent you everything from a flip-chart to an office. They also organize conferences, but the most frenetic bunch of trouble-shooters are to be found buzzing around the Hotel Praha (see p. 298), under the rather undynamic name of Conference Czechoslovakia Ltd, tel 333 81 11, ex 3241–4 (fax 311 80 44). They'll even hold a garden party for you. Finally, western businessmen should note that their Czech counterparts wear far fewer suits than they might be used to.

Other subjects that you may need to consider while living in Prague are:

Animals: Imported beasts have to be accompanied by an official bill of health in either English, German, French or Russian, which is no older than 72 hours. If your animal plans to stay for more than three months, it also needs a certificate from the State Vet at Těšnov 17, but it should be in tip-top shape—the Vet apparently has draconian powers of confinement and execution if he spots the pox or a suspect slaver. Assuming your pet survives, the butchers of Prague will be happy to sell you bags of entrails, and canned food is available at larger supermarkets. There's a 24-hour animal healthcare service at Šenova (tel 791 24 00), near Chodov metro (line C). Your mutt can be groomed at the Yoco Salon (tel 351 73 04). If you don't have a creature, but want one, check the 'Zvírata' columns of *Annonce*, where you can find everything from pythons to the lab rats with which to feed them.

Dictionaries: Don't rely on finding one in Prague. London's Collets International bookstore usually has a hefty volume in stock (see Further Reading for address).

Embassies: The British Embassy will replace lost passports, and fly your body home if you die alone, but otherwise it's useless. The US Embassy is slightly more helpful. As well as a few information pamphlets, it has a noticeboard with up-to-the-minute State Department telexes, warning US citizens which hotspots they have become unwelcome in most recently, which might come in useful if you're planning onward travel to Africa, Asia, or Latin America.

Furniture: There's a warehouse at Libeňský most. Plywood abounds, but the turnover is rapid, and it's been known to sell anything from walnut bureaux to ancient wirelesses. It's open from Mon–Wed 9 am–12 noon and 1–3 pm, Thurs 10 am–12 noon and 1–4 pm.

Homosexuals: Prague's gay scene, suppressed as a symptom of late capitalism for 40 years, is only slowly beginning to throb again. There are two clubs for men, the addresses of which are on p. 306. The pretty and the leathery are preferred at the T-Club, while U Holubů tends to be camper, but the distinctions apparently fluctuate. The Evropa café on Václavské nám. is a well-known haunt for both lesbians and gay men; and everyone can find love and/or thrills in the columns of *Annonce* (see Romance below).

Home Cooking: When you've had one *knedlík* too many, liven up some home cooking with the capital's best selection of spicy roots and powders at U Salvátora on Mostecká 4 (Mon–Fri 9 am–12 noon and 2–5 pm).

Keys: There's a cutting service on the third floor of the Máj department store on Národní (Mon–Wed and Fri 8 am–7 pm, Thurs 8 am–8 pm, Sat 8 am–4 pm).

Language Courses: The widest range of courses are offered at the Jazykova škola (see p. 322). A summer school is held every August at the Philosophy Faculty of the Charles University. Students come from across Europe, so places are limited, but if you're living in Prague and are happy to part with about £200 ($360), you'll be allowed to enrol. Apply early by dropping a line to 'Letní školy Slovanskych studií/ Fakulta Filosofická Karlova Universita/ nám. Jana Palacha 2/ Praha 1'.

Libraries: The British Council and US Embassy each maintain reading rooms at Jungmannova 30 and Vlašská 9 respectively. The State Library at the Clementinum also has an English section (Tues and Thurs 1–7 pm), and its main catalogue contains thousands of ancient and modern English tomes.

Newspapers: Britishers can keep up with the old country through the international editions of the *Guardian* and the *Financial Times*. Both steam off Frankfurt presses, and hit Prague's hotels, street vendors and bookstalls at about noon. US citizens may prefer the *Herald Tribune* or even *USA Today*. At the time of writing, the *European* is still afloat, published by the Bouncing Czech himself, Robert Maxwell. When you've finished with your papers, offer them to a friend who's learning English, since they're too expensive for most Czechs.

Radio: The BBC World Service broadcasts non-stop on 101.1 FM. President Havel hectors the nation every Sunday at 2 pm from his country retreat at Lány. Twiddle the knob to around 70 MHz until you hear his gravelly, smoke-filled voice. Prague's first, and mildly alternative, independent radio station has recently changed its name from Radio Stalin to Radio Ultra and can be heard on 92.6 FM.

Recycling: At the time of writing, the state paper recycling plant has closed down, with no replacement in sight. Almost any bottle that you buy from a shop can be returned to that shop, but different stores sometimes sneer at alien glass. Bottle banks exist in the suburbs, and if you have real problems, walk around with your vessels until you're accosted by an OAP who collects deposits.

Romance: You'll find several pages of lonely hearts under 'Seznámení' in *Annonce*. Both sexes and all preferences advertise; and the subsection marked 'Hezké chvíle...' ('Sweet moments') is for people who prefer to skip the preliminaries. The suggestions make for interesting reading, and often the friend who translates them for you doesn't have to be left out of the fun. To clinch, consolidate or repair your relationship, **flower deliveries** can be ordered at Moskevská 35. You have to pop in to choose your blooms, and only next-afternoon deliveries are possible (Mon–Fri 8 am–6 pm).

Students: If you're enrolled in a Czech college or university, you can pick up an ISIC card at the International Union of Students on Pařížská 25. You'll need a photo, some evidence of your status, and a handful of crowns (50 at the time of writing). The office is open from Mon–Fri 1–3 pm. British Airways offers a range of extremely cheap *return* trips to the UK from Prague. You get the best deals if you're under 26, but there are bargains available to anyone who's coming back.

Telephone Numbers: Emergency numbers are on p. 26. Directory enquiries are answered at 120 (Prague), 121 (for numbers elsewhere in Czechoslovakia), and 0149 (international code enquiries). The national operator is at 102; and English-speaking international operators answer to 0135. Overseas collect calls can be made through 0132. If you have your own phone, there are a few other services open to you, although you may have difficulty with them if you don't yet speak Czech. Telegrams are at 127, alarm calls at 125, the time at 112, and messages will be taken for you in your absence if you ask at 124.

Television: Three standard channels are now available in Prague: F1, which is nationwide; ČTV, broadcasting across the Czech Lands; and OK3, a babble of western services including CNN and BBC programmes.

Translations: Very rarely, you may have to submit a form in Czech in order to receive some benefit or avoid another burden. The best thing to do is to ask a friend for help, since Praguers are generally well versed in the hermetic language of their country's bureaucracy and can usually come up with the phrases, oaths and denials required. If the matter is more serious, the most reliable and expensive services are available at the larger hotels including the Palace and the Diplomat.

Tuzex: These stores, managed by the government and selling glitzy western imports in exchange for hard currency, used to be a lifesaver. As their monopoly is destroyed, they look to be collapsing into extinction, but at the time of writing they're still the only place in town to buy some specialized commodities like Benetton clothes, Finnish hunting daggers or French silk camisoles. You can get the addresses of those that have survived at PIS offices (see pp. 34–5).

Water: Toxins have been trickling down to Prague's water table for decades, and if you're in town for a few months you may want to limit the damage with mineral water. Every supermarket stocks a variety from Bohemia's spas, which are cheap and usually refreshing, but some have unwanted side-effects. To identify the gentler ones, compare the mineral contents (generally the less, the better), and assess the likely infirmities of other purchasers. Only buy the bottles marked *Karlovy Vary* or *Mariánské Lázně* if you have constipation or are following medical advice.

Day Trips from Prague

The Church of St Barbara in Kutná Hora

Karlovy Vary (Carlsbad)—Telč—Terezín and Litoměřice—Karlštejn and Křivoklát Castles—Kutná Hora

When you feel the urge to explore beyond Prague, the heart of Europe is your oyster. Some of the day trips below exemplify an aspect of Bohemia's history that throws the capital into its European perspective; others are simply destinations for lazy summer days. Two focus on the centuries of German influence in the country—from the tranquillity of the spa at Carlsbad to the very different silence of the Theresienstadt ghetto—while Kutná Hora contains some of the most superb Gothic architecture from the golden age of Bohemian independence. The latter is also the trip that many children will enjoy most, assuming that they're old enough to have developed a healthy interest in skeletons and tunnels. The Moravian town of Telč is among the most charming in all Czechoslovakia, a minuscule jewel spanning the Gothic and Renaissance, and the perfect destination for a drive and a picnic. Two Gothic castles—Karlštejn and Křivoklát—are covered in the penultimate trip; both are set in rolling hills and forests, and are the best choice if the cobbles and pressures of Prague have become too much, and you need to go wild in the country.

Orientation

All these trips are within $1^1/_2$–$2^1/_2$ hours of the capital. Karlštejn is the closest, and can be seen in an afternoon if you're pressed for time. They are all accessible by road and rail, but details of only the most convenient means of transport are provided. The railway and coach stations from which you set off are covered on p. 13. Car-hire details are on p. 12. If you aren't driving, be sure to establish how you intend to return to Prague as soon as you arrive; the last return time is often earlier than you'd expect.

329

Karlovy Vary (Carlsbad)

Carlsbad was for centuries one of the most elegant watering holes of central Europe. Goethe and Schiller drank deep of its draughts; its casino and promenades were the playground of Russian aristocrats and Europe's monarchs; and it's hard to name a Romantic composer who didn't take the waters.

The frolics ended in the troubled 20th century: as part of the Sudetenland it was stolen by the Nazis in 1938, and after the war the remaining toffs were dispossessed by the confiscatory Communists. But although the *beau monde* now frivols elsewhere and has been replaced by an annual reinvasion of German tourists, lovers of bygone charm will find few better spots in Bohemia. Le Corbusier once called Karlovy Vary a 'cream cake'; that's not much of a compliment from a man whose ideas of beauty involved glass skyscrapers and curved concrete, but less doctrinaire types will revel in the architectural confectionery.

The town, built along the bubbling Teplá river, climbs wooded hillsides in pastel blocks; and although most of the buildings are less than 150 years old, the tall autumnal façades, genteel lawns and summertime outdoor concerts make for a nostalgic amble back into an age when even gout could be romantic.

The town's fame sprang from its springs, The salty cocktails are forced up from subterranean hot rocks 2 km below, and reach the surface at temperatures ranging from 30–72°C. They first exploded into life during a geological shift about 500 million years ago, but little Wary was an unknown village of clean and healthy folk until Charles IV stumbled upon it in 1358. He immediately built a bathtower near by, and Wary received its prefix and a royal charter in 1370. Most of the houses still have private supplies of the water on tap; it feeds into the river at innumerable points (hence the name Teplá, which means 'warm'); and 12 of the 60 springs now have established medicinal benefits.

Getting Around/Lunch: The town is 130 km due west of Prague on the E48 road, which you can join on Milady Horákové, running north of Letná Park. Coaches leave Florenc regularly; and a private company, Čebus, also has a service, leaving at 7.30 am and 10 am and returning at 3.15 pm and 6 pm (its sales booth is nearby, on Kižíkova). The trip takes just over two hours. Trains leave from Hlavní nádraží, but are often considerably slower. On the other hand, the daily plane service (April–Oct) is very fast; tickets can be bought from ČSA (see p. 3), which will also arrange landing rights for your private jet, if you have one.

Within Karlovy Vary itself, the local bus service isn't of much use, given that the historic centre is only some 1¹/₂ miles long; but if you fancy a wander through the surrounding hillsides, there are two useful funicular railways.

The information given below progresses and digresses on a fairly logical route along the Teplá from the Thermal Hotel, a modern landmark of grey and glass which is very difficult to miss. While sauntering and sipping, beware of the hypochondriacal regulations that apply along the promenades—no dogs, smoking, or loud noises—and in the colonnades, where the prohibitions also cover prams and whatever is meant by the mystifying term 'long objects'. Hygiene police enforce the rules with on-the-spot fines, but insane though the bye-laws are, they're still less dire than they could be: you can retreat to a café or hilltop to smoke and scream, and Hassidic Jews are no longer regarded as a health hazard, as they apparently were for two centuries.

The town contains treatment centres for a variety of conditions from indigestion to quadriplegia. Courses and accommodation can be booked at overseas Čedok offices or at Balnea in Prague (see pp. 1 and 15). In the town itself, the *Kur* office next to the Vřídlo fountain (see below) can tell you whether Karlovy Vary can do anything for your particular ailment, but advance booking is all but essential in high season. If all that you're after is a dip, there's a public swimming pool filled with water from one of the (cooler) springs at the Thermal Hotel. The pool complex is set on the hill just behind the multi-storey hotel.

The town has a few dietary specialities that you may want to try. Look out for *oplatky*, sweet wafers which seem designed to mitigate the disgusting taste of the waters themselves; and the ubiquitous *becherovka*, a herbal tipple developed by town chemist Dr Becher in the 19th century. Despite rumours to the contrary, it contains no spring waters, but it's still proudly known as Karlovy Vary's 13th and most popular spring. Along with *becherovka*, the town's most popular souvenir is its Moser snifters, colossal glasses often blown up to balloon size which, insofar as they have any practical purpose whatsoever, are meant to make superior cognac taste even more superior.

The route through the town is lined with restaurants and cafés. The elegant **Elefant** at Stará louka 30 (opposite the Vítězslav Nezval Theatre), serves no food other than cakes and ice-cream as yet; but despite its dull decoration, it's a genuine survivor from pre-war days and a perennial favourite among the locals. If you can't find room there or anywhere else, the swimming pool of the Thermal has a vast coffee bar and restaurant attached; the ambience is similar to that of an airport lounge, but the view is pleasant enough and you're sure to find a table.

☆   ☆   ☆   ☆   ☆

To begin a trip through the town, find the Thermal Hotel, and continue walking down the Teplá. On your right is the Dvořákovy sady (Dvořák Park), with lily pond and the last of the garden's wrought-iron colonnades, the lone survivor of a Habsburg hunt for cannon metal during the 1914–18 war. Further downriver is the neo-classical splendour of the **Mill Colonnade** (Mlýnská kolonáda). Five springs hiss and gurgle to the surface here, and it's the favourite ambulatory of the town's hydrophiles, who stroll from fount to fount between the Corinthian columns, drinking through the spouts of their teapot-like *pohárky*. The locals all seem to have their favourite brew, but discrimination needs to be acquired, and you should exercise caution. In the unintentionally-honest words of one of the town's tourist brochures, 'even small doses have a striking effect on the alimentary tract', and it's no coincidence that there are well-marked toilets at the end of the colonnade.

The road veering right from the colonnade (Lázeňská) used to be named after Karl Marx, who visited three times. The delighted Communists thus had an excuse—as if one were necessary—to honour him with a statue, recently toppled, and the museum to your left. That's being reorganized at the time of writing; by the time you're reading this, it should have reopened under its former name, **The Golden Key** (U zlatého klíča), with a more balanced selection of exhibits from Karlovy Vary's past. The street winds into a little junction that was the heart of the medieval town. In the centre is the inevitable plague column from Bohemia's epidemic of 1715; every town in the country built one, although this one seems doubly superfluous if it's true, as the town claims, that the power of the waters has kept the bacteria at bay throughout its history. On your right is the wooden **Market Colonnade**, a replacement of a bronze victim of the Habsburg meltdown.

On your left is the fountain that was responsible for Karlovy Vary's rise to stardom. It's the **Vřídlo** ('Spring'), now housed in a glass temple built by the Communists and named until 1989 after another key man in their history of the spa, Soviet cosmonaut Yuri Gagarin (who visited twice and whose romper-suited likeness still stands—with an ever-growing air of impermanence—outside the main entrance). The fountain fizzes from rocks more than 2 km underground, and ends its journey in splutters and spurts of up to 12 m, at a temperature of 72°C. The various legends agree that Charles IV was on a hunt when he discovered the spring and brought the town its fame and prosperity, but the details are fuzzy: the most widespread story is that he was somehow led to Vřídlo by a deer; others claim that it was the yelp of a boiled dog that tipped him off; while the most intriguing tale insists that villagers carried him here after he had been grieviously wounded in hand-to-hand combat with a boar. The emperor was advised by his physician that, although the water was clearly holy, it was suitable only for bathing. The opinion is understandable when you taste the foul potion; but in 1522, the advantages of taking it orally were publicized by a certain Václav Payer, who steadily increased his recommended dosage until he was suggesting a daily intake of 60 cups and 12-hour baths. Even that was a chaser compared to the prescriptions of some later spa maniacs, but armed with a *pohárek*, you can work out your own optimum shot at the smaller outlets in the hall near the fountain.

If you return to the little junction with the plague column, a detour along the street running up the hill (Zamecký vrch) takes you to the spot where Charles is said to have ended his deer hunt. It leads past the circular colonnade of the **Castle Spring**, under the tower built by Charles and remodelled in the early 17th century (its viewing gallery is occasionally open). Follow the hill until you see a set of steps on your left (next to a house marked 'Marius'), then turn left again and take the second path on the right. The cobbles turn into a root-strewn path, which clambers up to **Stag Leap** (Jelení skok), the tall rock where Charles's quarry is said to have jumped/been wounded/been sighted. The legend was confused further by dotty Count Lützow in the 19th-century, who felt that only a goat could have stood on the crag, and an intrepid little chamois now gazes over the valley. Incidentally, Lützow also commissioned the construction of an iron cat on a pillar, for no known reason, at the other end of town.

Salvation of the soul has always taken second place to the perpetration and repair of sins of the flesh in Karlovy Vary, and churches are thin on the ground. Although Russian aristocrats built themselves an Orthodox church in the late 19th century (on Tř. krále Jiřího, near the junction with Petra Velikého), the town got only one Counter-Reformation masterpiece, the oval **Church of St Mary Magdalene** (Kostel sv. Marie Magdalena), built by K. I. Dienzenhofer in 1736. It's on the hill over-looking Vřídlo from the other side of the river, and one enjoyable, if roundabout, way of approaching it to take the funicular railway (*lanovka*) up the hill and walking down past the bulbous spires. The trains leave every 15 mins from Divadelní nám. 3; you'll find the so-called square in a crescent on your left if you resume your interrupted journey through the town centre. In the same square is the **Vítězslav Nezval Theatre** (Divadlo V. Nezvala), the construction of which was financed by what has always been a lucrative cottage industry in Karlovy Vary, the collection of toilet admission fees. Its stage curtain was painted in 1885 by three Viennese painter/decorators, who included a young **Gustav Klimt**. It dates from about a decade before he began his move towards the stylized beauties for which he's best known, and was one of scores of works that he and his decorative firm painted across Austria and nearby provinces. The curtain is a grandiose tribute to Theatre, filled with the nine Muses (Tragedy hogs the stage; she may well be an early Klimtian *femme fatale*); on the right is a band of troubadours, among whom is rakish Gustav himself, tootling on a flute. The box office is open from Tues–Sat 1.30 pm–6 pm; if you want to see the curtain, ask to speak to the young theatre manager, who is very friendly and knows the curtain intimately.

The journey through the town continues on the other side of the river with Stará louka (Old Meadow), containing some of the oldest houses in town, including the Krásná Královna (Beautiful Queen) café, home of Queen Maria Theresa during her visits to the spa. There's another funicular at the top of Mariánská, on the right at the end of Stará louka, climbing 200 m up the opposite hillside (9 am–4 pm daily). It takes you to an observation tower, a café, and a view that is so good that it's disillusioning, revealing the spa to be a tiny enclave of watery freshness and colour set within the greyness of a 20th-century town. Back at ground level, Stará louka and the Teplá swerve to the left, diverted by the 5000-bed **Grand Hotel Pupp**, the core of which is almost 300 years old but with suburban wings dating back only some 50 years.

The hotel marks the end of the town centre. A few hundred metres down Goetheova stezka is a bust of a very supercilious Goethe, who paid Carlsbad 13 visits, and broke his heart here for one of the last times when, in 1823, he spotted 17-year-old Ulrika von Lewetzow sipping the waters. She spurned the 74-year-old poet; according to legend he was consumed by a profound, if temporary grief, and penned his *Elegies* as he stormed out of town in his carriage. There's a gallery slightly further along the path with a small collection of 20th-century Czech art (open

Tues–Sun 9.30 am–noon and 1 pm–5 pm). If you feel like a climb, there's an observation tower on the hill next to the Pupp; and a final way of ending the walk is in the twilight splendour of the neo-Renaissance **Bath 1** (Lazně 1), next to the green opposite the hotel. It has a café on the ground floor, open on weekdays until 2.30 pm, and it's also one of the few places in town where you might get a treatment without having booked in advance. Exhausted walkers can choose from a variety of watery services, ranging from massages to low-voltage electrocution (open Mon–Fri 6.45 am–3 pm, Sat 6.45 am–noon). The pleasures have to be bought with hard currency—and if you have money to burn, and an evening in hand, the casino on the first floor opens at 6pm.

Telč

The minuscule town of Telč is one of the most stunningly beautiful in Czechoslovakia. It still has the feel of a medieval microcosm, a world within walls, but its fortifications and lakes now enclose the splendid luxury of a Renaissance chateau, and the pastel façades of a square which, on a sunny summer day, can make Prague's Old Town Square look hamfisted.

Getting Around/Lunch: Although the whole town is lovely, Telč's highlight is its chateau, and you should make sure that it will be open before setting off on this day trip. The opening times are given below, but broadly speaking, don't choose a Monday, Saturday or any month from November to March (inclusive). More generally, Telč isn't a town to visit out of season; for better or for worse, the town depends on the annual influx of tourists from nearby Austria, and it sinks into depressive melancholia as winter approaches.

Telč is about 120 km southeast of Prague, and the only practical way to reach it and return in a day is by road. If you're driving, pick up the Brno motorway from the south of Prague. The two largest feeder roads that loop into it are 5. května and Chodovská. Turn off at the E59 for Jihlava and then follow local signs. There's a regular coach service from Florenc station; the journey takes about 2¹/₂ hours.

The centre of Telč itself is so small that a bus would have nowhere to go. Once you've found your way to the centre of town, the sites are a stroll away from each other.

There are cafés scattered throughout the town square. In the summer, you'll be grateful to eat anywhere that has space, and if everything is full, you could try the *hospoda* up the hill running from the northern gate of the town, which serves beer, soups and dumplings. You might want to prepare a picnic before leaving Prague, in which case you can eat it next to one of the lakes that surround the town.

Telč seems to have originated in the early 13th century, but it emerges from obscurity only about a hundred years later, when prodigal John of Luxemburg pawned the town, along with several others in southern Bohemia, to keep the money flowing for his chivalrous jaunts overseas. His son Charles IV redeemed it, but after a spot of complex wheeling and dealing, it fell into the hands of the Hradec family, which constructed the town's fishponds, fortifications and chateau before extinguishing itself through various drinking and drowning mishaps in the early 17th century. The town then passed through innumerable noble hands until 1945, but it has hardly changed since the Hradec family left.

There are still only three gates through the town fortifications. From the bus station, you'll enter through the southern entrance, past the lonely Romanesque steeple of the first church in Telč, built in the early 1200s but now otherwise long gone. The cobbled lane emerges into the funnel-shaped town square, a 300-m long set of cinnamon, lemon and gingerbread façades that are too preposterously charming to be comparable to anything other than a film set. The Telč house is so distinctive that it's a byword for fairytale prettiness within Czechoslovakia itself—no mean feat in a country where every other village can lay claim to enchanted status. Each of the short buildings has a fiercely quirky independence—some combining *sgraffito* with crenellated rooftops, others surmounted with incongruous gables which double the height of the house concerned—but all have certain characteristic features. A Gothic arcade runs under the houses along the length of both sides of the square, and, pottering from gallery to café, you'll also notice how unusually deep they are in relation to their narrow jostling exteriors. They originated after a fire in 1530 and combine Gothic structures with Renaissance façades, with plenty of curlie-wurlie Baroque flourishes tossed in for good measure.

As you approach the narrower end of the square, you'll see on your left the towers and domes of the Jesuit church of St James, next to the Order's former college, and on your right the entrance to the Renaissance **chateau** (*zámek*). The home of Telč's lords for centuries, it dates back to Gothic times, but was reconstructed in its present form during the second half of the 16th century. As well as a sumptuous interior, it contains a museum of the town's history and an art gallery.

The small museum and the interior of the chateau are both open from Tues–Sun 9 am–4 pm (April, Sept, Oct), 8 am–5 pm (May–Aug), with a lunch break from 12–1 pm. The former would hardly merit a visit, were it not for an awe-inspiring electrical model of the Nativity, painstakingly constructed out of cardboard and papier-mâché by Telčian luminaries Mr and Mrs Vostry. Ask the curator to switch it on. His face will light up; and few visitors fail to be impressed as angels, cradle and sheep swoop, rock and graze with high-voltage fury in a landscape that's somehow redolent of both Heidi and the Arabian Nights. After taking in the other pinnacles of Telč's cultural history, you can buy a ticket for the guided tour through the chateau from the same ticket office. It leads through rooms that often combine Gothic cross- and net-vaulting with rich Renaissance stucco work and decoration; others with illusionistic painting; some gorgeous furniture and cassetted ceilings; and towards the end, impressive arrays of armour, and hundreds of hunting trophies. The latter collection includes what is claimed by many to be the largest elephant ear in central Europe, one metre in diameter.

The chateau also houses a gallery of the painting of Jan Zrzavý (1890–1977), at the end of the arcade in the gardens. Its complex opening hours are as follows: Tues–Sun 9 am–4 pm (April, Sept, Oct), 8 am–5 pm (May–Aug); Tues–Fri 9 am–4 pm, Sat 9 am–1 pm, Sun 9 am–4 pm (Nov–March). It closes from 12–1 pm wherever applicable. Zrzavý's art is some of the most distinctive and uncategorizable to have been produced by a Czech this century. The paintings on display span his entire career, during which his colourful and simple work teetered back and forth across the range from whimsy to profound humaneness; much of his finest art was produced between 1910 and 1930, under the (very indirect) influence of Cubism and then a form of social realism suffused with a powerful spirituality.

Terezín and Litoměřice

This trip is a none-too-lighthearted excursion through the final chapter of the German presence in Bohemia. Terezín is better known to the outside world as Theresienstadt, a 200-year-old fortress town that was transformed by the Nazis into a concentration camp for deported Jews from across Europe. It lay within the German-speaking Sudetenland,

and you can combine the visit with a trip to the nearby town of Litomě-řice—formerly Leitmeritz, and a thriving centre of the minority population until its violent expulsion after the war.

Getting Around/Lunch: Terezín is about 60 km to the north of Prague on the route to Teplice which you can pick up on Horňátocká, north of Holešovice. The journey by coach takes under 1½ hours; buses leave from Florenc station at 7.45 am, 10 am, 11 am and 11.30 am. There's also a service from Holešovice. Organized tours to the town leave Prague's Old Town Hall every Sunday morning; you can get the times and details from the Jewish Town Hall or one of the ticket offices of the Jewish museum (see p. 156). Trains go to Litoměřice, but the journey is long and involves changing at Lysá na Labem.

The bus to Terezín stops in the main square. The ghetto was in the town itself, and the nearby fortress was a prison, a distinction which isn't always appreciated by visitors. You should make sure to see both; they're separated by a walk of a few minutes. There's a regular bus service to Litoměřice (a 7-minute journey), leaving either from the same stop in the square at which you arrive, or the one just around the next corner.

Lunch can be a problem on this trip. If you only intend to visit Terezín, you have very little choice indeed. There's a *bufet* next to the bus station in the main square, and another on the way to the prison camp. If you're desperate, you could try downing a snack in the former SS canteen just inside the gates of the prison itself, although after a visit the prospect is often too nauseating. The atmosphere is more pleasant, but the selection little better, in Litoměřice. There's a dingy *kavárna* at the end of Dlouhá (on your right as you walk towards the square from the bus station); and three unappetizing diners on the northern side of the square itself. Your best bet is again to prepare a picnic before leaving Prague or to buy food from a store in the town, and then to eat in the quiet square in front of St Stephen's church.

Terezín was established by imperial fiat in 1780. Emperor Joseph II named it after his mother, but sentimentality ended there. Along with the nearby fortress (see below), the chess-board town was designed simply to defend Bohemia's northwest frontier. However, its eminently functional layout made it suitable for any project that required order, and when the Nazis began their *Aktionen* against Bohemian and Moravian Jews in 1941, they had little difficulty in turning it into a concentration

338

camp. Transports were soon arriving from across Europe, to be accommodated temporarily as the finishing touches were put to the Nazis' final solution of the Jewish problem. The first arrivals were put up in the barracks; but in June 1942, all of Terezín's existing inhabitants were expelled, and the entire town was taken over. The Nazis intended it to be the acceptable face of ghettoization; and International Red Cross representatives were shown around here, as and when the organization took an interest in what was happening to Europe's Jews. The relatively lax regime meant that the camp became a bizarre centre of wartime Jewish culture, with clandestine newspapers, plays and concerts, and even a jazz band ('The Ghetto Swingers'), despite a Nazi decree outlawing such Judeo-Negroid deviancy. However, the laxness was very relative indeed; only some 20,000 of around 140,000 deportees survived the war.

Terezín's former (Czech) inhabitants returned after 1945, but the town has a stillness that feels very different from the lazy calm that you might expect of a provincial town. The stark, but almost elegant neo-classical grid is permeated with the atmosphere of a terrible museum: after you've left, it's hard to remember seeing a child or hearing birdsong in the town; and little seems to drive on the broad and dusty roads save the occasional truck from its still-functioning garrison. If you leave the square along B. Němcové, and then turn left at Dlouhá, many of the street corners still show the overpainted German markings of the ghetto's blocks. On the right at the far end of Dlouhá is a disused railway terminal, and just beyond it a 100-m stretch of track. Trains carried 87,000 people to Auschwitz-Birkenau from here, of whom 3000 survived the war. The road parallel to the track (Bohušovická brána) crosses the vast ditch that rings the town and which could be filled by the river in moments of need. On the right, in arches set into the heavy fortifications, are funeral halls built towards the end of the war to impress the last Red Cross delegation. In one of the chambers, Christian services were held for those unlucky enough to be defined as Jews by Nazi race laws. Slightly further along the road, a path to the left leads to a graveyard and Terezín's **crematorium**. The inferno burned for the last three years of the war, and disposed of 30,000 bodies. It's now a museum, open from April–Oct 10 am–5 pm.

Apart from innumerable plaques and memorials, there's little more to see in the town itself. Retrace your steps to the main square. Walk towards the green on your left as you face Terezín's suitably desolate neo-classical church; and cross it onto Pražská. (The Nazis once built a playground on the lawn for ghetto children, just before Red Cross film-makers came to town.) Follow the road out of the town centre, turning right and then left across the Ohře river. It leads to the **Small Fort** (Malá pevnost), open daily 8 am–6.30 pm (summer) and 8 am–3.30 pm (winter). The fort was built by the Habsburgs, but again exploited most effectively by the Nazis. The Gestapo took over in June 1940 and 32,000 inmates passed through, either prisoners-of-war or pinko troublemakers. Their crime wasn't Judaism, and the treatment was correspondingly less harsh. As a result only 2500 died here, and another 5000 in death camps.

On your right as you walk to the main entrance is the **National Cemetery**, containing the graves of some 2400 people, and the ashes of some 25,000 others. The dates show how many were victims of the typhoid epidemic that raged through the town in the weeks after its liberation by Soviet forces on 8 May 1945.

After paying, turn left into the first courtyard, where prisoners checked in and were given uniforms and numbers. 'Arbeit Macht Frei' still greets you as you walk into the camp proper. In front of you are collective cells; and if you turn left and left again, you enter a street of solitary chambers for condemned prisoners and those under interrogation. The Nazis weren't the first to use them—and in the first cell on the right, the Habsburgs imprisoned **Gavrilo Princip**. Perhaps the most successful of the many trigger-happy anarchists of the turn of the century, Princip was the man who killed Archduke Francis Ferdinand, heir to the Habsburg throne, at Sarajevo in 1914. The assassination set Europe's war machines into motion, but Princip himself saw none of the action. He was manacled to the cell wall until tuberculosis crept in in 1916, and died in Terezín's military hospital in April 1918. The small exhibition contains mug-shots of Princip and five other members of the bungling Black Hand organization to which he belonged. Their slapstick efforts were consummated only when the Archduke's car stalled next to Princip, half an hour after another conspirator had lobbed a ball of dynamite which missed. The ludicrous Serbs became heroes of Tito's Yugoslavia, and this memorial was unveiled by the ambassador in the 1950s.

The next set of buildings contain showers, and the enamel basins and individual mirrors of a pristine shaving-room, constructed by the Nazis shortly before the 1944 Red Cross visit. Walk through the little passage nearby, and on the right is a gate (marked '19') which leads into one of the eeriest parts of the fortress, a dim tunnel stretching for hundreds of metres through its walls (closed in winter). That has nothing to do with the Nazis; but you emerge in front of a gallows and grassy bank where they shot and hanged some 250 inmates. Through the gate to the right is the overgrown site of a mass grave of 601 people, who were exhumed and reburied in 1945. Condemned prisoners arrived through the Gate of Death on the left. As you walk out of it, you'll pass the swimming pool and cinema used by the guards (unless the Red Cross were in town, in which case inmates were ordered to amuse themselves). The cinema now shows documentaries, although you'll need to amass a small group before the staff will show one. Just past the cinema on the left is a small memorial with earth from all the extermination camps fed by Terezín, and beyond that a courtyard and watchtower (the minute rooms to the right housed up to 12 people in the last months of the war). As you retrace your footsteps, there's a museum in the former SS barracks to the left; and the guards' canteen is just before the exit.

As you cross the Labe river on the short journey to **Litoměřice**, you'll see on your left Radobýl Hill, which contains a now-closed factory which belonged to the Flossenbürg concentration camp. 15,000 involuntary troglodytes worked inside the mountain during the war, and a third of them died there.

The centre of the town is in the direction from which the bus arrives. Cross the road and walk down Dlouhá towards the main square. A living town comes as a relief after the barracks and cells of Terezín, but unfortunately Litoměřice is an unkempt mess. There are some sights worth seeing, but you probably won't want to stay long after having had lunch. The town used to be one of the largest in Bohemia, but was almost completely wiped out by Swedes during the Thirty Years War (1618–48). Its recent history has been no happier, as you can begin to appreciate in the **Town Museum**, housed in the town hall, under the arcade on your right as you enter the square (open Tues–Sun 10 am–noon and 12.30 pm–5.30 pm). Scattered among the archaeological junk and standard medieval paraphernalia (including torture instruments and the tree-like stocks of the old town) are exhibits telling the story of the Sudetenland in microcosm, from swastika-laden soup bowls to photographs of the jubilant reception given the Nazis in 1938. However, what's missing is any mention of what happened to the town's Germans after the war. They were expelled, as they were throughout the Sudetenland—an understandable decision after you've been to Terezín, but one that led to the deaths of thousands, including Jews and relatives of concentration camp victims. For a decade, the area was filled with ghostly villages; and although Litoměřice itself was repopulated soon after the war, some of its façades are (very) muted echoes of Terezín, with faded German shop signs reappearing from under the fading paintwork. The museum also contains the *Litoměřice Prayer Book* (pre-1517), an important stage in the development of Czech printing. The titanic tome is usually open at a vibrant technicolour scene of alarmed Jan Hus preparing to meet his maker, and vice versa.

If you cross the square from the museum, and take Michalská on the left, you'll find the **North Bohemian Gallery** at No. 7 (open Tues–Sun 9 am–noon and 2 pm–5 pm). The small collection runs from Romanesque sculpture to sorry 19th-century efforts, but the most notable work is that by the Master of the Litoměřice Altarpiece, which marks the point in the early 16th century when Czech Gothic art joined the mainstream of the northern Renaissance. The work shows a close affinity to that of Lucas Cranach the Elder; and if you make your way from the gallery to the Jesuit **Cathedral of St Stephen**, you'll find work by Cranach himself decorating the interior. The church is in Dómské nám., which you'll reach if you walk to the end of Michalská and then head right for a couple of hundred metres. Unfortunately, it's closed except at services; but if you can't get in, the peaceful square in front of the church is a good spot in which to unwind after Terezín.

Karlštejn and Křivoklát Castles

Bohemia is full of Gothic castles. Many are mouldering ruins, caught unaware by the discovery of artillery and given up for dead by their fleeing owners, but these two, rising in majestic isolation from the rolling hills and forests to the west of Prague, are among the best preserved in the country. It's possible to visit both in a day, although you'd be pressed for time; the best idea is to plump for one and then spend some hours hiking through the surrounding countryside. Karlštejn is the closer, and probably the most popular tourist excursion of all from Prague, but beware—no matter what anyone else tells you, its most exceptional feature, the Chapel of the Holy Cross, is firmly closed for restoration until some time in the mid- to late-1990s.

Getting Around/Lunch: Both castles are always closed on Monday, and have convoluted opening hours (given below) that you should check before setting off. You can drive to Karlštejn by picking up the signs on Strakonická (southbound), the western embankment of the Vltava; and to get to Křivoklát, you have to then drive on to Beroun and follow local roads towards Rakovník. Most trains to Karlštejn leave from Smíchovské nádraží (the service is generally hourly). If you want to continue to

Křivoklát, catch a local train to Rakovník from Beroun, but be especially careful when working out your route back to Prague; if you miss a connection, you can easily find that over an hour has been added to your return journey. Karlštejn is 28 km southwest of Prague, and Křivoklát some 46 km almost due west of the capital; the rail journey to each takes about 35 mins and 1½ hours respectively.

Both castles are a short walk from their respective railway stations, and you can only wander through them in the company of a guide. Walking routes through the surrounding hills are marked on tree trunks, cairns and the like.

The road up the hill to Karlštejn is lined with small cafés, and although more private eateries are opening up to cater for the thousands of visitors who arrive hungry during high season, the best advice is, as usual, to be very grateful for anywhere you can find a free table. The castle road at Křivoklát isn't as jam-packed with either tourists or places to eat; but there's one cheap and moderately cheerful Czech café—U černých—which usually has space when all else is full. You'll find it at the top of the castle road, about ten minutes walk beyond the castle itself (open Tues–Sun).

Karlštejn: Open Tues–Sun: Mar 9 am–3 pm, April–May 9 am–4 pm, June–Aug 8 am–5 pm, Sept–Oct 9 am–4 pm, Nov–Dec 9 am–3 pm. Closed 12–12.30 pm.

Karlštejn is almost too perfect to be believable when you spot its slate roofs and towers from the train, perched on their limestone peak. By the 1700s, it had fallen into complete disrepair, the stalking ground of local peasants taking their pigs for a walk; and in the late 19th century it was restored according to the obsessively purist neo-Gothic theories of Josef Mocker (see pp. 72–3). Much of its interior suffered as a result, but it still contains enough to make the short journey from Prague worth while.

Most medieval castles were built as places to hide when the going got rough; but Charles IV had safe houses a-plenty, and his ideas for Karlštejn were very different. It was begun in 1348, and by the time its interior had been decorated in 1367, it had been turned into a vast symbol of the strange universe that the emperor inhabited. Its three almost separated components made no sense in defensive terms, but were designed instead to mark a mystical ascent from the mundane level of temporal power, represented by the emperor's quarters, up 260 m to the pinnacle of the castle, the Chapel of the Holy Cross. As a result of botched 19th-century restoration, the vagaries of guided tours, the closing of the chapel, and—perhaps most importantly—the lost mentality of an age, it's hard to re-create the pilgrim's way that Charles would have followed; but as you advance, there are a few highlights that you should notice in particular.

The first stage takes you through the lowest level of the building, including the richly-panelled Audience Hall, past an altar-piece by the north Italian Tommasso da Modena (1325–79)—a leading artist of his day, and one of those most often commissioned by the emperor—into the **Luxemburg Hall**. In the centre of the room is a minuscule model of how the original room looked (until destructive humidity led to the reconstruction of the room in the 16th century). Emperor Charles was less insecure about his position than many other monarchs, but he nevertheless swathed his dynasty in myth to be on the safe side; and the doll's-house room shows the characters whom Charles proudly claimed as his forebears—a lineage which somehow runs from Noah through Troy's King Priam to Charles's father, madcap John of Luxemburg.

The tour then leads up to the **Church of the Virgin**, in which the emperor is still honoured with a requiem on 29 November. It's here that spiritual concerns begin to take over. On the wall opposite the altar are the lively *Relic Scenes*, which are among the earliest known portraits of European art (*c.* 1357). They show Charles receiving a comprehensive set of oddments of the Passion, from Charles V of France (on the left) and an unknown king, and then depositing them in his specially-designed Reliquary Cross. That priceless trinket—which may be back on public display in Prague Castle's Chapel of the Holy Cross (p. 111) by the time you read this—contained niches for nails and splinters of the True Cross, thorns, and even a shred of the vinegar-soaked sponge. The other three walls are covered with scenes of the Apocalypse; they're sadly fading into undecipherability, but if you peer closely, you can still make out some of the most memorable hallucinations suffered by John on Patmos, including a city collapsing into topsy-turvy destruction, and the fiery seven-headed and ten-horned Beast itself. Next to the church is **St Catherine's chapel**, consecrated to one of Charles's innumerable patron saints, adopted by the emperor after she had saved his life on an Italian battlefield. The oratory is studded with the jaspers, amethysts and chalcedonies that so fascinated the emperor, set in gilt stucco; lining the side of the chapel are paintings of the seven Bohemian patron saints, and on the altar is a votive scene of the emperor kneeling under the Virgin. If you've already seen the Chapel of St Wenceslas in St Vitus's Cathedral (pp. 116–17), the decorative scheme of this chapel will be familiar—but it's in the third and last stage of Karlštejn that the fervent chiliasm of the emperor and his age reaches an unparalleled climax.

The **Chapel of the Holy Cross (Rood)**, accessible only via a corkscrew staircase and fortified with walls which are up to 5¹/₂ m thick, was designed by Charles to house his new crown jewels and Reliquary Cross; but to explain it in functional terms is to mislead. It ended the emperor's questing trek through the castle and represented the promised Heavenly City (an idea which recurs in the Chapel of St Wenceslas), in which he could contemplate the blissful relief of salvation after the tribulation of Revelation in the church below. Under its gilt vaults, studded with hundreds of glass stars, a moon and a sun, he would pray in the light of 1300 candles burning from iron spikes; and the emperor's painter, Master Theodoric (see p. 64) painted over 120 saints, prophets and angels to guard Charles and his jewels. The chapel is an extraordinary sight, but a combination of humidity, and utter stupidity meant that it had to be closed for long-term restoration in 1981. The ante-chamber shows the condition of the paintings immediately before the work began: not only were the annual exhalations of 300,000 breathless visitors threatening to unglue the chapel, but—almost incredibly—several of the irreplaceable masterpieces by Master Theodoric had been all but destroyed by tourists' graffiti.

Křivoklát: Open Tues–Sun: Feb–April 9 am–3 pm, May–Aug 9 am–5 pm, Sept 9 am–4 pm, Oct–Dec 9 am–3 pm.

Unlike the *via sacra* of Karlštejn, Křivoklát has never had pretensions to being anything other than a fortified country seat. Its towers, turrets and battlements rise with compact force from deep forest, once filled with the bears and boars so beloved of royal hunters everywhere; and its interior contains all the features that an owner would need, from chapel to oubliette and torture chamber. Rudolf II was the last Bohemian monarch to spend time in the castle—killing animals was one of his relatively healthy obsessions while young—and Křivoklát declined to merely noble status during the 17th century. However, minor royalty continued to invite itself along for a chase, most notably Archduke Francis Ferdinand, Habsburg huntsman *extraordinaire* until he found himself at the wrong end of a pot-shot at Sarajevo in 1914.

The castle originated in the early years of the 12th century, but its present appearance dates largely from its reconstruction in the late 15th century, during the reign of Vladislav II of Jagellon. As a result, the castle's architecture is typified by the flamboyant Vladislav Style of

Bohemian Gothic architecture (see p. 65), and among the rich figurative and organic encrustations, the castle is replete with net-vaults and spiralling pillars similar, if on a smaller scale, to those of Prague's Vladislav Hall. The guided tour leads through the castle hall and chapel, filled with panel painting, sculptures and exhibits from the castle's history, into the library of the Fürstenburgs, containing antique clocks, a piano and 25 books of fairy tales, which were apparently the noble family's favourite reading matter. If you're lucky, the exhibition of torture instruments in the round tower will have been reopened, perhaps with the six skeletons of starved debtors that were found inside during the 18th century. If not, you could go and look at the Huderka tower, at the other end of the castle, which is one of the several dungeons scattered across Bohemia where earless alchemist Edward Kelley is said to have jumped to his death (see p. 107).

Kutná Hora

Kutná Hora means 'mining mountain'. The town grew out of nothing in the late 13th century, when it was discovered that there was silver and copper in that there hill. The Přemysl kings muscled in on the operation, and the city boomed as it began to yield up thousands of tons of precious ores annually. It was granted a royal charter (1308), grew into one of the largest towns in Europe, and became the second home of King Wenceslas IV in 1400—and then in the mid-16th century, its silvery life-blood was finally exhausted. The panhandlers drifted away, the shanty-town suburbs evaporated, and apart from the standard Jesuit-inspired Counter-Reformation encampments, nothing of note was ever built again. But although its glory years were over, its crumbling Baroque and Rococo townhouses are peppered with some of the finest Gothic architecture in Bohemia, all monuments to a silver Klondike of the Middle Ages.

Getting Around/Lunch: To go by car, pick up route 333 on Vinohradská and drive for about 68 km. Buses leave Prague regularly, from either Želivského or Florenc (pay on board) and take about 1 1/2 hours to arrive. The train journey from Masarykova or Hlavní nádraží is often slightly longer, and sometimes requires a change at Kolín. Kutná Hora's tourist information office is in the main square, Palackého nám. You'll be walking for most of the time, and the town's filled with signposts which are only mildly confusing. If you want to get a bus to Sedlec (see below), buy a ticket from any tobacconist.

The town is perfect for a picnic on a fine day. Otherwise, there are several venerable tourist-traps (try **U havířů** on Šultysova), and a bubbling collection of new private cafés, often in one-time living rooms.

The highlights of the town are packed to the south of the main square. Walk down the narrow Jakubska and you'll be greeted by the **Church of St James** (sv. Jakub), its 82-m tower rising with incongruous magnificence from a curving lane of pastel cottages. The citizens started to build it in 1330, but splendid as it is, it was just a trial run for their later effort, which you'll see soon. To the east of the church is the **Italian Court** (Vlašský dvůr), open 8 am–5 pm (summer) and 8 am–4 pm (winter). The court was set up as a mint in 1300 by Wenceslas II after Florentine financial experts, summoned to advise him on monetary reform, suggested that he produce coins. Obvious really, and it worked; the *groschen* became an ECU of its time, used by merchants across Europe in preference to their flabby currencies. There are examples in the building's museum, along with the later *taler*, a name which originated in another Bohemian silver mine at Joachimstal (Jáchymov) and which eventually migrated across the Atlantic to become the dollar. Wenceslas IV moved his royal residence here in 1400, and the building contains his Session Chamber, used by the king whenever his troublesome nobles wanted to have a word. Diets assembled here into the 16th century, and in the far corner is a bench from 1511, which was specially designed—as your guide will gleefully demonstrate—to reverse direction with a flick of the wrist, to enable petulant councillors to turn their backs to their kings more easily. The paintings show the hall at moments of moment: one is of the election of Vladislav II of Jagellon; and the other depicts the issue of the Decrees of Kutná Hora, by which feeble Wenceslas IV agreed to gerrymander the electoral system at Prague's university. The same king built the neighbouring chapel, now smothered by garish neo-Gothic painting from 1904, but the sculptures are original. The hollow Man of Sorrows (*c.* 1520), once used as a safe, has the burly build of a Kutná Hora miner, and shows how closely linked the town's art was to its working traditions.

From the mint, it's a short walk to the **Hrádek Mining Museum** on Barborská 28, where you can explore more deeply into the town's history (open Tues–Sun, April–Sept 8 am–noon and 1 pm–5 pm, and in October until 4 pm). It contains a hoisting—original, but from another town—around which six horses would eke out their sorry lives lifting leather bags of silver and floodwater to the surface. The museum is built over a rediscovered mine shaft which burrows through the surrounding hill; it's the perfect spot to contemplate the drowning, burning and asphyxiation that were the most common forms of premature death in medieval Kutná Hora.

If you can find your way back to where you went into the museum, walk further along Barborská, which goes over the hill through which you've just been crawling—to your right is the former Jesuit College, built in the mid-17th century and their largest outside Prague; to your left is an avenue of the Baroque sculpture of which the Society of Jesus was so fond in Bohemia; and directly ahead of you is the **Church of St Barbara** (Kostel sv. Barbora), built from 1388–1558 and ranking among the most splendid Gothic churches in Europe. Its three steeples and web of gargoyle-bedecked flying buttresses can be seen from across the town; and the church is even more fantastic when you consider that it was no king but ordinary miners who financed it, in honour of their industry's patron saint (shared by anyone who faces sudden death). The church is open Tues–Sun 8 am–noon and 1 pm–5 pm (summer), 9 am–noon and 2 pm–4 pm (winter). Enter through the northern door; if it's closed, you can pick up a key at the Jesuit college opposite, through the door just under the tower.

Generations of Bohemia's finest architects worked on the church for over 150 years. Peter Parler or one of his students began the eight eastern chapels, and the most striking feature of the church, the wondrous flowers and stars of the nave's vaulting, was the work of Benedict Ried, who had just completed the equally ingenious Vladislav Hall in Prague (see pp. 123–4). The Jesuits moved in their Baroque baggage when they arrived—the long chapels at the western end have altars dedicated to their founders, SS Ignatius and Francis Xavier—but what remains of the original Gothic decoration is superb. Three of the chapels are covered with frescoes from the late 15th century: the Crucifixion and the Queen of Sheba; a colossal figure of St Christopher fording a fish-filled stream (he was traditionally a giant, but more importantly for Kutná Hora's churchgoers, he is another saint who'll have nothing to do with sudden death); and under one of the windows, pictures of miners at work. Again local traditions have influenced the art of the period, with striking effect when set in the church's architectural grandeur; the feature reappears at the south-west end, where an entire wall is covered with simple images of miners and angels, neither group more glorified than the other.

There are a few other sites worth seeing as you walk through the streets of the town, notably a late 15th-century **stone fountain** in

Rejskovo nám., and a **plague column** of 1715 at the junction of Husova and Šultysova, with detailed Latin inscriptions extolling the powers of various saints against the armpit-virus. There's also the ornate Gothic **Stone House** (Kammený dům) on Radnická, which also contains a small musuem. However, make sure to keep enough time to go to the incredible **ossuary** (*kostnice*) at Sedlec (open Tues–Sun 8 am–noon and 1 pm–5 pm (summer), 9 am–noon and 2 pm–4 pm (winter)). It's a couple of kilometres out of town; take any local bus from the stop at the beginning of Masarykova, and get off when you see a church on the right.

The church dates from around 1320, when the Cistercians in their abbey next door (now a factory) decided to build their very own French cathedral. It still has its original scale (the nave is three times higher than it's broad), but the vault is an 18th-century creation by Giovanni Santini. If the church is open, compare Santini's ribbing with Benedict Ried's in St Barbara's; the joyful abstraction of both is an excellent example of the continuity that linked Bohemia's Baroque and Gothic architectural traditions.

When they built the church, the Sedlec Cistercians weren't just joining the Kutná Hora construction boom. Their cemetery had been pulling crowds of pilgrims ever since Abbot Henry had returned from the Holy Land in 1278 and sprinkled a jar of earth from Golgotha over it. Within decades, it had become one of the most popular resting places in central Europe. Moribund believers headed for the area in droves, and corpses were trundled in from hundreds of miles away. Plague epidemics boosted business, and by 1318 the cemetery contained some 30,000 bodies—roughly the same as the population of London at the time—a state of affairs that gave rise to the creation of the ossuary. It's one of the most macabre sights that you're ever likely to see. You'll find it in the crypt of the All Saints' Chapel (1400), which is at the end of the small lane opposite the church, still surrounded by a functioning graveyard. As you approach, take a look at its tower, which has been an indirect victim of rapacious mining; the vagaries of distant subsidence have left it skew-whiff by 44 cm, and it tilts a few more nanometres every year. If the crypt is closed at a time when it shouldn't be, you can pick up the keys from the house next to the nearby shop, just back up the lane.

The ossuary dates from 1511, when a half-blind monk began gathering together all the bones from abolished graves and putting them in the crypt. It sounds an unenviable task, but it had a practical purpose and was the product of strange times; what's harder to understand is why as late as 1870, a woodcarver was hired to arrange the 40,000 sets of bones into pleasing patterns. Skulls and femurs have been turned into four monstrous bells, over three metres high; the Schwarzenberg family has been honoured with a skeletal coat-of-arms; and cheerful cherubs sit on top of obelisks of skulls, cradling grinning braincases in their laps. Woodcarver František Rint clearly wasn't superstitious—the writing on the wall is his own, a proud and bony signature. His *pièce de résistance* is the eight-branched chandelier that hangs over the crypt, composed of all the bones of the human body, several times over. On All Souls' Day (November 2), it's lit with candles and an intoning priest leads a requiem in the fiery charnel-house. 5 pm, if you happen to be in town.

Language

It's sometimes difficult to imagine how Czech could be more alien to English-speakers—although if you want to try, remember that St Cyril provided the Czechs with the script named after him when he arrived. The language seems to have given English nothing other than the words 'pistol' and 'robot' (although 'Semtex' will probably enter the OED before long); and, a few Germanic oddities like 'bratr' (brother) notwithstanding, the only English-tinged Czech words are the same 20th-century neologisms that the rest of the world has also borrowed. The language is Slavonic, with Latin influences, and in its modern form it dates from the 19th century. After 200 years of Germanization in Bohemia, it was painstakingly re-established by a few scholars, with the help of mumbling peasants, a few old texts, and Polish, Serbo-Croat, Bulgarian and Russian dictionaries.

If you try to speak a few words of Czech it's appreciated by most people, although Prague's surly waiters and shop assistants are more likely to treat you as an imbecile than to break into a kindly smile. The most widespread second language spoken here is still German, and almost all older Praguers can speak some, although lingering memories may make the words unutterable. There's a silent battle being fought in the country's schools between German and English (French is limited to a few sophisticates), but the young, encouraged by video nasties and the need to understand pop lyrics, are increasingly turning towards English. You'll almost certainly be cornered by someone eager to perfect his or her conjugations and learn a few more English obscenities. Two entire generations were forced to learn Russian—it's widely understood, but almost universally reviled, and even if you're fluent in the language, use it only as a last resort.

Czech is a phonetic language (pronounced consistently according to its spelling) with none of the shenanigans of silent letters and the like. That's simple enough—the problem is learning how to pronounce the letters. If the language of the English southern middle-class is used as a benchmark, the main differences are that *c* is spoken as 'ts', *j* is a vowel sound like the English 'y', and *r* is rolled at the front of the mouth. *Ch* is a consonant in itself—it's pronounced as in the Scottish 'loch', and you'll find it after 'h' in the dictionary. A *haček* (˘) above a consonant softens it:

thus *č* is pronounced 'ch' as in 'chill', *š* is 'sh', and *ž* is the 'zh' sound in 'pleasure'. With *ř*, you venture into territory uncharted by the English language, and every other known language in the world. Even Czech children have to be taught how to pronounce the sound properly; the closest you're likely to get to it is by rolling an 'r' behind your teeth and then expelling a rapid 'zh'. You'll amuse a lot of people by trying to say 'strč prst skrz krk'—it's a Czech tongue-twister which means 'put your fingers down your throat'.

Vowels are less complicated—*a* is the 'u' in 'up', *e* is as in 'met', *i* and *y* are both as in 'sip', *o* as in 'hot', and *u* as in 'pull'. The sounds are lengthened if the vowel is topped with an accent (´) (or in the case of *u*, also the symbol °)—they're pronounced like the vowels in, respectively, 'bar', 'bear', 'feed', 'poor', and 'oooooh!'. The letter *ě* is pronounced as though it were 'ye' and softens the consonant that comes before it. Accents affect only the sound of a vowel; and when pronouncing a word, it's *always* the first syllable that's stressed.

You don't use a subject (I, you, etc.) with a verb, since the ending in itself makes clear who's doing the deed. The English pronoun 'you' has two forms, as in many European languages: *vy* is polite and is used in most everyday situations (and always where more than one person is being addressed); *ty* is widespread among young people, and can be used to address anyone who you could call your friend (you can also use it to be contemptuous to someone you've never met before). Beware also of the bewildering number of endings any ordinary word can have, depending on which of the seven cases, three-and-a-half genders and two categories it belongs to; if you're looking something up in a dictionary, plump for whatever looks closest. Finally, be alert to the fact that Czechs generally say *no* or *ano*, when they're agreeing to something that's in doubt. Those who still feel eager to learn more can find details of language courses in the section on Living and Working in Prague.

USEFUL WORDS AND PHRASES

yes/no	*ano/ne*	You're welcome	*prosím*
I don't understand	*nerozumím*	Not at all	*není zač*
I don't know	*nevím*	I'm sorry	*promiňte*
Do you speak English?	*mluvíte anglicky?*	Call a doctor	*zavolejte lékaře*
I am English	*jsem angličan(ka)*	Let me through, I'm a doctor	*pusťt mě, já jsem lékař*
Please	*prosím*	Who?	*kdo?*
Please speak slowly	*mluvte prosím pomalu*	What?	*co?*
		Where (is)?	*kde (je)?*
Thank you (very much)	*děkuji (moc)*	Where (are you going)?	*kam (jdete)?*

From where?	*odkud?*	telegram	*telegram*
When?	*kdy?*	telephone	*telefon*
Why?	*proč?*	fax	*telefax*
How/what kind of?	*jak?*	I'd like to make a call to ...	*rád bych zavolal do ...*
How much/many?	*kolik?*	I'd like to reverse the charges...	*na učet voleného*
Do you have ...?	*máte ...?*	The number is ...	*číslo je...*
post office	*pošta*	I need the number of ...	*potřebuji číslo .*
pen	*pero*		
stamp	*známka*	telephone directory	*telefonní seznam*
envelope	*obálka*		
express-mail	*expres*		

soap	*mydlo*	headache	*bolest hlavy*
toothpaste	*zubní pasta*	cough	*kašel*
sun-protection cream	*krém na opalování*	sore-throat	*angina*
medicine for/against	*lék na/proti*	thermometer	*teploměr*
		plaster	*náplast*
		bandage	*obvaz*

CONVERSATION

Good morning	*dobré ráno*	Do you have a telephone?	*máte telefon?*
Good day	*dobrý den*	May I have the number?	*dáte mi číslo?*
Good evening	*dobrý večer*		
Goodbye	*na shledanou*	What did you say?	*co řikáté?*
Allow me to introduce myself	*dovolte, abych se představil*	What did you say? (very rude)	*co kecáš?*
Let me introduce you to ...	*dovolte, abych vám představil*	What are you looking at?	*na co se díváte?*
My name is ...	*jmenuji se ...*	What are you looking at? (very rude)	*co čumiš?*
I'm pleased to meet you	*těší mě, že vás poznávám*		
How are you?	*jak se máte?*		
Do you come here often?	*chodíte sem často?*		

HOTEL AND SHOPPING

Do you have a free single/double room?	*máte volný pokoj pro jednu osobu/pro dva?*	tobacconist	*tabák*
		supermarket	*samoobsluha*
		antique	*starožitnost*
I'd like the room for ... night(s)	*potřebuji pokoj na ... noc(i)*	book	*kniha*
		cigarettes	*cigarety*
May I pay by credit card?	*mohu platit credit card?*	crystal	*krystal*
		food	*jídlo*
How much does it cost?	*kolik to stojí?*	glass	*sklo*
		newspaper	*noviny*
laundry	*prádlo*	porcelain	*porcelán*

353

SIGHTSEEING

I'd like to go to a (concert)	*chtěl bych navštívit (koncert)*	May I take photographs here?	*mohu zde fotografovat?*
Two tickets for ... please	*prosím, dva lístky na...*	church	*chrám/kostel*
Do you have a map of the town?	*máte plán města?*	chapel	*kaple*
What building is that?	*co je to ze budovu?*	monastery/convent	*klášter*
How old is it?	*jak je to staré?*	castle	*hrad*
When are you open?	*jak máte otevřeno?*	cinema	*kino*
		theatre	*divadlo*
		gallery	*galerie*
		museum	*muzeum*

NUMBERS

zero	*nula*	twenty-two	*dvacet-dva*
one	*jedna*	thirty	*třicet*
two	*dva*	thirty-one	*třicet-jedna*
three	*tři*	forty	*čtyřicet*
four	*čtyři*	fifty	*padesát*
five	*pět*	sixty	*šedesát*
six	*šest*	seventy	*sedmdesát*
seven	*sedm*	eighty	*osmdesát*
eight	*osm*	ninety	*devadesát*
nine	*devět*	one hundred	*sto*
ten	*deset*	one hundred and one	*sto-jedna*
eleven	*jedenáct*	two hundred	*dvě stě*
twelve	*dvanáct*	three hundred	*tři sta*
thirteen	*třináct*	four hundred	*čtyři sta*
fourteen	*čtrnáct*	five hundred	*pět set*
fifteen	*patnáct*	six hundred	*šest set*
sixteen	*šestnáct*	seven hundred	*sedm set*
seventeen	*sedmnáct*	one thousand	*tisíc*
eighteen	*osmnáct*	two thousand	*dva tisíce*
nineteen	*devatenáct*	million	*milión*
twenty	*dvacet*		
twenty-one	*dvacet-jedna*		

COLOURS

black	*černý*	blue	*modrý*
white	*bílý*	pink	*růžový*
yellow	*žlutý*	violet	*fialový*
red	*červený*	golden	*zlatý*
orange	*oranžový*	brown	*hnědý*
green	*zelený*	grey	*šedý*

DAYS

Monday	*pondělí*	Friday	*pátek*
Tuesday	*úterý*	Saturday	*sobota*
Wednesday	*středa*	Sunday	*neděle*
Thursday	*čtvrtek*		

LANGUAGE

MONTHS

January	*leden*	July	*červenec*
February	*únor*	August	*srpen*
March	*březen*	September	*září*
April	*duben*	October	*říjen*
May	*květen*	November	*listopad*
June	*červen*	December	*prosinec*

TIME

What time is it?	*kolik je hodín?*	century	*století*
morning	*ráno, dopoledne*	tomorrow	*zítra*
afternoon	*odpoledne*	yesterday	*včera*
evening	*večer*	the day before yesterday	*předevčírem*
night	*noc*	the day after tomorrow	*pozítří*
minute	*minuta*	now	*teď*
hour	*hodina*	later	*potom*
(to)day	*dnes*	before	*před*
week	*týden*	after	*po*
month	*měsíc*	during	*během*
year	*rok*		
this year	*letos*		
next year	*příští rok*		

TRAVEL

How can I get to...?	*jak se dostanu na ?*	bus- or tram-stop	*zastávka*
I would like to go to...	*rád bych do...*	metro station	*stanice*
		(railway) station	*nádraží*
Where is...?	*kde je...?*	taxi-rank	*stanoviště taxi*
How far is it to...?	*jak je to daleko do...?*	aeroplane	*letadlo*
		bus	*autobus*
How long does the journey take?	*jak dlouha trvá cesta?*	tram	*tramvaj*
		train	*vlak*
How much does it cost?	*kolik to stojí?*	taxi	*taxi*
		car	*auto*
		small boat	*lodička*
May I have a ticket to...?	*prosím jízdenku do...?*	pleasure steamer	*parník*
		ticket	*lístek*
Can I buy a ticket on the bus?	*mohu si koupit lístek v autobusu?*	seat reservation	*místenka*
		on the left	*na leva*
Do I have to change?	*musím přestupovat?*	on the right	*na prava*
		straight ahead	*rovně*
When does the ... leave?	*kdy odjíždí...?*	nearby	*blizko*
		far away	*daleko*
Do I need a reservation?	*potřebuju reservaci?*	north	*sever*
		south	*jih*
May I have a couchette?	*mohu dostat lehátko lůžko?*	east	*východ*
		west	*západ*
What's the name of this station?	*jak se jmenuje tato stanice?*	crossroads	*křižovatka*
		street	*ulice*
Let me out	*pusťte mě ven*	square	*náměstí*
airport	*letiště*	bridge	*most*

355

MEALTIMES

Do you have a table for (one/two)?	*máte volný stůl pro jednoho/dva?*	Bon appetit!	*Dobrou chut!*
Is this seat free?	*je toto místo volné?*	breakfast	*snídaně*
Could I make a reservation for (one/two)?	*mohu reservovat jednou místo/dvě místa*	lunch	*oběd*
		dinner	*večeře*
		tea	*čaj*
		coffee	*káva*
May I see the menu?	*mohu vidět jídelny lístek?*	with lemon	*s citrónem*
		with milk	*s mlékem*
What would you recommend?	*co doporučujete?*	without milk	*bez mléka*
		milk	*mléko*
Do you have vegetarian dishes?	*máte bezmasé jídlo?*	lemonade	*limonáda*
		cola	*cola*
		juice	*džus*
Excuse me, I'm ready to order	*promiňte, mohu si objednat?*	mineral water	*minerálka*
		beer	*pivo*
That was delicious/ disgusting	*bylo to výborné/hnusný*	soda water	*sodovka*
		wine (white, red)	*vino (bílé, červené)*

THE MENU

dušené	braised	*obloha*	bits and pieces of onion and cabbage served as a side dish
na rožní	grilled		
pečené	roast		
smažené	fried	*polévka*	soup
vařené	boiled	*salát*	salad
hranolky	french fries		

MEAT, FISH AND POULTRY

bažant	pheasant	*kuře*	chicken
biftek	steak	*játra*	liver
divočák	wild pig (can also be used to describe sexually potent man)	*ledvinka*	kidneys
		maso	meat
		pstruh	trout
drubež	poultry	*pštrosů*	ostrich
hovězí	beef	*sekaná*	mince-meat
husa	goose	*srnčí*	venison
jeleni	stag	*štika*	pike
kachna	duck	*šunka*	ham
kapr	carp	*telecí*	veal
krab	crab	*uzeniny*	sausage
králík	rabbit	*vepřové*	pork
krocan	turkey		

FRUIT AND VEGETABLES

ananas	pineapple	*brambory*	potatoes
banán	banana	*broskev*	peach

česnek	garlic	*okurka*	cucumber
chřest	asparagus	*ořechy*	nuts
cibule	onion	*pomeranč*	orange
houby	mushrooms	*rajčata*	tomato
hruška	pear	*rýži*	rice
jablka	apple	*třešne*	cherries
jahoda	strawberry	*tuřín*	swede
meruňka	apricot	*zeli*	cabbage
mrkev	carrots	*žampion*	mushroom

DESSERT

koláč	cake	*šlehačka*	whipped cream
kompot	compote	*smetana*	cream
palačinka	pancake	*sýr*	cheese
pohár	ice-cream sundae	*zmrzlina*	ice-cream

Chronology

	Rulers	Events
c. 870	Bořivoj	
c. 894	Spytihněv I	
c. 905	Vratislav I	
c. 921	Wenceslas I (Václav)	
c. 935	Boleslav I (The Cruel)	Good King Wenceslas murdered
c. 967	Boleslav II (The Pious)	
999	Boleslav III	
1002	Vladivoj of Poland	
1003–		Dynastic struggle between
1034		Jaromír, Boleslav III
		Boleslav the Brave and Oldřich
1034	Břetislav I	
1055	Spytihněv II	
1061	Vratislav II	
1092	Břetislav II	
1100	Bořivoj II	
1107	Svatopluk	
1109	Vladislav I	
1117	Bořivoj II (second time)	Cosmas of Prague begins making up Bohemia's history
1120	Vladislav I (second time)	
1125	Soběslav I	
1140	Vladislav II	
1172	Bedřich	
1173	Soběslav II	
1179	Bedřich (second time)	
1182	Konrád Ota	
	Bedřich	
1189	Konrád Ota	
1191	Václav II	
1192	Přemysl Otakar I	
1193	Břetislav Jindřich	
1197	Vladislav III Jindřich	
	Přemysl Otakar I	
1212	(Kings)	Bohemia made a kingdom
1230	Wenceslas I	
c. 1235		Old Town receives royal charter; Jewish ghetto set up
1253	Přemysl Otakar I	
1257		Jews relocated; Malá Strana founded

1278	Wenceslas II	
1305	Wenceslas III	
1306	Jindřich of Carinthia	
	Rudolf of Habsburg	
1310	John of Luxemburg	
1346	Charles IV	Battle of Crécy; Black Prince steals three feathers from John of Luxemburg's helmet and puts them into Prince of Wales' crest
1348		Charles IV founds New Town; Europe ravaged by Black Death; most of Bohemia escapes
1378	Wenceslas IV	
1380		Bohemia ravaged by plague; most of Europe escapes
1389		3000 Jews killed in pogrom; survivors fined
1415		Jan Hus burnt at stake
1419		Prague's first defenestration
1420	Sigismund	Hussite Wars begin
1438	Albert of Habsburg	
1440	Ladislav the Posthumous	
1458	George of Poděbrady	
1471	Vladislav II of Jagellon	
1516	Ludvik of Jagellon	
1526	Ferdinand I of Habsburg	
1541		Fire on left bank
1556		Jesuits come to town
1564	Maximilian II	
1576	Rudolf II	
1598		Hradčany becomes royal town
1611	Matthias	
1618		Prague's grandest defenestration begins Thirty Years War
1619	Frederick of the Palatinate	
1620		Battle of the White Mountain (bílá hora)
	Ferdinand II of Habsburg	
1621		27 nationalists executed
1635		Treaty of Prague ends Thirty Years War; French start it again
1637	Ferdinand III	
1646	Ferdinand IV	
1648		Thirty Years War ends on Prague's bridge
1657	Leopold I	
1680		Plague returns
1705	Joseph I	
1711	Charles VI	

1715		Plague returns
1740	Queen Maria Theresa	
1743		French besiege Prague
1757		Prussians bombard Prague
1780	Joseph II	
1781		Edict of Toleration abolishes all religious orders which neither nurse nor teach
1784		Prague's four towns united into one municipality
1787		Mozart conducts *Don Giovanni*
1790	Leopold II	
1792	Francis I	
1835	Ferdinand V	
1848	Francis Joseph I	Year of Revolutions
1866		Prussians invade Prague and sign a peace treaty
1875		Horse-drawn trams appear
1891		Electric trams take over
1893		Demolition of Jewish ghetto begun
1916	Charles I	
	(Presidents)	
1918	Tomáš Garrigue Masaryk	Czechoslovakian independence
1935	Edvard Beneš	
1938	Emil Hácha (stooge)	Britain and France sell Czechoslovakia downriver at Munich
1939		Nazis invade; Protectorate of Bohemia and Moravia established
1942		Reinhard Heydrich assassinated; Lidice destroyed
1945	Edvard Beneš	Prague Uprising; city liberated by Soviet forces
1948	Klement Gottwald	
1952		Slánský show trials
1953	Antonín Zápotecký	
1957	Antonín Novotný	
1968	Ludvík Svoboda	Alexander Dubček elected First Secretary; Prague Spring; Warsaw Pact invasion
1969		Jan Palach burns himself to death
1975	Gustáv Husák	
1977		Charter 77 movement born
1988		Soviet foreign ministry spokesman Gennady Gerasimov asked what the difference is between perestroika and Prague Spring; replies '20 years'
1989	Václav Havel	Alexander Dubček becomes speaker of Federal Assembly
1990		Free elections

Further Reading

There is still a dearth of Prague-related literature in English, and most of what exists is understandably steeped in the politics of the cold war era. However, keep your eyes open for new translations and works. There are two shops in London specializing in books from eastern and central Europe: **Orbis Books**, 66 Kenway Rd, London SW5 0RD, tel (071) 370 2210; and **Collets International Bookshop**, 129 Charing Cross Rd, London WC2H 0EQ, tel (071) 734 0782. You could also try the library of the **Czechoslovak National House**, 74 West End Lane, London NW6 2LX, tel (071) 328 0131. It contains a restaurant, and plenty of émigrés with whom to discuss your forthcoming holiday.

Anděl, Jaroslav and others, *Czech Modernism 1900–45* (Museum of Fine Arts, Houston, 1989). Comprehensive survey of modern Czech art. The essays ramble, but there are lots of pretty pictures.

Bloch, Chajim, *The Golem: Legends of the Prague Ghetto*. The definitive versions.

Brook, Stephen, *The Double Eagle* (Picador 1988). An expedition through the post-war darkness of the former Habsburg empire, from the land of Kurt Waldheim to 1980s Prague. Marred by a tone that can become pompous when it intends to be scathing.

Chatwin, Bruce, *Utz* (Picador 1988). A gentle tale of claustrophobia, escapism and porcelain-collecting in post-war Prague.

Farova, Anna, *Josef Sudek* (John Murray 1990). A short biography of Prague's best photographer, with black-and-white shots that would do any coffee-table proud.

Fermor, Patrick Leigh, *A Time of Gifts* (Penguin 1977). Very English reminiscences of Fermor's trip through a late-1930s central Europe of crunchy snow and jackboots.

Garton-Ash, Timothy, *We the People: The Revolutions of 1989* (Granta 1990). Blow-by-blow account of central Europe's *annus mirabilis* by Garton-Ash, whose huge contribution to keeping the area in the news during the 1980s makes the self-glorifying flourishes of this book almost understandable.

Hašek, Jaroslav, *The Good Soldier Švejk*. Hašek was paid by the word for several of the Švejk stories, so pithy they ain't; the humour tends to come from somewhere between the bar and the toilet; but there are still chuckles a-plenty.

Havel, Václav and others, *Living in Truth* (Faber 1990), *The Power of the Powerless* (Hutchinson 1985). Two collections of political essays on post-1968 Czechoslovakia by opposition writers.
Hrabal, Bohumil, *I Served the King of England* (Abacus 1989). A waiter's coming-of-age against the backdrop of modern Czech history, encompassing brothels, Nazi convalescent homes, and a millionaires' prison.
Kafka, Franz, *The Castle* (Penguin 1990), *The Trial* (Penguin 1990). Two nightmares that make booking a restaurant in Prague seem a doddle.
Klíma, Ivan, *My Merry Mornings: Stories from Prague* (Readers International). The daily creation and destruction of dreams in Communist Prague. A collection of short stories has also been translated (*My First Loves*—Penguin 1989), as has his novel, *Love and Garbage* (Faber 1990).
Kundera, Milan, *The Joke*. The dangers of having a humourless girlfriend in post-war Czechoslovakia.
(Count) Lützow, *The Story of Prague* (J. M. Dent 1907). A readable introduction to the city's history, tinged with genteel nationalism.
Kovaly, Heda Margolius, *Prague Farewell* (Victor Gollancz 1988). Moving autobiography by the wife of an executed defendant in the 1950s show trials, beginning with her escape from a Nazi death-march and ending with Soviet tanks on Prague's streets.
Mlynář, Zdeněk, *Night Frost in Prague*, (Hurst & Co. 1980). The story of the Prague Spring told by one of Dubček's closest associates, and one of those taken to Moscow at gunpoint after the invasion. Times change: in 1989, Mlynář was the man that the KGB hoped to instal into power.
Pawel, Ernst, *Nightmare of Reason* (Collins Harvill 1988). An excellent biography of Franz Kafka, elegantly written and placing the author squarely within the Prague of his time.
Škvorecký, Josef, *Talkin' Moscow Blues* (Faber 1988). A collection of impressionistic essays on jazz, literature, film and political madness, told with the caustic humour of Škvorecký at his best.
Shawcross, William, *Dubček* (Hogarth 1990 edn.). Biography of an *apparatchik* who grew to fit extraordinary times. Hastily updated after 1989. The joins are often apparent, but the comments of the reformed Dubček of 1990 are a fascinating insight into how Communism destroyed its own dreams in Czechoslovakia.
Vaculík, Ludvík, *A Cup of Coffee with my Interrogator* (Readers International). Powerful collection of essays on the meanness and mediocrity of Czechoslovakia's post-1968 thought police, written contemporaneously and circulated underground.

Index